PROPHECIES OF LANGUAGE

Sara Guyer and Brian McGrath, series editors

Lit Z embraces models of criticism uncontained by conventional notions of history, periodicity, and culture, and committed to the work of reading. Books in the series may seem untimely, anachronistic, or out of touch with contemporary trends because they have arrived too early or too late. Lit Z creates a space for books that exceed and challenge the tendencies of our field and in doing so reflect on the concerns of literary studies here and abroad.

At least since Friedrich Schlegel, thinking that affirms literature's own untimeliness has been named romanticism. Recalling this history, Lit Z exemplifies the survival of romanticism as a mode of contemporary criticism, as well as forms of contemporary criticism that demonstrate the unfulfilled possibilities of romanticism. Whether or not they focus on the romantic period, books in this series epitomize romanticism as a way of thinking that compels another relation to the present. Lit Z is the first book series to take seriously this capacious sense of romanticism.

In 1977, Paul de Man and Geoffrey Hartman, two scholars of romanticism, team-taught a course called Literature Z that aimed to make an intervention into the fundamentals of literary study. Hartman and de Man invited students to read a series of increasingly difficult texts and through attention to language and rhetoric compelled them to encounter "the bewildering variety of ways such texts could be read." The series' conceptual resonances with that class register the importance of recollection, reinvention, and reading to contemporary criticism. Its books explore the creative potential of reading's untimeliness and history's enigmatic force.

PROPHECIES OF LANGUAGE

The Confusion of Tongues in German Romanticism

Kristina Mendicino

Fordham University Press

New York 2017

THIS BOOK IS MADE POSSIBLE BY A COLLABORATIVE GRANT
FROM THE ANDREW W. MELLON FOUNDATION.

Copyright © 2017 Fordham University Press

Fordham University Press also publishes its books in a variety of electronic formats.
Some content that appears in print may not be available in electronic books.

Visit us online at www.fordhampress.com.

Library of Congress Cataloging-in-Publication Data available
online at catalog.loc.gov.

Printed in the United States of America

19 18 17   5 4 3 2 1

First edition

for Rainer Nägele

Contents

PROPHECIES OF LANGUAGE

INTRODUCTION

. . . But often as a firebrand
arises conf(used)usion of tongues.¹ . . .

. . . Oft aber wie ein Brand
entstehet Sprachverw(irrt)irrung. . . .

In the midst of a fragment from his *Homburger Folioheft* (*Sämtliche Werke: Frankfurter Ausgabe* 7: 377), a notebook that contains several late elegies and odes and even more notes for poems that would never be completed, Friedrich Hölderlin registers the confusion of tongues.² His words arise among fragments written in several languages: his sentence appears to be written in German; a nearby marginal note in Latin reads, "sphere of the ecclesia [*orbis ecclesiae*]" (7: 374); several pages earlier, he records a passage in ancient Greek from Pindar's thirteenth Olympian ode, below the bilingual heading "Origin of Loyoté [*Ursprung der Loyoté*]" (7: 365). Thus, Hölderlin's sentence stands out, apart from the draft of the poem to which it seems to belong, as though to state yet again what takes place so often in these pages. The passage, "Oft aber wie ein Brand / Entstehet Sprachverw(irrt)irrung," might thus be considered the fragment of fragments at this late stage of Hölderlin's writing between 1803 and 1807, when he would produce the last poems to be published in his lifetime, as well as his translations of Sophocles's *Oedipus* and *Antigone*. But it is more than a manifestation of Hölderlin's late writing praxis. The excess at issue here, as tongues grow confounded with others and language emerges as fire, also speaks to the issues of translation, the origins of language, and prophecy that would preoccupy Hölderlin and many of his contemporaries, including Wilhelm von Humboldt, Friedrich Schlegel, and G. W. F. Hegel. No sooner does language emerge than the problem of its plurality and translatablity begins. And even before there is any talk of language, fire—an element associated with ancient prophecy, Pentecost, and the ἐκπύρωσις of the Stoics—heralds its coming, and forebodes its end before it can even begin: "But often as a firebrand, arises confusion of tongues."

But what does speaking in tongues say? And what could one say of it? Hölderlin's fragment speaks to the precariousness of any inquiry into the confusion of tongues and prophecy. For if one takes his comparison of linguistic emergence to a devastating firebrand seriously, one must confront the possibility that it may never be witnessed; that it could not be adequately addressed in any direct way or in any one tongue; and that language, as such, would not at first have been a means of communication, let alone transparent communication. Rather, Hölderlin's words imply that, every time it emerges, language will have been radically different from our understanding of words and from any words we understand, and that it will have been, from the start, other in and to itself. Unlike Enlightenment narratives of the origins of language, which also describe primal scenes of emergence for which there neither is nor can be a historical record, Hölderlin's poem dismisses the operative assumptions of Jean-Jacques Rousseau, Étienne de Condillac, and, to a lesser degree, Johann Gottfried Herder: namely, that language would have originated in the way we use and know it, and that the first language would have been one. Thus, Hölderlin's fragment demands a reconsideration of language as such. And, as I hope to show in the course of this book, the most intensive considerations of language in Hegel's, Wilhelm von Humboldt's, and Friedrich Schlegel's writings similarly call for a radical rethinking of language. Reading philosophical and literary texts of German Romanticism and German Idealism in relationship to Greek (and other) precursors, I argue in *Prophecies of Language* that a philological response to this demand not only uncovers aspects of these texts that would otherwise remain silent or ignored but also opens the possibility of questioning many tacit assumptions about what languages might mean. But how could this problem be addressed or pursued at all? What method or modus of writing could address it adequately, if the conventions of expository prose, too, must be placed in question by the nature of the issue? With Hölderlin's fragment, one quickly arrives at an impasse.

A detour is in order, to sketch a possible way to speak to the problems that emerge with Hölderlin's text more precisely. Precisely by speaking of "confusion of tongues [*Sprachverw(irrt)irrung*]," by asserting that it arises "often," and by situating it in no particular place or time, Hölderlin's fragment resonates with Jacques Derrida's "Des tours de Babel," his essay on Genesis and Walter Benjamin's essay "The Task of the Translator." There, Derrida also displaces the confusion of tongues from any univocal, original source, and he suggests, too, that such confusion, however frequent, cannot, properly speaking, be testified to, even though it necessarily affects every speaker of language. In this regard, his analysis of the very word "Babel" might provide a point of departure. For Derrida exposes "Babel" to be no mere "proper name" for the myth of language confusion, or for the city and tower that would fall (Graham 197)[3]—not least of all because it is now a common word in many European languages. At the same time, and for the same reason, "Babel" cannot merely be a term for "confusion" in any language, including Hebrew (Graham 192). Nor it is merely the derivative of the "Father-God" that its components "Ba" and "Bel" independently mean in "Oriental tongues," as Voltaire says in his attempt to explain the truth of the matter etymologically (Graham 192). Rather, all of these at once, and known to all languages that will have been estranged, "Babel"—the confusion of tongues, and more—would baffle any attempt to decide upon its linguistic source or status. Thus, it gives rise in its sheer dispersion to what Derrida calls an imperative to translate on the part of all lips,[4] precisely when it can no longer be decided what is to be translated (*l'à-traduire*) (Graham 208), or what orientation translation should take; when, that is, it cannot be decided in the first place whether a word is a proper or common name, from a proper or foreign tongue. This imperative is therefore, at the same time, impossible to satisfy, since it could not be said when or where such critical moments of linguistic indecision take place.

This is not the place for a full analysis of Derrida's own—highly complex—"Babelian performance," but for seeking preliminary orientation toward similar problems around the turn of the nineteenth century in Germany, what Susan Bernofsky has called the "golden age of translation" (ix). Such orientation will also help to draw out the specificity of the texts that will be addressed from this time, when the concern over language origins became—for at least some of its most critical writers—an acute concern for the plurality of languages, for the disclosure of their unfinished aspects, and, thus, for the possibility of an unheard-of language to come. Most importantly, it is the profound disorientation that emerges in Derrida's analysis of not only "Babel" but also Benjamin's "The Task of the Translator" that gives some indications of the ways in which the original plurality of language*s* might be addressed, as well as the consequences of this emergence for thinking and writing about them. If it is true that the confusion of tongues "takes place as trace or as trait, and this place takes place even if no empirical or mathematical objectivity pertains to its space" (Graham 208), then it may be approached only by tentatively following, as Derrida does, the singular, imprevisible—and therefore unsystematizable—ways in which texts register more than one tongue at once. Doing so will inevitably involve transgressing the lexical and grammatical limits of any single national language as well. For as Derrida shows in his own performance—and not only here—the only way to address the problem without falsifying it through a rhetoric that rests upon the assumption of transparent linguistic communication—even while commenting upon communication failure—would be to address each text in terms that come as close as possible to its "own," and to adopt as rigorously as possible a modus of writing that exposes the ambivalences and transgresses the limits of one's "own" language.

For example, in a critical passage from Derrida's essay, the futural "l'à-traduire" resonates with its near homophones, the substantivized infinitive "le traduire" and the privative "l'atraduire," which word does not, properly speaking, exist in French, but which might be heard here all the same, transforming the question of "the-to-be-translated" into one of "translating" itself. The sentence in question appears in Derrida's discussion of the way Benjamin cautions against defining the relation between a translation and an original in terms of reception, communication, or representation. It reads: "Ces trois précautions prises (ni réception, ni communication, ni représentation), comment se constituent la dette et la généalogie du traducteur? ou d'abord de ce qui est à-traduire, de l'à-traduire?" (215). Or: "These three precautions being taken (neither reception, nor communication, nor representation), how does the debt and genealogy of the translator constitute itself? or before this, that which is to be translated, the-to-be-translated / translating / nontranslating?" With this new turn, however, Derrida also renders the question of translating itself most uncertain, for his prose does not allow the reader a way to decide between the futural, infinitive, and privative constructions, between the three-word formulation "l'à-traduire" and the two-word alternatives: "le traduire," "l'atraduire." The questions raised in Benjamin's text are thus reprised, precisely in the way Derrida departs from them in order to write them further. Whether or not such a rhetorical performance is itself to be considered translation, one thing should be clear at this point: Derrida suggests through his writing—and *not* at the level of propositions, arguments, or judgments—that Babel can only be read and retraced when it is performed. Whereby "performance," in turn, would mean something like a forming that *per*vades and *per*verts the seemingly given forms of language, differently each time, for each instance of speech. As Benjamin will write near the start of his own essay, apodictically: "translation is a form" ("Die Aufgabe des Übersetzers" 9).

It should go without saying that any such performance would not be undertaken for the sake of merely exposing the nonsensical potential of language—the failures, for example, of the performative speech act, which no doubt enter crucially into Derrida's considerations of the "Babelian performance" in his reading of Joyce.[5] Rather, such performances would probe the limits of languages to expose the sense that they may bear when these limits are transgressed, or when they are no longer possible to demarcate in the first place. This critical indecision marks precisely where my readings will differ from those of others who have made similar claims about language and translation, but who revert to presuppositions that preclude a consideration of the linguistic plurality of each enunciation. George Steiner, for example, has insisted that language "alters at every moment" (18);[6] and asserted that, "when we read or hear [. . .], we translate" (28)— yet he continues to uphold the static notions of a "source-language" and "receptor-language" (28). By contrast, one might say that the intention of this book—but also of those texts by Hegel, Humboldt, Schlegel, and Hölderlin that will be addressed, analyzed in detail, and even partially translated anew—would be to touch upon those moments in these authors' languages, where, however fleetingly, language is indicated in an irreducible plurality that exceeds whatever it may convey in any one tongue, including the apparent limits of a single national language. Simply put, at stake is the exposure of the saying of what is said in more than one tongue at once—in distinction to its ostensible content or national-linguistic contour.[7]

Returning to Hölderlin's verses, "Oft aber wie ein Brand / entstehet Sprachverw(irrt)irrung," one may find a "trace or trait" of Derrida's Babel (Graham 208), insofar as Hölderlin dispels any attributions of its proper site, scene, or time, as well as any proper names. But Hölderlin's poetic text on the confusion of tongues also complicates the problems Derrida addresses and gives a new turn to "Des tours de Babel." For in arising like or as a fire, Hölderlin's "Sprachverw(irrt)irrung" would also, as such, destroy the site of its emergence, along with all that there may be to see or say—and perhaps, too, any trace of its happening. Thus, this particular metaphor for the "confusion of tongues"—Hölderlin's trope or *tour* of Babel—evokes a still more devastating origin than the one Derrida discusses in his text, and, at the same time, recalls the passage from the New Testament that figures as the counterpart to Babel—namely, Pentecost. There, the various tongues of the world come to the Apostles "like fire [ὡσεὶ πυρός, tamquam ignis]" (Acts 2.3),[8] allowing them to address the crowd of Jews—who "were confused [συνεχύθη, confusa]" (Acts 2.6)—in their respective idioms. But in his reprisal of this passage, which has been celebrated by writers such as Jürgen Trabant as a moment when "*all* languages are languages of the evangelium, none has a particular privilege" (*Apeliotes* 50), Hölderlin gives it a devastating turn. For whereas the "dispersed tongues [διαμεριζόμεναι γλῶσσαι, dispertitae linguae]" that descend upon the Apostles should undo the initial confusion of tongues by doubling it, the conflagration of language Hölderlin evokes veers from an echo of the Acts of the Apostles to the reemergence of "Sprachverw(irrt)irrung." Fire figures in Hölderlin's fragment as the trope that allows the original and originary plurality of languages to become all the more pronounced.

However, it is only by turning more closely to the context of Hölderlin's verses both within the New Testament and within his *Homburger Folioheft* that the prophetic dimension of the languages he evokes can be indicated more precisely, and with it, the "prophecies of language" to which the title of this book refers. Unlike the story of Babel in Genesis, what is at issue in the Acts of the Apostles is not the tower of a particular people at a particular place,[9] but the kingdom of God; not the name of the Father, but the name of the Son, which is said to save in the "last days [ἐν ταῖς ἐσχάταις ἡμέραις]" of time—or, as Peter's words read in the Vulgate translation, in the "new days [*in novissimis diebus*]" (Acts 2.17). According to the Hebrew prophet Joel, whom Peter cites, those days are the days when God "pours forth from his spirit"—as he also does on "this day," filling the Apostles and allowing, in the end, three thousand to be baptized in the name of Christ (Acts 2.41). According to Peter, this transmission of Christ's name across languages also turns all who would speak it into "prophets" and witnesses of divine signs and wonders, like the prophets and witnesses Joel had announced for the last (or new) days (Acts 2.17–19). Few words occur as frequently in this chapter of the Acts of the Apostles as "prophet" or "prophesize," though in this context, "to prophesize" could simply mean nothing other than bearing witness to the resurrection of Christ that has already taken place and that continues to take place with the many "wonders and signs" that "came to be through the apostles" (Acts 2.43)—foremost through the tongues that have been passed onto them. The prophet of these last days could announce nothing but the name of Christ, who has already fulfilled the announcements of the Hebrew prophets and departed. Thus, as the confusion of languages is resolved through its redoubling and all become prophets of God by speaking the name of the Son, there will be no further talk of speech, prophetic or otherwise, but for the fact that they are "praising God [αἰνοῦντες τὸν θεόν]" (Acts 2.47). Meanwhile, the dispersion of tongues gives way to the distribution of goods in the temple,[10] where all gather in concord (ὁμοθυμαδόν, *unanimiter*) and partake of the bread—the body of Christ—that nourishes them (Acts 2.45–46). In this temple, the distinction between the common and the holy collapses, and all that is said or sung is a vatic cantus with nothing else to say, no future or end of words or days—a vacant Vatican, and a voracious one, for the sole name that remains, in more ways than one, at the lips of each.

In this light, it is most significant that the words "der Vatikan" have come to denote the poetic fragment from Hölderlin's *Homburger Folioheft*, where tongues arise like flames, and where Babel and Pentecost will be confounded.[11] And here, where Babel does not fall, but burns, and the confusion of tongues does not resolve into Christian concord, Hölderlin writes, like Peter, of the last days of prophecy. But he does so in a way that conflates and exceeds the biblical eschata of the beginning and end, the Old and New Testaments, Genesis and the Apocalypse. His firebrand is—as the word "Brand" might also be used, according to the Grimm brothers' *German Dictionary*—abortive, untimely (2: 296).[12] If the biblical Babel marks, as Derrida writes, a myth of origins and, more precisely, "an origin not of language but of languages" in the plural (Graham 209), the verses that immediately precede Hölderlin's sentence of "Sprachverw(irrt) irrung" speak of "destroyed cities," "miasma," and Patmos—all heralded by "the guardian's horn"—and thus also reprise the salvos that announce the Apocalypse of John of Patmos, the last prophet, whom Hölderlin would address more expressly around this time in an ode of that name. And as only the owl—"well known from scriptures"—remains to speak "in destroyed cities," Hölderlin also reprises the apocalyptic destruction of nations that Isaiah prophesied, where the owl and the raven are said to dwell instead of men (Isa. 34.11), as fire and smoke perpetually lay waste (Isa. 34.9–10).[13]

Hölderlin's verses read:

> The guardian's horn tones, however, over the garden
> the crane holds the shape upright
> the majestic one, chaste, above
> in Patmos, Morea, in the plagued air.
> Turkish. And the owl, well known from the scriptures
> speaks, like hoarse women in destroyed cities. But
> They receive the sense. But often as a fire
> arises confusion of tongues.

> Der Wächters Horn tönt aber über den Garden (Aber)
> Der Kranich <aber> hält die G(a)estalt aufrecht (hält.)
> Die (V|)majestätische, keusche, drüben

> In Patmos, Morea, in der Pestluft.
> Türkisch. u[]nd []Die Eule, wohlbekannt der Schriften
> Spricht, (einer) heischer|n| Frau|n| gleich in zerstörten Städten. Ab[er]
> Die erhalten den Sinn. Oft aber wie ein Brand
> Entstehet Sprachverw(irrt)irrung. (7: 377)

And so, the emergence of language confusion follows the end. Or perhaps it coincides with the end and qualifies the owls' or cities' reception or preservation of sense—"die erhalten den Sinn"—from the start. Either way, beginning and end arise together here, so that these limits and, with them, any retrospective account of the world and its plurality of tongues, as well as any ultimate announcement of prophetic visions, are utterly eliminated. The speakers and bearers of sense are birds, the erstwhile mediators between men and the gods for the Greeks, but in a landscape that is utterly bereft of anyone for, to, or of whom they might speak, as well as any holy or common community their speech might found. Thus, where Hölderlin comes nearest to the universal prophecy of Christ that Peter pronounces at Pentecost—over the metaphor of fire—the "Sprachverw(irrt)irrung" of his poem would be foreign to what the tribes of the world witness among the Apostles. And as though to confuse matters even more, these verses depicting the miasma of Patmos may also bespeak an Apollonian plague. For soon, Hölderlin will go on to evoke Apollo by name, responding, perhaps, to the Italian humanist etymologies of the Vatican, which was a site of *vates* and originally rumored to be the location of a temple of Apollo (Trippe 786). But it would be still more precise to say that Hölderlin will go on to *re*voke Apollo at the Vatican, retracing the departure of this prophetic god, as well as his parting word: "And Apollo, similarly from Rome, of suchlike palaces, says Ade! [*Und Apollen, ebenfalls / Aus Roma, derlei Palla[] sten, sagt / Ade!*]."

The prophetic word thus turns out to be not "Christ," but "Ade," which itself marks a confusion of tongues. For this utterance—spoken by a Hellenic god—also parts from the German "Ade" as well as the French "Adieu," to echo the Greek ἄδε. And even in Greek, Apollo's word is not one: it could be the deictic pronoun "those there!" as well as the vocative substantive for "satiety" or "loathsomeness [ἄδος]," or the rarer, later homonym, "decree [ἄδος]." In other words, Hölderlin's Apollo—who, as Heraclitus once said, "neither speaks nor hides, but indicates" (Diels 79)—would, perhaps, point without indicating. He would, perhaps, utter a condemnation or injunction without imperative force. He would, perhaps, remain in parting. For his word could never impart a deictic gesture or divine judgment, so long as "Ade" may also be the word of farewell, nor could "Ade" bid farewell, so long as it may also indicate and enjoin. Apollo speaks, in other words—and in one word—at a limit of speech where multiple tongues meet, and where the modalities of the imperative, the interjection, and the indicative mingle, without revealing or concealing any one of them in particular. Thus it is only appropriate that here, Apollo takes leave of no place in particular—be it "Rome, [. . .] suchlike palaces," or the "Vatikan"—as the limits that might define the proper or the foreign in space and in language are eliminated.

Here, Hölderlin performs in his ode—in his *ade*—a modus of prophecy that is most intimately related to the confusion of tongues and the concomitant imperative to translate that Derrida retraces in his essay. For prophecy refers, as Greek usage testifies, to a speaking for or in the place of another, which at once confounds the source of speech and displaces whatever may be said. And beyond uttering the prophecy of *one* god or *one* other, Hölderlin's words speak for and in the place of the prophets of the Old and New Testaments, of ancient Greece and Rome. In each passage, several enunciations and speakers take place; each place is frequented by other tongues; and each instant, divided in this way, may itself be said to occur—like a firebrand—often, registering multiple instances of speech at once. These features of his text thus suspend, too, any decisive determination of *what* is said, and evince a most radical form of prophecy, on the verge of a language and a phasis that cannot arrive once and for all, for there is no single message to reach its receiver, and no single receiver destined for it.

For this reason, it can hardly be an accident that, as Hölderlin proceeds from the confusion of languages, from the Bible to Greece, he also echoes the names and topoi of two of the most celebrated poems by Friedrich Schiller, who was, beyond his general prominence, of the utmost personal and professional importance to Hölderlin throughout his career.[14] These are "The Promenade [*Der Spaziergang*]" and "The Song of the Bell [*Das Lied von der Glocke*]" (*Gedichte* 308–14, 227–39). They are concerned with the recuperation of classical antiquity and the establishment of Christian communal concord, respectively. But as Schiller's words turn up in Hölderlin's text, they are just as soon distorted and turned from at the end of his verses, as sharply as the fire of Pentecost reverts to the confusion tongues. And if attending more closely to the next verses of Hölderlin's poem may seem to divert from Babel and prophecy, they ultimately testify all the more to the foreignness of language that is at stake in both, as the words of even the most canonical and lauded poet of the time for Hölderlin become

estranged. After pronouncing his sentence on "Sprachverw(irrt)irrung,"
Hölderlin begins another, which reads:

> But as a ship,
> that lies in the haven, of evening, when the bell tolls
> of the church tower, and it echoes below
> in the innards of the temple, and the monk
> and the shepherd take leave, from the promenade
> and Apollo, similarly
> from Rome, of suchlike palaces, says
> Ade! impurely bitter, therefore!
> Then comes the hymen of heaven.

> Aber [w] ie wie ein Schi[ff]
> (L)Das lieget im Hafen, des Abens, wenn die Gloke lautet
> Des Kirchthurms, und es nachhallt unte[n]
> []Im[] (T)Eingewaid des Tempels und der Mönch
> Und Schäfer Abschied (,)nehmet, vom Spaziergang
> Und Apollen, ebenfalls
> Aus Roma, derlei Palla[]sten, sagt
> Ade! unreinlich bitter, darum(!)!
> Dann kommt das Brautlied des Himmels. (7: 377)

Here, the taking leave "from the promenade [*Spaziergang*]" that Hölderlin
speaks of takes place at least doubly, for the figures of the poem, as for the
poem itself. For whereas Schiller's "Promenade" closes with a triumphant
tone: "And the sun of Homer, see! she also smiles to us [*Und die Sonne
Homers, siehe! sie lächelt auch uns*]" (314), Hölderlin's monk and shepherd,
who depart from their departure—from their "promenade" or from *the*
"Promenade"—are aligned with a bitter Apollo, who is most closely related
to Helios, the sun of Homer in the Greek tradition and in Hölderlin's
poetic œuvre. And rather than greeting us, he takes leave with a more than
ambivalent word.

Likewise, the bell not only heralds "the hymen of heaven" but also
might be heard to echo Schiller's "The Song of the Bell [*Das Lied von der
Glocke*]." However, this bell does not culminate in the "Concordia" Schiller announces near the end of his poem, calling the bell a "voice [. . .]
from above, like the bright regiment of stars [*eine Stimme [. . .] von oben /
wie der Gestirne helle Schaar*]" (238). It does not, like Schiller's bell, promise
the reconciliation of nature with human art (238); the commemoration
of the deaths, births, weddings, and triumphs of the community; and the

testimony to us that he triumphantly extols, when he writes: "there it will loudly testify of us [*da wird es von uns zeugen laut*]" (228). In contradistinction to such song, Hölderlin's "hymen of heaven" may also be the hymen of the Apocalypse, distantly recalling John of Patmos's pronunciation of "the marriage of the lamb" (Rev. 19.7). After all, *an* end, if not *the* end is addressed in the verses that follow:

> Complete-end-peace. Gold-red. And the rib tones
> of the sandy ball of the earth in the work of God
> of express structuring, green night
> And spirit, an order of pillars, really
> total relation, with the With/Midst
> and shining

> Vollendruhe. Goldroth. Und die Rippe tönt
> (Tönt) Des sandigen Erdballs in Gottes Werk
> Ausdrüklicher Bauart, grüner Nacht
> Und Geist, der Säulenordnung, wirklich
> ganzem Verhältniß, samt der Mitt
> und glänzenden (7: 377)

Unlike the marriage that John announces, however, there are not even any "blessed" ones (Rev. 19.9) summoned to witness the completion of peace that arrives, and there is certainly nothing here that "witnesses" or "testif[ies]" of us [*von uns zeug[t]*]." Rather, the hymen resounds for none, and instead of serving a communal function, the "total relation" that emerges is one that relates only the architectonic elements of "the work of God"—a divine λόγος, not in the sense of the "Word," but in its more original sense in Greek: "proportion." Nor is there any woman to marry the sky but the "rib [. . .] of the sandy ball of the earth" itself, an utterly inhuman Eve for the heavens, in an apocalyptic repetition of Genesis without man. Even this familiar rhetoric of generation, however, will collapse as well, as the word for the hymen, or "song of the bride [*Brautlied*]" turns into a "structuring [*Bauart*]," a near anagram for "bride [*Braut*]" that renders it foreign to any traditional rhetoric of nature and earth.[15] Thus, while the "order of pillars [*Säulenordnung*]" that Hölderlin arranges in apposition to the other substantives of these verses may indicate the rise of a new temple—another Vatican, another space of song for the god—it would have to be as vacant as the first.

If Schiller shines through this poetic fragment, then, Hölderlin turns his contemporary's coordination of Hesperia and classical antiquity in "The Promenade" into a dynamic of departure, and he restructures the concord between nature and art in "The Song of the Bell" into one where human art is eliminated, and human witnesses are excluded from the transformation of the cosmos into a sheer order of measures. With and through the midst of Peter, John, Apollo, and Schiller—with and through traces of writers from classical and biblical antiquity, as well as Weimar classicism and his native Swabia—with and through a more than ambivalent "Mitt"—Hölderlin approaches in his text an utterly incommensurable language. He not only announces the frequent recurrence of the "confusion of tongues" but speaks of and to that confusion, with every word. He approaches, in other words, a prophecy of language that could never have been one.

Thus, "der Vatikan" marks a point of departure for pursuing the implications of translation, prophecy, and the origins of language, by setting us in their midst, throughout. Insofar as each word renders a singular configuration of tongues and speakers, and the next may involve utterly different ones than the last, such writing could never be systematized or reiterated as *a* language, so long as "language" were to be understood as a proper mother tongue, as a system of differential signs used by a community of speakers, or as the structured process by which a thought comes to vocal or written expression. For all the resonances that might be traced in a single passage of Hölderlin's text, it would be impossible to limit all that speaks at any one of them. Instead, the many determinate words that each single word evokes will have already been drawn out of the limits that might appear to lend them definitional integrity within the languages from which they seem to derive. This is a language of e-limination, which is why the emergence of language appears simultaneous with its confusion, why the scene of origination is depicted as a scene of destruction, why Genesis and the Apocalypse coincide, and why this most ambivalent event is to be reiterated indefinitely: "But often as a firebrand / arises confusion of tongues."

The limits that Hölderlin's poem approaches and transgresses will mark other texts from this time in Germany, too, where an intensive rethinking of prophecy and translation have been said to take place, but rarely considered in relation to each other, as two modes of speech that expose to an extreme the fundamental uncertainty over what language and its speakers are—an uncertainty that may, with varying shades, haunt every utterance. In his monograph from 2002, *The Rhetoric of Romantic Prophecy*, Ian Balfour brilliantly traces the emergence of various prophetic discourses in England and Germany, in the wake of the French Revolution, and of "a new way of reading the Bible—mythologically and poetically—that developed gradually in the eighteenth century and flourished in the years of political and intellectual tumult around the turn of that century" (2). Although he emphasizes the nonoriginary nature of speech that prophecy entails—"in the beginning, then, is the repetition of the [divine] word" (5)—translation figures only occasionally in his analyses, as when he discusses the work of Christopher Smart, whose "fascination with the [divine] letter turns into something of the order of the spirit through its very inventiveness, its proliferation of readings, its well-nigh infinite translations" (36), or when he turns to Hölderlin's remarks on Sophocles (245–49). In this way, Balfour's insights into the polyvocality of prophetic utterance incite readers to build upon his analyses and to consider the ways they speak to the equally critical importance of translation during the period he examines.

Similarly, those writers who have focused primarily upon translation around the turn of the century, such as Antoine Berman and Susan Bernofsky, have acknowledged the importance of the translation of sacred texts—most crucially, Martin Luther's German Bible—to the task of the translator, as it was conceived around 1800. Yet neither writer enters into the structural similarities between translation and prophecy, which both imply speaking for, with, and in the place of another. Doing so, however, would allow one to avoid the very presuppositions of national languages and clearly defined boundaries between the proper and the foreign that both writers so emphatically call into question through their readings, but nonetheless often recur to in their theoretical terminologies, writing, for example, of the different ways writers negotiated the relationship of original and "target language[s]" (Bernofsky 26). Berman and Bernofsky challenge these presuppositions most strongly in their analyses of Hölderlin's Sophocles translations, as when Bernofsky demonstrates several ways in which Hölderlin's texts conform to neither the German of his contemporaries nor to Sophocles's Greek, but develop instead an idiom involving traits that might be ascribed to both (foreign) tongues (105–06). In showing how Hölderlin recuperates lexical elements from Martin Luther's Bible translation, while introducing neologisms that approximate Sophocles's Greek (254–55), Berman exposes what he calls, quoting Heidegger, "a simultaneous double movement [. . .] that links the 'experience of the foreign' [. . .] to 'the apprenticeship of the proper'" (258), in a way that first produces the foreign and the proper, and con-founds them, in the strongest sense of the word.[16] In turning from the theoretical framework and vocabulary of their monographs, then, I hope to further the tendencies that their particular readings show, and by deviating, I hope to follow the lines of inquiry they open.[17]

One possible word for the confusion of tongues that Berman and Bernofksy register in Hölderlin is "prophecy," where the writer or speaker is always inextricably and indistinguishably beholden to the other(s) that speaks through her or him. Such a plurality of voices and tongues is, as Jean-Luc Nancy has shown in his reading of Plato's *Ion*, instantiated each time in a singular, unrepeatable, and thus unsystematizable way (*Le partage des voix* 67–68), and therefore the most pronounced challenge to the fiction of a static, coherent system that all too often makes up what is called, with the terminology of Saussurean linguistics, a *langue*. But by virtue of their singularity, prophecy and translation—or translation as prophecy—can never be the objects of theory or linguistics, but can be addressed only through close engagement with the languages of translator-authors. Following the work of Balfour, Berman, and Bernofsky—and with strong inspiration from Nancy—I seek to perform such engagement throughout this book, to expose how those texts I read and write with might call upon us to change the way we think about language.

Among the texts I examine are Wilhelm von Humboldt's *Agamemnon* translation, Friedrich Schlegel's *Aurora* project, Hölderlin's *Empedokles*, and the *Phenomenology of Spirit*, which G. W. F. Hegel introduces as a translation project in a draft of a letter to Johann Heinrich Voss, the most eminent German translator of Homer. All of these works solicit readings that respond to the questions Derrida provocatively poses near the start of his essay on Babel: "How to translate a text written in several languages at once? How is the effect of plurality to be 'rendered'? And if one translates with several languages at a time, will that be called translating?" (Graham 196). Each of these works also solicits readings that would address how, precisely, a prophetic modus would operate once Apollo has departed—not as speaking for and instead of the god, but as speaking for and instead of indefinite others; once the end of the biblical prophets has been pronounced; and once the place for the *vates*, inspired by a single god to announce his words or to address what may yet arrive, has been vacated. For as in Hölderlin's "der Vatikan," these texts also speak to a departure from biblical or classical models of prophecy and eschatology, as much as they deviate from any notion of translation that would presume the integrity of an original language. Thus, none can be described in terms of an "experience of the foreign," either, whether this would refer to the assimilation of another language or another's words into one's own or to the assimilation of one's own tongue and words to those of another, as Berman has suggested. To the contrary, the languages that these texts speak challenge any assumption of the proper that might authorize such a distinction and with it, the languages of constative, imperative—and thus binding—communal speech. Most radically, as languages that approach the limits of language, as languages of the limit—and therefore, too, of elimination—these texts must be read as texts that most rigorously register the experience of language *as* foreign.

In the first chapter of *Prophecies of Language*, I turn to the relationship between translation, philosophy, and prophecy in Hegel's *Phenomenology of Spirit*. For Hegel, it is philosophy per se that is to be translated. In a letter to Voss, he describes his forthcoming *Phenomenology of Spirit* as an attempt akin to Voss's and Luther's monumental translations of Homer and the Bible, respectively. "[S]o I will say of my striving," he writes, "that I will try to teach Philosophy to speak German," since "a people is barbaric and does not see the preeminence that it knows as its true property, so long as it has not learned it in its own language" (*Briefe* 99–100). Differently than his predecessors, however, Hegel does not seek to translate a canonical text from the Western tradition, but a philosophical language that was never spoken or written before. In this orientation toward a language that does not yet exist, his first major philosophical work—and translation project—is oracular, and it will turn out that the language of the oracle, which he addresses near the end of his work in his chapter on "Art-Religion," is pivotal to the genesis of philosophical language, as he strove to trace and produce it from the start. But it is pivotal in more senses than one. On the one hand, the oracle, which Hegel designates as the first language, and as one that, properly speaking, says nothing but that it speaks, prefigures the language of philosophy in its absoluteness. On the other hand, however, it implies an irreducible foreignness that even the most rigorous dialectical operations cannot sublate and surpass. For Hegel's discussion of the oracle is fraught with traces from those passages of the Hebrew Bible, Spinoza, and Homeric epic that he translates in his chapter—and only in tracing his German back through these texts and tongues can the logic of his remarks on language be unfolded. At the same time, these traces resonate with each other independently of his dialectic, and thus speak with and against his philosophical project in ways that open it anew. The confusion of tongues that a close analysis of his chapter reveals suggests that neither the oracle nor philosophy could be known "as [one's] true property." Instead, this complication in the language of philosophy is precisely what renders Hegel's translation other than the eternal, closed system he had set out to present.

The second chapter is devoted to Wilhelm von Humboldt's writings on language; I argue that his most original insights into the emergence of the word are presented not in his linguistic essays and treatises, but in the preface he appends to his translation of Aeschylus's *Agamemnon*, where the prophecies of Cassandra play the most crucial role. Humboldt operates upon different premises than Hegel, his future colleague at the University of Berlin, when he reflects upon the twenty years of labor he had invested in translating Aeschylus's *Agamemnon*. From the start, he stresses the untranslatability of the work in question, draws attention to the shortcomings of his own work, and makes no pretensions to producing a monumental achievement. Instead, translation and language are considered immediately according to their temporality: "For translations are [. . .] labors that test and determine the standing of language in a given point of time, as upon a remaining standard for measure, and should work upon and into it, and must always be repeated anew" (*Gesammelte Schriften* 8: 138). But from the moment that Humboldt's rhetoric shifts to time, measures, and work, the labor of translation becomes recast in dynamic terms that anticipate his famous definition of language as *energeia* in his last, magisterial treatise, *On the Diversity of Human Language Structure*. When does translation and, by analogy, language itself, emerge—and by what force? Only in addressing this question is it possible to delineate more precisely the way in which translations might work upon language at any "given point of time," along the lines of an incommensurable foreign text, where, as Humboldt puts it, one "can always only set against each utterly proper term a different one" (8: 130). And only then might one measure the possibility of renewing a given language through translation, thereby giving rise to language as it had never hitherto been spoken or written—which is what every translation, according to Humboldt, should promise. Here, the term that draws the various threads of Humboldt's text together will turn out to be the "symbol," which recurs with insistence throughout Humboldt's preface, and, true to its etymological root as a "throwing-together," marks a point of synthesis that is at once a moment of collision and contradiction—a *syn-ergeia*, which punctually takes place and has the potential to alter the status of all that would have been said before and after.

Humboldt illustrates this dynamic in his description of translation as a labor of setting words against words. However, the epitome of symbolic language will be Cassandra's prophetic outburst in the midst of Aeschyslus's tragedy, which "fills out the most horrifying moment of the piece" (8: 124), while suspending, at least temporarily, the otherwise relentless course of dramatic action and rhetoric. Her incendiary speech, which Humboldt depicts in analogy to the flash of a lightening bolt, comes to set her Greek against the Greek of the actors and chorus, her time against the time of the drama. Thus, with this account of a foundational fissure in speech, Humboldt translates the language of the *Agamemnon* already in his preface, and prepares for a reading of the tragedy that would disclose the way her language of prophecy works.

No reading of prophetic language, and no reading of Humboldt's reflections on language, could proceed without attending closely to Cassandra's speech in the *Agamemnon*, to which the next chapter is devoted. There, it will turn out that translation is the original problem of prophecy, as her utterances cross the registers of vision and speech, Greek and Trojan, human and divine tongues—whereby the divine source that is said to burn through her proves to be itself undecidable, at once reminiscent of the Furies and of their enemy, the oracular god Apollo. While Cassandra's speech has repeatedly been described in the terms of the sublime, beginning with the earliest Greek hypothesis appended to the play, through to Wilhelm von Humboldt's preface to his *Agamemnon*, what is most striking about her language is not the past and future horrors of the house of Atreus that her words appear to summon, but, as the chorus will say, her "speaking of an other-speaking city" (1200–01), in an other speech that also removes these Argive elders from their proper language.

Tracing the resonances of this "other speaking" in and beyond her scene, I analyze the way Cassandra demands a rethinking not only of prophecy—where gods, speakers, and tongues have become radically indeterminate—but also of the structures of action and temporality that are often understood to make up the grammar of drama. For she also interrupts the plotting that had culminated in Agamemnon's entrance into the palace, and that should have led to his murder. But more profoundly than this, Cassandra disrupts, through her speech, the presuppositions of continuity upon which any plot or time line would have to be based. In light of these pervasively unsettling effects, I return to what appear to be the more decisive remarks Cassandra makes, when she announces, laconically, "this day has come" (1301), and when she insists, more than thrice, that those whom she addresses should "bear witness to her." For how might "this day" be understood—before anything could arrive, and beyond all that could have come to pass? And what would witnessing her speech have to entail, when the status of events and speakers has been radically placed in question?

In contrast to the day that erupts with Cassandra's oracles, the next chapter revolves around Friedrich Schlegel's *Daybreak*, a poetic work that preoccupied him throughout his writing career. Based loosely on Jacob

Böhme's *Aurora*, and conceived before and after his conversion to Catholicism, Schlegel's *Daybreak* should have not only exemplified the new genre he would call "prophetic poetry" but also replaced Romantic poetry as the universal form of poetic (and prosaic) language. In one note, he will write, "every novel should [. . .], in a certain sense, be Aurora" (16: 497)—thereby reprising and parodying the conclusion of his most famous *Athenäum* fragment: "for in a certain sense, all poetry is or should be romantic" (2: 183). Characteristically, this work would come to fruition only in the form of posthumously published fragments, but in the first and lengthiest of these notes, Schlegel introduces *Aurora* as nothing less than a new cosmology on the basis of the mathematical infinite series, perpetually divided between 1 and 0. Besides translating Böhme into modern German, then, at issue is the translation of mathematical principles to language and the poetic metaphysics for which ancient cosmologies had served as models—a concern that Schlegel shared with his contemporaries such as Novalis. The order of numbers, however, does not transfer in this note into a language purified of semantic ambivalence. Instead, as a close reading of the fragment shows, in conjunction with a reconstruction of Schlegel's philosophical engagement with Friedrich W. J. Schelling's philosophy of nature and Plato's *Sophist*, the mathematical principle from which he derives the cosmos—the outbreak of his daybreak—has dire consequences for knowledge and for language. For it leads Schlegel to the premise of infinite divisibility that Plato's Socrates most vigorously contests in language, in order to establish the possibility of a propositional grammar that would allow for veridical distinctions. This consequence, which is registered in Schlegel's own syntax in a most remarkable way, results in a situation akin to the Babelian confusion of tongues. Still more precisely, Schlegel's fragment poses a challenge to the veracity of grammatical constructions. If Schlegel did not rewrite the world, and never even really wrote *Aurora*, his notes nonetheless reveal the possibility of a language of being and time that could be parsed in many ways at once, and that would therefore suspend those categories that make up the preconditions and tendencies of any possible order of knowing, predication, and timeless truth claims. Still more than this, however, Schlegel's text precludes, at least for a moment, all possible ends of prophecy and language, whether it be prediction of the future or the predication of a subject; the restitution of all that will have been, as in the Acts of the Apostles (Acts 3.21); or the command of the imperative.

In the final chapter of this book, I return to Hölderlin—not to his late poetic fragments, but to those poetological prose texts and drafts of a tragedy that he, like Schlegel, would never complete: namely, the drama that should have been based on the life and death of the ancient cosmologist and pre-Socratic thinker Empedocles. In line with the legend of Empedocles's plunge into Aetna, these texts reflect attempts to translate not a language, but a fire; specifically, the fire Hölderlin finds in his readings of Hesiod, Pindar, and Diogenes Laertes. Hölderlin approaches here a destructive elemental force, which turns out to be both the precondition for original speech and its preclusion. For Hölderlin, the logos is the prophetic or poetic *analogos* that follows upon (*ana*) a moment of burning—be it the fire sacrifices that a Greek mantic translates, the fires of Aetna, or the fiery "dissolution" of an entire fatherland, which tragedy reproduces after language and world have both gone under. At the tragic extreme, however, one must ask to what extent a prophet or poet might survive such flames, since they too belong to the world that burns. The poet-prophet Empedocles certainly does not survive to speak *his* dissolution in Aetna—and one might wonder what kind of speech would result if he could. For beneath Aetna lies Zeus's last Titanic rival, the fire-breathing Typhon, who has a hundred heads and at least as many tongues, as Hölderlin knew from his studies of Hesiod and Pindar. The pure possibility of tragic language is not an ideal totality, but a titanic one, in which all languages speak at once—a confusion of tongues *kat' exochen*. And although he would never complete his drama, its very nonachievement demonstrates the perils of an experience of foreignness in language, and shows how poetry, rather than philosophy, is where the limits and origins of speech are not only thought and spoken—but also silenced, dissolved, and disrupted, in their constitutive plurality. Yet the desire (*Ver-langen*) for and of the tongues (*langues*) that speak through Hölderlin's draft materials and that address Empedocles in Hölderlin's ode to this other "poet" cannot be extinguished, any more than the Titans can be definitively suppressed by the Olympians. By attending to and inscribing the tongues of this desire, Hölderlin exposes the saying of what is said, and gestures toward the prophecy of a language that would not foreclose the possibilities of speech beyond the orders of communication and the limits of one's proper tongue.

Another word for this desire of words and tongues might be "philology." And *Prophecies of Language* is committed precisely to this sort of philology—a philology that, in and through an inclination for language, takes neither its existence, structure, nor sense for granted, but allows itself to be most profoundly affected and addressed—and afflicted—by it.

THE PITFALLS OF TRANSLATING PHILOSOPHY: OR, THE LANGUAGES OF G. W. F. HEGEL'S *PHENOMENOLOGY OF SPIRIT*

In 1805, Hegel writes in a draft of a letter to Johann Heinrich Voss, the newly appointed professor in Heidelberg (from whom Hegel seeks support in procuring a professorship of his own):

> Luther made the Bible talk in German; you, Homer,—the greatest gift that can be made to a people; for a people is barbaric and does not see the preeminence that it knows as its true property, so long as it has not learned it in its own language;—if you will forget these two examples, so I will say of my striving that I will try to teach Philosophy to speak German. (*Briefe* 99–100)[1]

The "striving" to which he refers is the yet-unfinished *Phenomenology of Spirit*, and by tentatively ranging it among the achievements of Luther and Voss, Hegel seems to forecast his own fame or, at the very least, his philosophical promise. The promise that he makes, however, cannot be reduced to a rhetorical strategy to persuade Voss to appoint him to the Heidelberg faculty. Besides the fact that Voss may never have read these words—the letter Hegel actually ended up sending him is lost to posterity—Hegel significantly positions his project as the third and final term in a series of religious and artistic figures. He recapitulates—or precapitulates—the philosophical end and fulfillment of art and religion that the *Phenomenology* proclaims, differently, at its opening and close. Encrypted in this dead letter is the triad of spirit that Hegel will never cease to promulgate, in different configurations, from the *Phenomenology* to his *Encyclopedia* and his various lectures in Berlin. The repetition of his doctrine begins here—with the differences, however, that here, religion and art take the form of personified texts, who are made to "talk" (*reden*) a language other than their own (and thus to cease talking themselves, properly speaking); and that here, Hegel's philosophical culmination of these texts is presented first of all, like his predecessors', as a work of language and translation.

Thus, Hegel is a less unlikely figure to evoke than he may at first seem to be, when it comes to the question of translation around 1800, even though he did not enter into translation projects in the way that many of his contemporaries did, such as Johann Wolfgang von Goethe, Friedrich Schleiermacher, August Wilhelm Schlegel, and his friend Friedrich Hölderlin, all of whom sought to render in German specific texts composed in other languages, ranging from Plato's dialogues to William Shakespeare's dramas and Denis Diderot's satire *Le Neveu de Rameau*. Yet even more explicitly than these writers, Hegel inserts himself into the very line of major German translators that scholars such as Antoine Berman and Susan Bernofsky have named as the precursors to the new models of translation that would emerge in the early nineteenth century—namely, Luther and Voss. Yet neither Berman nor Bernofsky—nor more specialized scholars of Hegel, for that matter— have considered his writings within the context of those experiments and experiences in translation that were taking place precisely during the genesis of the *Phenomenology of Spirit*—and to which Hegel himself proclaims the *Phenomenology* to belong. Rather, when the question of translation does arise in studies of Hegel, his commentators most often focus either upon his translation from around 1805 of several pages from Aristotle's *de anima*, as Walter Kern has done, or upon Hegel's interpretation of concepts and terms from the Greek philosophical corpus, for which Alfredo Ferrarin's excellent monograph *Hegel and Aristotle* is exemplary.[2] Others reflect upon the difficulties and implications of translating Hegel's German into another lexis and syntax, as when Hegel's recent French translator, Bernard Bourgeois, considers the limitations imposed by the linguistic differences between German and French to be themselves functions within a generative cultural dialectic.[3] But reading the *Phenomenology* as a translation not only remains to be done; the book itself also presents unique obstacles that render the absence of such a reading less remarkable than it may appear to be. For a translation of "Philosophy" could have no textual precedent or basis—at least not in one single foreign language, or in one single text. And because there is no clear basis for this translation at either the linguistic or textual level, the most urgent questions become: what might translation mean for the *language* of Hegel's text, and what does the language (or languages) of the *Phenomenology* say about the extraordinary understanding of translation that Hegel implies, when he proposes to surpass the achievements of Voss and Luther with his own work in progress? These questions, in turn, cannot be pursued by recurring to those individual concepts and terms from ancient Greek that have guided philosophical interpretations of Hegel's more conventional labors in translation.

Here, it is not yet a matter of the philosophical concept (*Begriff*), which, as Hegel retraces it in his *Phenomenology*, should bring religious belief together with the transient, sensual intuition (*Anschauung*) from which it had hitherto been separate into an absolute knowledge that reconciles world and God. It is also not yet a matter of the progressive idealization in art that will culminate in the languages of ancient epic, tragedy, and comedy—and, finally, as the first-person speaker of drama collapses with his masked *persona*, end in a language of philosophical prose.[4] To be sure, these teleological transformations of speaking and knowing will ostensibly conclude the history that Hegel remembers, takes in, and organizes in the *Phenomenology*. But here—and implicitly, in the *Phenomenology* itself—it is a question of a thesaurus that would be available to all speakers of a language at any time, a trove of what one knows and owns, from the moment it has been learned in one's own language. Not the organic unfolding of the Hegelian concept, but a lexis, syntax, and grammar, would bring art, religion, and philosophy together to the German people, so that Hegel's task in writing the *Phenomenology* would be not only a matter of integrating the former pair into the universal system of philosophy but also, and first of all, of making Philosophy similarly available within his own language.

Furthermore, the language of Philosophy he aims to render in his book may not necessarily coincide with the more general features of Hegel's idiom that his readers have frequently noted. As is well known, the *Phenomenology* entails the destruction of the familiar forms of language, in Hegel's own German and in any related syntax. Early on, Hegel announces: "the nature of the judgment or proposition / sentence per se, which encloses in itself the difference of subject and predicate, is destroyed through the speculative proposition / sentence" (43).[5] With these words, Hegel not only proclaims that a logic of nonidentity—or, as Jere Paul Surber writes, of "dialectical identity-in-difference" ("Hegel's Speculative Sentence" 230)—will organize the writing that he performs throughout his book. He also begins to execute these principles in a writing that Judith Butler characterizes most aptly and succinctly at the opening of her analysis of the rhetoric of desire in Hegel's *Phenomenology*:

> Hegel's sentence structure seems to defy the laws of grammar and to test the ontological imagination beyond its usual bounds. His sentences begin with subjects that turn out to be interchangeable with their objects or to pivot on verbs that are swiftly negated or inverted in supporting clauses. When "is" is the verb at the core of any claim, it rarely carries a familiar burden of predication, but becomes transitive in an unfamiliar and foreboding sense,

affirming the inherent movement in "being," disrupting the ontological assumptions that ordinary language usage lulls us into making. [. . .] To read the sentence right would mean to read it cyclically, or to bring to bear the variety of partial meanings it permits on any given reading. Hence, it is not just that substance is being clarified, or that the subject is being defined, but the very meaning of the copula is itself being expressed as a locus of movement and plurivocity. [. . .] Hegel's sentences *enact* the meanings that they convey; indeed, they show that what 'is' only is to the extent that it is *enacted*. (17–18)

And in addition to Butler's observations, one might name a few other signature gestures of Hegel, such as his famous avoidance of proper names, lest the misconception arise that the subject of a sentence might be a fixed, independent entity; the chiastic turns in his rhetoric—for every progression from subject to predicate also imposes a sense of being "obstructed [*gehemmt*]," and "casts thinking backward" to the thought of the subject that has "gone missing," turning it around;[6] as well as the proliferation of reformulations that begin with the remark "or, what is the same [*oder, was dasselbe ist*]" (12, 18, 39, 79, etc.), whereby the disjunctive "oder" becomes the privileged conjunction for the elements of philosophical diremption.

But the transformation of grammar that thereby emerges would constitute less the translation of "Philosophy" from foreign tongues, as Hegel's analogy to Luther and Voss implies, than the grafting of organic teleology onto even the most basic elements of philosophical writing. As Butler's usage of the adverb "cyclically" suggests, Hegel's speculative sentences coalesce with the organic, teleological model of the concept that he will also elaborate in his preface, laying the ground for all that follows—"the science of knowing may only organize itself through the proper life of the concept" (38)[7]—for autodestruction is essential to the autoproduction of teleological causality. As Hegel's readers know, every part of every plant produces the whole that produces it, but only insofar as every moment of this eternal life cycle will also cancel itself, like the seemingly substantial subjects and predicates of basic propositions. To take Hegel's most well known example: the fruit refutes the bloom, which refutes the bud, which refutes the seed—which, in turn, reproduces bud, bloom, and fruit (10).[8] And, to the greatest extent possible, speculative propositions should also impart this autoreproductive logic; hence the necessary destruction of the form of the sentence.[9] However, in his letter to Voss, Hegel does not touch upon the way in which the logical grammar of subjects and predicates should, in the sentences of speculative philosophy, be reconceived as the immanent movement of a living, subjective substance that perpetually differentiates and reunites itself, and be reinscribed in such a way that reflects this motion. To be sure, Hegel generates a German idiom within which his thinking moves, as he emphasizes a rigorous dialectical teleology that would preclude any sustained reflection upon the particularity of the many foreign languages of religion, art, and philosophy that underlie his own masterful representation of the whole. Yet in speaking of translation explicitly, Hegel suggests in his letter there may be at least one other side to the revolution in language that he professes to Voss and executes in his text—one that would resist the universal turn of dialectical logic, and involve the very linguistic specificity it seems to suppress so restlessly.

Of course, one could not expect Hegel to preempt the arguments he will make in the *Phenomenlogy* in a letter draft about a job to one of Germany's most eminent translators. And, yes, it is, perhaps, arbitrary—or even violent—to begin approaching Hegel through an incidental, dead letter. But such incidental traces may be telling, and in any case, it is telling that, at least for a moment, Hegel presents his project as an operation in and of language that is not primarily logical or conceptual and that necessarily allows the foreign to persist. This is of utmost importance, for translation differs essentially from sublation, the primary gesture of Hegelian dialectic, insofar as nothing that is translated could be canceled out or subsumed. The "original" is precisely *not* "carried over," as the etymology of *translatio* suggests, in any proximation in a foreign tongue; it remains what it is despite every attempt to coax, say, Homer or the Hebrew prophets to speak German. Rather than being absorbed in a unifying, universal language or logic, the foreign speech of translation deflects the language of translation instead—or inflects it, as one can see in the extraordinary translations of Hegel's contemporaries, such as Friedrich Hölderlin and Wilhelm von Humboldt.

Hegel elides these aspects of translation in his letter when he accents the importance of learning "in [one's] own language" what one already "knows" and what is therefore already proper to one, as though translation were merely a reappropriation of the proper, rather than a necessarily incomplete transmission of the foreign that irrevocably estranges one's "own" tongue and eliminates any definitive horizon between the proper and the foreign. And indeed, as Rebecca Comay has shown in her monograph *Mourning Sickness*, Hegel, along with many of his contemporaries, considers translation to be an imperative, imperial gesture that would allow at once for the appropriation and exclusion of the foreign (8–25). Yet as she also argues, translation "points to a residue of materiality within language—an 'instance of the letter' that complicates any fantasy of transla-tion as regulated metabolic exchange, transfer, or passage," and it "disturbs the metaphysical foundation of such a transaction by undermining the very notion of commensurability or equivalence" (13). If Hegel's project to translate Philosophy might be read as one of the most far-reaching gestures of appropriation, then, it may also be read against the grain, to the opposite effect. Precisely in aligning his work with the major German translations of the modern era, Hegel hints toward a different way into his philosophical project than the one he will propose in his preface and introduction to the *Phenomenology*: a philological one, which would seek those traces of the foreign that are not overcome, but that persist as the many-tongued, and therefore incoherent, substance for the motions of Philosophy this substance at once grounds and crazes. With his letter to Voss, Hegel opens an approach to his text that would involve the most careful attention to his own gestures of translation.[10]

However, the unique object of Hegel's translation speaks against this possi-bility, at least at first. If Hegel's striving is, as its juxtaposition to the work of Voss and Luther would imply, also a work of translation, then it is a transla-tion of a text that does not yet exist. On the one hand, this is because, for Hegel, the history of thinking and knowing, as well as their various articu-lations, should culminate in Philosophy, which has not yet become formu-lated as a system or language in its own right, let alone in German—despite the explicit efforts of contemporaries such as Johann Gottlieb Fichte to do precisely this.[11] On the other hand, Philosophy is no one text, but the spirit that has always already spoken throughout all the texts of the Western tradi-tion, in all its tongues, as Hegel suggests in his early *Differenzschrift*, where he embraces Fichte's distinction between the spirit and the letter of Kantian philosophy ("Differenz" 5). Thus, one can hardly speak of Philosophy as a translatable text on a par with the Bible or the *Iliad*—until, that is, Hegel brings forth its presentation or *Darstellung* as a whole in his *Phenomenology* and thereby recuperates the spirit(s) of the entire Western tradition as his own, one book (see *Phänomenologie* 11). The translation of Philosophy would thus be its original (re)production. It would be the telos and the repetition of all that has come before, like the organic teleology that organizes the logic of Hegel's concept and sentences. This also means that "Philosophy" would neither come from a particular text nor be fixed in and as a particular text, nor, with any iteration, ever be foreign to itself—unlike the many letters in Hebrew, Greek, Latin, and French, among others, that had previously been inhabited by Spirit.

Philosophy is thus foreign to language as much as it is immanent to many different languages, so that its translation would have to differ from the translation of Homeric Greek, and, indeed, from any familiar praxis of "translation" itself. There are tensions within Hegel's references to translation in his letter to Voss, which cannot be resolved: Can one truly translate the Spirit(s) of the past into one tongue without utterly dissolving it? What would it mean to translate something that transcends any particular language, and, perhaps, language itself? Even Hegel's own German text of the *Phenomenology* cannot be easily and unequivocally identified with the Philosophy he personifies in his epistle to Voss, nor is the German of Hegel's writing necessarily the German that Philosophy should speak. In fact, it is possible to translate the final lines of Hegel's remarks to Voss differently and to read them as an indication that German Philosophy should speak a German that is not yet spoken: the grammatically nigh-impossible clause "daß ich die Philosophie versuchen will, deutsch sprechen zu lehren" could, diabolically, be rendered, "that I want to tempt Philosophy to teach German speaking"—as if Philosophy itself could be seduced into teaching a German that nobody knows, and as if Hegel, in speaking of his own promise (*Versprechen*), can do so only in misspeaking (*sich versprechen*). This interpretive possibility is critical, in that it casts the work of language that Hegel addresses and strives to carry out in his *Phenomenology* in a way that invites a reading of this work not only as a translation project but also as a prophecy of a (German) language to come, which would also be the language of Philosophy itself, and therefore no longer confined to the national linguistic horizons of German speakers at all.

In this respect, taking Hegel's letter seriously, taking him at his word, opens the *Phenomenology* in a way that has not been explored in the major monographs and articles devoted to Hegel's language. The "Frankfurt School" critics of Hegel, such as Theodor W. Adorno, accent the problem of taking Hegel's philosophy as a whole, as a system with clear intentions that one must presuppose in order to comprehend his individual statements, and of reading word for word, sentence by sentence, to the detriment of the system. As in this chapter, the language of philosophy is at stake in Adorno's essay "Skoteinos, or How to Read"—in particular, the constitutive tension between language and philosophy, whose pretensions to state clearly what is neither clear nor reified lead to the following paradox: "to that extent, all philosophical language is a [language] against language, inscribed by the mark of its proper impossibility" (*Drei Studien* 335). Yet in his articulation of this problem, Adorno—much like more recent Hegel scholars, who adopt a similar point of departure, such as Kevin Thompson and Chong-Fuk

Lau[12]—remains beholden to the presupposition that Hegel's texts are written solely in one language, as when he writes of a passage from Hegel: "this passage is interpretable through knowledge of the common Hegelian thrust [*des Hegelschen Gesamtzuges*], especially the conceptual construction of the chapter, but not from the literal words [*Wortlaut*] of the paragraph alone" (327)—presuming that the "literal words" can be read as such.[13] Even when Adorno not only calls for a Hegel philology that would address the historical associations that are operative within Hegel's prose but goes on to assert, "Hegel can *only* be read associatively" (370, my emphasis), his thinking moves within the limits of a monolingual framework that obscures the still more troubling possibility that the language of the *Phenomenology* is not one—not a homogeneous, unified medium, but a most complex product of translation from many tongues at once. Ernst Bloch comes closer to reading Hegel's writing as a variegated idiom, when he begins his monograph *Subjekt-Objekt: Erläuterungen zu Hegel* with a discussion of the recalcitrant foreignness of Hegel's language, remarking: "of the soft or usual there remains now no trace left over [*vom Sanften oder Gewohnten bleibt nun keine Spur mehr übrig*]" (18). Yet his reflections on the traces of Lutheran German,[14] and of southern German turns of phrase in Hegel's prose (19), as well as his remarks on the two different kinds of obscurities that obstruct a facile passage through any oeuvre—obscure subject matter, "which is exactly expressed as such," and obscure phrasing that merely covers what is "clear" (20)—do not give way to a more sustained analysis of Hegel's thinking on and through the languages interwoven in his texts. When, in the late 1960s, several monographs devoted to Hegel and language appeared such as Josef Simon's *Das Problem der Sprache bei Hegel* (1966) and Theodor Bodammer's *Hegels Deutung der Sprache* (1969), the problem was posed primarily in terms of Hegel's "universal determination of language [*allgemeine Bestimmung der Sprache*]" (Bodammer 149), either as the noncategorial presupposition of Hegel's entire philosophical system and logic (Simon 175–82, 201–04) or as the medium in which "spiritual contents objectivize themselves" (Bodammer 239). While these authors acknowledge the heterogeneity of the terms Hegel adopts and translates from the Indo-European philosophical, religious, and poetic traditions, they do so primarily in passing, via remarks such as "a critical commentary to the main works of Hegel would have, in this regard, a broad field of work" (Bodammer 156). And despite the more recent publication of collections of essays devoted to Hegel and language, such as Bettina Lindorfer and Dirk Naguschewski's *Hegel: Zur Sprache* (2002) and Jere Paul Surber's *Hegel and Language* (2006), this field remains to be worked through, insofar as the emphasis of current scholarship remains, with few exceptions, upon Hegel's remarks on language as such, rather upon than the confusion of tongues into which his articulations of absolute knowing may, in fact, dissolve.[15]

The future language Hegel projects in his letter to Voss might be a German that is foreign to every German speaker, but internally consistent and systematic in a hitherto unrealized way in the history of Philosophy, in all its tongues. This would be a language of speculative sentences that, on the one hand, involve grammatical peculiarities in their own right, but, on the other hand, do what they say, transforming the nature of subject and predicate, setting them in motion, and thereby disturbing the categories of predication fundamentally. Or it may be a German that bears traces of the many (foreign) articulations of spirit that preceded this latest (and first) textual incarnation of Philosophy, and that is therefore unfamiliar to any speaker. Hegel's language may be a universal German or a polyglottal idiom; a philosophical masterpiece or a philological labor of the most complex kind; the language of God or of Babel. Or maybe it is both.

Either way, there is no guarantee that Hegel's attempt—or seduction—succeeded and no easy way to tell what, exactly, success would mean for the status of his text. Before one could evaluate this, one would have to know the language of Hegel's *Phenomenology*, which his own testimony to Voss renders questionable. Above all, however, Hegel's ambivalent promise to Voss suggests a connection between the unique kind of translation he proposes and prophecy—which, however, should be the furthest from the language of Philosophy, if his pejorative remarks on the oracle in the preface to the *Phenomenology* are any indication. His promise would thus bode ill for his system and any other that would attempt to offer a homogeneous, unified language of concepts, however seductive such an attempt may be (47). For unlike Voss's and Homer's projects, Hegel's translation of Philosophy—or its seduction to teach German speaking—would indicate a language to come, and thus structurally resemble the prophetic address to a future that has not yet arrived.

Still more importantly, however, of all the foreign languages that Philosophy should teach to speak German, the oracle comes first, on several counts. In the *Phenomenology*, Hegel calls it the first language of the God—and therefore of the absolute—in his chapter on "Art-Religion." And like Philosophy, the oracle is a language that operates across many different tongues: after tracing the religions of Persia, Judea, India, and Egypt, Hegel remarks, when he arrives upon the art-religion of Greece, "The oracle of both the God of the artistic as well as of the previous religions is the necessary first language of the same [God]" (381).[16] For this reason, the oracle is always spoken and never yet spoken, and therefore fundamentally foreign. In fact, the oracle is not only the first but also the most foreign of languages, for it is, like Philosophy, foreign to language, but in the opposite way. Not spirit, but the incidental phenomena of birds, the trees, the seething earth are the stuff of oracles, Hegel writes, as he recounts the elements of Greek prophecy. As such phenomena, the foreignness of the oracle must be not only translated but entirely overcome if Philosophy is to mediate an absolute knowing with nothing left that is foreign to itself. Hegel's prophecy of Philosophy is contingent upon a restless translation of oracular utterance, which marks one of the most critical moments in the *Phenomenology*, as Jacques Derrida also stresses in the last pages of *Glas*, where he analyzes Hegel's chapter on religion, from light-religion—a "burning of all [*brûle-tout*]" that he brilliantly reads as a moment of sheer gift and sacrifice (266)—through to the Bacchic cults, which prefigure the Eucharist (291). In distinction to other readers on Hegel's chapter on religion, such as Alexandre Kojève and Jean Hyppolite, who do not address the oracle at any length in their commentaries on the *Phenomenology*,[17] Derrida isolates the oracle: "however, contrary to habit, there is a remainder in question after the hymn, and it makes for the object of a development that is longer and more encumbered" (287). He also reads it as a moment that might trouble Hegel's logic, not only because it introduces "chance, hazard, the throw of dice into language" but also because it inaugurates the demand for translation: "by a sort of division in two of the oracle: proper language and foreign language" (267–68).

Derrida's remarks come toward the close of his book, soliciting a reread-ing of the passages he cites and analyzes, and an attempt to reopen the *Phenomenology* through different questions—namely, what happens when the language of each sentence is not one, and when Hegel's first project is conceived as (oracular) translation? How might the initial speechlessness of the oracle be brought to speak as Philosophy—as the spirit of the letter in those foreign religious and literary texts that make up the Western tradition? And how would such a translation project fail to reappropriate the proper, persisting instead as a process that not only allows the foreign to remain but also transforms the language of translation? Are the traces of foreign speech—which would structurally resemble Hegel's oracle, insofar as they are foreign and, therefore not yet grasped or understood—truly an incidental matter that the philosopher-translator might overcome, suppress, or sublate?

No approach to these questions could proceed without a thorough commentary on Hegel's language and argumentation as he introduces the oracle in his *Phenomenology*. And any such close reading of Hegel's German oracle will have to be an estranging one that moves not only from word to word, as Adorno suggests, but also from each word to those other words in other texts and other tongues that it points toward, and that sentence it to move elsewhere than Hegel's dialectic would have it. Nor can Hegel's language be written about in a way that does justice to his text, without producing an equally sinuous English, where the grammatical ambivalences and deviations, the chiasms and figural turns of the text make up the substance of the argument, as the strongest readers of Hegel, such as Hamacher, Derrida, and Catherine Malabou, remind us—not to mention Hegel himself.[18] How else can one argue after Hegel? "That the form of the proposition is canceled out must not only take place in an *immediate* way, not through the mere content of the sentence. Rather, this antinomial movement must be uttered; it must not only [present] that interior blockage, rather, this retreat of the concept into itself must be *presented*. This movement, which makes out what otherwise the proof should achieve, is the dialectical movement of the sentence itself" (45).[19]

The unique status of Hegel's passage on the oracle will also call, however, for an excessive reading: one that exceeds the brief moment in which Hegel addresses the oracle in particular, extending to the moments of speech that precede and follow it and the foreign texts that underlie them. For the oracle is foreign to the progressive logic of the *Phenomenology*, standing between Hegel's discussion of the language of the hymn and the language of epic, as a first language that has already been surpassed by both. At the same time, insofar as Hegel calls the oracle the first language of the god (or, what is the same: God), he projects this speech back upon all previous religions—the religions of Light-Essence, of plants and animals, and of the Egyptian master-craftsman—and thereby calls for a reading of the languages implicit in those sections of the *Phenomenology*, too. Moreover, both his introduction of the oracle and the passages surrounding it entail echoes from Spinoza, Luther's Old Testament, Homer, and Sophocles, which will need to be accented to the same degree that Hegel underemphasizes them, in order to work through what oracular or philosophical translation might mean in its complexity. What is at stake is the way in which Hegel, his closed system, his Philosophy, and his German are themselves a philological undertaking that has not been opened up as such yet, and how his text, especially on the oracle, crosses the limits of philosophical language it otherwise seems to produce and circumscribe. Whereas Philosophy should end in a gesture of affirmation after universal history has not only been retraced but also grasped for the first time—and whose expression culminates in Hegel's "reconciling *Yes* [versöhnende *Ja*]" (362); a reconciliation, that is, which would no longer need to be mediated through Christ, no longer demands a translation of the foreign, and already renders "Absolute Knowing," the final chapter of Hegel's book, superfluous[20]—the oracle disturbs this closure with a foreignness in and of language that cannot be and is thus never yet overcome.

In his chapter on art-religion, Hegel introduces the oracle as the scission in the existence of God that first allows him to fully be, in any religion: "The *oracle* of both the god of the artistic, as of the previous religions is the necessary first language of the same [god], for in his *concept* lies just as well that he is the essence of Nature as of Spirit, and thus has not only natural, but also spiritual existence" (381).[21] Language would be the spiritual existence, or being-there (*Daseyn*), of god, who is also there in all of nature, but not in the same way, and not sufficiently to fulfill all that is comprehended in the concept of god. This premise seems straightforward enough, though already here, the ambivalence of Hegel's language makes it unclear whether the god to whom the "first language of the [god]" belongs is there at all yet. For at this critical point, the "oracle of the god" says nothing—not even "god." Even if it were nothing other than the pronunciation of its source, by marking the separation of the god's spiritual and natural existence, the oracle would announce the foreignness not only of this existence but also of god himself.

The articulation of this foreignness is carried out through Hegel's next sentences: "Insofar as this moment [of spiritual *Daseyn*] lies first in his *concept* and is not yet realized in religion, so language is, for the religious self-consciousness, language of a *foreign* self-consciousness. The (yet-for-eign-to-his-congregation) self-consciousness *is* not yet *there* as his concept demands [*wie sein Begriff fodert*]" (381).[22] The oracle says nothing, in fact: there is not only no god, but also no language of the god, if, as Hegel puts it, this moment of his concept is "not yet realized in religion," and he "*is* not yet *there* as his concept demands." However, in the very moment that god *must* be in language (since his concept demands it) *and* there is no language of the god, everything turns around. Under the pressure of a demand uttered by no one, "language"—*all* language, as Hegel's absolute usage of the noun implies—becomes "language of a foreign self-consciousness." There is a language of the god, then, after all. But it is for no one, for language itself has become the language of a foreign god, and therefore a foreign language. As soon as it is not "yet," divine language has already begun. As soon as any phenomenon is understood as a foreign message, even if the message itself is not understood, language is there. Reading a similar passage from Hegel's lectures on the philosophy of history, Hamacher writes, "where this speculative inversion [. . .] can take place, there must be a circular course between spirit and nature. Its logical form is the self-presupposition of spirit in its other—and 'spirit' is nothing, other than this self-presupposition" (*Entferntes Verstehen* 14). The gesture of presupposition reflects, in turn, a desire for appropriation and mastery not unlike the one that underlies translation. As John Russon makes clear when he reads the master-servant dialectic in the *Phenomenology* as a scene of reading, "to be a master means to be an interpreter. [. . .] Interpretation [. . .] involves totalization and unification, that is, the positing of a determinate extent as a signifier, and the positing of a determinate intent as a signified. Reading thus demands that one assumes that there is something to be read, and that this expression is the presentation of a unified meaning" (74). This iteration of what might be described as a characteristic gesture of Hegel's is not unrelated to the intentions he expresses in his letter to Voss, namely, to render the language of the god not only property, but "true property" of the Germans, by coaxing it surreptitiously "to speak German" (*Briefe* 99–100). Yet here, a translation has taken place, not from the foreign to the proper, but from an indeterminate "language" to the inconceivable foreign "language of a foreign self-consciousness." How, then, might this specific passage demand to be read—or not?

These features of Hegel's discussion of the oracle already suggest why Hegel would frame his own project as a translation project, and why the particular task of translation that arises when he finally arrives at the "first language" of the *Phenomenology* is inseparable from prophecy. The first language is and must be absolutely foreign, absolved from any relations that might limit it or reduce it to a matter of mere representation or historical contingency. Without such an absolute starting point, no equally absolute language of Philosophy could unfold. The transhistorical oracle, which Hegel determines in terms of privation—of not-being-there and of foreignness—fulfills precisely this demand of his logic, and in all that follows, it will be a matter of translating this incomprehensible and inaccessible speech into the proper terms of absolute knowing. The oracle cannot be defined any more closely than this, because it is, as Hegel presents it, separate from any speech that exists as spoken. But this nonspeech is not nothing, and Hegel must address prophecy in order to pronounce its end. A translation from the foreign to the proper must take place, and this is not only the promise, but also the demand of his text, which must be fulfilled if Philosophy is to begin to speak.

Still, Hegel's articulation of this demand is not so clearly comprehensible that such strategic, systematic presuppositions suffice to interpret it. The oracle of the god would be an initial estrangement of language per se. Since this language is the "necessary first language," regardless of where one begins—in Persia, Israel, India, Egypt, or Greece—it belongs to no particular place or historical moment, let alone to any particular speaker. This implies, too, that for all that might be spoken, no people would have a proper language (or a god), but for this unspoken demand ("Foderung") of an unspeakable concept. And alone, the phrase "as his concept demands" is stranger than it may at first appear. Not only could one read that god is not there in language "as his concept demands" him to be there; one might also read that god is not there in language "as his concept demands" him *not* to be there. Hegel's grammar precludes a choice one way or the other, leaving no way to determine, let alone satisfy, this demand that god exist or not in speech. At first, in other words, the oracular foreignness of language is an aporia, and thus an impasse to translation and progressive argumentation alike.

Yet Hegel proceeds by isolating still more radically the self of the foreign self-consciousness of the oracle. In the next sentence, he speaks only of the "self," so that the language and consciousness of this "foreign self-consciousness" also go missing, estranged: "The self is the onefold and thereby straightout *universal* being–for–itself, the one, though, that is sundered from the self-consciousness of the congregation, is only at first a *lone one*" (381).[23] One ends up with a "one," apart from the community (*Gemeine*) and, therefore, from all that is common, shared, accessible, speakable. Marked off further, with a dash—a gesture that scans the *Phenomenology*; denotes the caesuras in the rhythm of the Hegelian concept; and displays the graphic cuts and openings, the wounds, of the speculative text—this estrangement, at and beyond its limit, becomes reformulated as the proper: "—The content of *this proper and singular language* yields itself from the universal determination in which the absolute spirit *per se* is set in his religion.—" (381, my emphasis).[24] In the beginning was not the Word, but the One, and the One was itself a "proper and singular language," as though the proper could not be reached in its essence otherwise, if not by a *reductio* to a mere "one," to property and propriety at its barest and purest.

Hegel thus stages radical foreignness as the condition, and not the opposite, of the proper. This should not surprise, since such conversions are the only way any opposition can truly be overcome, as any reader of the Hegelian dialectic should know. And with this, one already knows the rest of the story: From here, it should be possible and necessary for this singular one to become a universal one, just as the singular "I," "here," and "now" in Hegel's chapter on "Sense-Certainty" show themselves, in truth, to be universal categories—although, as Paul de Man and Andrzej Warminski have shown, these universal categories can show themselves only by speaking again, against themselves (de Man, *Aesthetic Ideology* 91–104; Warminski, *Readings in Interpretation* 163–79). Yes, Hegel should be well on his way to the universal logic and language of Philosophy, and everything addressed in the passage on the oracle speaks in favor of a model of dialectical translation—and after this, sublation—that would overcome the foreign entirely, and that would operate at a conceptual level, where any variety of the singular and foreign—in and beyond any particular language—could be evoked and overcome in a few strokes. And yet the language of Hegel's passage also speaks against the logic of sublation.

The first proper language is a singling out of the foreign, unspeakable source of speech from any words that might circulate in common. If divisions and distinctions are crucial to any philosophy of language, here, it is not primarily a question of the division between a signifier and a signified, or of the differences that mutually determine signifiers within a given language, but of the absolute difference between speaker and speech. This constitutive foreignness of any proper self to common language is the split foundation for language as such, and it would seem to be an unmendable one, were it not that it also appears to repeat the split Hegel evokes and surpasses at the beginning and throughout the *Phenomenology*. The singular is always at odds with the universal, but—as the familiar story goes—only for a moment, for it *is* only as the universal. But here and now, Hegel does not proceed, as he did in his chapter on "Sense-Certainty," to universalize and reconcile this difference. Significantly, the singular language of the oracle *follows* Hegel's discussion of the first universal language of the hymn, which courses through—liquefying and electrifying—every singular self-consciousness of ancient Greece "as a universal one" and as the "equal *doing* of All" (380–81). He evokes the oracle, in other words, only *after* it has been surpassed by a language that should have already overcome its foreignness. It becomes a theme in his writing only *after* it has been translated into a language common to all, which is so immediate and so universal that Hegel will describe the spread of the hymn in terms of the communication of disease (*Ansteckung*) and electric heat (*Strom*).[25] On the one hand, this deferral of the oracle is yet another sign of Hegel's rigorous writing. If the oracle is by definition a language that is not yet there and not yet spoken, it could be addressed only after a universal language has come into being. Nonetheless, its belated introduction also means that the oracle itself gives pause, in that it interrupts this hot, hymnic current, which culminates in a polyptotic pulsation of "One." Here, Hegel writes, "the spirit has, as this universal self-consciousness of All, its pure inwardness just as well as the Being-for-Others and the Being-for-Itself of the single ones in One Oneness" (381).[26] As if to sully this pure One (and in Hegel's German, the "one" of "One Oneness," "Einer Einheit," flows into "One Purity," "EineReinheit"), Hegel begins a new paragraph with the sentence that introduces the oracle: "This language differentiates itself from another language of the god, which is not that of universal self-consciousness" (381).[27] Could it be, then, that the oracle is not only not yet there, but also a decisive, foreign eruption of the "not yet" within universal language or logic, even after it has begun? After all, it does short-circuit the hymn, the first universal language of the *Phenomenology*, as Derrida has also emphasized (*Glas* 287). And it could be that the oracle is, for this same reason, insurmountable and untranslatable, however one might think, parse, or cross through the demands of translation.

When it comes to the oracle, something different is happening in Hegel's language and logic than elsewhere in the *Phenomenology*. Before one could decide about the kind of course an absolute language of Philosophy might take and what kind of translation it involves, then, it will be important to dwell longer upon the foreignness of oracular speech, or to go back to those moments when it would have been implicit in the previous religions of the *Phenomenology*. What is more, there is a sign in Hegel's text that compels his readers to do just this, that introduces an obstruction in the text and cuts off its progress. For the passage in which he claims that "this proper and singular language yields itself from the universal determination in which the absolute spirit *per se* is set" begins and ends with a dash. The sentence thus stands doubly apart from what precedes and follows it, marked off with caesuras such that, in this context, the reader is cast back to the first "universal determination" of religion, the monotheism of "Light-Essence [*Lichtwesen*]." Of all previous religions, moreover, this one is primary, insofar as Hegel will call the god of the Greek oracle a "Light-Essence," too—which common name not only translates and reflects Apollo's proper association with the sun but also associates Zoroaster, Jahwe, and Apollo, as though these were all many names of the same One. Under the auspices of the oracle, then, Hegel solicits one to retrace, retrospectively, his trajectory from this essential light to the heat of the hymn.

When Hegel presents the first, monotheistic religion of "Light-Essence" and his oracles, the primary division between speaker and speech is already drawn, and in a way that promises the linguistic structure of all reality as a foreign message or emission. With the words "This-One is adorned with the manifold forces of existence and the figures of reality as with a selfless ornament; they are mere (bearing without their own will) messengers of his power, onlookings of his majesty and voices of his praise" (371),[28] the division within "the forces of existence and figures of reality" that can make them (both forces and figures and) emissaries, as well as the division within the god that allows him to be announced (and covered, clothed) by "the forces of existence and figures of reality," constitutes a primary (linguistic) articulation. The structure of this articulation, in turn, corresponds to the structure of the oracle Hegel will describe later. The lone, singular God is foreign to the range of foreign emissaries he emits. He is only in his absence from these emissions, and thus is "not there yet as his concept would demand," in all possible senses of the phrase. On the one hand, his emissaries should announce him, and only him; on the other hand, he should not be reducible or identifiable with any one of them. Thus, he should and should not exist or be there in their language. His detachment and absence, in turn, is what lends him his singularity, and thus his propriety, like the lone one that emerges toward the end of Hegel's brief paragraph on the oracle.

But here, the oracular, foreign language of "Light-Essence" is also foreign in another way. In its simultaneous openness (there is no limit to the manifold of messengers, or to their figurations, nor do they enter into relations among each other) and closedness (they all "mean" and glorify God alone, but as his adore(n)ment, they also render him absolutely closed-, clothed-off), this articulation amounts to: "God spoke ★ ★ ★." Or, what is the same thing, "Light-Essence" amounts to a language of limitless "names [*Nahmen*]" (371), which Hegel will present in such a way that they are absolute: absolved from any (Adamic) name giving as well as any systematic relations to each other that might allow them to mean. Yet if the origin of language depicted here is essentially meaningless, what does all the illumination of the world elucidate, when it comes to the language of Philosophy? And why does Hegel, after Luther, have to "ma[k]e the Bible talk in German" again, without any explicit reference or attribution to the biblical sources of his book?

Now it is possible that the implicit phrase "*God* spoke" suffices to originate language and the world, and that the utter foreignness of his many names is no real matter. But this moment in the *Phenomenology* is pivotal for the language of philosophy, and for language as such, as Paul de Man has noted in his reading of Hegel's *Lectures on Aesthetics*:

The monotheistic moment (which in Hegel is not or not yet the sublime) is essentially verbal and coincides with the fantastic notion that *die eine Substanz* could be given a name—such as, for instance, *die eine Substanz*, or the One, or Being, or Allah, or Yahweh, or I—and that this name could then function symbolically, yielding knowledge and discourse. From this moment on, language is the deictic system of predication and determination in which we dwell more or less poetically on this earth. (*Aesthetic Ideology* 111)

The *one* name, in other words, that originates the phenomena of the world and all other names to speak of would be enough for the foreignness of language to be overcome before it could even become a problem. And this one name could, as de Man suggests with his list, be any number of names, without their variations making any difference, insofar as everything comes down to the inauguration of this structure. Yet it remains significant that this passage is also Hegel's translation of the Old Testament moments of Creation and naming, in a philosophical language that competes with not only Luther's Bible but also the contemporary renditions of this scene one finds, for example, in Herder and Hamann. Hegel is not only translating, or carrying over, the transhistorical and translingual structure of the foreign oracle as the structure of divine language. He is also taking up the original structures of speaking and naming that occur in the Hebrew Bible in particular. And as he begins to reformulate human names or divine speech acts as "names" or tokens that arise through a "taking-in" or "taking-true [*Wahrnehmen*]" of divine substance, he translates them into his earlier rhetoric of perception in a way that functions less as a reappropriation of these foreign texts than as an expropriation of his own terms.

Immediately before his sentence on the "forces of existence and figures of reality" that announce God's power and praise, Hegel writes: "The content that this pure *being* unravels, or its true-taking [*Wahrnehmen*], is thus an inessential byplay on this substance. [. . .] Its determinations are only tributes-toward, which never coalesce into a standing-in-themselves, but remain only tokens / take-ins [*Nahmen*] of the many-tokened One [*vielnahmigen Einen*]"[29] (371). What substance or being un-ravels or de-vel-ops (*ent-wickelt*) is just as immediately taken back. This is why its "content" is uncontainable: it "contains" nothing other than the words that Hegel sets in apposition to it, as its own, always incomplete "taking-true" or "taking-in" (*Wahrnehmen*) of itself. Indeed, one might retain here Hegel's morphological reinterpretation of "Wahr-nehmen" or "perceiving" as "taking-true" from his early chapter on "Perception," since the true, for him, is always the proper, and the proper is what Light-Essence is consistently in the act of appropriating—without ever eliminating its foreignness to all, and the foreignness of all to it. The "taking-true" of "Light-Essence" is itself nothing other than its taking—and thus, it is no agent, no "taker," in any proper meaning of the word. The determinations or "at-tributes" of this substance, on the other hand, also demand a morphological reinterpretation akin to that of "Wahr-nehmung." For they are, in this passage, "tributes" (-tributa) "toward" (ad-) in the absolute sense: in the very moment they move toward the manifold exteriority that announces the glory of the One, they also move back toward this same One. In the same way, in the very moment they are emitted, these (at-)tributes are immediately taken back into and by the substance that manifested them, as "tokens" or "take-ins" (Nahmen) of the "many-tokened" or "many-taking" (vielnahmigen) One. With this, the structure of perception itself loses hold; it is so thoroughgoing that perceiving becomes a sieve.

But there is still more that might be sifted from this passage for both Hegel's presentation of divine language and for the status of translation in his text. For one, these "mere attributes" mark a rare instance in which Hegel avails himself of a Latinate word. This word is, in its own right, overdetermined in a way that exceeds the context—or subtext—of the Hebrew Bible. For "attributes" not only evokes the specific structure of naming that Hegel unfolds here, but also resonates with the relation of attributes to substance that Baruch Spinoza elaborates in his Latin *Ethics*, as an infinitude of expressions of the essence of substance, each to be taken in and perceived through itself (*Ethica* pt. 1, prop. 10).[30] Hegel can translate the language of the Hebrew Bible as well as Spinoza in one stroke, not only because the latter is, for him, the paradigmatic philosopher of the Hebrew God but also because Hegel presents the *Phenomenology* as the reserve of the entire history of spirit that thus holds both—and much more than both—among its contents. Hegel's book stages the organic, teleological unfolding of the concept, but it is also a thesaurus of Western thinking and speech. For the sake of the one goal, Hegel develops sentences with such precise syntax and word choice that each shift marks a new stage in processes he not so much describes, but per-forms, in the literal sense of the term outlined earlier in this book (4). But for the sake of the other, Hegel also writes a radical German, in which the roots—and rhetorical "flowers"—of every word, every morpheme, might have ramifications for his text in all of its senses, literal and metaphorical, etymological and poetic (see Hamacher, *Pleroma* 232–34.). Every sense of a word or a morpheme, including its foreign senses, can thus be, at any moment, a crucial attribute to the one concept that unfolds. And if there are still ways to describe this linguistic strategy as an organic process—which is *the* propelling metaphor for Hegel's language, insofar as it is the metaphor of teleology—this can take place only if the organic process is also understood as matters of grafting and wild overgrowth.

The God of the Hebrew Bible and Spinoza coalesce in Hegel's language here, so that the closer Hegel comes to a philosophical language that, in the byplay of its morphemes, etymological derivations, and foreign borrowings, says what it knows, the more his language branches out toward the foreign language(s) it should translate and surpass. To the extent that this is the case, even the conceptual translation of the foreign to the proper, which will have already succeeded with the language of the hymn, does not eliminate the linguistic foreignness that would continue to set the many underlying speakers of Hegel's *Phenomenology* apart. The oracle, which is the model of foreign language per se in Hegel's text, and which must have been overcome in terms of the absolute, may never be overcome. And if Hegel's text permits this reading, Hegel's language would be as much a testimony to this persistent not-yet, to the singular speakers that mark the foundational rupture of any common language or speech, as it is to the reconciling "Yes" that will culminate the appropriation of every singular "I" with the universal "Ja" (362).

The full consequences of this characteristic of Hegel's writing, however, will require more patience. To return to his lumenology, or light-logic: like the oracle that Hegel will only name later, this absolute language of attributes is absolutely foreign, even to itself. The Light-Essence, which recalls above all the sublime, Hebrew God who calls "Light" into being and wears "light as his clothing,"[31] is—because all the differences it can articulate are immediately taken back in its self-consumption—benighted. Similarly, in his 1805–06 lecture course in Jena, Hegel had proclaimed explicitly that light is "the Word that yet has no articulation on it." Indifferently all illuminating, the light itself is "the tenebrous being-in-itself that never imparts itself" (*Jenaer Systementwürfe III* 36).[32] In and as a language that is not (yet) language, God speaks and has always been speaking, from the beginning; even at the limit of human speech, there is no limit of language. The attributes of "Light-Essence" indicate clearly that this "necessary first language of the . . . [God]" is no limit of "language" at all, but its radical dislimitation, an excess of language that, in its ceaseless circulation and liquidation, obscures every meaningful distinction that might be seen, spoken, or heard. What is not "yet" there is not language, but the articulation of its differences that allow it not only to take in, but also to im-part.[33]

This imparting is what happens when the light of the god becomes the spreading heat of the hymn. The indifferent One of the oracle differentiates itself into the many "ones" of the hymn, as light gives way to heat (only for every distinction to be liquefied there, too). There, the language that is always not yet becomes the immediate, and therefore disappearing, presence of speech: the hymn "is the disappearing being-there; [. . .] it remains [. . .] too much enclosed in the self, comes too little to figuration, and is, like time, immediately no longer there, in that it is there" (382).[34] Later, Hegel will refer to this language, which is enkindled by and in each and every one, as a "pure language," a "reine Sprache"—and, indeed, precisely in its radical indetermination and ubiquity, this language is a pure speaking that only speaks, but still says nothing. Radical transitivity is, in other words, intransitivity, but that is no matter. The transmission of universal speech is all Hegel seems to need in order to translate foreign language to the proper language of God and all his emissaries alike, and eventually, perhaps, to translate "Philosophy" into a universal language. For what Hegel says of the languages of the oracle and the hymn translates well to what he otherwise says of the concept. One hears, for example, echoes here of Hegel's early philosophy of nature from his Jena period, where the all-spreading, selfless light eventually concentrates into the intensity of warmth, marking the beginning of material self-determination (*Jenaer Systementwürfe III*, 79–80). And this echo should not surprise: as Hegel had said of god in his introduction of the oracle, it lies within his concept that he is "the essence of nature as of spirit"—though, in the context of the heat hymn, one might call him more accurately the "essence of spirit as of nature."

But yet again, it is not only the teleological rhythms of nature that speak in this most crucial transition in the language of the *Phenomenology*, and it is not only the proper logic of the Hegelian concept that underlies the translation from oracle to hymn, from light to heat. Yet again, what appears to be a translation of religious language to Hegel's German Philosophy is fraught with foreign remnants that suggest his project has not yet suppressed or sublated the more traditional project of Luther and the foreign originals upon which it was based, and that the language of Hegel's writing is not one. One might recall, for example, how Hegel calls the electric course of the hymn, wherein the "essence" remains "by itself" (*bei sich*), a "pure thinking or devotion [lit: *toward-thought, Andacht*]" (380). As such, it has no object. That which is thought (*ge-dacht*) toward (*an*) in this "devotion" (*An-dacht*) can only be a thinking that is always upon the verge of something thought, and that thus loses itself. After noting how the prefix "an-"—from the Latin "ad (at, to, till)"—comes to express "the movement toward the action indicated by the verb" in German compounds (149), Katrin Pahl writes of "Andacht": "this figure of emerging thought skips the actual activity of thinking and jumps right away to a submissive devotion to ready-made thoughts, that is to say, to the posture of not needing to think anymore. Before it has even begun (*An-*), the thinking has already passed (*dacht* is the past tense of *denken*) and thus is *Andacht*" (150). And if this morphological, literal translation of Hegel's term seems to stretch the possibilities of the German language, it is worth noting that, in Luther's German, "andacht" refers not only to devotion but also to the very kind of solipsism that translates itself like a hot current throughout the selves of Hegel's hymn (see Grimm and Grimm, *Deutsches Wörterbuch* 1: 302). In fact, Luther's particular evocation of this word—which is perhaps more Hebrew than German—is the precondition to reading it in this passage of Hegel's own text. (One might begin to think that following Hegel's imperative from his letter, namely, to "forget these two examples" of Luther's Bible and Voss's Homer, would amount to eliding his own "striving [. . .] to teach Philosophy to speak German" [*Briefe* 99–100].)

In Luther's Bible translation, the phrase "to be in hot devotion" (*in heißer Andacht [sein]*) appears in the place of verbs for "heating" where the prophet Hosea accuses the people of preparing and heating their hearts like an oven, while letting their kings and judges die without calling to the Lord (Hos. 7.6–7). Whatever else these verses may say—and no commentary has yet exhausted them—in Luther's version of the prophet, the German word for "devotion" refers to a hot, empty, solipsism that contents itself with "idolatry" (*Abgötterey*) and thus remains away (*ab*) from god (*Gott*).[35] Nonetheless, Luther will elsewhere stress the connection between fire and prayer throughout the Hebrew Bible, to the point where he asserts, in a gloss on 2 Kings 23.5, "for overall in the Scriptures, incense [*Reuchwerg*] means prayer."[36] Hegel's streaming hymn of heat, "lit up in all" (*in allen angezündet*), is a purification and "pyrification" that translates this conventional conjunction of fire and devotion.[37] The essence of the hymn is to have always already been consumed in a fire that absorbs god and singer alike. In his German, Hegel operates with not only the "roots" of the German language as such but also its most profoundly significant translations, those scansions in the history of the language that not only made foreign texts "talk" in its tongue but also changed its own organization and sense. Furthermore, insofar as Hegel narrates the origin and spread of communal language over the confusion between the German "Andacht" and its Hebrew roots, Hegel's firebrand evokes Babel still more than the linguistic transparency of Pentecost—to which his imagery for this hymnic moment of sheer translation also most likely refers. And in this respect, Hegel's hymn resonates with the late hymnic fragment his close friend and contemporary Friedrich Hölderlin would privately note, around the same time that the *Phenomenology* was about to be published: "But often as a firebrand / arises confusion of tongues" (*Sämtliche Werke: Frankfurter Ausgabe* 7: 377).

Rather than surpassing his predecessor, then, Hegel radicalizes the achievements of Luther's translation. For here, his evocation of "devotion" (*Andacht*) in the spirit of the Reformation not only perpetuates Luther's association with prayer and fire; the hymn that should pay tribute to god also translates god himself. The "Light-Essence" goes from a foreign language to a tongue of lightning that, although it says nothing yet but its "Self," leaves "the purified soul" (*die gereinigte Seele*, 382) and "the pure language" (*die reine Sprache*, 403) behind. Yes, already in the hymn—which yields the "immediate, pure satisfaction of the self through and in itself" (382–83)—a communion or hymen is celebrated, in which god himself is imparted and taken in by the congregation that had hitherto remained foreign to the oracle. Yet, it is only by a radically impure, inexplicit logic, which involves multiple translations, texts, and voices, that any transition might occur here in Hegel's *Phenomenology*.

And there are still more problems in this passage on the hymn that give pause. Because the communication of this Lutheran, biblical speech is like lightning—or, as Hegel also puts it, "infection" (*Ansteckung* 380)—it is absolutely lethal and can only be supposed. More importantly, because it is most intimately "proper" to all who sing it, the fire of the hymn can have nothing to do with the foreign "Light-Essence." When Hegel says "this language differentiates *itself* from another language of the god," he implies that this language acts only upon *itself*. The carrying across that takes place leaves something foreign behind, and thus leaves the foreign language of the oracle intact and untouched. Even if this foreign "something" is nothing other than the character of foreignness itself, this remainder can, strictly speaking, enter into no relation with the philosophical translation of Lutheran devotion and divine light. The Hegelian fulfillment of religious speech depends, in other words, upon remaining incomplete. Meanwhile, the oracle and the hymn differ from one another as the "not yet" and "no longer"—there is only dis-juncture between them, so that, as these limits of speaking, neither the oracle nor the hymn could truly be—eliminated.[38]

Precisely because of its liminal status, the oracle—the foreign in and of language per se—is never quite "no longer," nor can it be positively uttered and understood. Hegel suggests as much when he rapidly traces the future of the oracle in the new paragraph that follows, up through the singular speakers of his early nineteenth-century present, whom it continues to haunt, with most uncertain effect. In other words, this transhistorical moment in and of language not only affects the previous religions he had traced in the *Phenomenology* but also the moment he writes. And by not translating, by precluding any definitive transition from it, the oracle speaks against any end, per se—against, that is, the teleological tendencies of Hegel's conceptual logic and philosophical language. A different strategy would be in order to lay the problems it raises to rest.

Just after the sentences that have been analyzed so far, where Hegel had concluded "—The content of *this proper and singular language* yields itself from the universal determination in which the absolute spirit *per se* is set in his religion—" (381, my emphases), he goes on to suggest that the language of the oracle never ceases, but becomes trivial: "The universal spirit of anabasis [*des Aufgangs*], which has not yet particularized its existence, speaks therefore simple and universal propositions of essence, whose substantial content is sublime in its onefold truth, but which, for the sake of this universality, seems at the same time trivial to the self-consciousness that builds itself further"[39] (381). Here, Hegel's method for avoiding the gravity of this incomprehensible, limitless language is to reduce its significance to a minimum. It may remain, but the tune has changed from Babel to blabla. And besides: no such foreign remainder would truly speak *against* the Hegelian circulation of spirit, because it does not yet speak anything at all, and the self-consciousness of god himself has shifted elsewhere. Arguing along similar lines, with respect to Hegel's criticisms of the obscurities and idiosyncracies of Johann Georg Hamann, John McCumber writes: "Where Hamann went wrong was not in recognizing that certain aspects of himself were ineffable, but in positing that ineffable dimension as his own essence and making it the governing factor in his relationships with others" (11). Yet by the same token, the perhaps trivial questions nonetheless persist: whether Hegel's primary articulation of language—which divides the speakable and unspeakable, the proper and the foreign—ever allows a Philosophy absolved from foreignness to speak; and whether the spirit of Philosophy can ever operate apart from the many dead letters that would inflect—and thereby deflect—her telos, in multiple directions at once.[40] If the latter is the case, then one of the most monumental achievements of philosophical writing and translation would indeed fall together with Babel. It would constitute, above all, not a system of spirit, but divergent testimonies to the traces of singularity that remain foreign to every system, to every order of subordination—and therefore testimonies to a language in excess of every philosophical enterprise to date. Making a case for this possibility is not, however, a merely destructive labor of negation. For if such a coincidence would speak to the detriment of Hegel's systematic intention, it would also mark his project as the extraordinary labor of translation he proclaimed it to be, when he aligned it with the works of Luther and Voss.

Without any particular existence, the oracle persists within one of the most linguistically overdetermined passages of the *Phenomenology*. After it is no longer the true speech of the god—after the speech of truth is no longer a foreign language, but, as Hegel will write, the "secure and unwritten law of the gods that always lives and of which no one knows from when it appeared"[41]—Hegel states that the oracle becomes the indicator of personal and particular matters, incidents that depend upon the equally incidental signs "from the birds, or from the trees or from the seething earth, whose steam deprives self-consciousness of its enlightenment" (382).[42] This follows, "for the incidental is the unlit and the foreign." And if one could have thought that the modern Enlightenment set the subject over and above such foreign and extrinsic forces, Hegel suggests that the consideration or superiority (*Überlegenheit*) of self-determination will have turned out to be no better than the lottery: what "underlies this self-determination," Hegel continues, is "the determination of the particular character," which "is itself the incidental." Thus, its knowing is "just such a knowing as that of those oracles or the lot" (382).[43] The oracle is never "no longer," it is always "not yet"—and, in his second paragraph devoted to prophecy, Hegel underscores its persistence as he redoubles the Latinate "Orakel" with the Germanic "Loos" in the phrase "oracle *or* lot [*Orakel* oder *Loos*]," which he repeats twice (382, my emphasis). The "Loos," however, is not just a word that translates the "Orakel" more properly into German. It is also Luther's translation of the biblical גּוֹרָל, κλῆρος, *sors* ("lot"),[44] so that Hegel's new formulation casts the "lot" backward and forward in time and language at once. Such is the complexity of his translational operations—which here, ironically enough, happen to multiply the very word he intends to leave behind definitively.

The foreign, singular self of the ancient oracle, meanwhile, turns out to be every singular self, which is no longer a "self," but a "particular character." This character, in turn, does not yet speak or act, but makes up the incidental, individual stamp of deliberation and decision—which, in its incidentality, is that aspect of the self that is and remains foreign, like the "daimon" of Socrates (381–82). In this paragraph, the god has shifted to a daemon; the oracle has shifted from the sphere of speaking to the sphere of practical action; and the categories of "singular [*einzeln*]" and "universal [*allgemein*]" have shifted to the categories of causality ("incidental" [*zufällig*]). And the shift that takes place here from "self" to "character" is equally critical. For the German "Charakter" is a transliteration of the Greek χαρακτήρ, an agent noun that originally referred to the "engraver" and, by extension, the engraved images and markings that appeared on coins and seals. Only through the comparision between a person and minted coin would it come to mean "character" in the modern sense of the word—which, for twentieth-century writers such Walter Benjamin, does not lose its original impression.[45] With the appearance of this precise word at this point, the transhistorical, translinguistic oracle—or lot, or character—turns out to be nothing other than an internalized hieroglyph or a dead letter. It marks the return of the engraved images of ancient Egypt that had posed "ambivalent, to them themselves riddle-holding essences," which, in turn, indicated first of all the riddle itself.[46] Concurrent with the "unwritten laws" that have replaced the oracle as the source of truth is, in other words, an indecipherable writing. And if every man, in reason and speech (λόγος), participates in the universal Word-made-flesh that speaks throughout the Gospel of John (and the corpus of Hegel),[47] every speaker is also the graven image, a riddling sign with no referent, no solution, no speech—yet.

With this trace, Hegel's primary linguistic division between speaker and speech becomes a perpetual given. And unlike the Word, this trace is foreign to genealogy and, above all, teleology. Not only is it "not yet," structurally and necessarily without end or fulfillment; Hegel had remarked on its external trace in Egypt, the hieroglyphic work of the master craftsman: "[it] yet misses, however, the figure and existence, wherein the self as self exists;—it misses yet this: to speak it out upon itself that it cloisters an interior meaning in itself; it misses language, the element wherein the fulfilling sense itself is at hand / beforehand [*worin der erfüllende Sinn selbst vorhanden ist*]" (374–75).[48] Here, yet again, an unspoken character—or, what is the same, an oracular language that is not yet language—is distinguished from the element of "fulfilling sense." This word, as a present participle, is always, in effect, "fulfilling" and therefore the model for the teleological language Hegel sets out to translate in his Philosophy, apart from the singular speakers and characters that would remain foreign to any such structure. As Brian Tucker points out in his reading of the artifacts of Egypt in Hegel's *Lectures on Aesthetics*, "not only is the object inadequate to the meaning it would express, but the meaning itself, as a purely negative moment, has only one formal property—its removal from life" (68). This "removal from life" is also what removes the work of the master craftsman from the teleological fulfillment that is always, for Hegel, organic and vital. And like so many other words in the *Phenomenology*, the foreign precedents for this "fulfilling sense" indicate what, from the spirit and past letters of philosophy, is at stake in its difference from the character or the dead letter.

For one, the process of "fulfilling" echoes the ἐντελέχεια, or the "holding-in-the-*télos*," of Aristotelian ontology, which Hegel will later evoke explicitly from Aristotle's *Metaphysics* to describe the thought that has itself as its content, so that form and content are the same—and therefore perpetually in an act of self-fulfilling (*Enzyklopädie* 399).[49] Language as Hegel describes it here would also be such a structure; and, as Hegel indicates throughout the *Phenomenology*, philosophical language should also be organized according to the self-fulfilling process of organic teleology. However, so long as the work of the craftsman never "speak[s] it out upon itself that it cloisters an interior meaning in itself," its sense remains unfulfilled. Interned, neither sense nor self "ex-ists" as such, and therefore never reaches, let alone holds in, its proper end or telos. At the same time, the words "fulfilling sense" echo the fulfilling (and overfilling) that is bespoken in the Christological πλήρωμα, which Derrida and Hamacher trace through Hegel's oeuvre, from his earliest studies onward. Then, it was also a matter of the distinction between form and content, or, more precisely, of attaining an infinite (*ein Unendliches*) object that surpasses any "Gefäß," or vessel (*"Der Geist des Christenthums"* 469). With their determinate objects, neither the forms of sensual intuition (*Anschauung*) nor representation (*Vorstellung*) allow this infinite object to be—nor would, for the same reason, any particular written mark—although Christ, the incarnate logos, or the incarnate love of God, should do so, according to Hegel's interpretation of the passages from the Gospel of Matthew and Paul's Epistle to the Romans, in which love is said to be "the fulfillment of the law" (Rom. 8.4). This love should overcome the limits and separations imposed by Mosaic law, or later, Kantian categories, as well as scripture in the broadest sense of the term; hence the insistence that Hamacher remarks in Hegel's corpus upon "the *unification* of the fulfilling with the fulfilled, [. . .] the *unity* of love and law," as "envisaged in the gnostic application of the pleroma-concept" (*Pleroma* 91).[50] Whether Hegel means the fulfillment of Aristotelian teleology or Christology when he writes of "fulfilling sense" in the *Phenomenology* cannot, on the basis of this passage, be decided conclusively. But insofar as Hegel is after the embodied, living Word, which would speak the "essence of nature as of spirit," the "language" of "fulfilling sense" could not be bound in singular characters that relate to nothing, not even to themselves. Without expression, realization, or comprehension, such marks of a radically untranslatable foreignness can only go missing from any affirmation of a universal, absolute knowing.

In this light, it only makes sense that Hegel counterposes an eternally living, unwritten law to this writing, to the oracle:

> The further-formed self that raises itself to *being-for-itself* is the greater agent over the pure *pathos* of substance, over the objectivity of the rising Light-Essence, and knows that onefoldness of truth *as the being-in-itself*, which does not have the form of incidental being-there through a foreign language, but *as the secure and unwritten law of the gods that always lives, and of which no one knows from when it appeared.*[51] (381)

No less absolute than before, the oracle is simply no longer suffered as foreign substance, nor is its "onefoldness of truth" any longer withheld as an incidental, foreign language—which would be, to put it crudely, pathetic. Truth has been transformed, and the oracle displaced—or rather, overcome (and thus submerged), by the "being-for-itself" that is now the "greater agent" over its pathos. And this suppression has to do with the emergence of a very particular kind of law that differs from any sort of written mark or oracular trace.

Hegel's wording here, near the start of "Art-Religion," recalls his prefatory remarks on its end, where Christ, the individual whom spirit chooses "as the vessel of its pain," wrangles with the unfigured, positive, universal power, until his pure action, "becoming the greater agent over it, has made *pathos* into its material" (378).[52] At the same time, the notion of an eternally living law, which Hegel adopts and translates from Sophocles's *Antigone*, resonates, too, with the law of eternal self-reproduction that governs teleology for Kant and Hegel alike. Christology and teleology—the logic of Hegelian Philosophy—come together here, as the oracle and its foreignness are to be definitely transcended. But on what terms? What this pathos is, and why the oracle has been rebaptized as a "pure *pathos* of substance," will only be legible (and then only barely, as a trace) after a closer attention to what, at the moment, the true word has become. Not the hymn, but the juncture—or disjuncture—between the oracle and the unwritten law turns out to be the crux upon which the possibility of a universal language of Philosophy, which no longer has "the form of incidental being-there through a foreign language," pivots. And more than any other passage analyzed so far, Hegel's articulation of this moment is a complex of translations that involves the foreign languages of ancient mythology, Homer, Sophocles, Kant—and the early Hegel himself.

For all its orientation toward the Passion, the pathos of substance that Hegel recalls here most immediately evokes the tragic pathos of Antigone, who first voiced the "secure and unwritten law" that now seems to triumph over the foreign form of oracular language. The rhetorical alignment makes sense only insofar as Christ, like Antigone, testifies to an *unwritten* law; his should fulfill (πληρῶσαι)—though it seems to cancel—the written laws of Moses and the division that cleaves the structure of a law per se. But that crucial moment remains, for the moment, distant; here, the word of the "raised" self is, even at first glance, no true ascension yet, and the reconciling "yes" remains a long way off. For here, in this singular passage, the "greater agent" over the "pathos of substance" only announces, but does not overcome, a law under which he remains subject. In this respect, the "over" is still an "under," and Hegel will state explicitly that "the universal truth, which was revealed by Light-Essence, has retreated here into the Inner or the Under"—which will prove to be no merely incidental matter (381).[53]

The displacement of the oracle comes down less to the "further-formed self" than to the character of this law. And the language of the law that interrupts the sequence of languages Hegel will trace in "Art-Religion"— here cited from Sophoclean tragedy, but translated into prose—is no chance ingression. The not-yet and no-longer of oracle and hymn are abruptly eclipsed by an eternal language that has always already "appeared" and that remains, living. Insofar as it has always already appeared, this law cannot rhetorically, logically, or chronologically follow the words that precede it, except as a law that does not "follow." Absolved from the rigorous course of spirit that unfolds in the *Phenomenology* (and as a mark of that rigor) the eternal law thus appears casually evoked, as though it could, again and again, always be casually evoked—and it is, indeed, the only citation that Hegel evokes twice in the *Phenomenology*.[54] (Outside the chains of causality, sequentiality, and writing, the secure and eternal law can only be, in other words, a parenthetical.)

This law, with no positive content except *that* it is an eternally living law, demands, like all else in Hegel's prose, to be taken literally. Set aside and within Hegel's discussion of the oracle, the sentence Hegel adopts from Antigone only posits the eternal life of an utterly indeterminate law per se. Alone, its position and articulation here renders this law foreign to the terms that govern many discussions of Hegel's reading of *Antigone* and of the function of the law in his system of speculative philosophy. If it is true that the law generally stands, as Peter Wake has recently argued in his reading of Hegel's early theological writings, as the figure for separation prior to any experience of unity or reconciliation (151), here, it plays the far less familiar role of overcoming the "incidental being-there through a foreign language" (Hegel, *Phänomenologie* 381), effecting a reconciliation of sorts with what is foreign to language. And if it is true that, as Dennis J. Schmidt has written, "the problem of law as Hegel understands it is clear and is to be understood according to the double imperative at work in the law: on the one hand, it is centered in the universalizability of a rule; on the other hand, it is inscribed in the irreplaceable, the unique life of the singular being in a concrete situation" (92), here, there is not yet any indication of injunction, conflict, or rule. Rather, the question of singularity is moot, insofar as "incidental being-there" is, at this point—if only for a moment—eliminated And it would not do to argue that this "law" might be interpreted with reference to the dualism of the state and the family, of the human and divine law, that Hegel elaborates earlier in the *Phenomenology* in his Antigonal presentation of the Greek ethical world. For although this passage evokes a rich byplay, including the burial rites that Antigone performs for Polynices according to divine "law" in the face of Creon's edict, for now, it would be a mistake to precipitously associate this citation of Antigone with burial and to lay the problems that arise in this passage to rest by situating it within a dynamic of oppositions and sublations that is foreign to the rhetoric and syntax of Hegel's sentence here. In fact, in both instances in which Hegel excerpts this passage from Sophocles in the *Phenomenology*, it stands apart from the opposition of human and divine law with which it is traditionally associated, demanding a reading on its own, before it can be related to the more familiar situations of conflict that Hegel reads in Greek tragedy. And as Carol Jacobs has shown in her exquisite reading of *Antigone* through Sophocles, as well as Hegel's and Luce Irigaray's analyses of his drama, the burial Antigone performs presents the "unconscionable menace to the patriarchal state that Hegel foresees" (909), when he posits the law she executes against the law Creon would uphold, but in such a way that itself remains unassimilable to the structure of opposition that predominantly orders Hegel's reading of tragic drama, as well as that of many subsequent commentators on his text, such as Michael Schulte, Christoph Menke, and Schmidt.[55] For when Antigone returns Polynices to the womb of the earth, uttering unintelligible shrieks akin to a mother bird who has lost her nestlings, she "assumes the place of destructive Nature," in a way that "does not give birth precisely, but rather death—and if not quite death then the dispersal of the corpse's (Hegelian) claim to completeness of shape, to universality, and to what Irigaray calls its 'final figuration'" (Jacobs 909). Antigone thus introduces a third, unassimilable term to the conflict between divine and state law that, ultimately, dissolves it: "In her role as mother [. . .], she *neither* preserves the family *nor* serves the state. [. . .] The forms that have enabled Hegel and Irigaray, and so many others in between, to organize *Antigone*—call them if you will family and state, matriarchy and patriarchy, woman and man, Antigone and Creon—become dis-engendered" (909). But even before Antigone can complicate the structural conflict Hegel maintains as the tragedy of Greek ethicality, all that Hegel insists upon in his citation of her words at this point in the *Phenomenology* is the sheer fact of an unwritten law, with no mention of any particular action that is commanded or forbidden by it, nor any hint of an impending collision. The first step to read this law is to abide by it, as it stands alone, apart from the particularities of the dialectical drama that has become foreign to it.

This is not to say that the law says nothing, however. As an eternally *living* law, the law is defined as a language fulfilled with life. This eternal life, meanwhile, is either one that does not end, in which case it would no longer be life at all, or one that is perpetually renewed, which would accord with what Hegel otherwise writes of the organic process of spirit as of nature. Insofar as the latter alternative is the only one that could make sense, let alone fulfill it, Hegel's words betoken the teleological principles that had preoccupied him since his earliest studies—and that he had contrasted consistently to every other model of providence, foresight, revelation, and wonder (and, presumably, oracles). Referring to the categories of "Ethicotheology" and "Physicotheology," which appear toward the end of Kant's critique of teleological judgment, Hegel would write to Schelling in January 1795:

> —If I had time, I would try to determine more nearly, how far we—could now, after the fixation of moral belief, use the legitimated idea of God backward, for example, in the explanation of the teleological relation, etc., [and] now take it from Ethicotheology to Physicotheology and now be permitted to rule there. This seems to me to be the course above all that one takes with the idea of providence—both *per se*, and with wonders, and, like Fichte, with revelation, etc.—[56] (*Briefe* 17)

The problem is, yet again, oracles—and the prophecy of a philosophical language or logos that would lay them finally to rest. Around the same time, when Hegel comments upon the verb προφητεύειν in the Gospel of John, he writes that this verb refers to an inspiration that has nothing to do with the "coincidence of something real, of something individual,"[57] but with "something fulfilled by spirit." It expresses nothing mechanical, or instrumental, but "the unity and intention of the whole [. . .] of the spirit."[58] Johanine "prophecy," in other words, translates to yet another name for teleology, or for the language of "fulfilling sense"—and is not to be confused with the foreign incidentality of any oracle. The providential insight of teleology, meanwhile, should provide an alternative to blind prophecy and wonder. No wonder Hegel contraposes law and oracle yet again at the decisive juncture in the *Phenomenology*, where it is a matter of translating the oracle, of turning singular language into the eternal, universal logic of Philosophy. Now, at this point in the *Phenomenology*, the terms have shifted subtly, and the oracle is contrasted to a living law from the language of ancient Greece, which, on the basis of its liveness alone, sets Hegel's argument on a similar course that should turn prophecy into providence.

The law of life according to Kantian teleology is such that the effect of the cause is the cause, each part of the whole produces the whole that produces it,[59] and every moment of the cycle is on hand and beforehand (*vorhanden*). Insofar as this causal model turns the linear, mechanical chain of causal succession back upon itself—and causal succession was, in Kant's *Critique of Pure Reason*, the ground for any objective temporal succession—the law of life is also the eternal exception to transience. (Teleology is what distinguishes the circular, true "infinity" of the Hegelian concept from the "bad"—or better: "straight"—infinity (*schlechte Unendlichkeit*) of endless, linear succession.)[60] For Kant, only living organisms may be judged as governed by a *causa finalis*—though artistic production offers a weak analogy for organic autopoiesis, and one could, as Kant remarks in a footnote, illuminate the ideal of the state "through an analogy with the above-mentioned, immediate natural ends."[61] For Hegel, these organic, artistic, and political analogies amount to one, final logos (or *lex*) in the Greek world of art-religion, which is also the world of the organic, ideal state, bound by an eternally living law that overshadows the oracle as the ultimate "onefoldness of truth."

The very counterposition of Antigone's living law to the oracle suggests, first of all, that true providence (and the truth of providence) is not the unfulfilled future of prophecy, but the eternal present of teleology. This reading becomes all the more plausible when one recalls the autopoietic nature of the Greek state that the *Antigone* citation had heralded earlier in the *Phenomenology*, as Hegel proceeded from "Reason" to his chapter on "Spirit," which began with the "ethicality" (*Sittlichkeit*) of Greece (236). There, the citation announces a world that, like the language that surpasses the foreign oracle, has, for the self, lost "all meaning of something foreign, just as the self [has lost] all meaning of a (separate from it, dependent or independent) being-for-itself" (238–39).[62] All "meaning of something foreign"—and thus, all meaning per se—is lost, because it is fulfilled. Nothing cannot indicate anything other than itself, and therefore cannot mean at all. There is no place here for the hieroglyphs, pyramids, or mummies that "cloister an interior meaning in [themselves]." Thus, in this world, "the *substance* [*die Substanz*] and the universal, self-equivalent [*sichselbstgleiche*], remaining essence [*Wesen*],—it [*er*] is the uncrazed and undissolved *ground* and departure point of the doing of all,—and their *end* and *goal*, as the thought *in-itself* of all self-consciousness" (239).[63] The state is not an ideal analogy to the teleological processes of nature, as it was for Kant, but a real circulation of willed production that engenders and sustains a world. And if the dashes that cut this passage, too, as well as Hegel's sudden grammatical shift from a feminine and neuter subject ("die Substanz und das [. . .] Wesen") to a masculine singular pronoun ("er") and a singular verb ("ist"), should give pause—this "uncrazed and undissolved ground" is absolutely torn apart in Hegel's syntax, which also leaves its initial subjects without a complement, hanging—these features of his prose do not speak against the kind of teleological ideal that the state of ethical substance realizes and that Kant had only supposed in a footnote. The state of this sentence is wounded through and through—graphically and syntactically—and *because* it is utterly dissolved and decomposed, it is an organic whole that eternally lives. But Hegel's words here are not only a translation of the organic rhetoric of Kantian teleology—they also conjure up those mythic gods who would be torn to pieces, then re-membered and re-generated, like Dionysos and Osiris, or the mythic monstrosities like the hundred-handed Briareus, whom Hegel had identified in 1803 with the living, teleological spirit of ethicality, and whose body is made up "of myriad eyes arms and other limbs, of which each is an absolute individual," so that this creature "is an absolute universal, and in relation to the individual, every part of this universality, each that belongs to it, appears as object, as end" (*System der Sittlichkeit* 328).[64]

In this teleomythology, each of its members tears up (*zerreißt*) the body of the state in order to take part in it and impart life to it. Such is its eternally living law, under which the incompleteness and foreignness of "Light-Essence," hierogylphs, and oracles are overcome and every singular trace should be absorbed and digested. And only through this process of dismemberment, ingestion, and reproduction that should cycle endlessly is every part of the state proper to it and appropriated as its "real and living" participants. As Catherine Malabou sums this movement in Hegel's thought more generally: "the individual 'devours' culture as if it were his 'inorganic nature,' and then reproduces in his own being that very destruction. [. . .] This is the only way the individual can *interiorize* culture" (153). And even if every single member in this life process remains subject to the temporal succession that leads to its ultimate end and irretrievable loss—everyone still must die—as a universal participant in ethical substance, each transient being recycles in the next generation of citizens. What Malabou says in her quite differently accented reading of the process of conceptual simplification in Hegel might thus also be said of this moment: "this life-destroying formalization is a guarantee of survival"—so long as one were to add that this survival pertains to nothing that enters into the process Hegel describes, but applies only to the process itself. The communion of this community entails *sparagmos*, or the tearing apart of the body, and *omophagia*, or the consumption of that raw, torn flesh. But it lives perpetually, like the gods of such myths, despite and because of its dis-memberment. Temporal and eternal at once, the "departure point" of the Greek state is, at the same time, always the "end and goal." Its sense is always there, always fulfilled beforehand, and always on its way to fulfillment. Communication thus operates upon a monstrous and violent premise that has not escaped readers such as Malabou, or Derrida and Hamacher, who have stressed the insistence with which Hegel's writing draws repeatedly not only upon the Eucharist but also upon the rituals of Dionysos. As the living law that governs this cannibalistic state of affairs overcomes the foreign speech of oracle, the metaphors for language and its reception, the tongue and the intake of substance, come to life, at the cost of all that might live: "This self-digestion of the absolute assimilating its own shape presents the exemplary model for nature and history alike. The religions still prior to history proper sought to procure conscious awareness of spiritual self-relation for themselves through the cannibalistic fetish-feast" (Hamacher, *Pleroma* 189). Yet this is not to say that the matter of intake becomes indifferent. This feasting without fill, this teleology without end, can be understood only so long as the different terms of Kant and Sophocles, as well as the myths of Dionysos and Christ, remain to be read within it, as the leftovers that Hegel's philosophical translation of Antigone's verses here cannot process and absorb fully, without losing all sense.

To be sure, the perpetual fulfillment it promises suggests that the living "law" (*Gesetz*) can and must replace the "onefold and universal sentences [*Sätze*] of essence" that Hegel had attributed to the oracular spirit of "anabasis" (*des Aufgangs*) and that were not yet, properly speaking, propositions (*Sätze*) at all. For it is the permanent proposition or purposition of all activity and production in teleology that first sets the incidental to work, makes it "real" or "worklike" (*wirklich*). The oracular pathos, or under-going, which is purely incidental, cannot but submit to the eternal law of teleological realization. ("Lawfulness [*Gesetzmäßigkeit*] of the incidental [*Zufälligen*]," writes Kant in a parenthesis, "is called purposiveness [*Zweckmäßigkeit*]" [*Kritik der Urteilskraft* 775].) The self under the eternally living law is indeed "the greater agent" (*Meister*) over the "little speech" that the "oracle" (*Orakel*) implies.[65] Or rather, whatever does not submit to this law, this fulfilling and fulfilled sense, is insignificant and "seems at once trivial to the self-consciousness that builds itself further" (Hegel, *Phänomenologie* 381). The proper language of Philosophy, in turn, is contingent upon the eternal repetition of natural, teleological law. Yet this self-fulfilling prophecy rests upon the Hegelian concept that not only *is* and knows itself as eternal truth but also grows mangled and tongue-tied in propositions that tear up the form of the proposition, and that parasitically feed from the words and myths of others in order to realize the organic movement they bespeak.

Therefore, like Hegel's earlier promise to try to teach "Philosophy" to speak German (or to seduce "Philosophy to teach German speaking"), this "eternally living" law cannot but be incomplete and misspoken. This is not only true because the tearing up of propositions is the only way to speak the propositions of organic teleology. Rather, the living law is a misspeaking per se. Just as Hegel considers John's usage of προφητεύειν to be a misnomer for teleology, he reads Antigone's usage of the word νόμιμα ("laws") as a misnomer for the principle that should govern the eternal life of the spirit. In an earlier commentary on these very verses of Sophocles, on *"the secure and unwritten law of the gods that always lives, and from which no one knows from when it appeared"* (381), Hegel had written: "Their [. . .] will was free, listened to its own laws; they knew no divine commandments, or when they called the moral law a divine commandment, it was given to them nowhere, in no written character; it ruled them invisibly (Antigone)" (*Hegels Theologische Jugendschriften* 222).[66] And in the *Phenomenology*, Hegel counterposes law to life consistently; or rather, he shows consistently how life overcomes the antinomies implied in any law.[67] Johanine prophecy is no oracle, and Greek "law," because it the living, should be no "law," properly speaking. It is not, like the Mosaic law that Christ fulfills, an external commandment that is abstracted from living reality, and thus never yet realized. Nor is it, like the character, an incidental trace, distinct from the interior meaning it cloisters and thereby withholds. Rather, it is always known and fulfilled beforehand, inherent in every member of the living polis, and *thus* invisible and unwritten.

Yet whereas the young Hegel characterizes the "law" of Antigone as a mere misnomer, any such slip of the pen could only bode ill for the language of the *Phenomenology*. Either Hegel misses a step in the course that should lead to the translation of Philosophy, or Philosophy can only be spoken in improper terms, and therefore cannot be spoken purely and truly at all. Either way, his crucial shift away from the language of the oracle would be the prophecy of his own failure; his own language would be foreign to his logic. But any such conclusion would also be all too easy to draw, and it would foreclose the question that the concept of Hegelian philosophy, at this juncture, demands: if Hegel knows and says often enough that any law is essentially dead, why would he perpetuate Antigone's misspeaking here?

Hegel ends his quotation from *Antigone* with a dash that marks yet again an impasse and a passage at once—this time, cutting back to the earlier sentence where he had appealed to this law, not as "law" (*Gesetz*), but as a "right" (*Recht*). There, although Antigone's law will introduce the living body of the Greek state, its immediate context suggests that its eternal life is that of the bloodless underworld, of a "life" that is no longer (or not yet) life. As opposed to his youthful enthusiasm for Antigone's words of "freedom," in the *Phenomenology*, Hegel will call this first articulation of teleological autopoiesis the "tautology [*Tautologie*]" (236), and then, the "pure category [*reine Kategorie*]" (238). If it is right that "not roughly now and yesterday, but ever there, / it lives, and no one knows from when it appeared" (236),[68] one can only always be right, but as the *pure* category, all that this right says is, "it is [. . .], because it is so [*es ist . . . weil es so ist*]," petrifying any accidental or subjective movement alike, and precluding any question of a future, foreign event or word.[69] One might even, in this context, be tempted to read the term "cate-gory," not only as a relatively fixed, philosophical *terminus technicus*, nor etymologically, as the accusation that took place in the Greek agora,[70] but also as a "talking down," which takes place in the κάτω, or "below" of Hades. After all, Hegel will write of the movement from the oracle to this tautological law, "the truth of the universal spirit of anabasis has retreated into the Inner or *Under*" (381, my emphasis), whereby the only way out is down, and the only alternative to "the universal spirit of anabasis," catabasis. Properly speaking, how could it have been otherwise?

Even if, incarnated in the polis, the "living" law seems to have overcome the pure formality of a tautological or categorical imperative, it has not yet become the living Word, which Hegel had emphasized earlier, too, when he called each singular member of the Greek world "the unreal shadow [*der unwirkliche Schatten*]" (251). The other side of teleology, it would seem, is the empty and dead tautology of a shadow that is only what it is, and therefore is not anything that one could predicate or integrate into a universal organization at all. However, this realm of shadows still differs from the singular traces of the oracle, insofar as the shades, as Hegel had said of the subjects of the living law, do not have "the form of incidental existence through a foreign language." To the contrary, as Hegel goes on to describe burial in the polis, the underworld becomes the only refuge for its singular members from the foreign, wild life of those birds, beasts, and elements that would otherwise devour their last traces—and that, in *Antigone*, make up the oracular signs of the illness of the state that have become, as Jacobs reminds us in her reading, "unintelligible" (904). Hegel says of Greek burial, which is a marriage between the corpse and the earth: "she thereby makes him [the dead] into a comrade of the commonwealth, which much rather overpowers and holds bound the forces of the singular matters and the lower vitalities that become free against him and would will to destroy him" (245).[71] And beyond burial—or as its extension—the eternal survival of these "unreal shadows" in Hades, too, would prevent such destruction. Death is what protects them against the excessive organic vitality that would overwhelm the human, overturn the state, and entail the utterly disorganized primacy of singular traces, beasts, and elements. Hegel's translations of Sophocles render teleology in such a way that amounts, at the same time, to the surrender of every end in itself and every end of oracular foreignness.

The shift from the oracle to the living law of *Antigone* leads down. It leads down, that is, to the ultimate thesaurus of speech and souls—to the underworld. This is also the place and source of the epic language Hegel will present next in his series of languages, for he will describe the singer of epic in terms of the Nekyia from Homer's *Odyssey*. Moreover, by calling epic the "first language [*erste Sprache*]," which contains "the full completeness of the world [*die Vollständigkeit der Welt*]" (389), Hegel transfers the erstwhile epithet of the oracle to this new form of speech, overwriting, if not overcoming, his first "first." And here, the primary linguistic division between speaker and speech, which had marked the oracle, the hieroglyph, as well as the "Light-Essence" and its emissaries, will be articulated differently, too—in a way that should yet again eliminate any traces of foreignness and inaugurate a language that is entirely proper. In epic, nothing is any longer "not yet"—but a permanent pastness. The pathos of the singer "is not the deafening force of nature," as it was for Apollo's mantics and for the corpses of the polis, "but Mnemosyne, the sensibility and the interiority that has come to be, the remembrance of the previously immediate essence" (389–90).[72] As a vessel of everything that has "come to be," remembered and internalized, and thus preserved from any devouring or dissolution—the epic "Bibel" or "Book" of a people is also the necessary precondition for any proper, national language, as Hegel will remark at several points in his career.[73] In light of all this, it would not be going too far to say that the epic underworld is also the privileged place and source of Hegel's own monumental, philosophical Book. When it comes to a proper speech, everything comes down, perhaps, to this. In the end, the primal scene of epic may be the last station to pause upon in tracing Hegel's competition with Luther and Voss, the Bible and Homer, in order to seduce Philosophy to speak, and to invent a German language that surpasses their translations.

Hegel's epic is not a narrative representation of the war in Troy or the return of Odysseus, but a summoning of speech, where the singer operates, like Odysseus, from a blood pit on the threshold of Hades. The only "Handlung" of this epic—the only action or plot that could be executed—is: "the injury of the calm earth, the pit that, besouled with blood, calls forth the departed spirits, who, thirsting for life, receive it in the doing of self-consciousness" (390).[74] However, the location of this action, which Hegel transfers and translates from Homer, as well as the implications of this decisive moment for the language of the oracle and for the language of Hegelian philosophy, cannot be limited to this threshold in the *Phenomenology*. While the scene that Hegel sets here has often been read as a preliminary stage in the evolution of religious language and philosophical consciousness by those readers who follow the conceptual developments of his argument, such as Bodammer in his study of Hegel and language (195–96), and more recently, Terry Pinkard (241–44), Denis Thouard has made the case that, insofar as the *Phenomenology* is designed to recover the spirits of history, the language of the entire book solicits a reading along the lines Hegel devotes to epic ("L'epos spéculatif"). And indeed, insofar as the pit of the epic singer both contains "the completeness of the world [*die Vollständigkeit der Welt*]" (389) and submerges the consciousness that creates it—the singer "is the organ *vanishing* within his content [*er ist das in seinem Inhalt verschwindende Organ*]" (390)—it also resembles those shafts that Derrida and David Farrell Krell have entered into most profoundly in their analyses of Hegel's *Encyclopedia*. There, Hegel describes the disordered, unconscious storage of image impressions as pits, which prove to be not only the foreign precondition for philosophical language and thought, as Hegel would have it, but also, as Derrida and Krell remind us, their constant: "The nocturnal pit can never be abandoned, all hierarchies of transition notwithstanding. To desire to ascend out of it is to surrender dialectic and to lapse into something approximating absolute oblivion" (Krell, *Of Memory, Reminiscence, and Writing* 220; cf. Derrida, "Le puits et la pyramide" 88).[75] The "action" of epic is nothing other than the opening up of song—or, what is the same, of the singer himself—to what cannot act, cannot speak, and cannot think; to the departed spirits that have also utterly departed from spirit, at least in the way its concept would demand. The grave he digs—the graphic wound that does not itself make sense, but can cut it, when it comes to mining for its possibility—thus becomes as placeless as it is limitless—much like memory, as Krell reads it in the *Encyclopedia*: "It is omnipresent in dialectic as the very moment in which all other functions, faculties, and activities of spirit are but particular gestures, including the gesture of egress. It is by virtue of the vagabondage of interiorizing remembrance in the hierarchy of transition that memory can be the transition to thought" (229). And insofar as the pit (or the "injury," or the "action") is the agent of speech here—the *pit* "calls forth the departed spirits"—it is also another word for the singer, who must therefore be himself the wound in the earth, the hollowed-out grave, and the vessel of blood Hegel evokes. As such, the singer both does and is the decisive action, the consciousness that gives "the departed spirits" life, blood, and voice—and gives up all of these things in the same stroke. By this primary cut, where the Homeric scene of animal sacrifice is translated as a moment of self-sacrifice, there would no longer be a distinction between speaker and speech, container and content. The singer himself is the subject and object of the first action that he performs, which opens him and his song to the other voices he conjures. At the same time, he is utterly contained in his speech, within which he disappears: "he is the organ vanishing within his content" (390). Like Homer's Odysseus, he is No-One—no determinate character or name, which might yet betoken a singular trace of foreignness. But he is also, split, no *one*—no purified oneness of God or any other subject of spirit. In the end, this most productive "organ" of speech turns out to be not the hand or the mouth or the word of the organic Greek state or any individual within it, but the wound.

This wound has not ceased to gape. With this passage, Hegel overturns the Greek world of ethical "sub-stance" into the world that "stands-under," or an "under-world"; he turns the body of organic metaphors that had pervaded his discussion of the Greek state into a bloody opening; he cuts the individual speaker out of this primal scene of speech entirely; and the oracular limit of the "not yet" has been crossed over and through with the epic past—which, as a grammatical tense in ancient Greek, is the "aorist"—literally, "without-horizon." Only here, perhaps, where the speaker and his speaking are at once absolutely open and enclosed, given up and taken in, could one locate a language in which everything has become internalized and appropriated—but only provided that this scene, neither here nor there, were thought as the end of all thought, the place of parting and de-parted spirits, through a cut that is uttered and suffered by no one, and that therefore cannot close.

There are other indications in the writings of Hegel that speak to the same end. For example, he will call language the "visible invisibility [*die sichtbare Unsichtbarkeit*]" earlier in the *Phenomenology* (179), marking the fatal effect of speech upon anything particular that one might immediately see or know—which, at the same time, should yield the eternal resurrection of all. Putting it more simply and explicitly for his students at the Nürnberg Gymnasium (and in terms that recall his epic singer), he writes: "the image is killed, and the word treads [in the place of] the image. [. . .] Language is the killing of the sensual world in its immediate existence, its becoming-canceled into an existence that is a calling-up, which resounds in all representing essences" (*Nürnberger* 437).[76] But the substantive "invisibility" also literally translates Ἀΐδης. Thus, in this context as in the *Phenomenology*, it cannot but recall the name for the Greek god of death and for the nether realm—the name that denotes neither a place nor a persona, exactly, and thus is never quite proper—which was popularly derived from the privative prefix ἀ- and the root ἰδεῖν (*to see*), which itself splits in significance between "see" and "know." Named properly, the visible invisibility of language marks the unknowable as well as all that Hegel would mean it to be, and is therefore incommensurable and estranged from the conceptual logic it would also sustain. From this horizon, without horizon, the medium of spirit turns out to be the u-topia of de-parted spirits; and it can, ultimately, be articulated only through and by this split. In this respect, Hegel's definition of language recalls the structure of the oracle, just as "Hades," who is also traditionally called "many named" (πολυαώνυμος), recalls the "many-named One [*vielnahmigen Einen*]" of Hegel's oracular "Light-Essence" (371)—or Jaweh, Zoroaster, and Apollo, all in one—who was foreign to language, and from whom Hegel had long since appeared to part ways.

This reading of Hegel's Germanic "invisibility [*Unsichtbarkeit*]" is not only possible but demanded by the concept of an absolute book that would enclose the world, that would encompass art and religion. For such a book would have to be a writing that always mingles, undecidably, with the other writings and foreign languages it translates. These, in turn, dissolve its limits—so that, at its most proper, it has parted from any other *and* itself. In the German language that Hegelian Philosophy comes to speak, one can no longer tell the difference among its Hebrew, Greek, Latin, and Germanic "roots"—to name a few of the foreign languages that Hegel incorporates in his Book. And perhaps the language that Heglian Philosophy strives to present can be heard only through the traces of the foreign tongues (and German translations) it translates, sublates, and suppresses and in the many names—or the *many-named* ones—that it famously strives to efface, in order to articulate the movement of spirit.

The oracular "pathos of substance" is not to be overcome, not even in Philosophy, but undergone, each time in an utterly singular way, and thus cannot *be* undergone, but, dislimited, demands its undergoing without horizon. And it is this pathos, which affects the entirety of Hegel's *Phenomenology*, that renders it an insuperable work of translation, as well as the prophecy of a philosophical language that could never have been one.[77] Yes, Hegel, like Christ, makes this "pathos" into his "material"; like his epic singer, he makes his book the "vessel" and medium through which Philosophy should come to speak; he completes the articulation of prophecy as providence, and of philosophy, art, and politics as teleology. Yet the translation upon which these gestures are contingent is the condition of its possibility as well as its impossibility.[78] And even *the* "Yes" that Hegel famously names in his *Phenomenology* as the culmination of his philosophy of spirit—an affirmative, Germanic root, which he nominalizes and provides with a definite article—is turned into a common noun or name that, as such, must remain apart from any proper act of affirmation in order to appear properly and absolutely universal.[79] What remains to be said further, the Hegelian culmination of the languages of religion, art, and philosophy, is not, like the language of the oracle, done—yet. When all appears to be said and done, no logic could operate without the singular, foreign traces it could not suppress without ceasing to speak, from Greek and Latin to birds and corpses. As Catherine Malabou writes, in a different context: "because there is nothing 'outside the text (*hors texte*),'" the text is placed "absolutely outside itself" (185). And even beyond the very last words of the *Phenomenology*—the chalice of spirit that spills over from the verses of Friedrich Schiller's *Philosophical Letters* to complete Hegel's book: "from the chalice of this realm of spirits foams forth to it its infinity"[80]—there remains a corresponding trace in Hegel's letters of nothing less than this, here, now, as the *Phenomenology* was about to appear:

—I hear from you that a logic should be coming out from Frommann or even from me; at the same time to give theological instruction,—and, indeed, the kind fit for the funnels, through which it should come further to the people,—and to write logic, you know very well, would be to be a whitewasher and chimney sweeper at once, drinking *infusum sennae compositum* and Burgundy along with it;—I, who nested all too many years on open stones by the eagle and was used to breathing pure mountain air, should now learn to feed on the corpses of dead or (the modern) stillborn thoughts and vegetate in the lead air of empty chatter; . . .—a contact, whose thought sets all my nerves trembling, as if the Christian church were a loaded galvanic battery, ε, ζ, η etc.—God give that this chalice pass from me! . . .

    Your

    Hgl.[81]

LANGUAGE AT AN IMPASSE, IN PASSING: WILHELM VON HUMBOLDT'S *AGAMEMNON* TRANSLATION

To date and sign the introduction to his translation of Aeschylus's *Agamemnon*, Wilhelm von Humboldt remarks:

> To conclude, I must still remark that I began [this translation] in 1796, reworked and ended it in 1804 in Albano, and that since then hardly a year has crossed that I had not bettered it. I say this not to credit myself with this carefulness as a desert, but so that it may serve as a pardon, if, perhaps, in this or that passage the lightness and suppleness [*Leichtigkeit und Geschmeidigkeit*] would be missed that often goes lost through more accumulated reworking [*durch häufigeres Umarbeiten*].
> —Frankfurt am Main 23 February 1816.[1] (*Gesammelte Schriften* 8: 146)

With this remark, Humboldt not only dates his tragedy and designates it a labor that lasted two decades of his writing career; still more than this, he unsettles the date he assigns it, recounting a period of "more accumulated reworking"—over twelve years after he had "ended [*endigte*]" it.

Through this profession of reworking, Humboldt turns any point of the text into one that might prove resistant to passage. Without the "lightness" or "suppleness" that would facilitate transition from this or that formulation to another, Humboldt's chronic revisions allow, instead, fluency to go lost. At the same time, while "reworking" might otherwise imply the erasure of earlier versions of certain passages—crossed out (*gestrichen*) with each year that "crossed [*verstrich*]"—Humboldt's formulation also suggests that the many iterations of his labor leave their mark upon the text, such that the time of this text is not one, but manifold. After all, "lightness" and "suppleness" are said to go lost "through more *accumulated* [*häufigeres*] reworking," and while "häufig" often means "frequently repeated," its association here with resistance suggests the substantive, "Haufe," or "heap," from which it comes. But if the layers of this history of revision might build obstacles, they could not be traceable in any chronological order, or even located with any certainty—as Humboldt suggests with his indeterminate reference to "this or that passage," and with his usage of the conditional: "would be missed [*vermisst würde*]." Rather, this accumulation would be perceived, if at all, as a lack—and because it could be perceived at any time, each passage entails a potential impasse and instant of standstill.

Coming from Wilhelm von Humboldt, who will emphasize the transitory, punctual essence of language, writing roughly ten years later, "language, grasped in its actual essence, is something that is constantly, and in each blink of an eye, passing" (*Gesammelte Schriften* 7: 45), these remarks on the temporal dynamics of his translation cannot be taken lightly. The reception of Humboldt's thinking on language may be divided according to whether writers take seriously the "priority" of "speaking [*Sprechen*]" over "language [*Sprache*]" in his writing (di Cesare 38), along with the consequences that choice entails—the first of which being that language cannot be approached as a fixed, determinate "object of thinking" (Borsche 44). In his monograph *Sprachansichten*, Tilman Borsche demonstrates the limits of those readings of Humboldt—most notably, Noam Chomsky's— that neglect to address the emphatic temporality implied in Humboldt's approach to language, whereby language becomes realized anew in each instance of speech, and, conversely, "what is spoken at any time also works back upon language itself and at once modifies what was seen as its fixed rules" (Borsche 42). This pivotal point in Humboldt's thinking has often been underscored, and even called "a perspectival inversion in the study of language" (di Cesare 38). However, even the most prominent commentators on Humboldt's writings, who have sought to retrace the development of his thinking on language over the course of his work, as well as to elaborate the "inner systematicity of his oeuvre" (Trabant, *Apeliotes* 166)—such as Jürgen Trabant and Borsche—do not address the way in which Humboldt's introduction to the *Agamemnon* speaks to the possibility of a singular instance of speech that does not come to pass at any one time or in any one language.

The time and language of this translation, as Humboldt presents it in his introduction, complicate his subsequent elaborations of language, while the remarks on language and translation that Humboldt sketches here already address issues that will preoccupy him throughout the years of his linguistic studies, culminating in his posthumously published *On the Diversity of Human Language Structure and Its Influence on the Spiritual Development of the Human Race* (1836). Nonetheless, most readers of Humboldt—including, too, those who have devoted monographs to Humboldt's reception of classical antiquity, such as Jean Quillien—have mentioned it only in passing. None but Hans-Jost Frey has posed the question:[2] what does Humboldt's theory of language look like, when it emerges out of—and perhaps as—a labor of translation?[3] And although scholars concerned with the issue of translation, such as Antoine Berman, Susan Bernofsky, and Josefine Kitzbichler, have devoted closer attention to this text, they have remained preoccupied with the relationship between the proper and the foreign, or the fraught articulation of "faithful" translation that emerges in Humboldt's introduction. But because these approaches presuppose an understanding of language—which the remarks that Humboldt will present, here and elsewhere, place in question—they pass over the more radical potential for rethinking language and translation that the text opens. For not only is the time of Humboldt's *Agamemnon*, and therefore its linguistic essence, more than ambiguous. It is also in no way certain what "language" Humboldt translates, if, as he will write, "language forms [*Sprachformen*]" are "symbols [*Symbolen*]" that arise "in spirit" (8: 131)—and emerge "out of nothing [*aus dem Nichts*]" (8: 130)—and if Aeschylus's *Agamemnon* itself, in its incomparable "sublimity [*Erhabenheit*]," sets forth, above all, "the pure symbol of human fates [*das reine Symbol der menschlichen Schicksale*]" (8: 119).

In this context, it is, at the very least, possible that Humboldt does not speak as the liberal humanist and systematic thinker that he is often made out to be, but for another language—and perhaps for something other than language—that would exceed any "empirically enlightened, linguistic anthropology [that] placed man at the centre of all language study," as James Underhill has recently summarized Humboldt's thought (96). For even if Humboldt's rhetoric of the symbol recalls Aristotle's opening remarks from the text that would be called *Peri hermeneias*—"there are symbols in the voice of the pathoses in the psyche [ἔστι μὲν οὖν τὰ ἐν τῷ φωνῇ τῶν ἐν τῷ ψυχῇ παθημάτων σύμβολα]" (16a 3–4)—the consequences of Humboldt's reformulation and reinterpretation of this sentence are far from evident, and what he evokes, far from univocal. For no thorough interpretation of Humboldt's remarks could ignore that the "symbol," in Aeschylus's *Agamemnon*, also marks the province of the prophet and the limits of insight, referring both to the phenomena that Calchas will interpret for the Acheans (ξύμβολα 144) and to the closing of the eyes—in sleep and in death—that the watchman of the prologue and later, the seer Cassandra, envision (συμβαλεῖν 15, συμβάλω 1294).[4] And at the same time, none could overlook the appearance of Friedrich Creuzer's *Symbolics and Mythology of Ancient Peoples, Especially the Greeks* in 1810—in the midst of Humboldt's "reworking"—where symbolic insight is said to arise "in a single stroke [*mit einem Schlag*]" (Creuzer 66), and where, in the extreme case, the finite and infinite collide in the blink of an eye, so that "straightaway the clarity of vision is annihilated [*vernichtet*], and there remains only a speechless astonishment [*nur ein sprachloses Erstaunen*]" (73). Like Aeschylus's tragedy, Creuzer's work struck Humboldt, too, with force: upon rereading it, he would write, "I am alternately attracted and repelled by it" (letter to Friedrich Gottlieb Welcker, 15 December 1822 [*Wilhelm von Humboldts Briefe* 67]), recalling the very terms with which Kant would describe the dynamic of the sublime, "i.e., with a rapidly alternating repelling and attracting [*d.i. mit einem schnellwechselnden Abstoßen und Anziehen*]" (*Kritik der Urteilskraft* 592). And Humboldt's linguistic symbols repeatedly register the suddenness, violence, and wonder that Creuzer evokes in his *Symbolics*—both in his introduction to the *Agammenon* and beyond, when he will write, for instance, in his speech "On the Comparative Study of Language" that language itself arises "in a single stroke [*mit Einem Schlag*]" (*Gesammelte Schriften* 4: 14).

This dimension of Humboldt's writing thus speaks to a sublime dimension of language that exceeds the measures of the human, and it demands that any reading of his theory of language be elaborated up to the limits of insight and speech, where they are destined to fail.[5] Although there are exceptions—Helmut Müller-Sievers, for example, remarks, "a tone of violence always resonates in Humboldt's description of linguistic sound production [*immer schwingt in Humboldts Beschreibung der Lautproduktion der Ton der Gewalt mit*]" (149)[6]—the general lack of commentary on this trait of Humboldt's writing is symptomatic of a tendency to paraphrase Humboldt and to take the sense of his language for granted.[7] However, Humboldt's writing resists this tendency, and the following chapter is intended to expose precisely this resistance, not in a conventional modus of academic exposition, but in a way that follows the halting rhythm of his prose and the complications involved in his words. Neither light nor supple, Humboldt's introduction to the *Agamemnon* stands at the crux of his aesthetic and philological studies, and his writings on the study of languages—as Frey has rightly pointed out (37, 61). Accordingly, it calls for a close reading in relation to his other writings on language, among others—where every word entails a potential impasse and instant of standstill—so that one might begin to attend to the unheard-of language that emerges in this text.

To return to the conclusion, with which I began: no one "then" for any one passage could be given or dated, though with each difficulty his translation presents, Humboldt suggests that the possibility is given—for the better—to read in it the work of translation, rather than reading the translation as a work. In this respect, what Humboldt says to his pardon is, at the same time, a promise that recalls what he had written more generally about translations midway through his introduction: "For translations are more labors that test and determine the standing of language in a given point of time, as upon a remaining standard for measure, and should work upon and into it [*auf ihn einwirken*], and must always be repeated anew, than they are enduring works"[8] (8: 136)—with the difference that Humboldt's translation itself reflects at least several repeatedly renewed labors. Consequently, the given point of time, the standing of language, and the standard measure that translations should test, determine, and transform will have shifted each time and become indistinct in the ultimately published version—but for the passages that prove difficult.

For instance, none who reads the edition of Humboldt's translation from 1816 would see how, in the prologue of the *Agamemnon*—as the first sign that will inaugurate the drama appears to be delayed—"the symbol of the torch" (8–9) that the watchman awaits has altered from version to version. The lines in question read:

καὶ νῦν φυλάσσω λαμπάδος τὸ σύμβολον,
αὐγὴν πυρὸς φέρουσαν ἐκ Τροίας φάτιν
[. . .] Φόβος [. . .] ἀνθ᾽Ὕπνου παραστατεῖ
τὸ μὴ βεβαίως βλέφαρα συμβαλεῖν ὕπνωι. (8–15)

And now I watch for the torch signal [lit: the symbol of the torch, *lámpados tò súmbolon*], the ray of fire bearing speech from Troy. [. . .] [. . .] Fear [. . .] stands beside me instead of Sleep, that I may not firmly close together [lit: symbolize, *sumbaleîn*] my eyelids in sleep.

In this passage, one symbol is set against another: the symbol the watchman looks for, and the closing together, or symbolizing, of the eyes that would preclude his lookout. Because the word "symbol [σύμβολον]" is formed from "together [συμ-]" and "to throw so as to hit [βαλεῖν]," it can double as the aim of the watchman and as its foreclosure. And between these moments, the symbol itself doubles as the "torch signal" and its elaboration, "the ray of fire bearing speech from Troy." In an earlier draft, Humboldt adheres to the order of the original, where the evocation of the symbol is followed by its elaboration. He writes of a "torch sign [*Fackel Zeichen*]," then a "gleam of flame [*Flamme Glanz*]," which "sends [. . .] us news from Troy [*die [. . .] von Troja Kunde her uns sendet*] (*Gesammelte Schriften* 8: 205). The

watchman, meanwhile, remains with "fear at his side, that sleep per-
chance close too tightly the tired lashes [*Furcht zur Seite, dass der Schlaf
zu fest vielleicht die müden Wimpern schliesst*]" (8: 205). But in Humboldt's
published version, the watchman expects a "torchlight [*Fackellicht*]" and
"sign of flames [*Flamme Zeichen*]," fearing that "slumbering, the eyelid
firmly close [*schlummernd, schliesse fest das Augenlied*]" (8: 148). In this
version, the "sign [*Zeichen*]" shifts from the product of the torch to the
operation of the flame, as though the "ray [αὐγὴν, *augên*]" stood where
"symbol [σύμβολον, *súmbolon*]" is set in Aeschylus's Greek. At the same
time, the "lashes [*Wimpern*]" become altered to an "eyelid [*Augenlied*],"
and thus to a word that reprises the phonemes of the original "ray
[αὐγὴν, *augên*]." Through these displacements, the "sign [*Zeichen*]"—or
"symbol"—not only becomes associated with an element rather than a
conventional instrument. The "ray [*augên*]" that has assumed the place
of a "sign [*Zeichen*]" also returns, literally, in Humboldt's translation
of "eyelid-closing / symbolizing" (βλέφαρα συμβαλεῖν, *bléphara sumbaleîn*)—as its German homophone, the eyelid, or "*Augen*lied." Through
these complex operations, which can be read only between Greek and
German, Humboldt thus brings together the doubling of "symbol
[σύμβολον / *súmbolon*]" and "closing together [συμβαλεῖν / *sumbaleîn*]"
in Aeschylus's text. And in closing in on this doubling, Humboldt alters
the sense of all the words involved, such that "Augen" can no longer be
said to mean "ray [αὐγὴν /*augên*]," "symbol [σύμβολον / *súmbolon*]," or
"eyes [*Augen*]," but condenses all of these at once, in a singular instance
of language that is not one.

   This instance of Humboldt's labor of translation, from the prologue
of Aeschylus's tragedy, is not simply one among others, but one in which
the poetic terms of the translated text intersect with those of his prose
introduction.[9] It shows, in a preliminary way, how Humboldt works in
and upon German and Greek, making the ray (*augê*) meet the eye (*Auge*)
in a symbolic collision of language that unworks the limits of the terms
σύμβολον, αὐγή, *Zeichen*, and *Auge*. In this reworked passage of the
drama—and in its resonance with his introduction—Humboldt opens,
with the *aug*–, insight into the symbolic optics that will inflect his account
of language and its time in his later works on language, which are scanned
by a rhetoric of vision, light—and lightning. And he demonstrates how
radically one might interpret his remark on "language forms" as "symbols" from his introduction. For when he writes, "all language forms are
symbols, not things themselves, not conventional signs, but sounds, which
find themselves with the things and concepts that they present [. . .] in

an actual, and if you will, a mystical connection, [and] which contain the objects of actuality dissolved, so to speak, into ideas," and then goes on to remark, "these symbols can be underlain with a higher, deeper, more tender sense" (8: 131), Humboldt does not suggest that these symbols are contained within any one language, but speaks of them absolutely. If this implication could be overlooked at first, any presupposition of fixed linguistic boundaries dissolves in a flash, as the *"aug-"* shifts between Greek and German and opens both to a language that belongs properly to neither.

The *aug-* also exposes, however, the difficulties inherent in Humboldt's remarks on a "remaining standard for measure," as well as the "standing of language" that translation should "test and determine." What stands, and what can be understood, when the only "standing measures" (*Maßstäbe*)— or, more literally, "measuring sticks"—are the letters (*Buchst*äbe)—the sense of which can always alter, in an instant? And how might this potential alterity, which cannot be contained, relate to the rhetoric of actuosity that pervades Humboldt's work, including, above all, his assertion that the labor of translation "should *work* upon and into" the "standing [*Zustand*] of language" in a "given point in time [*Zeitpunkt*]," as upon its "measure [*Massstab*]" (8: 136)? After all, any or all of these masculine nouns could be referred to with the pronoun "ihn" in Humboldt's German phrase—"work upon and into it [*auf ihn einwirken*]"—so that the condition, time, and measure for this activity, as well as its object, grow as opaque as the *aug-* of his translation.

In this passage, no term sticks. Insofar as the standing of language or standard for measure that Humboldt evokes is only what it is at the time of translation, it could not preexist the work of translation—which is said to test, determine, *and* change it at once. And insofar as this standard can be indicated only *as if* it were steady and constant—translations are measured *"as upon a remaining standard for measure [wie an einem bleibenden Massstab]"*—it would appear never to exist or consist in anything but this conditional modality, in the process of perpetual modification through translation. Other readers, such as Denis Thouard, have emphasized the importance of modification not only to the work of the translation but also to the (re)production of any linguistic form.[10] But it has not been stressed emphatically enough that, according to Humboldt's formulation here, the original of any translation—and with it, the standing of all languages into and from which it might be translated—would change each time. Consequently, Humboldt's assertion that translations "must always be repeated anew" cannot mean the reiteration of an act that would ever be the same, but must mean a reprisal of the transforming that other translations have performed and that is itself transformed from the moment it begins. Each translation would bear further, each time, previous modifications that have worked upon the work, and bear them beyond any measure or moment that might be taken for a given. This would be true whether a translation were completed within one year or over twenty, since the logic of translation and the point in time in which it operates—into and upon which it should work—are first marked by the process of translation, and are therefore already transgressed at each instant of work. In this repect, Humboldt's remarks on translations—which do not differentiate between the proper and the foreign, the newer or the older language, but speak only of "language" per se—presage yet again what he will say, differently, on language as such twenty years later in *On the Diversity of Human Language Structure*: "Language, taken up in its actual essence, is something constantly and in each instant passing [*in jedem Augenblicke Vorübergehendes*]," and, a bit later: "[Language] is, namely, the eternally repeating labor of the spirit. [. . .]"[11] (7: 45–46).

Language as a whole, all that could be or have been said, is constantly spoken and eternally evoked, revoked—and thereby re-evoked (that is: bearing the mark "-" of vocal hiatus, between the repetition and cancellation of what could have repeated, if it were not already transformed before the fact)—in each single, passing instant of speech. And Humboldt will insist, repeatedly, that language exists only in each instance of speech,[12] and that all language is at stake in each single instance. But if each instance is sudden, singular, and as such, indivisible—"the striving of spirit which produces speech individualizes in the very same blink of an eye [*Augenblick*] and in one stroke [*mit einem Schlag*] sound, word, and fusion" (6: 143)— each actual expression conjures all others *in potentia*. Besides the being of language, which is only in its being uttered, is the nonbeing of all other possible expressions that might supplement it, and thus make it what it could be, but never yet was. Speech is enacted, Humboldt writes, "as if at once, instinctively, the entire web to which this singularity belongs were present";[13] likewise, "the possibility is given" in each single word "to build from its elements a number of others, which actually proceeds indefinitely" (7: 57). But whether what is actually said announces, beside itself, all other possibilities, or whether the possibilities of one utterance actually proceed to be realized indefinitely, language is also necessarily never entirely uttered, and therefore, "from the start in need of new labor" (7: 46). The actuous ontology that underlies Humboldt's thinking on language—the "foundational essence [*Grundwesen*]" of "force [*Kraft*]" that each linguistic "phenomenon" brings to light, without ever revealing it as such (6:

127)[14]—is thus characterized not only by positivity and possibility but also by privation.[15] If, in the philosophical tradition that Humboldt also evokes in his rhetoric, being was posed as a function of positing—culminating in the "acting-deed [*Tathandlung*]" of Johann Gottlieb Fichte's *Doctrine of Knowing*, namely, the "I" that posits itself in his foundational proposition: "the I *sets itself by itself*, and it *is*, by virtue of this sheer setting through it itself [*das Ich* setzt sich selbst, *und es ist, vermöge dieses bloßen Setzens durch sich selbst*]" ("Grundlage" 259)—Humboldt deposes the speaking subject by suggesting its every proposition is sentenced to lack the very language it calls for and calls forth. Those who speak language, bespeak in the same stroke a need (*Bedürfnis*) for language. And because of this lack, each positing (*Setzung*) would not only evoke in each moment those possibilities that would, strictly speaking, correspond to it as *its* proper language. By virtue of the fact that any possible proper language would have to be missing with each utterance, each utterance in any one language may also call for other ones.[16] In other words, through this lack—which cannot be reduced to the merely human need to "develop [his] spiritual forces and to attain a world view" (7: 20)[17]—the work of language demands, in any given moment, labors of translation (*Übersetzung*) that fundamentally displace and supersede every positing (*Setzung*). Thus, Humboldt emphasizes the way that the perpetual operation of language, in and upon itself—and after the possibilities it misses—elapses as an ellipsis, that it is ever at once that which is to be actuated, and thereby in need of itself, as of another.[18] And if each word or utterance actually presupposes all others, the essential, constant passage of language also renders its every instance, as well as its proper possibilities, lost and missed—"going over [*vorübergehend*]," it is going and gone over before it could be grasped—and therefore always at an impasse.

Yet at the same time, because every passage—every translation or utterance—works upon the "standing of language in a given point of time," language must still be or exist in some way, albeit differently than the transitory instant of speech that would speak to and from it, and thus it must be divided from itself. This dilemma poses an obstacle to every encounter with Humboldt's remarks on the temporality of language, for, as Borsche writes at one point: "the object of linguistic science is not 'something constantly and in each instant passing over,' for something actually fleeting cannot be an object at all" (61). But since, as Borsche also notes, Humboldt "at no time gives what one would call clear definitions" (63), one cannot proceed by supplying the definition of language that Humboldt seems to pass over and attempting to supplement this perceived lack once and for all. One cannot turn his texts into the objects that they never claim to be, either. Rather, such absences solicit commentary in their own right. And insofar as any approach to one language is always already in the midst of another one, which is equally fleeting and contingent, there is no means of metalanguage that would allow one to master another. For lack of definitions, when it comes to Humboldt's insistence on the radical temporality of speech, one is compelled to look more closely to the temporal horizon of speaking, as Humboldt opens and describes it, and to speak as closely as possible with Humboldt.[19]

"Throughout," Humboldt writes in *On the Diversity of Human Language Structure*—where it is a question of "the study of language" as such, and thus of languages in the plural—we find ourselves "displaced in a historical midst"—in the midst, that is, of speaking a language that has already "received material from previous generations out of a prehistory unknown to us [*uns unbekannter Vorzeit*]" (7: 47). This reception implies a kind of continuity, in which we find ourselves a "member of an infinite conversation" (Trabant, *Apeliotes* 11); it does not merely suggest that the speech of each speaker, for all the singularity of his utterance, "takes place in the middle of a valid language" and "must be intelligible [. . .] for other subjects" (Borsche 309). It also means that each act of speech would be given over to an "unknown [*unbekannt*]," and therefore *foreign*, given—which Humboldt no longer even calls a foreign language, but neutralizes as something stranger still. He writes, instead, that the activity of expression is not simply "productive [*erzeugend*]," but "always at once directed toward *something already given* [*immer zugleich auf* etwas schon Gegebenes *gerichtet*]" (my emphasis).[20] And since no speaker knows this indeterminate given, but nonetheless is always "reshaping [*umgestaltend*]" it (7: 47), in so doing, he could never have received it.[21] The historical midst that is spoken of here is thus not a matter of in media res, nor is it at any point between instantiations of speech that would hold proper places in a historical time line, or standing tradition. For what comes "out of a prehistory [*Vorzeit*] unknown to us," belongs, strictly speaking, to neither history nor time, and is therefore radically "displaced [*versetzt*]," from the beginning. The exchange that is enacted through this interim—this "historical midst" that is the only history to speak of—exceeds—in rendering the given, in thereby transposing and replacing it, and in presenting the received as not yet granted—any proper destination to which it might be addressed or attributed, and thus any limit that might give it measure.[22] Our "historical midst" would be a mean, then, without measure, a dimensioning of sheer distances that take place "throughout" our speaking, out from every through, and thoroughly out of sync.[23] Oriented in this way toward a measure and a date that it would produce in trespassing it, before as after, each translation, like each speech act, could only be incommensurable with its proper measure and incoincident with its proper date.

This date, other each time, altered as it is uttered, would thus have to be the "new" from, into, and past which it operates "anew [*vom neuem*]," and a "new" that would, in turn, emerge only after the fact. Hence, Humboldt will write in *On the Diversity of Human Language Structure*—this time, with the "age of time [*Zeitalter*]" as his subject—"alone in the inworking [*Einwirkung*] that each [age of time] exerts upon the one that follows after it, does it become clear what [inworking] it itself experienced from its prehistory" (7: 34).[24] A definite date or age *is*, in other words, *as* the premise and promise of speaking and translation alike. Likewise, speaking and translation would be prophetic of the language they will have transmitted, transformed, and thereby abandoned through receiving it.

The word for this dynamic and the temporal structure it entails is, here as in Humboldt's introduction to the *Agamemnon*, "Einwirkung," which often-repeated term in Humboldt's lexicon might be translated literally as "inworking,"[25] in the sense of acting upon and into something that is therein affected. As an expression of effective force, it would bespeak the actuosity of language that erupts in a single stroke. At the same time, however, the word is drawn from the register of textile labor, where it refers to working a thread into a weave, which sense is made explicit in many passages of *On the Diversity of Human Language Structure,* as when Humboldt remarks that language works "as if at once, instinctively, the entire web to which this singularity belongs were present" (7: 80). "Einwirkung" thus describes, at once, the intersection of actuality and potentiality—while implying the opening, if not the privation, that renders both possible—which is decisive, in Humboldt's words, for each instance of speech, as well as translation. But "Einwirkung" is itself a translation of foreign terms and texts into Humboldt's oeuvre—and thus in need of further commentary. In the midst of Humboldt's introduction to the *Agamemnon*, the central word of his sentence for translation still gives pause: "For translations are more labors that test and determine the standing of language in a given point of time, as upon a remaining standard for measure, and should work upon and into it [*auf ihn einwirken*], and must always be repeated anew, than they are enduring works" (8: 136). And indeed, no reading of the status of language in Humboldt's text, or the work of translation upon it, can proceed without pausing to elaborate this word—which is not one.

Picking up one traditional trajectory, Humboldt says through this metaphor that the operations of speech are akin to weaving, specifically, to working in a thread—"Einwirkung" in the more technical sense of the term. Humboldt's insistence upon this web, which will repeat throughout his work,[26] not only suggests that every instance of speech that comes to pass passes through a text, making each act of speaking into one that is relatively bounded, if not entirely prescribed. He also suggests, as before, that each time, the text will be construed and interpolated differently, and he indicates that, insofar as interweaving takes place "instinctively," and therefore unconsciously, the web that speech implicitly presents at any given time is unknown to every speaker. With this, then, Humboldt takes up the comparison Johann Gottfried Herder had drawn in his own major treatise on the origins of language between the circumscribed, compulsive art of the spider and the unlimited purview of human work. Since Humboldt's earliest commentators, the debate over the degree of Humboldt's indebtedness to Herder has been prominent in Humboldt scholarship, from Heymann Steinthal's discussion of the resonances and differences between the two writers in his commentary on Humboldt's *Kawi* introduction (198–203) and Rudolf Haym, who asserts that Humboldt "repeats Herder's basic thought" (408), to, more recently, Martin Manchester's and Kurt Mueller-Vollmer's treatments of Humboldt's Herder reception. However, the debate primarily revolves around parallels between the two writers' arguments, rather than the particular metaphors that are operative in the texts of each author, along with the implications of their transfer from one text to another. Beyond the notion that, for example, "the category of force is of equally great meaning for Humboldt, [. . .] as for Herder" (Steinthal 199), an operation of weaving binds their texts, whose force cannot be measured in such terms.

For Herder, the art of the spider is as refined and precise as its sphere is narrow, and its world of work and expression is never other nor wider than its web. The instinctive skills of any living being work in inverse proportion to the extent of its sphere. Without any such predetermination, however, the human "sphere of work"—man's "Würkungskreis" (Herder 714)—is entirely open; hence, man is, accordingly, without any leading instinct, at once directionless and helpless. Language is what will replace this lack, which turns out to be less a failing than the very freedom that distinguishes man from animals and their—blind—instincts. In transforming Herder's description of the spider's web into a metaphor for human language, then, Humboldt also implies that human language is at once more complex and less free than his predecessor would have it, and that the operations of speech are at least twofold: its active inworking and its being interwoven, instinctively, within an unknown and unknowable foreign context. As he will put it in his later, posthumously published essay fragment on *The Foundational Traits of the Universal Language Type* (1824/26), "[t]hrough the very same act by virtue of which man spins language out of himself, he spins himself into it, and each language draws a circle [*einen Kreis*] around the nation to which it belongs, out of which it is possible to go only insofar as one at once steps over into the circle of another language" (5: 387–88).[27] Through the ins and outs of Humboldt's rhetorical turns, each single instance of speech thus seems inextricably entangled within an encompassing net that only grows with each intervention and that would seem to grow more binding each time. Nonetheless, insofar as this process is provoked by an *instinctive* instigation that expresses not only compulsion but also a puncture, each particular inworking may also unravel the text in which it involves itself. Translation, when one "steps over into the circle of another language," would be the extreme development of this possibility, but because "no one understands by a word precisely that which another does" (5: 396, 7: 66), working even within one's nearest network is bound to pierce it. For Humboldt also implicitly takes the "point" or "stigma" of "instinct" more literally than Herder, when he goes on to write that what comes together in language is, each time, "at once a going asunder [*zugleich ein Auseinandergehen*]" (5: 396, 7: 65).

This "at once [*zugleich*]" makes all the difference, and if the work of speaking is not, for Humboldt, as immediately free and unlimited as Herder originally proclaims it,[28] it is also not so inherently constricted as the "narrow circle [*enge [. . .] Kreis*]" of a spider's "actuality" or "working" (*Würkung*) (Herder 712). It is in the works of being done and undone, at least in part—and apart from the conscious intentions of any speaking subject. "Inworking" is, as one could also say in German, "too like [*zu gleich*]" unworking for these distinct tendencies not to cut across each other and thereby intersect, "at once [*zugleich*]," in the historical midst of imparted speech. But only in that split of a second would there be a time for language to develop and unravel differently, and only then would an interstice open for something more to be said further.

If the labor of translation thus works "upon and into" the "standing of language in a given point of time," this would have to mean that it at once complicates and undoes the text of its original, as well as the text of the translator that is in the making. At the same time, because neither text is distinct at this point—at this point between languages, where it is a question of "the standing of language" as such—this instant of inworking would at once be the point of their coincidence, as well as the point where they go asunder. That moment, however, cannot, as such, be identified with the product of translation, and would therefore, at the same time, seem to leave no trace, thereby posing yet another impasse to reading the implications of Humboldt's remarks on translation. What takes place in the moment of "inworking" is still unclear, and can begin to be broached only by breaking it asunder and turning to the point where it intersects with yet another word, in another language. For Humboldt's "Ein-wirk-ung" also translates, precisely, the morphemes of the Greek ἐv-ἐpγ-εια. This word, which Aristotle elaborates at greatest length in his *Metaphysics*,[29] is crucial not only to Humboldt's sentence on the labor of translation but also to his most often-cited definition of language, where it appears in between the two passages cited above on the "transitory [*vorübergehende*]," "actual essence" of language and its definition as an "eternally repeating labor of spirit":

> Language, taken up in its actual essence, is something constantly and in
> each instant passing over. Even its maintenance through scripture is always
> only an incomplete, mummy-like preservation, which first needs again that
> one seek to sensualize the living delivery. It itself is no work (ergon) but an
> activity (Energeia). Its true definition can thence be only a genetic one. It is,
> namely, the eternally repeating labor of spirit. [. . .][30] (7: 45–46)

Perhaps even more than those passages in which Humboldt speaks in the language of Herder, this sentence on "Energeia" marks the point where scholarship on Humboldt most sharply diverges.[31] Martin Heidegger assevers "that Humboldt determines the essence of language as *energeia*, understands this, however, in an entirely un-Greek way in the sense of Leibniz's *Monadologie* as the activity of a subject" (*Unterwegs zur Sprache* 238).[32] Donatella di Cesare argues that Humboldt's entire project cannot be understood apart from Aristotle's *Metaphysics*. Whereas in Leibniz's *Théodicée*, "the actuality of things is, from the beginning, contained in virtuality," and therefore can never "exceed potentiality" (43), Humboldt, like Aristotle, presents the actualization of ἐvἐpγεια as prior to potentiality, both in the logical and ontological senses, in that "it is the act of speaking in which the realization process of language is each time carried out and each time begun anew" (44).[33] Denis Thouard, on the other hand, contends that Humboldt adopts and adapts Aristotle's usage of ἐvἐpγεια, "not from the *Metaphysics*," but from the first paragraph of the *Nicomachean Ethics*. According to his reading, the telos of ἐvἐpγεια, when it comes to language, would be the praxis of human speech, and would be continuously renewed in view of further "interaction" ("La difficulté de Humboldt" 4).[34] All of these interpretations, however, emphasize exclusively the positivity implied in Humboldt's "energeia," whether it is the egological positing of a subject, or the actuality that, in Aristotle, has ontological and logical priority over possibility and privation.

"Energeia" operates differently, however, as "Einwirkung," and does not correspond to what has been described by others as an emphasis upon an "original, creative process [*ursprünglichen, schöpferischen Prozeß*]" (Cassirer 86), or as a "free [. . .] creative activity [*eine freie [. . .] schöpferische Tätigkeit*]" (Coseriu 143).[35] Humboldt's usage of "Einwirkung" reprises other aspects of Aristotle's discussion of ἐνέργεια in the *Metaphysics*. In particular, "Einwirkung" works in tension with the double temporal aspect that defines ἐνέργεια for Aristotle—which no commentator on Humboldt has elaborated at length. And as "Einwirkung" comes to pass as a function of tense, it opens a horizon for reading the structure of its operation, prior to and apart from any visible effect—as a critical a priori, then, that defines the conditions of the possibility of translation and speech. Time is at least twofold, when Humboldt writes: "For translations are more labors that test and determine the standing of language in a given point of time, as upon a remaining standard for measure, and should work upon and into it, and must always be repeated anew, than they are enduring works" (8: 136). For if translations "should work upon and into" the "standing of language in a given point in time," they must destabilize that very standing, which may be why their effectiveness can only be projected in terms of what, as Humboldt puts it, "should" happen. At the same time, this instability is definitely why—with no guarantee that translations ever will have worked, and no certainty over what they will have worked upon—by virtue of their sheer having been done, they "must always be repeated anew." The work of translation is therefore, possibly, powerless; its time, actually past—and thus, at once, yet to come. In between what "should" be effected and what "must" be done again, would be the instant of "Einwirkung" itself, which is elided in Humboldt's sentence—hence translations are "more labors [. . .] *than* enduring works [*mehr Arbeiten [. . .] als dauernde Werke*]." And because the work of translation would thus be always already beyond doing, translations are "more labors [*mehr Arbeiten*]" even "*as* enduring works [als *dauernde Werke*]" (8: 136). The more or less duplicitous status of translations, meanwhile, belongs to the structural inaccessibility of the moment of translation itself, and the necessary doubt over whether it ever will have worked as it should. In other words, the uncertainty surrounding the time of translations *is* their doing, and in this respect, the "point in time [*Zeitpunkt*]" of this work could only have been a puncture, a stigma, and a blind spot, where nothing could be said to work or not. Hence, a temporal dimension opens therein, for that point to be repeated, hollowed out again—or, as Werner Hamacher has said in his remarks on philology, whose philology has inspired these remarks on Wihelm von Humboldt, throughout: wiederhöhlt . . . .[36]

This structure forms the precise negative of Aristotle's ἐνέργεια, wherein end and praxis coincide, such that energetic doing is always already done,[37] at every moment taking place and having taken place, and therefore a permanently repeating, actual essence. Thus it is no accident that, in the interpretation of Humboldt's contemporary Hegel, ἐνέργεια marks teleological fulfillment per se—marred as this will have turned out to be in his corpus. Just as Humboldt's "should [sollen]" and "must [müssen]" indicate a redoubling deficiency, Aristotle's examples include, repeatedly, present and perfect tense verbs, conjoined "at once [ἅμα]," to denote a constant efficacy, as when he writes: "It is such that one sees and at once has seen, [. . .] thinks and has thought [. . .] and having seen and seeing is, at once, the same, [as is] thinking and having thought [οἷον ὁρᾷ ἅμα καὶ ἑώρακε [. . .], νοεῖ καὶ νενόηκεν [. . .] ἑώρακε δὲ καὶ ὁρᾷ ἅμα τὸ αὐτὸ καὶ νοεῖ καὶ νενόηκεν]" (Aristotle's Metaphysics 1048b 22–34).[38] Here, as in Humboldt's text, each moment will have surpassed itself, which is how energetic activities, as opposed to others, are always perfectly complete, even as they continue: "the telos and the praxis [τὸ τέλος καὶ ἡ πρᾶξις]" (1048b 22–23). But what is fulfilled for Aristotle is inscribed in Humboldt's "Einwirkung"—at least at this point in his introduction to the Agamemnon—as an opening, at once like Aristotle's terminus, and like the punctuality of blind instinct that Humboldt derives from Herder—and therefore unlike either "original" source.

Although Humboldt's transliteration of ἐνέργεια seems to occur only once in his oeuvre,[39] the double temporal aspect of Aristotle's ἐνέργεια returns throughout his work, which thoroughly divides activity by its proper deactivation and reactivation. With a different emphasis, drawing an analogy between the emergence of a word and the vision of an artist, Humboldt will say in his introduction to the Agamemnon that the "ideal shape" that arises in artistic fantasy "cannot be taken from anything actual, but emerges through an energy [Energie] of spirit, and most properly understood, out of nothing; from this blink of an eye [Augenblick] onward, however, it enters into life and is now actual and remaining."[40] Humboldt thereby replicates, perfectly, the momentary coincidence of the present and the perfect tense—which in Greek indicates not only the completion of an action but also, at once, the instantiation of a condition whose effects are permanent[41]—in Aristotle's primary example of ἐνέργεια: "one sees and at once has seen [ὁρᾷ ἅμα καὶ ἑώρακε]." One might translate this sentence anew, with Humboldt: "from this blink of an eye onward, seeing is now actual and remaining." But even here, where creative production seems to transpire through spirit, and its work appears to endure, this activity is essentially inoperative and broken. Through an energy of spirit—through this revision of Aristotle's ἐνέργεια—the glimpse Humboldt provides into the actuation of artistic vision—which arises from *nothing*, but is suddenly "actual and remaining"—discloses it yet again as an instant of radical privation. In one stroke, the possible and the actual are taken back, when artistic vision "*cannot* be taken from anything *actual*," and spirit must have departed, too, if "through the energy of spirit" means, at the same time—and "most properly understood"—"out of nothing."

Only from the "blink of an eye [*Augenblick*]"—with nothing and no one to see—does vision emerge as "actual and remaining." And if one might object at this point that the structure Humboldt describes corresponds to subjective actuosity in its most radical formulation—namely, Fichte's, where the "I" operates as a sheer positing—one cannot but see that here, activity is positively "nothing." In pursuing the logic of energetic activity to its most proper consequence, all talk of a subject, as of energy itself, becomes impotent and void. The same would go, moreover, for the present view that appears to have been permanently instantiated and can now be taken for granted. For precisely because whatever is "actual and remaining" is "now" in view, its sight would, strictly speaking, preclude any glimpse into its foregone inexistence, as if what has come to pass had never taken place. At the same time, however, if constancy is indebted to an instant of "nothing," the permanence of what is "now actual and remaining" also is thoroughly instable, and could, at any moment, disappear out of nowhere. From this perspective, the status of language as Humboldt presents it—the instant of its division, where it passes for and after itself, in no time—implies that the "en" and "ein" of "energeia" and "Einwirkung" could not denote a unified immanence, nor an intensification of effective force, but the interstice of a breach, and therefore, at once, the "out" of language, and all its apparent givens.

Into and through this "out," speech, as translation, comes to pass. It comes to pass along a way that cannot be seen or known, where the instant of each utterance, each intervention and inworking in language as a whole, also cuts off further passage, in the blink of an eye. In this way, the operations of language would resemble the language of the *Agamemnon* as Humboldt presents it, preempting his apology at the conclusion of his introduction with which I began:

> With every new reworking I have striven to take ever more distance from whatever did not stand sheer in the text. [. . .] I have sought to shield myself from ungermanness and obscurity, alone in the latter respect one must make no unjust demands that hinder what is to be more highly preferred. A translation [. . .] may not include any obscurity that emerges from wavering word usage and skewing conjunction; but where the original merely indicates, instead of clearly speaking out, where it allows itself metaphors whose relation is hard to grasp, where it leaves out mediating ideas, there the translator would do injustice in arbitrarily bringing in of his own accord a clarity that would distort the character of the text. The obscurity that one sometimes finds in the writings of the ancients, and that the *Agamemnon* preeminently bears upon itself, emerges from the brevity and boldness with which, with disdain for mediating conjunctive clauses, thoughts, images, feelings, remembrances and premonitions are aligned with one another as they arise out of a profoundly moved mind.[42] (8: 133)

Throughout this passage, Humboldt emphasizes middle terms, from mediating ideas and conjunctive clauses, which are omitted and avoided, to metaphors, which are permitted, but "hard to grasp," such that the relation they draw would hardly transmit to any receiver. What stands in the text seems to work and move in sheer isolation, as so many "thoughts, images, feelings, remembrances and premonitions" that are merely "aligned," but other than that, unrelated in any sequence that might facilitate passage according to the analogies of metaphor or syntheses of logic. Neither supple nor light, but resistant at every point, the rhetoric, thought, and syntax that are said to characterize the *Agamemnon* redouble the difficulties for which Humboldt begs pardon at the close of his introduction and attributes to his "more accumulated reworking." This redoubling marks the point where introduction and translation alike begin, at once, to unravel. The difficulties for which Humboldt later apologizes cannot be mistaken as marks of overwrought style, but as replications of the elliptical brevity of Aeschylus's original, to which Humboldt professes "troth [*Treue*]" throughout (8: 130, 132, 133). Humboldt's "accumulated reworking[s]" thus turn out to be a matter of ever further removal: "with every new reworking," he has "striven to take ever more distance from whatever did not stand sheer in the text." This formulation, in turn—to return to the opening of his introduction—reprises the way that Humboldt had described the incomparable sublimity of Aeschylus's drama, whose significance might be

glimpsed only now. For there, he had also emphasized how "each motivat-
ing ground drawn from incidental personality is removed [*entfernt*]," and
"all things merely human and earthly, annihilated [*vertilgt*]" (8: 119). All
of these parallels throughout his introduction—at the beginning, middle,
and end—come down to this: the original point that translation envisions,
where it would coincide with the tragedy itself, should be the punctual,
negative moment of "Einwirkung," which unsettles the standing of language, in order to set it working in the first place. In translating the *Agamemnon*—or, at least, in describing his work—Humboldt strove to translate
neither Greek nor German, but the "energeia" of language, beside itself.

Everything in this text stands sheer apart, and the truth of the matter is,
as in Kant's accounts of the mathematical and dynamic sublime, no matter
at all, but a distancing and annihilating of all that might be a mediated
object of interest, of human or earthly predication or comparison; of all
that might, in other words, pass for familiar in any logic or tongue. Unlike
Sophocles's language—which Humboldt calls "so tenderly melded, so supple and nearing the conversation [*so zart verschmolzen, so geschmeidig und
sich dem Gespräch nähernd*]" (8: 129), the text of the *Agamemnon* in no way
communicates transitively. Thus, Humboldt cannot but remark: "Such a
poem is, according to its proper nature, and in a much different sense than
can be said of all works of great originality, untranslatable" (8: 129).[43] The
very impotence and impossibility that this word implies, however, is what
also distinguishes the *Agamemnon* as the text where, in Humboldt's view,
the energetic precondition for any transmittable or translatable language
might be pointed out. Hence, Humboldt cannot but avoid the register of
words and speech in the passage where he refers to the elements of the
drama, which he calls, instead: "thoughts, images, feelings, remembrances
and premonitions" (8: 133). Beyond the Greek language, or any other, the
Agamemnon would be, rather, a prophecy of language, destined to fail itself.
And indeed, the register of prophecy is not absent from the language of
Humboldt's introduction, either. For his assertion that Aeschylus's text,
in places, "merely indicates, instead of clearly speaking out"—recalls the
oracular God of whom Humboldt may have read among the fragments of
Heraclitus in Plutarch: "The lord, whose oracle is at Delphi, neither speaks
nor hides, but indicates [ὁ ἄναξ, οὗ τὸ μαντεῖόν ἐστι τὸ ἐν Δελφοῖς οὔτε
λέγει οὔτε κρύπτει, ἀλλὰ σημαίνει]" (Diels 79).

Whether or not Humboldt's discussion of the *Agamemnon* resonates
intentionally with the prophetic signs of Apollo, however, Humboldt's
further indications that all places in the text—from metaphors to syntax—
operate in precisely this suggestive way openly imply that his translation is

directed toward something other than a language that might correspond
to any one could presume to know or grasp, ancient or modern. Hence,
too, the unmediated leap that occurs, when Humboldt moves from his
assertion of the untranslatability of the *Agamemnon* to a discussion of language as such. Comparing the origins of a word to the visions of an artist
from nothing, then abandoning these registers to present the forms of
language still more primarily as symbols, he indicates, in other words, that
his translation addresses, first of all, the energy and emergency of language
per se, the "gift [*Gabe*]," as he will call it later, that will have befallen before
any dates (7: 17).

Once the *Agamemnon* is pronounced untranslatable, the disparity of different languages comes into view—"each expresses the concept somewhat
differently, with this or that secondary determination, a step higher or lower
on the scale of sentiments"—and from this perspective between languages,
Humboldt imagines how a "synonymics of the foremost languages, also only
of Greek, Latin, and German" would be "preeminently worthy of thanks"
(8: 129).[44] If language is a gift, and if the textual tradition from Greco-Ro-
man antiquity might be a given, the language of Aeschylus's *Agamemnon*
does not carry over, and instead of being translated, or posited over again—
über-setzt—its resistance disposes the translator to a reflection on his lack of
means, in any one language or another. Dispossessed of any way to proceed,
Humboldt proposes a synoptic and synchronic view of languages, whereby,
however, their "synonyms" would not denote equivalences among words,
but mark constellations around concepts that no one term in any one language could entirely grasp or designate. No concept "can emerge [*entstehen*]
without the [word]," nor could it otherwise "be held fast," but even when
both word and concept stand out and seem at hand for use, their existence in
a language does not speak against the possibility that each word also, at once,
loses hold of what it was intended to grasp. For each synonym "expresses the
concept somewhat differently [*etwas anders*]," turning it into something different, which no word in any language can contain. And if no word is "equal
[*gleich*]" or "like [*gleich*]" any synonym in one language or another, each concept would have to be many named and anonymous at once. This anonymity cannot be understood, however, in the sense that objects and concepts
would have preexisted their designations, and that their true being would be
revealed through a gathering of all synonyms, as the French Enlightenment
authors of synonym lexica, to whom Humboldt most likely alludes here,
had thought.[45] As Humboldt says in his speech before the Prussian Academy,
"On the Comparative Study of Language": "All attempts to place, in the

midst of the separate, singular ones, general signs for the eye or the ear, are mere abbreviated translation methods" (4: 22). More radical than this, the anonymity Humboldt implies here would have the structure of privation, such that, namely, objects and concepts, which can only be by name, lack it, and they must lack it from the very moment they are so called, because each single appellation could have taken place otherwise. That Humboldt's remarks may be read in this way is suggested not by the words he writes, but by the impasse he reaches at this point in his writing. For only when the un-translatability of the *Agamemnon* renders thinkable—at least for a moment—the anonymity of objects or concepts, only when the translator is at a loss for words, does Humboldt begin to consider of the origins of a word—as the unspeakable origin of different ones. And in this respect, the logic of the *syn-* that Humboldt implicitly works through here may even have touched upon the singular-plural origins that Jean-Luc Nancy describes—albeit in other words ("avec," "cum," "co-"), and in an ontological register—in his monograph *Être singulier pluriel*.[46]

At this point, through a metaphor that will repeat throughout his later writings on the *Foundational Traits of the Universal Language Type* (1824/26) and *On the Diversity of Human Language Structure*, among others, Humboldt's initial discussion of word formation begins:

> A word is so little the sign of a concept that the concept cannot emerge without it, let alone be held fast; the indeterminate working of the force of thought draws itself together in a word, as light clouds emerge upon a clear sky. Now [*Nun*] it is an individual essence, of determinate character and determinate shape, of a force that works upon the mind, and not without the capability to propagate itself.[47] (8: 129)

Before anything can be "held fast," grasped, or conceptualized, the "force of thought [*Denkkraft*]"—a sheer subjective activity (*Denken*), but one that, as force (*Kraft*), exists only in its utterance—must gather itself, and in intensifying, express something else. This exercise of energy would be the product of no decision, and certainly no act of any personal will, taking place as clouds condense upon a clear sky, as Frey has also pointed out in his elaborations on this passage (55).[48] Rather, Humboldt's metaphor transfers the sphere of word formation from the human to the heavens; casts it as an utterly fortuitous event—which would therefore never take shape the same way in any other language—and thus deprives it of thought. For once it exists, its sheer "force" (*Kraft*)—now divorced from any thinking (*Denken*)—is said to work upon the mind and to be capable of self-propagation. Out of nowhere, it is "now [*nun*]," as Humboldt puts it, in a condition of perpetuation, and it is thus already past the limits of Humboldt's metaphor: no transient cloud of nebulous, changing shape, but coined with a "determinate character and a determinate shape." Like the coincidence of the present and perfect tempi that had characterized the operations of ἐνέργεια, the emergence of a word is unthinkable apart from its already having emerged. And like the upsurge of artistic vision—to which Humboldt will compare word formation next—it is there in the blink of an eye: instead of any transition, the instant of emergence itself is marked in Humboldt's text only by the punctuation of a single point, "." The blink of an eye itself, however—the *Augenblick* of inauguration, which Humboldt will explicitly name in his artist simile—is absolutely closed to view and thought, absolved from any mediating terms that might bridge the cloudlike condensation of force and the "now [*nun*]" of the word that has emerged. Precisely because the analogy Humboldt draws does not carry the word over this breach, precisely because the "now [*nun*]" could have followed nothing, Humboldt revokes it immediately, proceeding from the actuality of the word, to the possibility of its emergence, to the impossibility of viewing or imagining any such instant: "If one should wish to think the emergence of a word in a human way (which is, however, already impossible, because speaking it out presupposes the certainty that it will be understood [. . .]) [. . .]" (8: 129).[49] And yet as the text Humboldt will have translated makes lucid, the "Augenblick" *is* the symbol, which, in its verbal form, βλέφαρα συμβαλεῖν (*bléphara sumbaleîn*), denotes the closing of the eyelids. And in his version of the *Agamemnon*, the symbol (σύμβολον, *súmbolon*) is inseparable from the ray of light (αὐγή, *augê*) that meets the eye (*Auge*)—and that should "bring a call from Troy [*bringend Ruf von Ilion*]" (8: 148), before a single word.

What this unspoken symbol and invisible *Augenblick* might mean for the language that Humboldt envisions at this point in his writing, however, can be pursued only by reading the traces of its impact in other texts, where the light that flashes between a nebulous force and its propagation is rendered more explicitly. Later, Humboldt will modify his metaphor in his *Foundational Traits of the Universal Language Type*, writing, "Everywhere, where freedom moves within the bounds of finitude, there is a series of determining foreign influences in the instant [*Augenblick*] of its working, but it can also, like lightning [*Blitz*] out of cloudless ether, suddenly step out from them and become self-determining" (5: 398).[50] He then likens this lightning to the word: "since it is now the property of the word to call forth the concept through the tone, as through an electric shock, so too does the effect of it radiate through the entire soul, out in all directions."[51] And still later, in *On the Diversity of Human Language Structure*, more explicit remarks to this effect follow, in a further elaboration of the analogy between thought and language, in which each sound, in the blink of an eye, erupts like a bolt of lightning:

> Intellectual activity, thoroughly spiritual, thoroughly inward and in a certain measure passing over without a trace, becomes external and perceptible for the senses through the sound in speech. [. . .] It is, however, also in itself tied to the necessity of entering into a bond with the spoken sound; otherwise thinking cannot attain to clarity, representation cannot become concept. [. . .] The correspondence of sound and thought thus falls clearly to eye. As the thought, comparable to lightning or a bolt, gathers the entire force of representation into One Point and excludes all that is contemporaneous [*alles Gleichzeitige*], so too does the sound resound in abrupt sharpness and unity. As the thought grips the entire mind, so too does the sound possess preeminently a penetrating force that shudders all nerves.[52] (7: 53)

In advance of anything that might be said but for the saying itself, the intonation of language and thought shocks, in a collision akin to the concomitant strike of thunder and lightning. Through this extended simile, however, Humboldt not only attempts to present the purely impersonal conjunction of intelligence and sound in language; he not only reprises the way, in his *Agamemnon*, the "ray [αὐγὴ, *augê*]," and not the "symbol [τὸ σύμβολον]," becomes the first sign to arrive; he suggests, too, that the time of the word strikes apart from all that is simultaneous and therefore, too, apart from all that belongs to a temporal continuum. The initial time of the tone stands out from all such measures, like "the sudden [τὸ ἐξαίφνης]" that, in Plato's *Parmenides*, is said to belong to no place and no time, between and before any shift from stasis to movement or vice versa (156 d3–e2), and that, in Aristotle's *Physics*, is called the ecstatic interval of each change, imperceptible due to its utmost brevity (222 b15–29). Unlike Aristotle's articulation of ἐνέργεια, which hinges upon the "at once [ἅμα]" that conjoins "seeing and having seen [ὁρᾷ ἅμα καὶ ἑώρακε]," Humboldt's translation of the force of language is absolved from "alles Gleichzeitige" in the most radical sense—from all similarity or equivalence (*Gleichheit*) to any moment, as well as any other temporal (*zeitige*) category. And it might now be said more precisely than before how privation is the effect of this force. The nerve-shuddering vibrations of the first tones, which are not words or concepts, expose the very thought they should incorporate and express to its shattering and suggest that the emergence of language can be experienced only at the point of utmost peril for speech and thought alike. In the beginning, the inworking and unworking of language must have coincided. And in this respect, one might almost be reminded of the fall of Babel, if the notion of an edifice—a tower—were not so improper to the registers Humboldt evokes here. Yet it is through a confusion of tongues—the tongues he names in his speculation on synonymics—that the tone, so critical throughout his oeuvre, strikes a note of exigency.

In short, Humboldt implies that to intone thought is, at least at first, to *tonare*—the Latin verb for those bolts of thunder that strike with every lightning flash—and he thereby implicitly places the emergence of the word sheer under the sign of Zeus—without any "mediating ideas" or "conjunctive clauses" to render the metaphor easier to grasp. Words would not arise in the mind of man, but descend in a flash,[53] and the tenuous hold of these metaphors notwithstanding, it would, at the very least, be in no way thinkable "in a human way [*auf menschliche Weise*]" (8: 129). In this respect, this coordination of thought and sound comes very close to the mystical concurrence that Friedrich Creuzer had depicted in his chapter "Ideas on the Physics of the Symbol and of Myth," from *Symbolics and Mythology of Ancient Peoples*, which Humboldt had read repeatedly and explicitly cites elsewhere.[54] In it, Creuzer writes: "It [the symbol] is like a suddenly appearing spirit, or like a lightning bolt, which at Once lights the night. It is a moment that takes our entire essence in demand. [. . .]" (69).[55] And although Creuzer suggests that this demand could be withstood, and that the spirit might "return, enriched," he also draws the consequence that Humboldt will not explicitly get across: namely, that the symbol may also mark the end of speech before it has begun. "Here the inutterable overpowers," Creuzer writes, "which, in that it seeks expression, will ultimately burst the earthly form through the infinite violence of its essence, as a container that is too weak. The clarity of vision is hereby annihilated, and there remains only a speechless astonishment left" (73).[56]

However, whether or not Humboldt's related metaphors for the emergence of the word propagate Creuzer's elaboration of the symbol, or translate the traditional epithets of Zeus—who is the "cloud-gatherer [νεφεληγερέτα]" (*Il.* 1.517),[57] "the thunderer on high [ὑψιβρεμέτης]" (*Il.* 1.354), and "the lightener [ἀστεροπητής]" (*Il.* 12.275)[58]—the "divinely free [*göttlich frei*]" arrival of language will always already have befallen a people. Its imprevisible incidence and immeasurable effect underlie the register of the sublime throughout Humboldt's many pronouncements of the wonder and astonishment that language inspires.[59] And this arrival will have befallen a people at "One Point" that could neither be repeated, traced, nor survived—a fatal "Gift [*Gabe*]," toward which they are ever destined to tend: "a gift fallen to them through their inner destiny" (7: 17).[60] This inner destiny—a fall of and in language—arrives beforetime and is now permanently withdrawn from thought, word, and sight. And it falls together with the intoned forms that make up any language—as the remains of an untraceable event that nonetheless marks all that may henceforth come to pass. In his introduction to the *Agamemnon*, Humboldt tentatively calls these remains the "dead elements" of language, which determine "in no small way the moral and political fate of nations," and through which living speech always and at all times is borne out:

> In the judgment of languages and nations, one has attended much too little to the, in a certain measure, dead elements, to the external delivery [*äusseren Vortrag*]; one always thinks one will find everything in the spiritual. Here is not the place to carry this out, but it has always seemed to me that the circumstance, how in a language letters bind themselves to syllables, and syllables to words, and how these words relate to one another in speech according to duration and tone, preeminently determine or denote the intellectual, and even the moral and political fate of nations in no small way.[61] (8: 135–36)

Here, "dead" cannot only mean, in the sense that Humboldt sometimes used it, "mechanical."[62] It would also mean the legacy of the dead that each speaker inherits, and that remains, like the "mummy-like preservation" of "scripture," inert until uttered again, with "living delivery" (7: 45–46).[63] All the while, however, these remains are the aftereffects of the instant when language will have been inworked and unworked at once, and thus, they are not simply reactivated in the present, but permanently inscribed in the spirit of the living, as Humboldt writes in *On the Diversity of Human Language Structure*: "language has gone through the sentiments of previous generations [. . .] and preserved their breath [. . .] in the same sounds of the mother tongue" (7: 62).[64] In these sounds, before and with any word that is uttered, one is already spoken for as one speaks, and only ever speaks as others have spoken before. External "delivery [*Vortrag*]"—where the "pro- [*vor-*]" conjoins with the verb "to draw, to bear [*tragen*]"—draws out this pro-phetic dimension of expression, which works in all that verbal delivery might otherwise bear upon, protracted toward a future that could not be foreseen and a past that forbears all speech of its own. Thus, Humboldt will point to the prehistory of this fateful gift, as well as the date of its emergence, as the impassable "cleft which separates something from nothing [*Kluft, welche das Etwas vom Nichts trennt*]" (7: 39). This impasse, however, is nonetheless an a priori given that can in no way be received,[65] a foreign antidote to all linguistic and historical data—and therefore, at once, a rift through our midst.

Throughout his writings, Humboldt addresses nothing less than the cleft between something and nothing; the sudden initiation of expression that will have arrived before any "now [*nun*]," past or present, and any word that will henceforth be spoken. What he addresses, in other words—and each time through other words, drawn from other tongues—are exceptional instances of disjunction before the establishment of all that could be binding in language. Like the anonymous points where the synonyms of diverse languages would con- and diverge at once, Humboldt speaks to a "syn-" at the punctual origin of language before any word, which marks nothing, other than its foregoing vanishing point. Minimal as it is, this point is crucial for the labor of translation, which can come to pass only insofar as it, too, undergoes such an impossible instant, when it would work into and upon the standing of language, and thereby—for a moment—unwork any language that is hitherto and henceforth spoken. Although this moment would seem to take place without a trace,[66] its structural necessity—at the point when, most properly understood, nothing comes to pass—entails the weak possibility that, through translation, language might be absolved from whatever may now be bound in it; that translation should not only "work upon and into" it, but also "determine" or "attune" (*bestimmen*) it in an utterly different way.

Thus, more than in any subsequent text, Humboldt will emphasize this "syn-" throughout his introduction to the *Agamemnon*, from his early reference to synonym lexica to his later pronunciation on the symbolic formation of language. For in this text, he will emphasize more forcefully than ever the fragility of the linguistic bonds between sound and sense, where the actual connection they effect is, at once, the point where the objects of actuality dissolve:

> All language forms are symbols, not the things themselves, not conventional signs, but sounds, which find themselves with the things and concepts that they present, through the spirit in which they have emerged and always emerge further, in an actual, and if you will, a mystical connection; and which contain the objects of actuality dissolved, so to speak, into ideas, and now, in a way for which no limit can be thought, can change, determine, separate and bind.[67] (8: 131)

On the one hand, these symbols are the aftereffects of the instant when language would have emerged, for only then can they work as fully operational conjunctions of past and present: "they have emerged and always emerge further." Yet at the same time, as the medium through which the "objects of actuality [are] dissolved," these symbols can "now [*nun*]" not only "determine" but also "change"; not only "bind" but also "separate." Neither words nor concepts, symbols mark the limit of linguistic expression and contain, properly speaking, nothing but the preliminaries for any possible composition and decomposition. These possibilities are limitless, because there is no limit for the limit itself—which can in no way be fixed, and which therefore demarcates nothing a priori. The fact that Humboldt provides no object for the infinitives, "change [*verändern*], determine [*bestimmen*], separate [*trennen*], and bind [*binden*]," means that he breaks the grammatical prescription of transitivity, thereby rendering each verb infinite, but with nothing to act upon, and thus infinitely active and impotent at once. This breach, in turn, testifies to nothing, and it is this lack that perhaps renders indefinite—if not infinite—possibility thinkable. Either way, Humboldt emphasizes through this breach within his own prose that the point where sound and sense connect is, at once, their breaking point.

These symbols may be the effect of blind fate, initially instantiated by the first concomitant outburst of thought and intonation, but they are also the site where everything can change and fall out of sync. As Humboldt knew from the Greek language, συμβαλεῖν not only denotes closure but also breaks down into a "dashing (-βαλεῖν) together (συμ-)," which he will elaborate explicitly in his more concise definition of the term several years later. Beginning with the standard notion of the symbol as a synthesis—"in the symbol, the sensual and unsensual, pervading one another mutually, is seen as One [. . .]"—he dashes this more conventional notion,[68] with the gloss: "idea and bodily matter fall together [*fallen zusammen*]" (5: 428).[69] And if this reformulation displaces and alters the sym-bol to a sym-ptom—from συμ-πίπτειν, "to fall together, fall upon, happen to" (*OED*)—Humboldt's later gloss sheds light on the passage from his introduction to the *Agamemnon*, too. For only as an accidental col-lapse—only as the "together" of a "fall"—can symbols be said to *"find* themselves in an actual, and if one would like to call it thus, mystical connection," rather than being invented at will, or predetermined *a priori* by necessity. If all language forms are symbols, then the gift that will have "fallen to [*zugefallen*]" any given people "through their inner destiny" (7: 17) must also be an accident: *Zufall*. And as an inexplicable and incalculable emergence, in which "accident [*Zufall*] also reigns" (7: 74), language might also happen to be free. The connection that the symbol denotes thus entails as its necessary counterpart the freedom for every conjunction to miss, or fail—one morphological correlate of συμ-βαλεῖν is, after all, con-jecture—as well as the freedom for all that conjoins at the point of encounter to fall asunder.

Thus, these remarks on the symbol re-evoke the dynamics of "Einwirkung," where what comes together in language is also "at once a going asunder [*Auseinandergehen*]" (5: 396). They re-evoke the point between languages, when nothing elapses, but without which the labors of translation could not test, determine, and work into and upon language at any given point in time. And they re-evoke the way that Humboldt proclaims, at another juncture in his introduction, that the truest translation does not convey the original in similar terms, but collides with it, in that it "can always only set *against* each utterly proper term, a different one" (8: 130, my emphasis)—which he will illustrate, as has been seen, when the ray (*augê*) meets the eye (*Auge*) in a symbolic collision of language that unworks the limits of the terms σύμβολον, αὐγή, *Zeichen*, and *Auge*—at once.

Humboldt will subsequently attempt to limit the consequences of this radical formulation of language by confining the symbol to only one possible aspect of linguistic presentation—and by asserting that it must be suppressed (*niedergedrückt*), lest it impede the discourse of thought, through an "inclination to dwell by the obscure and mysterious connection" (5: 430) it effects.[70] But in his introduction to the *Agamemnon*, he opens a glimpse into the impasse that each word, absolved from its definitional limits, might pose to the compulsory trajectories of speech and action that will have befallen any speaker, at any given time. And he thereby points out a way through which, at the risk of stunned silence, language might be rethought, labored upon, and elaborated differently. Perhaps his task, as the translator of the untranslatable *Agamemnon*, compelled him to do so; perhaps the words of his introduction are the fallout of a fortuitous encounter with Aeschylus's Greek and Creuzer's *Symbolics*, among others. In any case, the symbol is none other than the point of Aeschylus's tragedy.

In the opening paragraph of the text, Humboldt introduces the *Agamemnon*:

> Among all works of the Greek stage, none equals the *Agamemnon* in tragic sublimity. As often one goes through this wonder-replete piece anew, one senses all the more deeply how meaningful every speech, every choral ode is; how all singularities, though they outwardly appear loosely bound at first, inwardly strive toward One Point; how each motive drawn from contingent personality is removed; how only the greatest and most poetic ideas are the ones that reign and rule throughout; and how the poet thus annihilates all

that is merely human and earthly, so that he succeeds in setting forth the
pure symbol of human fates, of the righteous reign of godliness, of the eternally retributing doom, which mercilessly avenges debt through debt until a
god, full of sympathy, reconciles the one that is accrued last.[71] (8: 119)

In this passage, what emerges foremost is the prominence of the "One
Point" toward which each spoken and sung utterance inwardly strives.
Every single element, which otherwise appears "loosely bound," is nonetheless beholden to it, so that going through the text anew would less reveal
the outward meanings of each speech or song than it would allow one to
sense an intensive tendency throughout. Each apparent utterance would
therefore be "meaningful," not insofar as it speaks of or about something
else, but in that it means unto itself, and thus tends toward a minimum
of meaning in any conventional sense. Thus, what Humboldt formulates
here is no description of poetic production or poetic work, but a radical
withdrawal, where Aeschylus's work strives to subtract all that might seem
positively binding from human motives and personality to "all that is
human and earthly." What Humboldt exposes as its working intention—its
en-ergeia—can therefore be understood as a zeroing in upon the "nothing
[*Nichts*]" that will have preceded any artistic vision or linguistic symbol.

Therein lies the incommensurable "sublimity [*Erhabenheit*]" of this work,
in the sense that Kant describes in the *Critique of the Power of Judgment*,
where the sublime is felt as "solely *negative* [*nur* negativ]," and as "a privation
[*Beraubung*] of the freedom of the power of imagination through itself"
(606)—before the prospect of sheer annihilation.[72] However, if Humboldt's
rhetoric converges to some extent with Kant's, what he indicates here is a
nihil before any prospect. For the "pure symbol of human fates" could only
be the symbol of *all* possible destinies and destinations—and must therefore
be pure of any single one of them, as well as any fateful contingency. As
such, however, it would also have to be the instant of sheer contingency,
where all possible destinies and destinations must have, together, fallen
asunder.

This structure is not contradicted, but affirmed, when Humboldt proceeds to align "the pure symbol of human fates" with a form of serial retri-
bution, and extends this "One Point" to a line of debt. For the "retributing
doom," which "mercilessly avenges debt through debt," cannot merely
refer to the particular courses of vengeance taken in Aeschylus's tragedy—
not if "all that is merely human and earthly" is annihilated at this point.
Rather, it must be understood foremost as intrinsic to the structure of sheer
contingency that Humboldt sets forth. Whether it refers to a "dashing

together" of sound and thought; of idea and bodily matter; or of two halves
of a bone or other object, which "contracting parties broke between them,
each party keeping one piece, in order to have proof of the identity of
the presenter of the other" (Liddell and Scott), the symbol is, only when
it is broken. As the bond *of* a rift, it would therefore betoken, even in its
purest form, the need for a complement. And in its purest form, this need
would have to be limitless, for if the symbol is "pure," it could not conjoin
two particular, determinate counterparts like sound and intelligence, but
before this, it would have to work, like ἐνέργεια, between a sheer, absolute
punctuality and eternal, equivalent consequences. It would have to work,
in other words, like language as such, where any single utterance evokes
those possibilities that, strictly speaking, correspond to it, and also calls for
others—where it is, at any and all times, no sooner actualized, than "in
need of new labor [*einer neuen Arbeit bedürftig*]" (7: 46).[73] But at the same
time, regardless of which particular direction fate may take, any one will
have been constituted in an instant of accident, and would thus have to
potentially be different.

It is to this possibility that Humboldt speaks, when the particular scene
he indicates as incommensurably sublime—"Nothing in all antiquity
attains to the sublimity of this scene, is equally shuddering and stirring
[*Nichts im ganzen Alterthum reicht an die Erhabenheit dieser Scene, ist gleich
erschütternd und rührend*]" (8: 124)—happens to be the one point when all
the workings of the plot reach an impasse, and when all the language of the
play appears revoked, in order to emerge anew: the Cassandra scene. This
is the moment when *nothing* happens—"the one between Agamemnon's
entrance into the palace, by which his fate is no longer doubtful, and
his murder" (8: 124)—and it is the closest the drama comes to the point
that Humboldt sets forth at the outset. Thus, when he writes, "Cassandra
fills out the most horrifying [*schrecklichsten*] moment of the piece"[74]—the
fullness of the instant cannot refer to any dramatic event. Rather, as a
moment of inaction, it would be the fulfillment of the intensity "toward
which each spoken and sung utterance inwardly strives," and thus where
all that might "outwardly appear"—including every debt—defaults. This
moment is therefore, at the same time, "most horrifying," not in the sense
of the horrors Cassandra will utter, but in the original sense of *Schreck*:
"rupture, rip [*sprung, risz*]" (Grimm and Grimm 15: 1659). In other words,
in interrupting the course of dramatic action, Cassandra fulfills the intentions of the play by reducing all that has and will come to pass to nearly
naught, and thus to the breaking point.[75] The fault line of this rupture
runs through Humboldt's words too, which outwardly might seem to be

simply about it. For the remark, "Nichts im ganzen Alterthum reicht an die Erhabenheit dieser Scene, ist gleich erschütternd und rührend" (8: 124), is at once a positive assertion of incommensurability—"nothing [. . .] is equally [*gleich*] shuddering and stirring"—and a moment when nothing, beyond all comparison, shudders and stirs—"nothing [. . .] is at once [*gleich*] shuddering and stirring"—and is thus itself a translation of that very scene, in the works of shattering.

Elaborating this moment further—this instant between something and nothing—Humboldt suggests that this Trojan prophetess initiates the language of the drama anew, in a foreign tongue. Without speaking it clearly, Humboldt indicates as much when he says that her "stark silence [*starres Schweigen*]" dissolves, beginning with "bare inarticulate sounds and outcries [*blosse unarticulirte Laute und Ausrufungen*]" (8: 124). This formulation is stunning, coming from Humboldt—who elsewhere insists that the "*articulated* sound [*articulirte Laut*]" is the minimal linguistic phenomenon that can be described (7: 65), and that no account of its origins can be given, because the "cleft, which separates something from nothing," "withdraws from our observation" (7: 39). For with these words, he revokes his own explicit premises for linguistic science, in order to re-evoke the inarticulate interjections that open narratives of the origins of language by Enlightenment and Romantic writers such as Condillac and Ferdinand August Bernhardi.[76] Before any articulate forms of vocalization, the sounds Cassandra utters come from nowhere, and therefore shock, like an origin of language—and like the nerve-shuddering emergence of lightning that Humboldt, like Creuzer, will propagate as the first sign of voiced sound. Thus, they at once emit a symbolic promise of language—and the concomitant possibility that sound and thought might be so thoroughly shaken, they would end before they begin, in a flash. Cassandra's language, which will erupt between Greek and Trojan, and is therefore unlike any other, would thus be the most radical prophecy of another one—a sheer beginning that might, for all its horror, initiate and ignite—i(g)nitiate—an utterly different delivery and thus a deliverance to a different fate.

This moment also marks the impasse, beyond which no reading of Humboldt's introduction can go further, without turning to Aeschylus's Cassandra. But in it, Humboldt will have opened a theory of language to the point where language does not come to pass at any one time or in any one tongue, where its energy and expressive force are contingent upon a radical privation, and where, therefore, speech might also happen to be free. If he will, in his later writings, withdraw from the radicality of the formulations he sets forth here, those writings register tremors that cannot be fully suppressed by any systematic synopsis of his works and that deeply trouble any instrumentalization of his language. Humboldt opens, through the midst of his introduction to the *Agamemnon*, insight into the rift in language, through which it will have come to pass, to date, to sign, and at which instant all means of passage—stop.

PROPHECY, SPOKEN OTHERWISE: IN THE LANGUAGE OF AESCHYLUS'S *CASSANDRA*

This day has come.
ἥκει τόδ᾽ ἦμαρ
—Cassandra

The work of the *Agamemnon*, the fate it dramatizes, is the end of the hero in more senses than one. The offstage murder of Agamemnon is the obscene point—to modify Humboldt's synopsis of the play—toward which every speech, if not every choral ode, tends.[1] But this incontrovertible tendency is eclipsed, ephemerally, by a different speech. Agamemnon's murder is concealed, elaborately plotted in secret, and prepared, and it will, indeed, take place precisely as planned, so that Clytemnestra can call her act of vengeance a "victory of old [νίκη παλαιά]" (line 1378), even as she stands over the fresh corpse. And yet just before it is about to happen, it is set forth, envisioned, and decried by Cassandra, in a scene of prophecy that defers the decisive moment, even while her utterances "tie [*knüpfen*]," as Humboldt puts it, "the entire sequence, from its origin onward [. . .] to one another in the most sublime of ways" (*Gesammelte Schriften* 8: 120), from the earliest bloodguilt in the house of Atreus through the Trojan War to the pardon of Orestes in Athens. Telling what is to happen, in other words, temporarily disrupts and undoes the sequential logic without which plotting—especially the plotting of reciprocal vengeance that drives "the entire sequence"[2]—would be unthinkable and ineffective. The same would have to go for heroic deeds, too, such as the sack of Troy, as well as the sublime net—"higher than all overleaping [ὕψος κρεῖσσον ἐκπηδήματος]"—that Clytemnestra boasts to have woven around Agamemnon (1376), topping the "leap [πήδημα]" from the Trojan Horse that had culminated her husband's own intrigue (826).[3]

But there is no point dwelling on these things if we are trying to listen to Cassandra. For Cassandra's prophecies intervene before the end of the hero, and beyond a logic of ends, in such a way that calls for a different approach to the *Agamemnon* than a "mimesis of a praxis" with a "beginning, middle, and end" (Aristotle, *Aristoteles Peri Poietikes* 1449b 24, 1450b 26–27). And if Humboldt nonetheless says that Cassandra's prophecies "tie" everything together "in the most sublime of ways," the accent must be placed upon "the *most sublime* of ways"—lest her incommensurable speech be mistaken for a representation of connections along the lines of a causal or temporal order, in which events follow one another like vengeance, or, as Humboldt formulates this nexus of sequence and reciprocity earlier in his introduction: "so that under the direction [of Justice and Retribution], event unrolls out of event [*so dass unter ihrer Leitung Begebenheit sich aus Begebenheit entwickelt*]" (8: 119).

Cassandra disrupts. And in saying that she "ties" what seems to be a straightforward "sequence, *from its origin onward* [*von ihrem Ursprung an*]," Humboldt borrows Aristotle's description of plot in terms of "binding [δέσις]" and "loosing [λύσις]" (*Peri Poietikes* 1455b 24). But since her utterances disrupt sequential continuity, as well as the plot, his words imply, at the same time, that her operation upon this "sequence [*Folge*]" would have to differ from the linear continuity it seems to be made up of. Furthermore, his remark suggests that such continuity is not itself binding—for it can be knotted differently—and that, therefore, no linear form necessarily defines events or their times.[4] One might read along these lines the many nominal phrases and instances of asyndeton in Cassandra's opening lyrics, which the chorus cannot unravel, any more than it could disentangle its own premonitions from before, when it said, upon Agamemnon's entrance into the palace: "now it [my tongue], pained in spirit, mutters in the dark and hopes to unravel [ἐκτολυπεύσειν] nothing timely, my breast ablaze with living flames" (1030–34). And whereas other commentators, like the medieval scholiast Demetrius Triclinius, take the word ἐκτολυπεύσειν simply to mean "to fulfill the appointed lot [ἐκπληρώσειν τὴν μοῖραν]" (Smith, *Scholia* 183), "to accomplish" (Fraenkel 1: 153), or "complete [*parfaire*]" (Judet de la Combe 2: 205), Humboldt works its more specific sense into his translation, writing: "But in the dark it murmurs now, breeding melancholy, and no longer hoping to *uncoil the threadwork* at the apt time [*Doch im Dunkel murrt es jetzt, schwermuthbrütend, und nicht* das Gespinnst *zur gebührenden Zeit zu* entknäueln *noch hoffend*]" (8: 179, my emphases).

This coil is the clew to the "tying" that Humboldt speaks of in his remarks on Cassandra as well—whose speech is untimely and inconsequential, and whose visions also blaze obscurely, winding up to be out of line with philosophical principles or rhetorical persuasion, while striking the chorus to the core. Even as the chorus fails to understand her, and proclaims itself "to be with no means" to make out her "blinding oracles [ἐπαργέμοισι θεσφάτοις]" (1112–13), it testifies to the immediate impact of her language by launching from iambic dialogue into strophic lyric, in responsion with her; by reprising her words in its own speech—and by comparing the effects of her words to those of a fatal wound: "To my heart there rushes a drop of saffron dye, the very one which, to men fallen by the spear, arrives together with the rays of setting life" (1120–23). Above all, this striking effect is exactly why Cassandra, condemned to "persuade no one nothing" (1212), can nonetheless be said to speak "in the most sublime way," as Humboldt—a reader of Pseudo-Longinus's sublime highness (ὕψος) as well as Kant's *Erhabene*—would have known: "for sublime things [literally, those things that are supernatural, τὰ ὑπερ-φυᾶ] lead listeners not to persuasion [πειθὼ], but to ecstasy [ἔκστασιν]" (Longinus 1.4).[5] Or, as Longinus more frequently states, such things will have knocked the audience out, left them stricken with "astonishment" (ἔκπληξις, from 'out-' [*ek-*] and 'strike' [*plêssô*])—not unlike the emergence of a word per se, as Humboldt sees it (see above, 69, 82–85).[6]

Cassandra, the "choicest flower of many war spoils [πολλῶν χρημάτων ἐξαίρετον ἄνθος]" (954–55), is a knockout, in more ways than one. And no discussion of prophetic language could proceed without pausing, stunned, upon the Cassandra scene of the *Agamemnon*. There, not only dramatic action but also language itself seems to temporarily fail with Cassandra's incendiary outburst of song and speech—which, according to the anonymous author of the opening synopsis, "arouses wonder, for its astonishment / strikingness [θαυμάζεται ὡς ἔκπληξιν ἔχον]" (1: 88).[7] Well before Agamemnon is "struck [πέπληκται]" down offstage by his wife (1343–45)—in a perversion of the erotic connotations that πλήσσω ('strike') had borne up to that obscene point[8]—Cassandra's language strikes,[9] just when she had appeared to be a mute figure, unable to "receive the speech [δέχηι λόγον]" of Clytemnestra (1060), and unable to respond to any address.[10] However, her language strikes not only because she seems at first to be "a silent actor," as Bernard Knox suggests in his essay, "Aeschylus and the Third Actor" (111), nor merely because, as the chorus will say, it is "stricken, as with a murderous sting [πέπληγμαι δ'ἅπερ δήγματι φοινίωι]" (1164), when it hears her "shrieking [utterances that are] shattering for me to hear [θρεομένας θραύματ' ἐμοὶ κλύειν]" (1165–66). It is not just the cries of her dirge, or θρῆνος, that traumatizes the chorus, when Cassandra breaks her silence, wailing to—and against—Apollo, "who is not," it remonstrates, "one to meet upon the dirge [οὐ γὰρ τοιοῦτος ὥστε θρηνητοῦ τυχεῖν]" (1075).[11] Nor is her impact even primarily due to the horrors that she sings, "from their origin onward" (Humboldt 8: 120), decrying Thyestes's consumption of his own children (1095–97); the murder of Agamemnon (1107–11, 1125–29), then of herself (1146–49); before lamenting the destruction of Troy (1156). Above all, the awestruck chorus "wonders [θαυμάζ[ει]]" at her because she, "raised beyond the sea, speaking of an other-speaking city [ἀλλόθρουν πόλιν λέγουσαν]," nevertheless "hit the mark, as if [she] had stood by [ὥσπερ εἰ παρεστάτει]" the bloodshed that had taken place in Argos a generation before, when Thyestes feasted upon his own children (1199–1201).

Her language astonishes, in other words, for its radical otherness and its simultaneous nearness to Argos—just as her language allows her now to appear to have been a bystander for events that took place overseas, and before she was born. Yet if the latter function of her speech seems most extraordinary, one would have to bear in mind that, since Homer, the prophet is one who—like the seer of the Argive army, Calchas, whom Aeschylus's chorus will have impersonated in its opening lyrics—"knows the things that are, that shall be, and that were before [ὃς ᾔδη τά τ᾽ ἐόντα τά τ᾽ ἐσσόμενα πρό τ᾽ ἐόντα]" (Il. 1.70). Knowing a past before her time, then, cannot be what strikes this prophetic chorus as strange, and furthermore, as a vessel for divine inspiration, the mantic would always be on standby for the mantic god Apollo,[12] who not only knows the will of Zeus—who "brings the days to fulfillment" (Hesiod, Erga 565)—but also "has never said anything concerning a man, woman, or city upon his mantic seats that Zeus, the father of the Olympians, did not command" (Aeschylus, Eumenides 616–18).[13] It cannot be simply the vision Cassandra conveys that surprises the chorus—besides, her vision, when it comes to Thyestes's feast, is one that the chorus already knows. Above all, it is her language that the Argive chorus explicitly wonders at, and as it does so—still more astonishingly—it gets carried away to the point that Argos and Argive Greek become, themselves, displaced.[14] For the "other-speaking city" [ἀλλόθρουν πόλιν]" that the Argive chorus names must refer to its own, as Pierre Judet de la Combe argues (2: 508–10), citing Humboldt's translation of the line, "you speak of a city of a foreign speech [von fremder Sprache Stadt erzählst]" (8: 186).[15] And not only do the chorus members, upon hearing Cassandra, suddenly reflect upon their city and tongue as foreign, beside (παρά) themselves in witnessing her bystanding (παράστασις). Besides this, the terms in which they do so also entangle them in the very language that had struck them with pain and bewilderment from the start. For the throes implicit in their "other speaking," or ἀλλό-θρουν, reprise, otherwise, the verb they had spoken to describe Cassandra's stinging cries, θρέο-μαι, as well as the word for her dirge to Apollo, or θρῆν-ος, which the chorus had not found meet. Even the wonder (θαῦμα) of which the chorus members now speak, upon hearing her "hit the mark," echoes the shattering wound (θραῦμα) her opening utterances had inflicted, differing from it, literally, by a single letter (ρ). Thus, when the Trojan priestess Cassandra is said to speak of an other-speaking city, Greek has become another tongue, for Cassandra as for the chorus. Her shattering language is also a shattering of language, for all speakers involved in this scene. With "other-speaking [ἀλλόθρουν]," the chorus's words, too, become "shatterings to hear θραύματα κλύειν]"—or shards of Cassandra's own broken speech. To revert to Humboldt's metaphor: no wonder everything unravels from here, precisely as the source and status of speech become convoluted. This effect is at least as important to the prophetic speech of Cassandra as the events she bewails, and, in bewailing, temporarily *threa*tens.

When Cassandra remains unresponsive to Clytemnestra's attempts to coax her into the house, this pause—first silent, then voiced in prophecies that extend for over two hundred lines—has been interpreted consistently as a caesura in the action that, at the same time, illuminates the past and future of the entire *Oresteia*. Seth Schein points out: "At this point, with his characteristic boldness, Aeschylus suspends dramatic time" (13). Judet de la Combe calls her speech a "profound accident at the heart of the work," which, addressed to no one, thus has no relation to the drama—and for this very reason expresses the true, most immediate revelation of the horror of the trilogy (2: 395, 403–04). Above all, her revelatory force has been emphasized in proportion to her ineffectiveness at the level of dramatic praxis, in a dialectic of impotence and affect. She "does not act," writes Judet de la Combe succinctly (2: 404). Contrasting her to the prophets of the Hebrew Bible, Bernard Knox asserts, "she has no advice to give, no call to action or repentance, no moral judgment, nothing except the vision of reality, of what was, is, and will be" (116). Her words, according to scholars such as Judet de la Combe, Simon Goldhill, and Laura McClure, distinguish themselves from the attempts of the dramatis personae, especially Clytemnestra, to manipulate language to effect desired ends. Thus, the knot of the drama—to return to the language of Humboldt's synopsis—would seem bound up with a figure whose speech complicates the "reciprocal murder [*Wechselgemord*]" (Humboldt 8: 120) that ties the lineage of Pelops in mutual annihilation, to the point that it dissolves. And in this respect, one might even go on to say that Cassandra already realizes the interruptive justice that will conclude the *Oresteia* at the Areopagus in Athens, not in terms of a decision or an action—which would affirm an order of effectiveness in its own right—but, still more radically, in her language.

Only when her language could be heard or read, then, could the ethical and dramatic implications of Cassandra's prophecies be, at least provisionally, unfolded. But how might this be done, when it is not certain what language she speaks—and when, above all, her speaking astonishes and absorbs those who witness it? It is not enough to play the role of the interpreter that the chorus seems so desperately to need, and to bring her allusions to the slaughtered children of Thyestes, the murder of Agamemnon and herself, and the return of Orestes to hermeneutic completion. From such a perspective, the dramatic content of her message, rather than her language, would become the premise upon which a discussion of her prophetic speech would proceed. Yet it is also not enough to say that Cassandra speaks apart from the other actors of the drama, or that her words constitute an impotent, yet powerfully revealing pause—although these points are of utmost importance and have been rightly stressed by readers of the *Agamemnon*. For even a rhetoric of interruption risks missing the mark, insofar as it is bound to subsume her ecstatic speech within the plot of the drama to some extent, rather than concentrating upon what makes it stand out.

And yet, in nearly all of the commentaries on her scene—themselves relatively few in number, as Robin Mitchell-Boyask remarks in his detailed study of bridal imagery in the episode (270)—the question of her language has not been posed radically enough, with few exceptions, such as James I. Porter's excellent analysis of the challenges that the "idiom (language) of the play"—which Cassandra "knows all to well [ἄγαν [. . .] ἐπίστα[τ]αι]" (1254, qtd. in Porter 43)—poses to hermeneutics.[16] In his essay, Porter reads against the grain of a long-standing scholarly tradition—namely, the assumption that "meaning" in the *Oresteia* is "proleptically driven towards its solution," or that Aeschylus orchestrates a "movement from enigmatic utterance to clear statement" (32). In this respect, his reading furthers the pathbreaking work of Simon Goldhill, whose monograph on the *Oresteia* consists precisely in his "analysing (reaching towards rigour) how the (rigorous) search for meaning (δεσπόσω λόγου) is outplayed (eluded) by the play's own working—πέφευγε τοῦπος" (4). But Porter does not pursue the question of what implications Aeschylus's "idiom" might have for the meaning of language, when respite from the toil of reading "will never arrive" (45), and when each apparent clarification of ambivalence "is always a matter of 'other words'" (35). And when he adds, "the Aeschylean self-alluding and 'homophonic' text is in ceaseless motion, and its self-motions spread in all directions simultaneously" (35), by placing an emphasis upon "*self*-alluding" and "'homo-phonic'"—however ironically this selfsame "homophony," set in quotatation marks, must be understood—Porter does not broach the particular problem that Cassandra's "other speaking" poses to any language of self-referentiality, and to "language" itself. In his discussion of the Cassandra episode, Goldhill emphasizes, as he does throughout his book, the ruptures in "the process of signification," and "the problematic of the exchange of language," in particular, the way in which here, where "we have referential language, language that is not only true, but also capable of accurate prediction," that "language [. . .] is incapable of being received" (81–82). But he does not enter into the further complexities of the scene—which involve the disruption of the single (Greek) language in which the drama appears to be composed—nor does he dwell upon the astonishment Cassandra provokes, and the implications it has for language in the play. Wilhelm von Humboldt, however, solicits readers to do precisely this, when he introduces, as we have seen in the previous chapter, some of his most radical remarks on language in his introduction to the *Agamemnon*—in terms of a sublime, shattering force that threatens the language to which it will have given rise, and in which it is always, energetically, at work—and when he considers Cassandra's "prophecies [*Weissagungen*]" to be the consummate expression of this force, in "the most sublime way" (8: 120).

The wisdom (*Weisheit*) of her sayings (*Sagungen*) is nothing, other than this superlative way (*Weise*), which, over and above the sayings themselves, conveys divinity (θεοφόρητος [1140]), and with it, the "brilliance of godspeak"—to translate her "blinding oracles [ἐπαργέμοισι θεσφάτοις]" (1112–13) in yet another possible way. Cassandra's "other speaking" is at once, in other words, other than words; her language is also not one. And although it may seem anachronistic to speak of the sublime at this point, one must also bear in mind that the punctuality of the sublime, as Humboldt presents it, involves the annihilation of temporal and causal sequence—which is precisely what takes place here. At the same time, the synchronization of vision and language that distinguishes sublime expression—or: "explession"—for writers such as Longinus, and thus simulates the obliteration of linguistic and temporal mediation alike, is exactly what appears to be at stake in Cassandra's utterances, as they cut to the quick, sublime *avant la lettre*. "Look, look! [ἰδοὺ ἰδού]" (1125), she cries, repeatedly, to point out the rapid fire of what, at once, springs to the eye. For, she interjects—and in verses that have always troubled commentators, for their deviations from meter and grammar[17]—"*papai* such is the fire it comes upon *ototoi*" [παπαῖ οἷον τὸ πῦρ ἐπέρχεται ὀτοτοῖ] (1256). Such divine fire outstrips her speech, comes up too quickly to come upon "her," and provokes a cry of pain instead, thereby going further than even those flames that had overcome the chorus in its own premonitory song shortly before this passage—where its heart, as we have heard, was nearly "outstripping the tongue [προφθάσασα καρδία / γλῶσσαν]" (1028–29), its breast "ablaze with living flames [ζωπυρουμένας]" (1034).

If ever there were an instant when the distinction between speech and vision is nearly blended out—so that, "overcome by inspiration and pathos, you seem to see that which you say, and you set it below the eyes of your listeners [ἃ λέγεις ὑπ' ἐνθουσιασμοῦ καὶ πάθους βλέπειν δοκῇς καὶ ὑπ' ὄψιν τιθῇς τοῖς ἀκούουσιν]" (Longinus 15.1); if ever there were a moment when "what is spoken nearly outstrips the speaking agent himself [τὰ λεγόμενα ὀλίγου δεῖν φθάνοντα καὶ αὐτὸν τὸν λέγοντα]" (Longinus 19.1), it would be Cassandra's visionary prophecies, or "*Weissagungen*"—which word is itself an articulation of saying (*Sagen*) and seeing (*Weise*, from "**ueid*, to see, to know" [Grimm and Grimm 28: 1012]). But still more extreme than the rhetoric of vivid illustration, or ἐνάργεια, that Longinus provides, Cassandra's prophecies limn the eclipse of speech and vision for the audience of her "blinding oracles [ἐπαργέμοισι θεσφάτοις]" (1113). This phrase, which crosscuts the registers of vision and speech, is most telling. Struck by their failure to immediately understand her visions—"not yet do I understand, for I am now [. . .] without means [οὔπω ξυνῆκα· νῦν γὰρ [. . .] ἀμηχανῶ]" (1112)—the chorus calls her words "blinding," where the word is ἐπαργέμοισι, the pathological variant of ἐνάργεια, from ἀργός ('brilliant,' 'white'), which refers to the appearance of white spots upon the eye that obscure vision. Yet at the same time, in the same stroke, the chorus lights upon the point of all that Cassandra has said thus far, for the enigmatic site of the murderous scene she depicts and the obscure topic of her oracles, here and now, is none, other than what they say: Argos. The trope of "white spots [ἐπάργεμα]" prevents insight, so long as the visual sense of the word outshines the place-name it also contains—which turns out to be the chorus's blind spot.

Thus, when the chorus members speak, they are already spoken for in Cassandra's prophecies, and they can be said to visualize precisely what Cassandra expresses—but not as auditors who find her message "below their eyes [ὑπ' ὄψιν]" (15.1), as Longinus would put it. Rather, they do so, insofar as they participate in her visionary rhetoric blindly, and therefore speak a language that they do not, and cannot, themselves understand. Hence the frequency of ἔοικεν ('looks like' [1084, 1093]) in their exchange, as well as its derivative, προσεικάζω ('liken to' [1131]), as the chorus simulates insight in lieu of knowledge—which nonetheless manifests the truth.[18] Hence, too, the many similarities between what appear to be the chorus's words and hers, from lexical repetitions (e.g., "lustrate" φαιδρύνασα [1109] / φαιδρύνει [1120]) to echoes between etymologically unrelated words (e.g., the "stretchings [ὀρέγμα-τα]" (1111) that echo, deranged, in the midst of "blinding [ἐπ-αργέμ-οισι]" (1113) two lines later). Likewise, when the chorus shifts from iambic trimeter to strophic responsion, it adopts the rhythm of Cassandra's song;[19] and—most astonishingly—it does so just after her imperative: "Let insatiate Sedition [Στάσις] raise to the race an exulting shout [κατολολυξάτω] over the sacrifice that merits stoning [θύματος λευσίμου]" (1117–18). With this, they not only enter into "an affective community" with Cassandra "despite their incomprehension," as Judet de la Combe writes (2: 454). For in thus answering her call, the chorus also becomes the likeness of the very sedition she calls for and calls forth, even before they will themselves threaten the new rule of Aegisthos with "curses of stoning [λευσίμους ἀράς]" (1616), and before they will reappear, in the Eumenides, as the chorus of Erinyes whom they now raise, in question: "What sort of Erinys do you call to raise [her voice] upon this house?" (1119–20). As opposed to those explanations of the chorus's failure to comprehend Cassandra's prophecies, which rely upon the assumption that the chorus is composed of sovereign psychological subjects, who simply do not want to understand that the justice of Zeus may well entail the slaughter of their king (Scott, "The Confused Chorus" and Musical Design 66–67), or that the chorus's extreme agitation, to which they testify in their immediately preceding song, physically prevents them from registering the purport of her words (Thalmann),[20] one could speak instead with Cassandra, and say of them: "all too well do they know her speech."[21]

Whereas recent scholarship on deictics and tense by classicists such as Egbert Bakker and Pauline LeVen has renewed the debate on enargeia,[22] in order to show how grammatical nuance can draw narrated events nearer to their audience in ancient Greek poetry and prose, the exchange between Cassandra and the chorus stands out, to the point where the distinction between language and sight is, nearly, eliminated.[23] No sooner does Cassandra express what she sees than her audience is struck in no time, appearing as her visions and uttering them further, blindly and unwittingly. In this respect, what bears out is a scene of commutation that nearly eliminates, too, the distinction of speaker and auditor, much as Cassandra herself is, at the same time, a vehicle of the god (θεοφόρητος [1140]). And the language of this scene—which communicates beyond comprehension and is itself, more than any dramatis persona, the shifting subject of speech—cannot but affect the god, too, who is also indefinite. For the one to whom Cassandra so intimately appeals as "*my* Apollo [ἀπόλλων ἐμός]" (1081 = 1086) is far from evident at this point, and any familiar Pantheon figure, as the chorus's bewilderment suggests, is a long shot. At the same time her utterances "tie the entire sequence, from its origin onward" (Humboldt, *Gesammelte Schriften* 8: 120), then, all subjects and objects of vision and speech threaten to disappear in a flash, and the optics of *enargeia*, the language of Cassandra's blinding oracles, and the temporality of her scene are—eclipsed.[24] Such would appear to be the effect of the fire that comes, over her, upon Argos (ἐπ' Ἄργος), in prophecies of a language that is not only not one, but that unworks, enargetically, all that one might seem to know about language. This must have been the point that struck Humboldt—who repeatedly returns, as we have witnessed, to a rhetoric of violence and vision, strikes and lightening, in order to illustrate the force of linguistic expression—and the point where all such imagery is drawn blank. And yet there is more to say, when nothing is said and done. Beyond "the last of time [ὁ δ'ὕστατός γε τοῦ χρόνου]" (1300) and "as one who is dead [ὡς θανοῦσ[α]]" (1317), Cassandra announces—"this day has come [ἥκει τόδ' ἧμαρ]" (1301)—and solicits her hearers to "bear me witness in this [μαρτυρῆτέ μοι τόδε]" (1317).

At "this," the time has come to turn back and listen for what this prophetic day—when all days should come to light, in speech—may have looked like. The time of Cassandra's word is a different time, which bears, first of all, upon the singular time to which the drama begins, where a watchman waits in the dark for a torch signal that will announce the fall of Troy. There, we recall, the day breaks after the signal of conflagration is sighted. We have heard of this moment before, when Humboldt translates the scene of waiting in such a way that utterly obscures the medium and organ for vision, making the ray (*augê*) of light meet the eye (*Auge*) in what I have called a symbolic collision of language that unworks the limits of the terms σύμβολον, αὐγή, *Zeichen*, and *Auge*. But the time has arrived to hear it again, otherwise. As at the opening of the *Agamemnon*—a scene of waiting, followed by fire, then sun—the word of Cassandra proceeds, after a prolonged a silence, to burning outcries; then to a word that should "no longer peer out of veils" (1178), but should instead "seem [. . .] to dart to the risings of the sun [ἔοικε ἡλίου πρὸς ἀντολὰς / [. . .] ἐσάιξειν]" (1181)—only to go up again in flames (1256). The words of this Trojan princess thus emerge like the original words in the play—or these emerge like hers—where the first word was itself not yet a word, but a "ray of fire bearing speech from Troy [αὐγὴν πυρὸς φέρουσαν ἐκ Τροίας φάτιν]" (9).[25] Although her day will have to be considered in relation to the cycles of sunlight in the drama, then, the initiation— the "ignitiation"—of her very first words calls for closer attention first.

At least one reader, Wilhelm von Humboldt, has stressed the arrival of her language as an originary, incendiary moment of language per se, when he introduces Cassandra's outcries in his preface to the *Agamemnon*, tying her rhetoric together with the topoi that had structured Enlightenment and Romantic narratives of the origins of language along the lines discussed in the previous chapter: from the emergence of words through inarticulate cries and onomatopoeic responses to strong sensations, to the primarily verbal-participial character of these first "names." He writes: "The daughter of a king, who now serves as prisoner, dissolves bit by bit her stark silence; breaks out first in laments, bare inarticulate sounds and outcries, then in prophecies; at first in dark ones; and thereupon [. . .] she removes every darkness; unveiled, the seer's dictum should step counter to the sun" (8: 124–25).[26] And much as in Humboldt's depiction, Cassandra begins by uttering cries, "otototoi popoi da / Apollo, Apollo [ὀτοτοτοῖ ποποῖ δᾶ / Ἄπολλον, Ἄπολλον]" (1072–73 = 1076–77); the vocalisms of her cries—o and α—condense in "Apollo,"[27] a word of pain that at once denotes and denounces the fire that courses through her, and in so doing has already "destroyed [ἀπώλεσας]" and appalled her (1082). In his translation, Humboldt amplifies her inarticulate sounds by literally disarticulating, or removing the consonants, between the opening o's: "O o o o weh, o weh, ach" (8: 181), and by rendering her initial interjections with the same ones that Herder had evoked as the original, painful "language of nature" in his *Treatise on the Origin of Language*, before they crystallize as the name "Apollon": "Weh" and "Ach."[28] And if, in Greek, Cassandra's apotropaic outcries are conventional enough to be recognized by the chorus as a "dirge [θρῆνος]" (1075); if they are, in the language of tragedy, inscribed repeatedly at moments of mourning and lexicalized in the verb ἀνοτοτύζω, "call out *ototoi*" (1074),[29] Humboldt's reinscription of them as an origin of language nonetheless translates this moment of speech in a way that strikes to the heart of what is happening when she, a Trojan "raised beyond the sea," and "speaking of an other-speaking city [ἀλλόθρουν πόλιν λέγουσαν]" (1200–01), begins to speak a Greek that, for all its similarities in lexis and syntax to the language of her auditors, remains unheard of. Hearing "Apollo," the chorus protests that "Loxias [Λοξίας] is not such a one to meet upon a singer of dirges" (1075), and that it does not "become the god [τὸν θεὸν] in any way to stand by [παραστατεῖν] in lamentations" (1080), before it sees that the divinity she addresses is not only by or near her but also inspiring her speech—"the divine [τὸ θεῖον] remains in her breast, enslaved though it is" (1084). This insightful acknowledgment, however, culminates in a degradation of the name of the god that follows the one she performs, even as the chorus remonstrates against her blasphemy. It, too, turns the god away, as it rhetorically shifts from the proper name, "Loxias," to the noun, "the god," and, finally, to a "divine" quality—which gradual shift indicates that it has only grown more uncertain who or what is speaking.

Cassandra's denomination of "Apollo" is itself a painful and pained denunciation that undoes a familiar name, in such a way that the source of her inspiration appears obscure. It *is* "Apollonian," but only in the sense that the one whom she calls "*my* Apollo (ἀπόλλων ἐμός)" (1081) destroys (ἀπόλλυσι). And even before this apostrophe, her cries of lament to the god—ὀτοτοτοῖ—turn to and away from Apollo at once, as an expression of mourning that is, in the same stroke, the expression of apotropaic prayer.[30] As she is alone, Cassandra's mourning is unsettling—and not only because it is addressed to the god. Women's mourning, as Nicole Loraux has shown, was considered in itself a potential danger to the order of the polis in Attic Athens, to the point that laws prohibited threnody in the public funerary ceremonies and limited the presence of women during the ceremonies, in order to contain those expressions of passion and lack that could disturb the militaristic, civic order.[31] But Cassandra's outcries are excessive even on this empty stage by the house of Atreus, exceeding the commemoration of any single loss, as she bewails all the dead, past and future. The potential threat of this excess is underscored by the parallel between the chorus's description of her as "insatiable of the cry [ἀκόρετος βοᾶς]" (1143) and Clytemnestra's later evocation of the insatiable daemonic bloodlust in the house of Atreus, whose "eros [ἔρως] feeds its craving for blood," by yielding "new pus" even "before the old suffering relents [πρὶν καταλῆξαι / τὸ παλαιὸν ἄχος]" (1478–80).[32] However, beyond the extreme mourning Cassandra performs—which overturns even the chorus's minimal expectations that a corpse be present,[33] and that the mantic god be far from the scene—her utterances turn out to be cries of deflection, much like the outcries of Aeschylus's chorus in the *Suppliant Women*,[34] when the Danaids wail:

ὀτοτοτοτοῖ
μᾶ Γᾶ, μᾶ Γᾶ † βοᾶν †
φοβερόν ἀπότρεπε
ὦ βᾶ Γᾶς παῖ Ζεῦ (889—92 = 899—902).

Otototototoi mother Earth, mother Earth
turn away the fearful † shout †. O king, child of Earth, Zeus.[35]

And much like the Danaids, who have fled to Argos and now decry the arrival of their pursuers—their cousins, who have followed them from Egypt and wish to marry them—Cassandra cries out first of all against her own unwanted lover, *her* Apollo, who had been "stricken with desire [ἱμέρωι πεπληγμένος]" for her before she refused him (1204).[36] (Hence, her punishment to "persuade no one nothing" [1212] fits the crime, for in resisting the consummation, she is denied the seductive, erotic power that "persuasion" (Πειθώ) carries in Greek.[37]) Unlike the passage from the *Suppliant Women*, however, this is no longer the place to speak of distinctions between pursuer and protective god, or distances between pursuer and pursued. At this point, unlike the Danaids, Cassandra doesn't have a prayer. For the god himself, Apollo, has "led [ἤγαγές]" her to Argos as a husband would (1087)—which Mitchell-Boyask has pointed out in his extensive study of the way Aeschylus casts Cassandra as the bride of Apollo.[38] The addressee of her plaints is thus the very lover she fears, the "destroyer [ἀπόλλων]" who has, she says, already "destroyed her [. . .] utterly for the second time [ἀπώλεσ[ε] [. . .] οὐ μόλις τὸ δεύτερον]" (1082). The only saving grace is this: his name is also "destroyed," in turn, through her speech—and in this respect, the chorus was right to call her "blaspheming [δυσφημοῦσα]" (1078), albeit for reasons it could not know.

Cassandra's apotropaic lamentations are blasphemous, and the gesture of turning away that she performs pervades her speech so thoroughly that the Apollinian language that originates with her utterances turns out to be catastrophic. At nearly every turn, at every term of Cassandra's opening strophes comes a question or an imperative directed at and against the subject of her mournful visions and the subject of her speech. The house of Atreus is undone when she cries, "Ah, wither hast thou brought me? to what kind roof?" (1087) and then, ignoring the chorus's answer, "To that of the Atridae" (1088), declares: "one hated by the gods, bearing witness to ills of kindred murder and beheading, a slaughter place for men, a place where ground is sprinkled" (1090–92). Later, she pleads with her listeners to hold Clytemnestra off from Agamemnon, now beasts on the verge of a fatal entanglement: "Look, look! Hold off the bull from the cow!" (1125–26). But her deictic imperatives immediately take a downturn: in a new verse, in asyndeton, she declares, "one strikes, one falls [τύπτει· πίτνει]" (1128)—whereby not only the ones she speaks of but also the words she speaks for each action and agent, as near anagrams of each other, collapse in one stroke. At the same time, in other words, that everyone is struck, nothing could be said to befall anyone yet. This means that no name or verb is certain, and that Cassandra's Apollonian denomination defers any names with the same speed she evokes them—much as Longinus had written of sublime uses of asyndeton, which "bear an emphatic agony, which at the same time impedes [ἐμποδιζούσης] and chases [speaking] on [συνδιωκούσης]" (19.2). In the case of Cassandra, however, this dynamic brings about an instant, where her prophecies will have circumvented the future they rushed past. On this day, everything said to take place may have already been foregone.

Cassandra's way of speaking is, therefore, superlatively demanding: she repeatedly calls places, figures, and actions into question, and calls upon her listeners to act, only to dash the possibility that anything could have happened to be acted upon. When the chorus professes it cannot master the "term [τέρμα]" (1177) of her pathos—its end or its turning point—it is not only because, as seen above, the limit between its speech and hers has blurred to the point of invisibility, but also because every moment of her prophetic language is at once an end and a turn, an enunciation that summons and averts what she says and sees, and thereby eliminates it. One can say of Cassandra's lamenting prophecies what Gershom Scholem will say in 1918 of the language of lament (which is, he writes, "the nearest relative to the language of tragedy"): her language is "language on the limit, language of the limit itself"—as well as the "language of annihilation," which must necessarily extend to the limit as well as everything else (128–29). If her speech is "immediate," as so many commentators have asserted,[39] then it is immediate insofar as she inquires and demands that which only exists in the demand—which will just as soon be surpassed—leaving no means for the demand to fail or be fulfilled. It is immediate, insofar as Cassandra calls forth by calling into question and names by denouncing. Diverting every term, every limit is raised and razed—erased—with each word.

"How shall I say the end [τέλος]" (1108), she asks at one point, then answers in the next verse: "for quickly this shall be [τάχος γὰρ τόδ' ἔσται]" (1109). This end, here and now, is to be. Cassandra does not speak it; she speeds it, questioning, soliciting, and turning it away, only for it to approach with interminable swiftness. The time of her language is not a time of past, present, or future, but of a—destructive—tempo. No adverb recurs with such frequent insistence in her episode as "quickly [τάχος]" (1109, 1124, 1161, 1172, 1240), and only at one other point does the word occur so frequently in the text: namely, in the description of the torch signal that arrives from Troy to inaugurate the drama. Unlike the many moments of speech and song that address what has been worn down and awaited in (or with) time (χρόνωι 126, 463, 521, 551, 702, 807, 857)—and χρόνος, in this drama, is consistently evoked as a μῆκος, as a length, stretch, or attenuation (2, 196, 610)—Cassandra's prophecies arrive "in speed [ἐν τάχει]" (1240). If, in epic poetry, χρόνος refers primarily to conditions of hindrance, lack, delay, or fruitless activity (Fränkel 2), but also, in Pindar and Aeschylus, to periods of maturation and, ultimately, to the entirety of days and events realized under the rule of Zeus,[40] who "brings the days to fulfillment" (Hesiod, *Works and Days* 483), the speed of Cassandra's speech and the arrival it heralds would be the antitime, the antidote to duration, growth, and progress toward teleological fulfillment. After all, Cassandra herself will, at the end of the scene, reject the chorus's appeal to the value of endurance—"But the latest time is the eldest and best [πρεσβεύεται]" (1300)—with the astonishingly lapidary pronouncement: "This day has come [ἥκει τόδ' ἦμαρ]" (1301), and with the implication that it will have already come to naught.

This day has arrived—in no time. And in this respect, the day Cassandra announces begins to look very similar to the first message that arrives in the drama, in yet another way, when the "ray of fire bearing speech from Troy [ἀυγὴν πυρὸς φέρουσαν ἐκ Τροίας φάτιν]" (9) had outstripped the dawn from the east. Her words are akin, that is, to the "fast-travelling [ταχύπορος]," "fast-dying [ταχύμορον]" (486) torch signals Clytemnestra had orchestrated. These are another speedspeak—which, like the indeterminate "term [τέρμα]" of Cassandra's prophecies, is described by the chorus as the rapid-spreading "female limit [θῆλυς ὅρος]" (485), and thus no limit at all,[41] but a process of elimination that sets Argos ablaze and destroys its distinction to Troy.[42] For no sooner does the last light "strike this roof of the Atridae" (310)—and it "strikes [σκήπτει]" like a thunderbolt (σκηπτός)—than Clytemnestra sends it past its final destination, raising fire sacrifices throughout the city, so that all altars "flame [φλέγονται]," and "torches, from here and there, rise up heaven-high [ἄλλη δ'ἄλλοθεν οὐρανομήκης / λαμπὰς ἀνίσχει]" (91–93). Gloria Ferrari has read these flames as a conveyance of the Erinyes, as they are depicted carrying torches in Aeschylus's oeuvre and in visual artifacts (19–24); John J. Peradotto sees them as "ill-omened for the house of Atreus," since they are "kindled from the burning city of Troy" (389). These fires "from Troy [ἐκ Τροίας]," however, are also the sign *of* Troy, where, as Agamemnon reports upon arrival, "by smoke the conquered city is well signaled [εὔσημος] even yet / and storms of blind ruin live [ἄτης θύελλαι ζῶσι]" (818–19)—so that its distance and distinction from Argos will have gone up in smoke.

Furthermore, and beyond even this, Clytemnestra's fires are the sign of a day that is absolved from any astrological order, as the fires dawn before the sun, "a daylight of night [νυκτὸς ἡμερήσιον φάος]" (22–23). One could therefore go further than Peradotto, who argues that, in this play, "daylight is really the sunless night into which he and the house of Atreus have sunk" (390), and propose: Clytemnestra rapidly induces an artificial day with ruinous fires—the *téchne* of all *téchne*—which are thus similar to the fires Cassandra receives and conveys with her "divine-inspired *téchne* [τέχναισιν ἐνθέοις]" (1209). Like the daylight of night, these missives pierce the chorus's heart like the very "saffron-dyed drop [κροκοβαφὴς σταγών]" that "also arrives to men fallen by the spear, together with the last rays of setting life [βίου δύντος αὐγαῖς]" (1120–23). And as light and death, sun and blood, bleed into one another, the traditional Homeric epithet for the dawn, "saffron-robed [κροκόπεπλος],"[43] transforms into a "saffron-dyed [κροκοβαφής]" drop (239, 1121).[44] At this point, where daybreak and night-fall converge yet again, the chorus breaks off abruptly, and envisions what remains of Troy and Clytemnestra's torches despite itself: "and blind ruin is swift at hand [ταχεῖα δ'ἄτα πέλει]" (1124)[45]—with the further implication that *this* sun sets in the east.[46]

Thus, the day that Cassandra and Clytemnestra usher in with their incendiary speech eclipses the sun and arrives ahead of time, setting the solar system off course at the house of Atreus. This disturbance is immeasurable. No actor will begin to speak without addressing the day, with the exceptions of Cassandra, who addresses "her Apollo," and Agamemnon, who is preoccupied with other stars: namely, the setting of the Pleiades that had marked the leap of the Trojan horse (825–26). The accent placed upon the day in Clytemnestra's, the messenger's, and Aegisthos's opening speeches resonates, in turn, with the traditional status of the day in the archaic Greek poetic tradition, where men are "creatures of a day [ἐφήμεροι]" (Aeschylus, *Prometheus* 253)—exposed to what the day brings upon them—and where

justice itself depends on the order of the days.[47] One must know the days—
though, even at the end of the *Works and Days*, Hesiod declares that few do
(824)—and in the end, one can only know the apportioned day of return,
enslavement, or destruction, when it is thick upon one. "For," the ghost of
Clytemnestra explains, "sleeping, the mind lights up for the eyes, but in the
day, the fate of mortals is unforeseeing [ἀπρόσκοπος]" (*Eumenides* 104–05).
And more generally, the days of tragedy—often limited to one period of
the sun, as Aristotle remarks—are such imprevisable times, as Hermann
Fränkel argues in his study of day creatures in archaic Greek poetry (35),
which is why the time of the day must be the time of the future, and a time
to be greeted, for better or worse. "And the future," as the chorus had said
just before Clytemnestra's opening lines—"when it comes thou mayst hear
of it; let it be greeted in advance—but that is equal to being lamented in
advance, for it will arrive clear together with the rays of dawn [τορὸν γὰρ
ἥξει σύνορθρον αὐγαῖς]" (251–54). This is why it must be the time of prophecy as well. But the night is what dawns upon Cassandra, the chorus, and the
protagonists of the drama alike, such that "this day" marks an incalculable
turn of times and speech.

It would not be the first time. When Cassandra calls upon the chorus to hear the Erinyes "sing their song, [. . .] the proto-inaugural ruin
[πρώταρχον ἄτην]," and to witness how, in turn, "spit at the bed of
the brother" (1191–93), she recalls the adultery that began the hostilities
between Atreus and Thyestes. In so doing, however, she also obliquely
evokes the moment when Zeus reversed the course of the sun and stars,
which came to pass, at least according to Plato's version of the myth, "as an
apparition concerning the dispute told of Atreus and Thyestes" (*Statesman*
268e 9–10).[48] But the solar eclipse that takes place now may be, nonetheless, the only time. Clytemnestra's artificial dawn had seduced even the
watchman—who professed from the outset, "I know well [κάτοιδα] the
assembly of the stars at night, and those bright potentates conspicuous in
the sky who bring winter and summer to man" (4–6), but swiftly forgets
all he knows, greeting the "daylight of night [νυκτὸς ἡμερήσιον / φάος]"
(22–23). And when Clytemnestra herself welcomes the dawn as the daughter of Night—whom she designates with the euphemism, "well-minded
mother [μητρὸς εὐφρόνης]"—she also invokes, as many commentators
have pointed out, the other progeny of Night: namely, the Erinyes.[49] These
figures of vengeance not only bear the torch of *her* pyrotechnical dawn but
also dwell perpetually in "sunless darkness [δυσήλιον κνέφας]" (*Eumenides*
396)—so that if their day has truly come, it would not simply signal "a
daylight of night," but inaugurate a potentially interminable one.

There is no foreseeable limit to this night, especially once the similarities between Clytemnestra's and Cassandra's speech begin to shed further light on the source of prophetic inspiration here. For Cassandra's Apollonian prophecies also ring of the Erinyes. From the start, her language is more closely aligned with fire than sun,[50] and with dirges rather than paeans, all of which suggest a more furious inspiration than her appeal to Apollo may at first seem to suggest (993). Furthermore, Cassandra's song of the Furies is heralded by the choral ode that immediately precedes the Cassandra scene, as the chorus sings "the dirge of the Erinys [θρῆνον Ἐρινύος]" (992) against its will. The chorus is an "autodidact [αὐτοδίδακτος]" on autopilot (992), driven by the song that rises up in and through it, "unbidden and unhired [ἀκέλευστος ἄμισθος]" (979). The series of alpha privatives in this passage only affirms their assertion, being the signature grammatical feature of the Erinyes' language in the *Eumenides,* as Naomi Finkelstein has argued at length in her dissertation devoted to negation in Aeschylus's oeuvre, writing: "The abundance of alpha privative language through which Aeschylus characterizes the Erinyes echoes and reamplifies all of the earlier alpha privative language and represents these goddesses as its culmination" (7). Alone, the chorus's later designation of Cassandra's outcries as threnody would therefore imply a connection to its *un*-song—all the more so, since her initial utterances open almost exclusively with ἀ- (ἄ-πολλον, ἀ-γυιᾶτε, ἀ-πόλλων, ἀ-πώλεσας) and thus sound much like the chorus's language of negation, despite all semantic differences between her words and its. For, as seen above, Cassandra's verbs of abolition and gestures of apotropeia produce an effect in language that is similar to the impact of the chorus's and the Erinyes' privatives, even though none of the opening alphas in the list I have provided (parenthetically) are privative prefixes. But beyond even this, as Cassandra begins to utter her visions of murder, the chorus compares her to a hound on the trail of blood—"Keen-scented like a hound [κυνὸς δίκην] the stranger seems to be, and she is searching for the murder of those whose murder she will find" (1093–94)—which comparison will return in the *Eumenides* to describe the Erinyes, the hunting dogs par excellence, here and elsewhere.[51]

Surely, Cassandra is eventually said to approach the clarity of the sun in the line that, for Humboldt, reflects the completion of the emergence of her language from inarticulate cries (8: 124–25)—"no longer" should her oracle "peer out of veils" (1178); instead, it would "seem [. . .] to dart to the risings of the sun [ἔοικε ἡλίου πρὸς ἀντολὰς / [. . .] ἐσᾴξειν]" (1181).

But even this is no indication that Phoebus Apollo, the bright one, now prevails over prophetic speaking. For in the very same passage, Cassandra will ask the chorus to "run along [συνδρόμως]" (1184) with her,[52] as she scents "the track of the ills enacted long ago" (1185)—again like a hunting dog. And again, her pursuit lights upon the Erinyes, who have settled as a blood-drunk *komos*, or group of revelers, in the palace, who sing—like and through Cassandra—the "proto-inaugural ruin [πρώταρχον ἄτην]" (1192) of the house. In the moment her prophecies move toward the sun, then, Cassandra not only nears but also becomes the Erinyes whose presence she sniffs out and whose song she also utters at the moment she evokes it. And at the same time, in urging the chorus to follow her, she—if only ephemerally—plays the ghost of Clytemnestra, who will enjoin a sleeping chorus of furies to awaken and hunt Orestes in the *Eumenides* (131–39). Cassandra's Apollonian burning thus carries the torch of Clytemnestra and the Erinyes.[53] When, at the end of her speech, Cassandra claims to "make a hit, like an archer" (1194)—like, that is, Apollo—this marks only one moment, then, in a language that transforms speaker and speech rapidly, throughout.

Here, one might object that Clytemnestra's fires seduce her audience utterly, while Cassandra's inspire horror; that no one sees through Clytemnestra's falsehood, while none recognizes Cassandra's truth. In her sensitive analysis of the parallels between Clytemnestra's and Cassandra's speech—including the way they are compared to dogs—Laura McClure underscores their distinction along precisely these lines: Cassandra, in her genuine language of lamentation and inspiration, reveals the guileful rhetoric of Clytemnestra that seduces everyone else (*Spoken like a Woman* 99). However, one cannot fail to see that Clytemnestra's visionary speech—another "other speaking" from Troy, which razes any linguistic and spatial limits to speak of—affects her auditors in the same "most sublime way [*erhabenste Weise*]" as Cassandra's does, her rival from foreign shores (Humboldt, *Gesammelte Schriften* 8: 119)—and who will, when she is alone with the chorus, temporarily assume her place.[54] As McClure points out (93), Clytemnestra's phosphoric missive, like Cassandra's, strikes the chorus with awe. When Clytemnestra relays her torch signals for a second time—this time in words—it responds: "but as for these words, I would like to hear and wonder [κἀποθαυμάσαι] at them again, from beginning to end, as you say it" (318–19).[55] And according to the same, sublime compulsion that drives the chorus to incorporate Cassandra's visions into its own speech—albeit blindly[56]—the tidings Clytemnestra conveys cannot but appear, at first, to be "good [εὖ]." For they are "good" not—or not only—because she announces victory, but because, in closing one of her speeches with the phrase "may the good reign [τὸ δ'εὖ κρατοίη]" (349), she echoes the language of the chorus's thrice-repeated refrain from before: "may the good prevail [τὸ δ'εὖ νικάτω]" (121 = 139 = 159).[57] Thus, the chorus members cannot but respond to her imperative and let "the good [τὸ εὖ]"—as a word, an echo, and therefore a substantial force—temporarily prevail over themselves, too. They cannot but say, swiftly persuaded by her εὖ-angelium, that she speaks "like" or "according to [κατὰ]" a "wise and temperate man [ἄνδρα σώφρον[α]]"—for she speaks like them (351). Yet the linguistic similarities that prevail here have shifted valence; Clytemnestra's translation of their speech takes place in terms that only simulate its reprisal, and thereby estrange both moments of utterance alike. Clytemnestra, according to the chorus, is "*well*-minded [εὐφρόνως]" (351)—that is to say, they all are, alike, benighted.

On this day, everything is other than it seems, borne by the energy of a visionary language that obscures as it illuminates, to the point where the more one looks, the less one sees—and this may have been what Humboldt had meant when he wrote, as we have heard:

> Among all works of the Greek stage, none equals the *Agamemnon* in tragic sublimity. As often one proceeds anew through this wonder-replete piece, one senses all the more deeply how meaningful every speech, every choral ode is; how all singularities, though they outwardly appear loosely bound at first, inwardly strive toward One Point; how each motive drawn from contingent personality is removed; [. . .] and how the poet thus annihilates all that is merely human and earthly [. . .]. (8: 119)

In any case, this is a day where the Olympian and chthonian gods have become indistinguishable or are not yet distinct. It is, instead, the day of apparitions that displace every semblance of identity, human or otherwise, and render all language foreign to its speakers. Thus, the divinity or divinities that are said to befall and inspire Cassandra and Clytemnestra will receive the designation "daemon," when the chorus says to the Trojan prophetess: "some overbearing daemon [δαίμων] falling upon you [ἐμπίτνων], sets you to singing mournful, death-bearing [θανατηφόρα] sufferings [πάθη]" (1174–76), and when the chorus—in nearly identical language—responds to Clytemnestra's boasts over the corpses of Agamemnon and Cassandra by addressing the "daemon [δαῖμον], who falls upon [ἐμπίπτεις] the home and the two-natured Tantalidae," "singing a tune discordantly [ἐκνόμως ὕμνον ὑμνεῖν]" (1468–74).[58] And as Cassandra—who was initially conceived as "god-bearing [θεοφόρητος]" (1140)—is said to utter "death-bearing sufferings," the bright world of Argos turns out, catastrophically, to be the underworld: "these gates of Hades here ['Άιδου πύλας δὲ τάσδ[ε]]" (1291). Hence, phantoms take shape not only in Cassandra's prophecies—where the foremost question is always, implicitly or explicitly, as she once put it: "what is this that appears? [τί τόδε φαίνεται]" (1114)—but also throughout the rhetoric of the *Agamemnon*. These phantoms manifest in yet another way the visionary language of the play, as a phenomenology where the light (φάος) in which each figure appears is none, other than a shade.

The chorus announces itself in its entrance song: "no stronger than a child, [. . .] a day-phantom dream [ὄναρ ἡμερόφαντον]" (81–82), and soon, this chorus of twelve will appear to Cassandra as the twelve slaughtered children of Thyestes. When Cassandra claims to trust in "these witnesses here, these babes here, weeping the slaughter and roasted flesh, devoured by the father" (1095–96)—the deictic markers, combined with the agreement in number and characterization, all point to the chorus as the dead she envisions and adopts in her visionary speech. It has remained a puzzling matter of debate why the number of Thyestes's slaughtered children in Aeschylus' *Agamemnon* is twelve (cf. Fraenkel 3: 758–60 and Judet de la Combe 2: 740–42), but at this point, one cannot overlook that there is a real body of twelve onstage within Cassandra's field of vision as she speaks: the chorus. There is a real group that had been wailing, too, before she speaks: the chorus. For the choral song that comes between Agamemnon's entrance into the palace and Clytemnestra's attempts to speak with Cassandra surges up, "unbidden" (ἀκέλευστος, 979); it entails a presentation of the chorus members' bodies as mantic objects; it is specifically designated a "lament" (θρῆνο[ς], 992)—like Cassandra's own outcries, but for the fact that the chorus's lament is specifically the "lament of the Erinys" (θρῆνο[ς] Ἐρινύος, 992). The song the chorus sings works in a complementary way with hers: its dirge is answered with the dirge she performs, which is likewise unbidden, and which she attempts to avert even as she sings it, from her very first words. The originary, prophetic moment of speech in this drama splits between the chorus and Cassandra; it, meanwhile, is an absolutely other moment of divine inspiration that splits between the Erinyes and Apollo. It evolves over the course of translations—further otherings of this other language—as the chorus's song translates into the wailing Cassandra claims to hear. As soon as she evokes the children's wailing, in fact, her dochmiacs give way to iambics—which is the prevailing meter of the chorus's preceding stasimon. The chorus's mantic bodies, in turn, translate into the bodies she encounters in her mantic visions. Speaking before twelve interlocutors, she sees the twelve children of Thyestes; having heard their mourning, she claims to hear the mourning, slaughtered infants.

And this moment is not the only one that indicates how the horizon of Hades swiftly spreads throughout the drama, even if it may be the most striking one. Earlier, the chorus likens Paris to a boy chasing after a "flying bird [ποτανὸν ὄρνιν]" (394), who has thereby "set an unbearable affliction upon the city" (395), while a "phantasm [φάσμα]" of Helen "will seem to rule the house" she has left behind, until—and perhaps so long as—Menelaus likewise pursues her. Like the flitting shades of the *Odyssey*, "mournful dream-phantoms [ὀνειρόφαντοι]" are "present [πάρεισι]" for him, a "vision [ὄψις]" that will have "shifted aside [παραλλάξασα]," just as he would try to grasp it (419–26).[59] And Clytemnestra, too, will disavow her status as the wife and murderer of Agamemnon, telling the chorus: "Phantasming [φανταζόμενος] itself into this dead man's wife, the ancient fierce spirit [ὁ παλαιὸς δριμὺς ἀλάστωρ] that takes vengeance for the misdeed of the cruel feaster Atreus has now rendered this full-grown man as payment to the young, a crowning sacrifice" (1500–04). The very fact that, as Helene P. Foley has argued, one might doubt even this denial of culpability (*Female Acts* 203) only proves the point: everything seems other than it is, including anything that is said to seem. Even Cassandra herself figures as a dead child of sorts, when she contrasts her early days on the Scamander River to her current future: "now [νῦν], it seems [ἔοικε], swiftly [τάχα], it is by Cocytus and the banks of Acheron that I am to chant prophecies [θεσπιωιδήσειν]" (1161–62)—whereby the swiftness of her and Clytemnestra's speech will also soon appear as a predicate of the waters of Hades: "the swift-flowing [ὠκύπορον] passage of the stream of woe [πόρθμευμ᾿ ἀχέων]" (1557–58).

But if this is what the day comes down to, what could it mean to have witnessed it? It may be that all addressees of Cassandra are sped toward these waters of woe, and not only because her prophetic utterances— among others—are said to bear death; or because her lamentations exceed all human limits, making Cassandra seem like "one, insatiate of lamenting cry, [. . .] moaning Itys, Itys, a life flourishing on either side with ills, a nightingale" (1142–45). Her repeated injunctions to "bear witness to me, upon oath" (1184, 1196, 1317), bare of any call but to witness, may be nothing other than an appeal to the Styx, the boundary of the cosmos, which is, as Jean Bollack has argued, the ultimate definition of the oath.[60]

In any case, there is nothing to testify to, beside the limit of all that could be said or seen. Prophecy would culminate in the oath to have witnessed the prophecy, to swear blindly to a speech that one cannot understand, by a god one cannot grasp, revere, name, or call. And it would therefore seem to achieve nothing—to speak with the chorus: "What good saying [ἀγαθὰ φάτις] from oracles is accomplished [τέλλεται] for mortals?" (1132–33). Surely no good news, no εὐ-angelium.

Yet at this point, Cassandra's language parts decisively from Clytemnestra's, too. Whereas the queen ultimately prays for the final execution of all her daemonic plans—"Zeus, Zeus accomplisher, accomplish my prayers [Ζεῦ Ζεῦ τέλειε, τὰς ἐμὰς εὐχὰς τέλει]" (973)[61]—the prophet speaks past every *télos*, and asks for the impossible: "Bear witness, swearing in advance not to have seen [τὸ μὴ εἰδέναι] [or: that I have seen, τὸ μ'εἰδέναι] in speech the ancient transgressions of this house here" (1196–97). Commentators cannot decide whether to read "not to have seen [τὸ μὴ εἰδέναι]" or "that I have seen [τὸ μ'εἰδέναι]," nor can they agree whether the subject of "not to have seen" refers to the chorus or to Cassandra (Fraenkel 3: 548–51). It is equally ambivalent whether she asks them to take an oath before her now or pleads with them to swear in the future before the Argive public about the truth of her oracles (West, *Studies* 211; Judet de la Combe 2: 504–05); or whether the chorus's subsequent failure to perform any oath can be attributed to its incomprehension, or to the tension between her rhetoric—which appears to have "strange legalistic tinges"—and the fact that "courts of law seem to be non-existent in Argos" (Fletcher 52). But still more undecidable, in light of all that has been said, is what anyone will have seen in speech, and what anyone could knowingly say thereof. Any "swearing in advance" could only be a forswearing, when every "this" that is bespoken and envisioned has already passed upon arrival—which even goes for the "end [τέλος]," of which Cassandra says, as we saw, "How shall I say [it]? for quickly this shall be" (1009).

For this reason, there can be no answer to her appeal, and the chorus does not swear, but asks instead: "And how could the fixing of an oath, innately fixed, become something healing [καὶ πῶς ἂν ὅρκου πῆγμα γενναίως παγὲν / παιώνιον γένοιτο]?" (1198–99). Surely, there is nothing healing to expect here, any more than there is any end to be prayed for or "accomplished" through this utterance. There is no paean to be heard, and no Apollonian Healer in sight—Cassandra will say herself: "no Paean / Healer [Παιὼν] presides over this speech [τῷδ' ἐπιστατεῖ λόγῳ]" (1248). And we are a far cry from the imperative the chorus had addressed to Clytemnestra in its entrance song: "become a Paean / Healer of this anxious care [παιών τε γενοῦ τῇδε μερίμνης]" (99). But when the chorus asks Cassandra, "and how could the fixing of an oath, innately fixed, become something healing [καὶ πῶς ἂν ὅρκου πῆγμα γενναίως παγὲν / παιώνιον γένοιτο]?" (1198–99), the word "innately [γενν-αίως]" begins to blend with "becoming [γέν-οιτο]," while the "healing [π-αιῶν-ιο-ν]" echoes and unsettles its near anagram, "innately fixed [γεν-ναίω-ς π-αγὲ-ν]," such that the fixed limits of the oath and the terms of healing are loosened, along with all that could be set in this language. The density of phonetic resonances here parallels that of Clytemnestra's prayer for a final accomplishment——"Zeus, Zeus accomplisher, accomplish my prayers [Ζεῦ Ζεῦ τέλειε, τὰς ἐμὰς εὐχὰς τέλει]" (973)—to no end. Thus, with the uncertainties that emerge in its question—which, at first glance, verges on a straightforward dismissal—the chorus begins to testify, despite itself, to a possibility that cannot be guaranteed, by oaths or other bonds, if it is to be at all. And through their words, where oaths and healing become other than themselves—and therefore other than their opposites, too—the possibility of speaking beyond the terms of execution, accomplishment, and violent remedy that otherwise govern the drama is spoken to.

This speaking would differ from any definitive promise, from any forward-looking plans, as well as from those prognostics in which the future becomes indifferent—as the chorus had already indicated, from the start: "and the future [τὸ μέλλον], when it comes thou mayst hear of it; let it be greeted in advance [προχαιρέτω]—but that is equal to being lamented in advance [ἴσον δὲ τῷ προστένειν]" (251–54). But the language the chorus speaks here, when all seems past healing, opens speech to an imprevisible future, which is other than any that could be predicted, and which therefore may still come differently—if not for the citizens of Argos, and not for the rest of the *Oresteia*, then in the moment these words are uttered or read. It is therefore more than fitting that this question immediately precedes the chorus's expression of wonder at Cassandra's "speaking of an other-speaking city [ἀλλόθρουν πόλιν λέγουσαν]" (1200–01). Witnessing Cassandra's prophecies demands an openness to speaking otherwise that cannot be completed, anticipated, or affirmed with any surety, but that may be furthered nonetheless. And when there is no way to tell the telos, and nothing to say that could be done, speaking other than one could claim to know may yet open the way for this day—to break.

PROPHETIC POETRY, AD INFINITUM: FRIEDRICH SCHLEGEL'S *DAYBREAK*

Beginning and end of history is *prophetic*,
no object any longer of pure inquiry.
Anfang und Ende der Geschichte ist *prophetisch*,
kein Objekt mehr der reinen Hist[orie]
    —Friedrich Schlegel, *Fragmente zur Poesie und Literatur*

Around 1800, among papers containing "Ideas for Poems [*Ideen zu Gedichten*]," Friedrich Schlegel first takes note of a project that would preoccupy him through his last fragmentary notes on literature and philosophy: namely, *Aurora*. Marginal to his published oeuvre—and marginal in scholarship on Schlegel—*Aurora* marks nonetheless one of those motifs in his writing that, to borrow the words of Walter Benjamin, "the writer rescued over from the decay of the [Romantic] school into his later life's work" ("Der Begriff" 16). Specifically, *Aurora* becomes affiliated in 1807 with the genre Schlegel will tentatively call "prophetic poetry," and before this, he writes among his philosophical notes from 1802, amid fragments concerning the possibility of a philosophical encyclopedia: "(*Aurora*) πρ [Prophetie]" (*Kritische Friedrich-Schlegel-Ausgabe* 18: 458).[1] Whether it be a philosophical prophecy or a prophetic poem, however, *Aurora* continues, intermittently, to evoke what Ian Balfour has read as a "marginal and privileged category" in the early Romantic period—"marginal, insofar as 'the prophetic' is hardly an omnipresent concern among theorists, yet privileged when the aphoristic speculations of a Novalis and a Schlegel are read 'in themselves'" (39). And *Aurora* continues to be evoked in relation to this category even after Schlegel explicitly aligns it with the "presentation of mystic Catholic philosophy," following his official conversion in 1808.[2]

Reading the traces of Schlegel's *Aurora* among his notes would therefore promise to shed light on the category of "the prophetic," beyond the context of Schlegel's early fragments, and askance of those tendencies in his later writings that Bernadette Malinowski traces in her recent work, in which she shows the function of the prophet to be subsumed within the paradigm of a teleological philosophy of history, and presumed to have the ability to effect historical change (230–37). A reading of the poetic and philosophical stakes raised through Schlegel's *Aurora* fragments would also complicate the distinction that is still often drawn between his early and late writings, despite the analyses of Philippe Lacoue-Labarthe and Jean-Luc Nancy in *The Literary Absolute.*[3] In their monograph, they not only register the "monolithic," and even "papal" traits of the Schlegel brothers' authoritative practice, already as the editors of *Athenaeum* (18). They also complicate any such interpretation of Romanticism, demonstrating how these traits do little to explicate "the prodigious labor" of the Schlegel brothers' achievement (19), let alone the way in which the structures of critique, theory, literature, and subjectivity developed in Jena around the turn of the nineteenth century remain, in many respects, current (27).[4] And if any text should have manifested the "literary absolute," it would have been *Aurora*, not only because it repeatedly returns in Schlegel's literary and philosophical notebooks, to the dissolution of any boundary between these two modi of writing, but also because Schlegel himself says: "all to be dissolved in *Aurora* [*Alles in die* Aurora *aufzulösen*]" (17: 81). But beyond even this, would not the recurrence of *Aurora* fragments among Schlegel's reflections from 1800 to 1823, together with his perpetual deferral of the project, render it *the* ultimate paradigm—or parody—of what Lacoue-Labarthe and Nancy have described as the fragmentary structure of "progressive universal poetry," that is, of a poetry that "cannot but perpetually become, and never accomplish itself,"[5] but that, in its very inachievment, functions "as the immediate projection of that which it nonetheless unachieves" (63)? After all, Schlegel himself will write at one point, "Every novel should actually, in a certain sense, be Aurora [*Jeder Roman sollte eigentlich in einem gewissen Sinne Aurora sein*]" (16: 497)—thereby paraphrasing, parodying, and potentiating the conclusion of his famous *Athenäum* fragment on Romantic universal poetry: "for in a certain sense, all poetry is or should be romantic [*denn in einem gewissen Sinn ist oder soll alle Poesie romantisch sein*]" (2: 183).

What happens, in other words, when "Romantic poetry" becomes *Aurora*, after Schlegel is no longer affiliated with the Jena circle, and no longer involved in the collective project of Romanticism that had figured so crucially in the composition of the *Athenaeum*? It cannot be the same—alone, by virtue of the fact that these unpublished notes do not occupy the position within Schlegel's written oeuvre that the published fragments had. But if one might be tempted to call *Aurora* a hyper-Romantic survival of certain tendencies from Schlegel's earlier writings, an afterlife of Romantic poetry, perpetuated beyond the dissolution of the group—and thus projected as its last prophecy—this tentative categorization would have to fail, on several counts. Such a designation would fail to represent the dispersion of *Aurora* fragments, which themselves resist being gathered as representatives of a category—or of even each other. And it would fail to represent Romanticism, for, although the period of the *Athenaeum* marks a criticial moment of its history, on principle, further iterations of reflection would be integral to its products. Early Romanticism is, as Lacoue-Labarthe and Nancy have shown, inscribed by this tension between its historical specificity and infinite demands,[6] so that it must remain a question, for now, whether and how it could be said to continue, or survive, itself, or whether its inception was already its afterlife. In any case, no one among Schlegel's scattered forecasts for *Aurora* is more developed than any other, nor do the notes, for all their variations, show a clear trajectory of development, as Ernst Behler has remarked in his edition of Schlegel's *Fragmente zur Poesie und Literatur* (17: xi–xv). And unlike the concept of reflection that Benjamin traces from Schlegel's early published fragments through the lectures on philosophy that Schlegel would deliver in Paris and Cologne after the dissolution of the Jena circle, no systematic elaboration of *Aurora* comes to fruition in his corpus. Where to begin, then—but elsewhere?

Even if *Aurora* were to have remained only nominally the same, the name alone provides some direction for approaching Schlegel's project. *Aurora* is the title of the seventeenth-century mystic Jacob Böhme's first published book from 1612, *Daybreak Ascending: That Is, the Root or Mother of Philosophia, Astrologia and Theologia* (75),[7] which was read, discussed, and engaged in various ways by many writers associated with the Romantic movement, including Ludwig Tieck, Novalis, Friedrich W. J. Schelling, and G. W. F. Hegel.[8] Whether Schlegel's *Aurora* was to be "a translation *of Böhme* [*eine Uebersetzung* des Böhme]," as he proposed several times (16: 422, 18: 439), or whether it was to be differently related to its namesake, as the "*root* of all poetry" (17: 333)—and thus, as a variant of Böhme's original[9]— Schlegel's *Aurora* remains oriented toward this book, whose scope would therefore be illuminating to view, if only briefly.

Böhme describes *Aurora* already on his title page—

A description of nature: how all things were and came into being in the beginning; how nature and the elements became creatural; and of the two qualities of evil and good; from whence all things had their origin; and how it all stands and works now; and how it will come to be at the end of this time; as well as about the constitution of God's and Hell's kingdom; and how human beings work in a creaturely way upon each thing. All diligently composed

out of the right grounds in the knowledge of spirit and in the sway of God /
through Jacob Boehme in Görlitz in the year 1612.[10] (75)

As Cyril O'Regan has emphasized in his excellent and erudite monograph
on Böhme, "the very title" is "self-consciously apocalyptic" (90). Böhme
announces from the outset the eschata of nature—such is its scope—which
come to be articulated throughout his text in various ways, beginning with
"all of *Philosophia, Astrologia, and Theologia*, together with their mother,"
which he compares to a "splendid tree that grows in a garden of delight"
(77), but that withers itself through its own sap, until is "cut off and burned
up in the fire" (79).[11] This opening simile, in turn, initiates a series of similar
ones, for, as Böhme will later indicate in *De tribus principiis*, "just as we see the
heavens, the elements, as well as the Creatures, so too do we see in the material world the likeness [*das Gleichnis*] of the paradisal, ungraspable world"
(53)—with the implication, as Karin Schuff has pointed out, that insight into
God takes place solely "per analogiam" (492). Along these lines, Böhme will
also, for example, describe the nascence of all things literally—at the level of
their minimal linguistic elements—beginning with the opening phonemes
of Holy Scripture, "in the beginning [*am Anfang*]" (*Aurora* 526/27). The
pronunciation of "am Anfang" recapitulates, first, the fullness of Creation
and the Fall—as "*am*" is said to "mean that sound has gone out from the heart
of God and encompasses the whole *locus* of this world, but as it is found evil,
so the sound retreats back to its locus" (527). But the first words of Genesis
also encompass the world's apocalyptic end. "The last push *ang*" closes with
a voiced stop that "retains for itself [. . .] the tone [. . .] in the back of the
mouth," which "means that the innermost spirits in their depravity, are also
not at all pure, and thus need purification [. . .] in fire, which at the end
of this time will happen" (529). Böhme's work is thus itself a translation of
sorts, of the trajectory of the entire Christian Bible into two words, and of
biblical words into letters. This latter tendency can be traced along the lines
of Kabbalistic mysticism, as Schuff (499–500) and O'Regan (112–15, 193–209)
have demonstrated.[12] Yet it differs, at the same time, from that tradition, in
that "meaning is embodied in sound, understood as much in terms of how
the sound is produced as the sound itself" (O'Regan 107). And in this respect,
Böhme's biblical hermeneutics resembles, too, Schlegel's own pursuits of the
character of each alphabetic letter in his literary notebooks—with reference
to *Aurora*, Böhme, and Plato's *Cratylus* (16: 377–79)—which are likewise
construed with a view to "cosmogony" (16: 377) and the "grounding formula
of the construction of the earth" (16: 379), if not with a view to its beginning
and end.[13]

Analogical structures pervade Böhme's text, then, to the letter—and to
the point where the relata of the analogical relations he traces dissolve, along
with the words or *lógoi* to and through which they are drawn. The analogy of
the material world to the paradisal one turns out, after all, to be an analogy
to a "likeness"—and thus, not unlike the structures Michel Foucault has
analyzed more generally, in his signature work, *Les mots et les choses* (32–59).
But whereas the modi of similitude, analogy, and signature to which Foucault refers are largely contingent upon an original divine deposition—"the
names were deposed upon that which they designated, like the force written
in the body of a lion, the royalty in the regard of the eagle" (51)—analogy
is pervasive in *Aurora* because, Böhme insists, paradise and God themselves
are immanent to the world, as is dead matter (which is itself nothing but
the remains of God's light, ever since Lucifer burned out).[14] And if, in this
collocation of matter and spirit, the "external birth" of dead matter is all
that can overtly be grasped[15]—and therefore, too, all that can be seen or
said—all of this cannot but be, simultaneously, a semblance with reference
to divinity itself, which, however, "has, beyond nature and creature, no
name" (*Mysterium magnum* 632).[16] As Peter Rusterholz emphasizes rightly,
"Böhme's similes are certainly not illustrations of abstract principles drawn
from nature, but relations of analogy among structurally equivalent natural,
anthropological, and theological processes" (210). But one might draw further consequences for the structure of meaning and eschatology that Böhme
elaborates: if there is no proper speech for God, then there is, by the same
token, no proper speech for the material world, either. By taking things
differently than they seem—and thus taking them as semblances in the first
place—Böhme opens every word and morpheme to mean otherwise. As
a consequence, every word may be rendered fundamentally undecidable,
and in a trenchant formulation of this crisis, Böhme will write, in the midst
of his description of the heavens: "Now when I write of trees, bushes, and
fruits, so must you not understand [them] in an earthly way, like to this world
[*Gleiche diser weld*], for it is not my meaning that, in the heavens, there grows
a dead, hard, wooden tree or stone that stands in earthly quality, no, rather
my meaning is heavenly and spiritual"—only to continue: "but truly and
properly, as such, I mean no other thing than as I set it in letters [*Aber doch
wahrhafftig vnd eigendlich also / Ich meine kein ander ding / Als wie ichs Im buch
staben setze*]" (172/73). However, if he cannot say what he means and always
nonetheless means what he says, Böhme's language would be able to address
not only material nature but also—because it is ultimately the same—the
way that things will be when, in the end, the division inherent in all things
will itself be judged, decided, and split for good.[17]

Thus, Böhme can already now turn to the devil, and announce the Day of Judgment: "as of then you will receive a house and the locus where now the earth stands [. . .] for you will receive the salitter in the external birth which you yourself have established as an eternal dwelling place. But not in the form as it stands now. Rather, all will separate itself in the inflamed fire of rage" (501). And such instances of direct address can take place at any moment, insofar as the scission at stake here is inscribed throughout Böhme's prose, as it is throughout the world. If, as O'Regan has demonstrated through a systematic approach to Böhme's oeuvre, Böhme's later works show a general tendency to illustrate "divine becoming" (123), along the lines of Valentinean Gnosticism (141–209), *Aurora* might be called thoroughly apocalyptic, not only insofar as it perpetually reminds of the coming end of time but also insofar as it aims to have brought this end about, and already always conveys the decisive separation yet to come.[18] Hence, Böhme repeatedly reminds the reader that the crisis of the end—in the sense of an ultimate scission of scissions—is not only near but imminent, and—more nearly still—"at hand [*ver Handen*]" (570/71; cf. 168/69, 554/55).[19] And in his concluding words, appended to the second edition of his manuscript, Böhme will himself confess that the daybreak heralded by his title should already have been, in fact, the new one: "I impart to the God-loving reader that this book BREAK OF DAWN is not completed / for the devil thought to make a break of it / since he saw that the day wanted to break forth therein."[20] In other words, *Aurora* should have been *Aurora*, but for the fact that—by virtue of the very same qualifications of speech that render daybreak possible—the break is broken, confused with dichotomies of the present, disjected, and therefore: diabolical.[21]

In Schlegel's notes on *Aurora*, the eschatological tendency of Böhme becomes more pronounced.[22] Around the midst of its conception—and just before Schlegel's decision to break from the Protestant church and convert to Catholicism—Schlegel writes in 1807: "The poetry of AURORA (as presentiment of the new evang[elium] <apocalypse etc>) must not be treated as a *kind* or *form* of poetry—but rather [*sondern*] the inner essence of poetry must here break forth, thoroughly newly and magically engendering, and with constitutive force.—It would thus have to be observed, not as an element of epic but rather [*sondern*] as apart from every series, entirely for itself" (17: 105).[23] Thus, Schlegel implies that the poetry of *Aurora* would not only be prophetic of the "Apocalypse" but rather, as a *poetry* of dawn— as its "making," or "poiesis"[24]—it would, at the same time, have to give rise to creation in the first place. Whereas in fragment 116 from *Athenäum*, "progressive universal poetry" would "reunite all separated genres" (2: 185), here, the accent has shifted to severance, and to a sheer poetry of production that should not be treated like a "kind or form" at all.[25] Furthermore, insofar as the poetry of *Aurora* would have to be observed "apart from every series [*außer aller Reihe*]"—and thus, apart from any genealogical, chronological, or causal succession—the crisis in poetry here marks a scission from the scissions of existant poetic "*kind[s]* and *form[s]*." It would thus indicate nothing less than the kind of end that Böhme had announced. For even if Schlegel at first presents *Aurora* parenthetically as the "presentiment of the new evang[elium] <Apocalypse etc.>," rather than the daybreak of the Apocalypse itself, this poetry would itself be "magically *engendering*" and would exercise "*constitutive* force."[26] And in so doing, it would operate analogously to the most all-encompassing products of God and man, nature and statecraft, while being distinct from all past and current instances of each—themselves being various *kinds* and *forms* of poetry, in the most encompassing sense of the word. Like genre, which, as Werner Hamacher writes, is generated "only on the condition that it does not take place, only on the condition that it is not and never is what it is" (*Entferntes Verstehen* 201)—whence there are "disparate genres" (202)—*Aurora* would be what it is, only under the condition that it, qua presentiment, is not yet. But at the same time, Schlegel's new project entails a constitutional violence that no longer resonates with the rhetoric of reconciliation he had deployed in his earlier writings, when it (approximately) came to the "reunification of genres" in Romantic poetry. At stake is the end of the world as we know it and the beginning of an entirely separate one.

The *poetry* of *Aurora*—that is, not any poem or poetic product, but its making, made permanent in the substantive "Poesie"—would engender a new world and constitute a new order of sheer engendering and constituting. But it would also be misleading to suggest that these "new" tendencies differ quite as severely as they might sound from those that Schlegel had shown during the years of Jena Romanticism. And in fact, the rhetorical similarities to his earlier writings are critical to Schlegel's articulation of the ends he envisions in 1807. For precisely in calling it a "presentiment of the new evang[elium]," Schlegel also projects *Aurora* as a new announcement of the "Kingdom of God [*Reich Gottes*]" that he and Novalis had envisioned years before, under the auspices of G. E. Lessing, who in his late text "Education of the Human Race [*Die Erziehung des Menschengeschlechts*]" had proclaimed the coming time of "a new eternal evangelium": "It will certainly come, the time of a new, eternal Evangelium, which was promised to us already in the elementary books of the New Bond" (*Werke* 96).[27] The late Lessing had spoken of a new Evangelium of a coming time, and the early Schlegel had thought the time had come, writing to Novalis in 1798 of his plans to compose the new Bible and thereby to contribute to the new religion that he believed to be emerging through Schleiermacher's writings—as well as through Tieck's studies of Böhme (Schlegel, *Kritische Friedrich-Schlegel-Ausgabe* 24: 183, 206–07). It thus comes across as an intensification of these previous tendencies—to the breaking point—when Schlegel writes here that *Aurora* would break forth "thoroughly newly," implying that this novelty could not be new in relation to anything that had hitherto been. And indeed, it is precisely through these echoes of and departures from his earlier pronouncements that Schlegel performs the very separation he calls for, in order to announce a decisive *novum* that should no longer be mixed up with poetological reflections on kinds and forms or with any previous evangelical writings.

This performance cannot but be, like Böhme's, undercut by its presuppositions and therefore cannot make or do what it is supposed to. But aside from its perpetuation of earlier Romantic tendencies and the future it never attains, what does this fragment, read closely in its own right, disclose? Thoroughly new, the poetry it bespeaks would have to be the first, all-pervasive emergence of the inner essence of poetry, and a breakthrough of sorts is traced in Schlegel's note. The mere "presentiment" of a new evangelium and apocalypse is, at first, enclosed in parentheses and proposed as something to be "treated [*behandelt*]," or "made into praxis [*be-handelt*]."[28] Then it suddenly erupts—a subject for itself—after a dash that sunders it from what came before, in order to "here break forth, thoroughly newly and magically engendering, and with constitutive force." With this, the "inner essence" of poetry must have, it would seem, come into existence—all by itself, in this very text. But only for a moment. And for this moment, there could be no time or words. Insofar as the poetic operations Schlegel describes should be nothing other than engendering and constituting, *Aurora* would also have to be other than the words and punctuation marks that appear to name and draw it forth. (One might be reminded of Hamacher's remarks on the reunification of genres projected in Schlegel's fragment 116: "This would have to be an instance—or process—of which nothing is yet said, so long as it is spoken of in the concepts of a logic of positions or oppositions. It would be an instance of sheer speaking, over which nothing can be said, as it always solely speaks itself" [*Entferntes Verstehen* 201].) The poetry of *Aurora* would have to be, in other words, absolute—as Schlegel had remarked in his very first recorded note on *Aurora*, in the margins of his notebook, "Fragments on Literature and Poetry" (16: 173)—and thereby absolved from even this text.[29] Such is the paradox that Schlegel inscribes in his note, and that renders the achievemenet of his textual performance—the breakthrough of his *Daybreak*—no completed action and no inauguration of a new era, but a conditional, if not counterfactual utterance. Accordingly, the imperatives ("must [. . .] must [. . .]") that repeat with insistence in Schlegel's note shift from the indicative to the conditional: "It *would* thus have [*müßte*] to be observed, not as an element of epic but as apart from every series, entirely for itself" (my emphasis).[30] And in distinguishing it from any *epos*—which in ancient Greek may mean "word" or "myth," as well as "epic poetry"—*Aurora,* in its sheer separation, would not only differ from the kinds and forms of poetry that Romantic universal poetry should have reunited. It would also differ from what Schlegel had, in his essay from 1796 "On Homeric Poetry," distinguished analogously, describing the "Epos" as the "simplest" "kind of poetry [*Dichtart*]," which "orders an unlimited manifold of possible, external objects, bound through causal connection, through the equivalence [*Gleichartigkeit*] of matter and the curve of contours to a sheer sensual unity [*zu einer bloß sinnlichen Einheit*]" (Schlegel, *Kritische Friedrich-Schlegel-Ausgabe* 1:124).

Neither like the first poetry, then, nor the last, *Aurora* would have to be the most radical break from poetry that also breaks from itself. But what if its exceptional status were the source of its "constitutive force [*constitutive Gewalt*]"—which phrase recalls the "constitutive power [*konstitutive Macht*]" Schlegel had addressed earlier, in his political essay from 1796? Another echo resounds in Schlegel's note that simultaneously speaks to the potential of his newest project and constitutes a breach in its proclaimed autonomy. In his essay "On the Concept of Republicanism," Schlegel will say that, as a sheer foundation, "constitutive power" can be founded in nothing else, not even the consent of the constituted:

The constitution is the central concept of the permanent relations of political power and its essential components. The government, on the other hand, is the central concept of all transitory expressions of the force of political power. The components of political power relate among each other and to their whole as do the different components of the cognitive faculties among each other and to their whole. The constitutive power corresponds to reason; the legislative power, to the understanding; juridical power, to the power of judgment; and executive power, to sensuality, the faculty of intuition. The constitutive power is necessarily dictatorial: for it would be contradictory to make the ability of political principles, which should contain the basis of all remaining political determinations and abilities, dependent upon these; and for precisely this reason, it is only transitory. Without the act of acceptation, political power would not be represented, but ceded, which is impossible.— The constitution impacts the form of fiction and the form of representation.[31] (7: 18–19)

This "power [*Macht*]"—which grows forceful, even violent (*gewaltig*), in the *Aurora* fragment—is sheer exception. But it could be only as "dictatorial [*diktatorisch*]" and absolute, as it would have to be utterly "transitory [*transitorisch*]." A far cry from any stable institution or social pact, "the constitution impacts the form of fiction and the form of representation" (7: 19), whereby dictatorial "representation" would be itself cast, in retrospect, as a fictive invention. The duplicity of this constitution would lie in the way the foundational "acceptation" that should underlie it must itself be its "act"—"without the *act of acceptation*, political power would not be represented, but ceded, which is impossible" (7: 19, my emphasis). Yet such a conjunction of actuosity and reception—with nothing to receive—is precisely what also renders the political power to be made here, "die politische Macht," impotent, and thus that "which is impossible [*unmöglich*]" after all.[32] Furthermore, if the exceptional moment of "constitutive power [*konstitutive Macht*]" would have to take place once and for all in order to work, the exceptionality of *Aurora*—which should stand "apart from every series"—is articulated over a *series* of asseverations that thereby undermine what they dictate. The sheer point of departure that *Aurora* constitutes is imparted only through the successive sunderings that Schlegel repeats—by including two dashes and two instances of "rather [*sondern*]" in his text, and then by opening his next note: "The *Aurora* entirely separated-off—[*Die Aurora ganz abgesondert—*]" (17: 105).

In this light, the poetry of *Aurora* speaks against its supposed determination as the object of theory (*Betrachtung*) or praxis (*Behandlung*) from the outset. It leads to a sheer contradiction when Schlegel pretends to represent a *poiesis* that could no longer be thought of as the middle term to mediate the two, as its Kantian correlate, the power of imagination (*Einbildungskraft*), supposedly does.[33] And even as a "constitutive force" that corresponds to what Schlegel once aligned with the reason of state, *Aurora* is rhetorically executed in a way that subverts its every claim to power. Thus, thought to its ultimate consequences, neither perceptible nor producible, Schlegel's daybreak, as the inner essence of poetry per se, could only break off—like Böhme's *Aurora*. *Aurora* would mark not only the end of time but also the end of *Aurora*, and with it, the structures of engendering and constitutive force that, far from new, Schlegel intended to resurrect and reinstate as the subject and object of his prophecy. Solely such an utter antidote to *poiesis*, perhaps, could have been *thoroughly* new—if it were not that, at the same time, Schlegel also posits the "inner essence" of this poetry, with the implication that it must have always been, like the inner heaven and divinity in Böhme, even if it has never yet broken forth. And if it must have always been, everything may henceforth proceed as it always had. Here, too, where Schlegel's *Aurora* may appear far from Böhme's, it is oriented, essentially, to a similar end, and to an end that is the same as what ever was.

Of course, no discussion of *Aurora* could simply end there. Before and after, throughout the course of his career, Schlegel will waver between planning to compose *Aurora* in terzinas or in stanzas;[34] between writing it as a translation of Böhme and as a work in which Böhme would figure in addition to Dante, Plato, or Aristotle—or not at all;[35] between conceiving it as philosophy or mythology and as a poetry or cosmogony that would do without mythology altogether.[36] He will proceed in his notes from the suggestion that "[e]very novel should properly, in a certain sense, be *Aurora*" (16: 497) to "doubt over *Aurora* at all" (16: 501), and, ultimately, to the categorical declaration of its imminent necessity—"Aurora, indeed necessary, in order to set in the place of *Paradise Lost* and the *Messias* something else, something truly poetic and Christian" (17:51).[37] Not to mention its transhistorical character, as the root of all poetry: "Aurora is, so to speak, the root of all poetry" (17: 333).

A "central poem [*Centralgedicht*]" without any fixed formal, generic, thematic, genetic, or historical status to speak of (one could say: a center that is everywhere, with no periphery):[38] this is how *Aurora* comes to appear more than any other project over the last two decades of Schlegel's literary and philosophical notebooks.[39] In other words, it appears to be at least as elusive, pervasive, and decisive for him as "Romantic" poetry once was, if not more so, to the point that it seems most prominent among his unrealized plans and, simultaneously, nothing other than a name signifying so many different orientations, that it nearly says nothing, and certainly never says quite the same thing. Schlegel himself nearly says as much, when he remarks of it: "The *Aurora* belongs nowhere and is not understandable alone [*Die* Aurora *gehört nirgends hin und ist einzeln nicht verständlich*]." He then immediately aligns it with yet another one of his unrealized projects—"except in the *Dodecamerone*" (16: 352)—which leads, ultimately, nowhere.[40]

Therefore, one could characterize it only proximately, if at all. Nonetheless, Schlegel's notes reflect, from beginning to end, a relatively persistent tendency to imagine this poem as one that, like Böhme's *Aurora*, should present a Christian cosmogony—whether it would synthesize all myths, as "their chaoticiza-tion and dissolution into Christianity [*Chaotisierung derselben und Auflösung ins Christenthum*]" (16: 351); constitute a sheer "presentation of the *Trinity*" (17: 60); or make up the Christian poem in which all is "unified" (17: 340).[41] This ten-dency toward totalization manifests itself equally in Schlegel's designations of *Aurora* as a "poetic poetry" and as an "absolute poetry."[42] And through his later notes on poetry, Schlegel frequently writes toward a more particular end along the lines of the Apocalypse, as Böhme had done before, when he proclaimed: "the day of revelation and final judgment is now near" (Böhme 168/69), echo-ing the verse from Revelation: "the time is near" (Rev. 22.10). This apocalyptic resonance is registered in Schlegel's succinct remark, *"Aurora.* Apokal[ypse]" from around 1807 (18: 575), and in his suggestion that *Aurora* should replace Friedrich Gottlieb Klopstock's *Messias*—a New Testament epic that anticipates the Apocalypse throughout, as Götz Müller has argued (44)—or the Nordic *Edda*, which, according to Schlegel, ends the same way (17: 51, 320, 409).[43] And in his last entry on *Aurora* from 1823, he writes: "It could be that a poem takes place as a *parting* from all *hitherto* poetry—and a turning point of the transition to new poetry—to the *Aurora*. First it must lead into the holy *wasteland*, into the *night*—from which, then, the new dawn blooms upward" (17: 471)[44]—as though the occurrence of an obscure, anonymous poem could be all it takes for the new poetry of *Aurora* to arise and the synonymous dawn—or *Daybreak*—of a new age that would take place with it.

Still, there is nothing final about this beginning and end, even if it happens to be Schlegel's last words on *Aurora*. The rhetorical strategies differ here from those Schlegel deployed in his fragment from 1807. Yet the pivotal precondition for *Aurora* is still, as it always was, a moment of unmaking and an antidote to *poiesis*. It is still figured, as it was, in terms of a scission and departure—as a cutaway or "Ab-schied" from all other poetry—now said to take place, accordingly, in a way that leads to a "holy wasteland [*heilige Einöde*]," and thus to a space barren of all generation. And supposing another poem were the prophecy of this poetry—which Schlegel suggests by echoing Isaiah ("I am about to do a new thing; now it springs forth, do you not perceive it? I will make a way in the wilderness and rivers *in the wasteland [Denn sihe / Jch wil ein Newes machen / Jtzt sol es auffwachsen / das jr erfaren werdet / das ich Weg in der Wüste mache / vnd Wasserström in der* Einöde]" [Isa. 43.19, my emphasis])[45]—this does nothing to mitigate the contradiction implicit in Schlegel's concurrent assertions of rupture and transition, *Abschied* and *Übergang*. Meanwhile, what lends his words their apocalyptic force is not their novelty, but the echoes they entail: of the Hebrew and Christian prophets, of Böhme's and his *Aurora*.

If the anonymous poem Schlegel imagines here does not recur in his notes, beside all the particular projects he names, one can follow a parallel thread in Schlegel's texts on poetic genre from 1811–23. Some call the calling of poetry most generally "to make the divine Word visible in all its glory, and to foreshadow <how it will be,> when it will be restituted" (17: 320). Others present the idea of lyric as future songs that would address no time to come, but its apocalyptic end.[46] And in one note, Schlegel improvises a gloss on "poetic justice [*poetische Gerechtigkeit*]" in drama with the remark: "<Vision of action and character from the point of view of the *Last Judgment*>" (17: 345).[47] But if the apocalyptic restitution of the Word—or restitution of all that will have been (Acts 3.21)—can be foreshadowed, if the point of view of the Last Judgment can be presumed, if the end can be known and said in advance, and if its images are already drawn in the book of the Bible—then any poetry configured along these lines could only reiterate an end that is given. It could only approach a datum, if not a date, that has already come before—and one that therefore will never (have) come decisively. There would be nothing new about the new time that should break forth on these terms and that cannot but—again, and again as before—break off. Thus, when "progressive universal poetry" turns into *Aurora*, nothing all that new could be said to take place, either. The rhetoric, syntax, punctuation, and figures may differ, but the structure of prophetic speech seems to be similar throughout. If one could speak of "conversion" here, one could do so only with reference to the inversion of those absolute tendencies already at work in Schlegel's published fragments, which would yield a return to the same. If it ever were to be the radically new prophetic poetry that Schlegel projected, *Aurora* would have had to begin differently.

However, in the first and lengthiest note that he would devote to *Aurora* or its poetry, and before it is properly named ("Aurora" would be written later, in the margins of this notebook entry), Schlegel will conceive the project otherwise. Reading this note reveals that Schlegel will have been, even around 1800, no less concerned with the language and logic of prophetic poetry, and no less concerned with Böhme than he will be to the end. And consequently, he will also prove to be no less concerned with the eschatological figures that dawn upon him ever more over the coming years. But there, the eschaton Schlegel envisions is a beginning that could not end, depicted over allegories on the beginning of the world, its generation and its passion, drawn from Böhme, among others. Whereas Paola Mayer, one of the few readers to devote attention to this fragment, comments solely upon the way Schlegel's prose evokes only a few "striking poetic images" from Böhme's *Aurora*, in order to argue that there is no evidence, at this point in his writing career, that Schlegel had "much firsthand knowledge of [Böhme's] works" (171),[48] there is much more to be worked through in this text, and only through a close, detailed commentary can its full purport be proximated. I quote in full:

> To the Dithyrambs.
>
> The Διθ [dithyrambs] = Cosmogony + παθ / ο [absolute pathos]. The world as χα[chaos] and χα[chaos] for the world.—The *universum* is eternal and unchanging, but the *World* as κοσμος is in eternal becoming.—*Evangelium* of poetry; thus *poetry of poetry.*—<It must begin with the *spirit* and his inner force of creation.—> Orgies of fantasy; to close, poetry as the word of the riddle.—Choruses of children, maidens, boys, mothers, men, priests etc.—the priests sing the origin of the world.—The mothers and children must express love / the boys and maidens, nature.—Alleg.[ory] <of the> *tree of life / source of joy*—*love* is the divine spark through which the dead universum is vivified into nature, and through reason nature lifts itself again to divinity.—The whole = mysteries of nature—and orgies of beauty or of love.—All images are true. <All images are true.> *Light* is life and love; all matter is human, and all form, divine. The return to the elements is what properly distinguishes men from animals and plants.—*Paradise.*—Aspect of painting? *Adam and Eve.*—The heaven, internal, as in Böhme.—Plenitude of alleg[ories] and visions.—*Presentation of heaven.*—A *realm of light* as in Dante.—Humanity, an immediate emanation of divinity.—Also animals, plants and elements idealized according to the character of that [divinity]. Immediate onlooking of the sun, and also the otherwise original sense that is now lost. Perception of the music of the spheres of love in nature. Playing angels as in Böhme. The primitive language reimaged as much as possible. / *Titans* very good to denote the wild nature of men after the first explosion.—The wildness after the first explosion—the golden time after the first accidental revolution—Then again an accidental disturbance; otherwise the age of love would have been eternal.—[49] (16: 198–99)

To begin with, little could be said about the "dithyrambs" toward which this sketch professes to tend, aside from the way that the abbreviation "Διθ" already points to the dichotomy that most immediately follows, marking nothing less than the cosmos itself—which is beside itself, in passion.[50] More and less than the generation of all, at once, "absolute pathos," or "παθ / ο," should be added to "cosmogony," in a mathematical construction that becomes reformulated and redoubled in the relations: "the world *as* [chaos] and [chaos] *for* the world"—only to turn into the articulation of eternal being and eternal becoming. Such is Schlegel's extremely condensed prologue to the dithyrambs—which poetic products are no stable works, if they are truly to emerge from or dissolve into the combination of cosmogony and absolute pathos that Schlegel says they do—or into the plethora of images that follows, drawn largely, but not exclusively, from Böhme's *Aurora*. These include the "playing angels," which Mayer reads as an allusion to the "life of the angels as eternal play in love and amity" in Böhme, as well as "the allegory of the tree of life" (Mayer 171). The "divine spark through which the dead universum is vivified into nature" recalls, moreover, Böhme's remarks on God's "reignitiation" of earthly matter, after Lucifer had dessicated and deadened it,[51] while "chaos" may also be evocative of Böhme, although this word does not designate an image in his corpus, but "the eye of the unground [*Auge des Ungrunds*]" of all things, eternal and temporal, before their unfolding (Böhme, *Mysterium magnum* 6).[52] But if no trace of what Mayer calls "Böhme's metaphysics" can be found here (156), elements from his texts—absolved from the ends to which he wrote them—would still have to be taken as a source of truth in this passage, for—"All images are true. <All images are true>."

But what version of metaphysics is implied in the images that fracture this fragment, and in the assertion of truth that justifies their proliferation? Nothing of this text can be understood, nor can the words that it comprises be truly read, until this question is answered. To be sure, this fragment at first appears to present yet another succinct sketch of what would belong in poems that would never be. But in the end, it explodes, and from the start, Schlegel's note refracts and disperses in more ways than one, which render it the more proper starting point to address the thoroughly new poetry and revelation Schlegel would abandon as he reformulates *Aurora* through to the end of his career. And beyond this, the fragment concisely presents one of Schlegel's most condensed philosophical and poetic remarks—in response not only to Böhme but also to Schelling and Plato—when it comes to his thinking on being, truth, and language. The possibility of thinking through a cosmogony is proposed, in similar terms, in Schlegel's contemporaneous philosophical notes,[53] only to return, differently, in his lectures delivered in Cologne a few years later.[54] The intersections between his philosophy and the language of this literary project thus open the possibility, if not necessity, of reading this fragment together with that prose. They open his disparate texts to each other—and to others. They open the question of the relation between a love of knowledge and poetic production, when it comes to an articulation of the beginning of all, or its end. And as such an inchoate poetry, the fragment opens the question of a prophetic language that would differ in structure and character from the conjurations of the Apocalypse to which Schlegel would later resign himself. Here, the a priori of the world, and thus of its history—before all chronological sequence, organic cycles of generation and decay, and progressive developments—turns out to be proper not to philosophy (φ), or to poetry (π), but to a literal combination of the two ($\pi\varphi$), which Schlegel explicitly glosses as "prophecy" in earlier notes and fragments (16: 112, 2: 207)—and only later confers the proper name: *Aurora*.[55]

This combination would be a necessary one, if prophecy is to address what is not yet, or more accurately, what is not and has never been. And what has never been would, ultimately, have to be the beginning or end of the world, through which all, including history, is mediated, and which is therefore imminent at any given moment. Insofar as philosophy, like epic, "always begins in the midst [*in der Mitte*]" of things (2: 178)—even when it is a question of their end—and insofar as it would likewise always do so according to a lexicon of traditional images and tropes (for example, "in media res"), only a poetic philosophy—a philosophy that would produce, rather than grasp, what it would know—could provide insight into whatever may be said of this radical nonbeing. And at the same time, strictly speaking, it could also never know or say what it does, before having done so.[56] Meanwhile, as for the "Dithyrambs," which Schlegel will rename *Aurora* in the margin to this note, Schlegel articulates precisely such a combination. He does so, namely, through his thetic philosophical prologue to the fragment and the poetic fragments that follow it, even if it is the imagery, and not the theoretical prose, that should, by his own lights, confer truth to his plan. But before even poetry and philosophy, or their combination in and beyond the dithyrambs, Schlegel adds pathos to generation in the initial formula of his text, and thereby suggests that any cosmology or history, philosophical or poetic, would rather have to begin there.

Where Schlegel pairs absolute passivity to total productivity, he cannot have done so in such a way that would lead to the neutralization or mutual cancellation of both terms, definitively aborting the production of nature before it could even begin. Should anything come out of this conjunction at all, this pairing must be thought of differently than as a simple opposition. To the contrary, in his formulation, Schlegel implies that something other than genesis operates as the necessary condition for a cosmos, as well as anything it might entail, to come to be. Sheer generation, absolute productivity—whether one calls it cosmogony, nature, or something else entirely—is not enough for anything to be, even in appearance. For, as Schlegel had read in Schelling's *First Draft of a System of the Philosophy of Nature*—whose derivation of the universe from a "first explosion [*ersten Explosion*]" Schlegel will take up at the end of his note,[57] and with whom he is in dialogue from the beginning: "If nature is [. . .] originally *only* productivity, there can thus be nothing determinate in this productivity, (for all determination is negation), and thus, through this, it cannot come to products" (I,8: 44).[58]

Nothing can begin without a hindrance, though at the same time, nature, as a subject of sheer activity, is all, and therefore cannot be affected by anything else in order to pause and thereby allow anything particular to emerge.[59] Rather, for Schlegel as for Schelling, whose premises he adopts and adapts in his fragment, there can be no single, absolute productivity, no actual *unus*, or *universum*—unless it is divided. "Nature," Schelling writes, "must originally become itself an object for itself, this transformation of the *pure subject* into a *self-object* is unthinkable without an original dividing in nature" (I,8: 44).[60] Likewise, Schlegel inscribes this original division in his text through the fraction entailed in his opening formula, as well as the separation his addition of (productive) cosmogony and (passive) pathos marks. Yet Schlegel's approach in his condensed poetic passage to the problems that Schelling addresses in his philosophical oeuvre, as well as Schlegel's departure from his contemporary, can be elaborated only by further nearing the philosophy of nature from which Schlegel's *Aurora* will break.

Alone, Schelling's word "productivity" already bespeaks a necessary split in nature, since, without moments of limitation that would yield a product, there would be no productivity, properly speaking, and vice versa. To abstract one of these polar tendencies would be to eliminate both at once. Each operates only in and through its opposition to the other, which also means that, even as each tendency tends toward itself, it tends toward its own annihilation. Sheer productivity without products would eliminate itself and its opposite. Yet no such point of annihilation can be reached, because polarity was, Schelling argues, congenital to nature in the first place (I,8: 53–54). Schelling will call this thoroughgoing polarity, which tends toward neither negation nor identity, "indifference,"[61] and he will derive from its utmost concentration the first point of explosion that gives rise to the world—which Schlegel echoes at the end of his note. But through cosmogony and pathos, Schlegel will begin to reformulate Schelling's contemporaneous solution to the productivity of nature. And at the same time, he begins to radicalize it, insofar as no substantial product, no entity (even in appearance) enters into his equation, but rather absolute passion and passivity, which Schelling explicitly denies to nature, writing: "in nature, depite its being limited, there is no passivity if the limiting is also positive, and if its original duplicity is a contest of really opposing tendencies" (I,8: 45).[62] In fact, in the introduction to his *Entwurf*, Schelling insists that negation is as *positive* as natural production and coterminal with it, so that in every moment, every product of nature persists, only insofar as it is constantly being annihilated and reproduced, and thus infinitely splitting (I,8: 45)—without nature ever suffering anything but its own doing.

However, since nature, as an original, absolute productivity, would have to be conceived at first as one—or as "pure identity [*reine Identität*]" (I,8: 44), as Schelling puts it—there is nothing else yet to speak of. Thus, the scission in question can be articulated only as one between 1 and 0, with the consequence that neither nature nor its negation ever entirely is: "It is without a doubt very comprehensible," he writes, "that the series 1−1 + 1......, thought *infinitely*, is neither = 1 nor = 0" (I,8: 45). Which is not to say that this series is a sequence, as though the positive were followed by its opposite, and then by a subsequent repositioning of itself. For Schelling had immediately preceded this remark with the statement: "The product must be thought *as in each moment annihilated*, and *in each moment newly reproduced*" (I,8: 45). The "product" of nature is, in other words, a perpetual fractioning, in *each* single moment, and Schelling will reformulate his "series" in the next sentence: "this series, thought infinitely = 1/2 [*diese Reihe, unendlich gedacht = 1/2*]" (I,8: 45).

With this, Schelling adopts the solution to the problem of infinite alteration that had been proposed by Guido Grandi and Gottfried Wilhelm von Leibniz to yield the average of its terms, although the debate in mathematics at the time revolved precisely around "whether this series has a definite limit value at all"; after all, the possibilities of what the series may yield at any given moment may differ infinitely between 1 and 0 (Ziche 112, 326–28; see also Reiff 65–70). Schlegel, for his part, will articulate the duality at stake here differently, but consistently, throughout his philosophical and literary notebooks and lectures between 1800 and 1805, as a series that would be represented not by 1 and 0, but by 1/0, for infinity,[63] and its reciprocal, 0/1, for the infinitesimally small. At one point in his philosophical notebooks from around 1800, he writes: "All finite numbers lie in the middle between 1 or 0 and 1/0 : 0/1. The *prime numbers* make up the positive pole—the decimals, the negative one [*Alle endlichen Zahlen liegen in d[er] Mitte zwischen 1 oder 0 und 1/0 : 0/1. Die Primzahlen bilden d[en] positiven Pol—die Decimalzahlen d[en] negativen*]" (18: 415, cf. 18: 412–22). This revision to Schelling's formula will have implications for Schlegel's own elaboration of nature and consciousness, as John Smith shows in his excellent discussion of Schlegel's references to infinitesimal mathematics, writing, "in this infinite space between the 0 and the 1 consciousness unfolds over time, its two limit concepts being 'chaos' and infinite knowledge, also called 'allegory'" ("Friedrich Schlegel's" 250–51), with reference to the notebook entry in which Schlegel writes: "the world to be construed from chaos and allegory. *History of nature* from the 0/1—1/0 [*Aus Chaos und Allegorie die Welt zu construiren. Geschichte der Natur von jenem 0/1—1/0*]" (18: 422).[64]

But one could break down the significance of this formula further, with respect to other problems in Schlegel's writing, and with a view to *Aurora*, where "chaos" does not appear related to consciousness, even as its opposite. At one point, Schlegel notes, given an infinite *one*, or the "the presence of unity at once with that of infinity," "the possibility *per se* of a system of numbers" is also given, and with it, "the one infinite great and small number [*die eine unendliche große und kleine Zahl*]." This "one" number, in turn—infinitely split between the infinitely great and the infinitesimally small, and thus infinitely inverted and reversed as 1/0 and 0/1[65]—yields the universal formula for all thinkable fractions, in excess of any numeric system: "from 1/0 and 0/1 can be made all thinkable fractions" (12: 384). And this decisive formulation of the infinite as two simultaneous, reciprocal infinities articulates a differential dualism that differs from Schelling's solution—and opens the possibility of a conjunction between cosmogony and absolute pathos, at once.

The primary opposition in Schlegel is therefore not, or not only, the opposition of the infinite and finite, which many excellent commentaries on the philosophical thinking of Friedrich Schlegel have explicated, as when, in his detailed treatment of temporality in the writing of the early Romantics, Manfred Frank poses the problem of temporality in terms of the opposition of infinity and the finite (22–96).[66] It is the infinite split of "the one infinite great and small number," from which all else might be derived and dissolved. Thus, even the well-known and often-cited binary of Schlegel's thinking—namely, that of "autocreation [*Selbstschöpfung*]" and "autoannihilation [*Selbstvernichtung*]"—could be reconsidered along these lines. For its structural similarity to Schlegel's formulas, 1/0 and 0/1, and to Schelling's philosophy of nature suggests that it is yet another variant of these articulations of mathematical and metaphysical problems. And if this were the case, the processes of autocreation and autoannihilation could not be understood as a sequential alteration (e.g., a poem transforms and thereby destroys, while surpassing, "itself"). Rather, Schlegel would have called for the thought of an a priori oneness and noneness, which, like the fractions 1/0 and 0/1, are equally infinite, and therefore processual solely in tandem. In fact, without this simultaneously infinite and infinitesimal "number," no world and no transient moment of autocreation or autoannihilation could take place.

It is, in this respect, also no wonder that the formulation "1/0 and 0/1" implicitly recurs in relation to Schlegel's poetic project under the heading "To the Dithyrambs," if, as Schlegel had already noted in 1798, "[i]n the form of the $\Delta\iota\theta$ [dithyrambs] much spirit of algebra, because of the magic—" (18: 273). This "magic" would not only reside, as Winfried Menninghaus has written, in the integration of presentation and the presented in mathematics, so that mathematical language, it could be said, "'makes out a world for itself,' in lieu of merely representing a presupposed 'world'" ("Die frühromantische Theorie" 50).[67] Above all, it would derive from the infinite possibilities of parsing to which it gives rise, with implications for causality, temporality, and language. For like wonders and magic, in the familiar sense of the words, the infinite possibilities of parsing that Schlegel's algebraic formulas present cut all three from any order they may happen to be in at any given moment. These formulas, which are also implicit in the opening sentence of his first *Aurora* fragment, "The $\Delta\iota\theta$ [dithyrambs] = Cosmogony + $\pi\alpha\theta$ / 0," are also precisely what would allow *Aurora* to be, as he would later put it, "the root of all poetry" (17: 333), as well as the root of all history. Everything that could be made, or made to happen—as well as unmade and undone—comes down to this particular formulation of dualism, whose consequences Schlegel draws out, throughout his notes. For in addition to all numeric and linguistic constructions, all possible temporal scansions are given through Schlegel's 1/0 and 0/1 as well, as Schlegel indicates later in his lectures,[68] when he describes the simultaneous emergence of temporal intervals and infinitely great and small velocities in analogous terms to the emergence of a system of integers and the one infinite / infinitesimal quantum—this time, out of the initial scission of space, which is full (1/0), and time, which is not (0/1), which Schlegel calls "becoming [*Werden*]."[69] What becomes of the world thus becomes through such fractioning, too, and it is in this sense that the sentence from "To the Dithyrambs," "the *World* as κοσμος is in eternal becoming," could begin to be broached.

The scission of the one marks the beginning of time and world at once. It might be articulated more precisely as the pathos of natural productivity, rather than its product, which is what Schlegel will do at the start of his note on the dithryambs. Nor would Schlegel's reformulation of Schelling's

"1—1 + 1" as "cosmogony + παθ / ο" be a mere metaphor, carried over
from his mathematic speculations to a more poetic construction—for the
pathos of nature is also articulated as such elsewhere, more or less clearly,
for Schelling, too. Although he later categorically rejects an original passivity in nature, Schelling had asserted earlier, in his *Ideas toward a Philosophy
of Nature*: "Nothing that is or that becomes can be or become, without another at once being or becoming [*Nichts, was ist oder was wird, kann seyn oder
werden, ohne daß ein anders zugleich sey oder werde*]" (I,5: 138). It is the pathos
implicit in this sentence that Schlegel radicalizes in his *Aurora* fragment, at
the level of logic and language—and adopts nearly verbatim elsewhere in
his fragments and published writings, noting, for example, emphatically:
"*No one understands himself insofar as he is solely himself and not at once also
another* [Niemand versteht sich selbst, in so fern er nur er selbst und nicht
zugleich auch ein andrer ist]" (18: 84).[70] And it is this sentence—from which
Schelling himself will, it turns out, turn away—that allows the incisiveness
of Schlegel's cosmological intervention, with *Aurora*, to be read. Its tren-
chancy is, in fact, due in no small part to Schlegel's divergence here from
Schelling, to whom he is otherwise so near.

On the one hand, Schelling's remark presents the assertion that each
thing that is or becomes is coordinated with the being or becoming of
something else. Since this coordination is formulated two sentences earlier
in terms of an economy of giving and receiving—"nature has allowed
nothing [. . .] that does not [. . .] incessantly give back what it received,
and that does not receive again in new form what it had given back" (I,5:
138)—passive receptivity is implicit in the process of exchange that he
describes. Yet the sentence must also be read otherwise, for the structure
of natural productivity that Schelling elaborates here does not allow the
presupposition of a stable natural product that could be the subject of cause
and effect. When he writes, "nature has, in her whole economy, allowed
nothing that could exist for itself and independently of the whole nexus of
things," this "whole nexus of things [*Zusammenhang der Dinge*]" has less to
do with "things" than with the utterly ephemeral products of "effect and
countereffect [*Wirkung und Gegenwirkung*]," which, as products of forces, are
always changing and will always change further. In this economy, passivity and pathos—that is, undergoing—must be conceived differently, apart
from a stable subject, and the grammatical subjects of Schelling's remark
"nothing that is or that becomes can be or become, without another at
once being or becoming" suggest how it might work. For the other that
"at once" is or becomes might be not the correlate but the transformation
of what initially "is or becomes." Counterintuitive as it may sound, this

reading is supported by the fact that Schelling does *not* write, "nothing that is or that becomes can be or become, without at once being or becoming another." For if everything in nature is processual—and therefore other-ing—nothing that undergoes this othering could be called in the same way or referred to as the consistent subject of Schelling's sentence. Hence the shift in subject in his formulation: "Nothing that is or becomes can be or become, without another at once being or becoming." In other words, nothing that is or becomes ever comes to be a something, but rather, splits between a nothing and another, neither at once.

There is no way to decide between these two possibilities—for another is another as another—though Schelling does indicate explicitly that pathos is as essential to the scission he marks as generativity, concluding his sentence: "and even the perishing of a product of nature is nothing other than the payment of a debt that it has taken upon itself against the entire rest of nature [*und selbst der Untergang des einen Naturprodukts ist nichts als Bezahlung einer Schuld, die es gegen die ganz übrige Natur auf sich genommen hat*]" (I,5: 138). Nonetheless, insofar as Schelling lends primacy to the one and the whole—and here grants more wholeness and substantiality to natural "products" than his logic otherwise seems to allow—he elaborates the pathos of othering as the perishing of a finite something. And only via this contradiction to his own premises can he proceed to formulate change over time as an order of debt, thereby paraphrasing Anaximander's famous proposition: "But that from which beings have their origin also gives rise to their passing away, according to what necessitates; for things render justice and pay penalty to one another for their injustice, according to the ordinance of time."[71] This formulation may also reflect the way Leibniz would write on the problem of the infinite series, which Howard Pollack cites in his study of Novalis and mathematics: "just as the calculation of probability prescribes that one must draw the arithmetic mean, i.e., the half of the sum, so, too, does nature observe here the equal law of justice [*das gleiche Gesetz der Gerechtigkeit*]" (qtd. in Pollack 134). However, this analogy of equivalence and equity cannot truly be integrated into the arguments Schelling had initially advanced, where neither production nor product was prioritized, and neither *is*, let alone is equal to itself. And it is solely by taking the none with the one even more consistently than Schelling that Schlegel departs from his contemporary to propose that sheer productivity would be itself nothing/other than absolute pathos—"cosmogony + παθ / 0"—at once.

Before any other temporal distinction, then—and entailed in all temporal distinctions—there is the critical scission of the one, which is also the scission of each single moment, marked by the adverb "at once [*zugleich*]" in Schelling's text, and by the "+" of Schlegel's initial formulation on the dithyrambs. Before any time, in other words, there is simultaneity,[72] and when the "+" of cosmogony and absolute pathos marks their coincidence, Schlegel can reformulate the world—which is the "cosmos [κοσμος]"—*as* "χα [Chaos]," too: "the world *as* [chaos] and [chaos] *for* the world" (16: 198). This chaos, in turn, would, given the mathematical order to which Schlegel is indebted, have to be a chasm or scission—the utter fragmentation of any world or order—and thus, at the same time, an opening *for* the world, which only comes to be through this opening: "and χα [Chaos] for the world." This thoroughgoing scission will, as in Böhme, entail implications for language and meaning, too. But it is not, as it was for Böhme, a scission that could or should be ultimately decided, nor is it the scission of good and evil, God and devil. Rather, it is simply double. The absolutes of 0/1 and 1/0 would always allow all thinkable breaches, but no ultimate end. And this means, too—at least at first—that there would be no law or order of time with the emergence of temporality, no causality or succession to speak of—but the sheer chaos of scissions—"all thinkable breaches [*alle denkbare Brüche*]"[73]—which is reflected—or rather: refracted—in the nigh absence of transitive verbs in the fragments that follow in Schlegel's note, most of which entail nothing other than substantives set apart by dashes or joined by the copula. But even before this, the conjunction of chaos and world has other consequences for the language through which any such world and chaos might be articulated: for the linguistic correlate to the simultaneous—as Schlegel displays by reformulating his initial equation in terms of the relations "as," "and," and "for"—is the similar.

Everything is as another, even as itself, and therefore for another, as for itself. Thus, the chasm—the world as chaos—turns—in a chiasm—and cuts a figure that crosses through every possible oppositional configuration of genesis and pathos.[74] Accordingly, the only pathos to speak of in Schlegel's note is "love," from its sheer emanation as light and song, to the chaotic unions of orgies. These instances of sexual union, however, do not so much produce anything as they perpetuate themselves—for there is no genesis of the generations in Schlegel's note, but the simultaneous appearance of "children, maidens, boys, mothers, men, priests etc." Yet at the same time, because all it takes is an "accidental disturbance" for the register of harmonies and emanation to shift to that of Titans, wildness, and explosion, one could also just as well call the absolute pathos of Schlegel's chaotic cosmos "hate." Similarly, Schlegel's universe describes the turn of the eternal one to the eternal becoming of the world, which, *as* eturnal, turns out to say the same thing differently—as a process of perpetual differentiation, and over the scission of an adversative "but": "The *universum* is eternal and unchanging, but the *world* as κοσμος is in eternal becoming" (16: 198).

But before any universal tendencies are evoked, Schlegel displaces ontology through semantics,[75] with the "as" and the "for." And this thoroughly simulated ontology has far-reaching resonance—both in his note and in Schlegel's contemporaneous remark in his "Theory of the World," where he writes: "From *allegory* (elucidation of the existence of the world) follows that in each individual there is only so much reality *as it has sense, as it [each individual] has meaning, spirit*" (12: 40).[76] The reality of any individual, in other words, is contingent upon the degree to which it means something else,[77] and would increase in direct proportion to such divisions in its meaning—which, in turn, approach the infinite, which is one. Schlegel calls the modality of this meaning or being "allegory"—literally, an 'other' (ἄλλος) 'speaking' (ἀγορεύειν)—both in his note on the dithyrambs and in his philosophical theory of the world. There, he will also call it "love," and designate it, in turn, "the point of indifference [*der IndifferenzPunkt*]"— thereby signaling its relation to the problem of the one that he had adopted from Schelling, but solved otherwise (12: 52–53). And in the "Theory of the World," as in his cosmogonic fragment on the dithyrambs, Schlegel makes it absolutely explicit that allegories operate much like the breaches of his mathematical formulas—but now formulated otherwise, as a positive "intercalation [*Einschiebung*]"—in order to mediate the individua of the universe with the universal—which he now calls "Substanz"—by dividing them from themselves, as and for their meaning.[78] For the essence of any individual, Schlegel writes in his "Theory," is not indivisibility, but "infinite divisibility [*unendliche Theilbarkeit*]."[79] This divisibility follows from the mathematical principles underlying his arguments: an individual, in the strict sense of the word, would have to be understood as $1/0$, and it would therefore be infinitely divisible, as its correlate $0/1$ suggests—so that any individual most truly is by meaning what it is not, and again what it is not, ad infinitum, eternally being in becoming other, and thus in becoming per se. Meanwhile, any given moment of splitting, seen positively, could be grasped only as an utterly temporary and provisional—and partial—"*image or presentation, allegory* (εἰκών) [. . .] of the *one infinite substance*" (12: 39). This ultimate meaning, of course, is itself necessarily meaningless, be it none or one—which nonetheless amounts to the same. But at the same time, by the same token, this indifferent one can be approached only by differing, and thereby meaning, or loving—or hating—as distinctly much as possible. Said otherwise, "the result is the concept of *assimilation* [*das*

Resultat davon ist der Begriff der Assimilazion]" (12: 40), which here can only mean: a tendency toward similarity through dissimilarity, a simultaneous incrementation of meaning and oneness through scissions. If this throughgoing allegorical structure resembles, in many ways, the pervasive analogies through which Jacob Böhme organizes his words and his world, the accent will have shifted from one upon propriety—"but truly and properly, as such, I mean no other thing than as I set it in letters [*Aber doch wahrhafftig vnd eigendlich also / Ich meine kein ander ding / Als wie ichs Im buch staben setze*]" (*Aurora* 172/73)—to the expropriation of every meaning toward another, which will lend even the proliferation of images that Schlegel adopts from Böhme a different kind of truth than their author may have intended.

Hence, in his fragment on the dithyrambs—on the poetry that should announce poetry and "therefore" be the "poetry of poetry"—as the poetry of genesis and pathos per se—Schlegel prescribes: "Plenitude of alleg[ories] and visions [*Fülle d[er] Alleg.[orien] und Gesichte*]." And before this, he iterates twice, once in the main body of the text and once in the margins: "All images are true. <All images are true.> [*Alle Bilder sind wahr. <Alle Bilder sind wahr>*]" (16: 199). These remarks, which appear amid a plethora of imagery—mostly, nonetheless, with a very particular orientation, namely, toward the light ("the divine spark," "a *realm of light* as in Dante," "immediate onlooking of the sun" [16: 198–99])—are the precise correlates of the cosmogony Schlegel concisely notes at the start of his fragment.

All images must be true, insofar as images are all that can be grasped or presented of the becoming that most truly is. All images are true, in other words, because all of them are other than what truly is, and none of them *are*. However, if all images are true, there could also be no immediately apparent criterion to distinguish truth from untruth but what does not appear, so that the nontrue would seem to be neither visible nor thinkable—and with it, the "true." Nor would it be adequate to say that all images are true in this fragment, insofar as they tend toward the luminous source of truth and being that all of Schlegel's most apparent literary and philosophical sources here reflect: namely, the light that constitutes the essence of God in Böhme's *Aurora,* the Gospel of John, and the *Paradiso* of Dante—which begins, as Schlegel also puts it, with an "immediate onlooking of the sun" (16: 199). However, the identity of Schlegel's source is, like everything else, thoroughly divided. In accordance with the premises underlying—and undercutting—the entire text, his image may refer, in addition to Dante's *Paradiso,* to the light that distinguishes philosophical knowing in Plato, and that gives rise to the world in Schelling's philosophy of nature, as "the first and positive cause of universal polarity" (I,6: 92) or "*becoming itself*" (I,7: 220). The light source for refraction does not and cannot matter, nor does the fact that this image appears to be the privileged "one." If all images are true, then this statement would have to be true for all others, too. And in this light, no distinguishing criterion seems imaginable, at least not according to the philosophical tradition that would constitute truth as the correspondence of a representation and an object. For an image is neither a representation nor an object, and no such terms of distinction precede Schlegel's evocation of images here. Nor could truth be regulated according to the principles of noncontradiction and of sufficient reason—the two main criteria for correctness in logic that Leibniz would posit and that Schlegel would approach, critically, throughout his philosophical notebooks and his later lectures (cf. 12: 4, 314–23, 18: 46, 71). Images cannot be true for any reason but their being images—without, however, being anything that could enter into a relation of contradiction or identity with themselves: each image is only as an image of another, and were it to differ instantaneously, the image would be nothing other than another, equally true image.

With this dictum, which Schlegel singles out and reproduces in the margin of his note for *Aurora*, his words of truth turn and lead to another's: namely, the anonymous Eleatic Visitor's discrimination of appearances that forms the inquiry of Plato's *Sophist*. This text is yet another one that was or came to be critical for Schlegel's conjunction of genesis and pathos in his *Aurora* fragment; for the eternal, unchanging universe and the world of endless becoming that he articulates there; for the "as [*als*]" and "for [*für*]" that structure the relations of all that is and its otherness—and that may translate not only the principles of Schelling's philosophy of nature but also the ὡς ("as") and πρὸς τί ("for / in relation to") that pervade Plato's text;[80] and for, most evidently, Schlegel's assertion of the truth of images. In fact, just as one and none prove to be the decisive terms for Schlegel's mathematical metaphysics, the Eleatic Visitor's elaborations of being, truth, and language derive from his analyses of "being" (ὄν) and "nonbeing" (μὴ ὄν)—which he glosses as being "other" (ἕτερον)—and are most closely related, too, to the pronunciation Schlegel adopts and adapts from Schelling as the ontopoetological premise for his *Aurora*, and beyond: "Nothing that is or that becomes can be or become, without another at once being or becoming" (I,5: 138). Thus, it is a reading of this Platonic text that will open a way to read the images, which, after his prologue, make up the remainder of Schlegel's *Aurora* fragment. And only by turning to Plato before returning to the details of Schlegel's fragment will it be possible to read Schlegel's assertion of truth as the radical intervention it truly marks. If Schlegel never carried out his plans to translate Plato, which had preoccupied him around the same time he wrote "To the Dithyrambs,"[81] his first *Aurora* fragment translates his readings of the *Sophist* into a new poetic world that could have dissolved all as we know it.

Whereas Schlegel emphatically repeats, "All images are true," in the *Sophist*, the conclusion that "all is true [ἀληθῆ πάντ' εἶναι]" (260 c1–2) would exclude the distinction between true and false, and with that, the existence of images—as well as philosophy and, ultimately, speech itself. This is because there can be a true appearance of something that is "another such one, likened from and to the true one" (240 a7–8) only once the distinctions and interrelations of the same and the other—that is, for Plato, nonbeing—are sorted out; and once it can be said that, because they are mixed in all, their proper relations can be mistaken, presented as other than they really are, and therefore falsely. The false is not—as Theatetus falsely says it at first—"saying things that are, not to be, and things that are not, to be [τά τε ὄντα λέγων μὴ εἶναι καὶ τὰ μὴ ὄντα εἶναι]" (241 a1), but presenting something as other than it is, in the likeness of a true statement: "The true [speech] [. . .] says the things that are *as* they are [. . .] and the false [speech], things that are other than what are. [. . .] It says things that are not, then, *as if* they were [λέγει δὲ αὐτῶν ὁ μὲν ἀληθὴς [λόγος] τὰ ὄντα ὡς ἔστιν [. . .] ὁ δὲ δὴ ψευδὴς ἕτερα τῶν ὄντων [. . .] τὰ μὴ ὄντ' ὡς ὄντα λέγει]" (263 b4–9, my emphases). The true relation of being and nonbeing is determined by their proportions and relations, by their logos. For both being and nonbeing have "gone through" (259 a6) or been "dispersed" (260 b8) among all (the Greek verbs are διέρχομαι ['go through'] and διασπείρω ['scatter'], respectively), so that everything can be as itself and, in certain ways, as another. It is those proportions and relations that should be rendered in the true speech (or: logos), which is a result of their "interweaving [συμπλοκή]" (see 259e 5–6). Thus, the true or false can be said solely when speech itself is shown to be analogous to the proportioning and apportioning that structures all that is, and only then can it also be said that "everything is necessarily full of images and icons and even phantasms" (260 c8–9); that is, full of disproportionate likenesses to the true.[82] Otherwise, every statement would have to be admitted, and insofar as we only truly know what we can say,[83] every appearance would have to be true, too. Nothing could be an image, whose existence is to be proven from the start in this dialogue with the "Sophist"—the maker of images who himself does not appear in person, but who will be produced and refuted in effigy through the Eleatic Visitor's speech (268 d1). Every truth of the dialogue pivots upon the vertiginous evocation of "image" production and its opposite, whose turns cannot be retraced in full here, but have been elaborated at length by scholars such as Maria Villela-Petit and Stanley Rosen.[84] In fact, this construction of an absent persona is, perhaps, the truest proof for the existence of images in language in this dialogue with the sophist, who is said to debate as one who "has no eyes [οὐχ ἐχεῖν ὄμματα]" (239 e3).

But for something to be said to be false, more than its name—or its "not"—would need to be said, as the Eleatic Visitor makes clear toward the end of the *Sophist*. Alone, every word, like every image or appearance, is neither true nor false, or—what is the same—they are all "true." Words alone are not only not speech, and certainly not true or false speech. Rather, even when they are spoken, even when they are strung together at length, they "do not illuminate any action or inaction, nor any essence of a being or a nonbeing [οὐδὲ οὐσίαν ὄντος οὐδὲ μὴ ὄντος]" (262 c2). Illuminating neither "a being nor a nonbeing," words cannot be taken for anything at all, lest speech and reason—that is, the proportions of being and nonbeing that determine all that truly is—go lost: "to accept someone saying that a name is something would not have any speech/reason [λόγον οὐκ ἂν ἔχον]" (244 c11–d1).[85] And in excess of every proportion or order, individual words, divided from the synthesis of the minimal syntax that the Eleatic Visitor is just about to formulate,[86] and dividing all without end, mark the vanishing point of speech: "For [. . .] to undertake the separation of all from all [καὶ γὰρ [. . .] τό γε πᾶν ἀπὸ παντὸς ἐπιχειρεῖν ἀποχωρίζειν]," the Eleatic Visitor remarks toward the end, "is disharmonious and, in all respects, [the mark of] one who is unmusical and unphilosophical. [. . .] It is the utmost vanishing of all speeches to dissolve each thing from all things [τελεωτάτη πάντων λόγων ἐστὶν ἀφάνισις τὸ διαλύειν ἕκαστον ἀπὸ πάντων]" (259 d9–e5). In this respect, words are much like nonbeing—and likeness is as close as things can get—for they would be (like) the "other," whose "nature appears," as the Eleatic Visitor had previously said, "to be cut through and through, just as knowledge is [κατακεκερματίσθαι καθάπερ ἐπιστήμη]" (257 c7–8). Except that words are exempt from all that they could say or know of anything else, including "is" and "is not." And they are therefore exempt, too, from the ontological order of divisions into being and nonbeing, movement and stasis, same and other, that will be set forth—and replicated in grammar and syntax—as well as from the distinction between appearance and reality, and, ultimately, true and false. Words alone would appear to be sheer scission, and if this is what must render them negligible for the Eleatic Visitor, it is precisely what cuts them out to be the true substance of Schlegel's cosmology and to mark the most radical breaches of his *Daybreak*.

Like the other philosophers the Eleatic Visitor alternately ventriloquizes and critically questions in his dialogue, who maintain an absolute distinction between being and nonbeing, but in so doing, silently presume a "third beside those two" (243 e2–3) without which their logic would be inoperative, he silences words as words. Yet words cannot but emerge as the ultimate "allegory," or speaking otherwise, that is other than all that can be spoken, even as they allow each speech to speak. Thus, before and apart from all that is or is not, and as the division that opens all others, words are the truth of this dialogue. They are what truly allow it to operate—also on its own terms of what "truly" or "really" is (ὄντως ὄν)—whereby the word for "truly" is not the predicate "true" (ἀληθής), but the adverbial modification of being itself (ὄντως): "I say," says the Eleatic Visitor, "that every such thing that has acquired any power either to make something other, whatsoever its nature may be, or to undergo even the slightest pathos by the slightest degree, even if it should take place only once, [I say every such thing] to really/beingly be [ὄντως εἶναι]" (247 d8–e2). Yet words do so only and precisely by being utterly inoperative in and of themselves and by being what, taken in and of themselves, might dissolve each and every speech or appearance or knowing they make possible. Theirs is not the truth of true or false sentences, but one that comes before either, and one that Schlegel proclaims by adapting the Eleatic Visitor's statement: "All images are true. <All images are true>" (16: 199). Here, the image, like the word, cannot be taken as a visible "something," or as a likeness to anything else, or as a nothing, but only—between and apart from the one and the none, being and nonbeing—as a sheer function of this difference that would allow anything else to be said, seen, or meant.[87]

However, the consequences of this premise—that all words and all images are true—are nigh impossible to follow or carry out in thinking and writing. It is one thing to proclaim their truth, and another to write or speak a language of imaging or wording itself. Yet the accomplishment of this task is what truly would make up the prophetic poetry Schlegel had envisioned for *Aurora*, as a language that addresses what is not yet, or more accurately, what is not and has never been; as language that speaks to nonbeing more radically than anything one could say, when it comes to addressing the end or beginning of the world and all that takes place in between. Such writing or speaking would have to speak other than any that operates according to the order of logical affirmation and negation that arises with and as the distinction between the true and the false. And this would mean that it could not operate according to any conventional, predicative syntax—at least not truly. But before returning to Schlegel's fragment, where syntax and the ontology it implies are precisely at issue— in the sense of being on their way out—the *Sophist* has more to say. For as Plato's Eleatic Visitor says, when one sets an action (πρᾶξις) together with an agent (πράττων [262 b10]) or object (πρᾶγμα [262 e12]) through nouns and verbs, one can at last call this interweaving of words a speech (λόγος) and judge it to be true or false.Being and nonbeing themselves are exempt from this logic, however, since neither would belong to the Eleatic Visitor's register of praxis, and if everything is and is not, according to the pervasive intertwining of being and nonbeing (that is: being-other), then affirmations of any being would amount to little more than saying a word alone. And in fact, the first statement the Eleatic Visitor proves to be false—"Theatetus, with whom I now speak, flies" (263 a8)—is not even false because of a mismatched conjunction of an action with an agent, but because of the misplaced deictic "with whom I now speak" and, more truly, because of the response it solicits. Not even a deictic—which involves pointing toward an ostensible reality, in a speech that should demonstrate truth and falsehood through words alone (since the Sophist, as we saw, "has no eyes" [239 e3])—can guarantee anything. Nothing is true or false until Theatetus himself responds, saying that it is he who is meant, and that things "concerning me [περὶ ἐμοῦ]" are not as the Eleatic Visitor had said. What truly makes a difference is not other words or *the* other of the Eleatic Visitor's ontology, but rather, the words of another.[88] Only you can tell me whether I speak the truth. Words alone, however, would testify to the vanishing point of sheer scission, to the opening of all "thinkable breaches," and this other way of speaking would operate apart from any conclusions of truth or falsehood.

Words prior to predicative truth are precisely what Schlegel exposes throughout his text "On the Dithyrambs." Thus, nothing could happen in Schlegel's dithyrambs but the production or reproduction of images, without priority among them or transitive interactions between them. Most often, nothing more is said than a series of nouns, names, or images, separated by dashes: "Orgies of fantasy; to close, poetry as the word of the riddle.—Choruses of children, maidens, boys, mothers, men, priests etc. [. . .] Alleg.[ory] <of the> *tree of life / source of joy*—" (16: 198–99). When the occasional verbal construction does appear to denote activity—e.g., "the priests sing origin of the world," "mothers and children must express love"—these actions have no predetermined limits, and, perpetuated indefinitely, would still be no different than instantaneous images. Even the vivification of the "dead universe" through the "divine spark" and the re-elevation of "nature [. . .] to divinity"—which imply change and even goals of motion—are presented in the present tense, and thus could be conceived as taking place without end. Nor would there be any way to say, in this particular context, according to Schlegel's chaotic formulation of cosmogenesis, whether the "dead universe" was ever once alive, or whether nature, "lifting itself again," was ever once fallen; or whether these processes preceded the singing of the priests and the generations of mothers, children, maidens, boys, and men that Schlegel had evoked before. There is no distinction between past, present, and future, no articulation of anything that could begin or end—which is also, perhaps, why imagery drawn from the chronologically disparate texts of Dante, Böhme, Schelling, and Plato can all appear gathered at once. Thus, in the end, it nearly appears that everything in the beginning was always in media res and heading nowhere. Likewise, the very images of cosmic order—such as song and love—are torn apart and posited without relation to one another, so that they may just as truly be in the midst of forming chaotic discord, with no way to tell the difference: "The world as χα[chaos] and χα[chaos] for the world" (16: 198).

At the same time, this chaotic order means that anything can happen, which Schlegel indicates by ending his note differently than he began, with what seems to be the conclusion of a conditional clause: "—Then again an accidental disturbance; otherwise the age of love would have been eternal [—*Dann wieder eine zufällige Störung; sonst würde das Zeitalter der Liebe ewig gewesen sein*]" (16: 199). What can happen, in other words, is the happenstance of an accident, or a fall—not the fall of Lucifer, or the fall of man, as in Böhme, but an utterly indeterminate "accidental disturbance," itself without agent or cause. And from here, it seems that everything happens in the most familiar of ways. In this case, the disturbance entails consequences—so that causal determination will seem to have emerged, too, at once, with and as nothing other than this disturbance. Likewise, a "first accidental revolution," which distinguishes a "golden age" from a previous "wild nature," introduces a "first"—and, as a result, temporal succession— to the world as well: "—The wildness after the first explosion—the golden time after the first accidental revolution— [—*Die Wildheit nach d[er] erst[en] Explosion—die goldne Zeit nach der ersten zufälligen Revoluzion*]" (16: 199). By ending as he does, then, Schlegel appears to conclude his prophetic poem not with an impending outbreak of a new order and genesis that would end time, poetry, and thinking as we know it, but with the emergence of time as succession and of causal conditions. He would seem to break off his note, that is, with the temporal modi of the known world, and with possible objects of historical inquiry and veridical predication, as well as with the syntax in which these things might be articulated. He would, in the end, already no longer speak to a time that would have truly been different from that of the world as we know it.

And yet it would be utterly mistaken to read in these developments a genetic or mythic account of a world in which the laws of causality, succession, and noncontradiction can thenceforth be presumed to have eternal and universal validity. There is no such constitutive power at work here. To the contrary, even with the appearance of a syntax similar to grammatical norms, Schlegel undoes predication and any veracity predicated upon it in the most sophisticated of ways. For if causality and succession, as Schlegel's writing suggests, are the by-products of an accidental disturbance, they could never be eternal laws of nature, and even if they were to become operative as laws, they could not be entirely binding. Rather, in order to be consistent with themselves, they would also have to remain bound up with the accident that gave them rise. And in fact, this breach within the logic that seems to emerge in Schlegel's fragment leaves its mark in the conclusion Schlegel draws, on several counts: It cannot, according to the principle of noncontradiction, be true that the "age of love" would have continued were it not for an accidental disturbance, because the "age of love" was no "age," until the very accident that disturbed it. Therefore, it only ever was as a result of this disturbance, after its loss. Similarly, it could not be true that the age of love could ever have been eternal if was an "age," and therefore temporally limited. Thus, it could never have been what it would have eternally been, had it not been disturbed. But even before this, the first part of Schlegel's conditional sentence is an incomplete clause, a nominal phrase that ends with a semicolon, thereby resembling the fragmentary substantives that had preceded it—"[t]hen again an accidental disturbance;" Without a protasis and without clear syntactic indications of the relation of the "accidental disturbance" to the words that follow, the apodosis that Schlegel gives—"otherwise the age of love would have been eternal"—is given away as something other than the consequence of a cause. Hence, one cannot but conclude that the structure of conditionality he appears to evoke is itself disturbed. And consequently, it also cannot necessarily be true that the accidental disturbance Schlegel names causes anything to begin with or that what follows its evocation truly follows from it.

And then again, beyond this, the phrase alone "otherwise the age of love would have been eternal [*sonst würde das Zeitalter der Liebe ewig gewesen sein*]" troubles any logic that could determine what era, precisely, has ended, and whether any era has been after all. The more usual way to say "otherwise the age of love would have been eternal" would have been "sonst wäre das Zeitalter der Liebe ewig gewesen." In this (nonexistent) version, "wäre," the third-person singular subjunctive of *sein* ("to be"), would indicate a past counterfactual, with the implication that "the age of love" had once been, and that it could have been eternal, but that presumably, as a result of something else, it ended and turned out otherwise. Insofar as "würde" can be used as an auxiliary verb in subjunctive constructions in place of the main verb, Schlegel's sentence also says as much. But by writing "würde" instead—the third-person singular subjunctive of "werden," which means "to become" and which also serves as an auxiliary verb with the infinitive to build the future tense—Schlegel implies, at the same time, that the age of love never was nor could have ever *been* eternal. For his clause may be no past counterfactual, but a counterfactual future perfect: namely, the counterfactual of the indicative clause, "das Zeitalter der Liebe wird ewig gewesen sein," which would mean: "the age of love will have been eternal." Thus, Schlegel presents the counterfactual of a possibility counter to any possible fact: the vertiginous possibility of an eternity that could have been finished and with it, the equally vertiginous possibility that the age of love in fact remains to come. Perhaps, then, its potential eternity has not been yet; perhaps it may still be on its way to becoming one that will have been.

The turns of Schlegel's universe of one and none cannot but be vertiginous in precisely this way. And there is no way to decide among the grammatical possibilities in his *Aurora* fragment, where past and future utterly intersect, distinct and yet indistinguishable at once. In this respect, Schlegel anticipates at the end of his note the more straightforward definition of eternity he will provide in a philosophical note a few years later in his lectures in Cologne: "There is a twofold eternity through the annihilation of the poles (of future and past) and through the annihilation of the present—as the binding, hindering indifference.—Total presence would be death.—Eternity is infinite temporal fullness, not temporal absence" (19: 58).[89]

More than this, however, Schlegel speaks the language of this temporality in his earlier fragment, where all tempi—the infinitive (*sein*), the future subjunctive (*würde*), and the past participle (*gewesen*)—are intertwined: "otherwise the age of love would have been eternal [*sonst würde das Zeitalter der Liebe ewig gewesen sein*]." And he thereby shows that such a language would operate only on the condition of sheer conditionality. Eternity, he suggests, would be thinkable and speakable only with the suspension of all that is—including eternity itself—as it crosses and is crossed with the past (*gewesen*) and the *irrealis* (*würde*). And if this language of being and time could truly be parsed in all such ways at once, Schlegel would have done even more than defer an interpretive decision and, with it, the temporal or modal status of the "age of love"—which should, presumably, come first and last. He would have done more than suspend, as he did before, those categories—transitivity, succession, causality—that make up the preconditions and tendencies of any possible order of knowing, predication, and logical truth. He would have done more than utter the impossible possibility that even those conditions—through which all that can be known or done is determined—are contingent upon accident, and that their supposed universal validity could not therefore be true for all time.

And for once, he would have also precluded all possible ends of prophecy, whether it be the restitution of all that will have been, as in the Acts of the Apostles (Acts 3.21); the institution of an entirely new order of poetry, as in Schlegel's later fragment; or the annihilation of the fallen world, and the scission of scissions between good and evil, spirit and matter, as in Böhme. For this one critical moment of his *Aurora* project—before it will have been called *Aurora*, and before he will have decided for the apocalyptic direction he will pursue thereafter, to the end—Schlegel speaks beyond prophecy. For this one moment, then, Schlegel may have been, as Christ would say of John, and as he will say of Christ—but in a very different way than Christ or Schlegel themselves would have ever said—"*plus quam propheta* [more than prophet]" (19: 328). And as such, he may have said: in the end, anything can happen but the end.

EMPEDOCLES, EMPYRICALLY SPEAKING—: FRIEDRICH HÖLDERLIN'S *TRAGIC ÖDE*

With the break of day, I thought to say to you the word,
the stern and long withheld one . . .
Mit Tagesanbruch dacht' ich euch das Wort
Das ernste langverhaltene, zu sagen . . .
—Friedrich Hölderlin, *The Death of Empedokles*

The tragedy that Friedrich Hölderlin intended to devote to Empedocles never came to an end. Suspended between the heavenly fire that had dawned—and broken—upon him and the fire of Aetna into which he longs to plunge; between the word that he had intended to offer the people of his city, and the sign that he wishes, in burning, to become, Empedocles would be the prophetic figure of Hölderlin's poetic oeuvre, whose enunciation remains irrevocably withheld. His drama—which never takes place—revolves around an incendiary word that he should have delivered as a parting gift to the Agrigentians, then doubled by burning himself. Such are the burning points of the drama, which structure its course without ever being touched—and which would have been destined either to rejuvenate the polis or to pronounce its end, and with it, the beginning of a new era. If Hölderlin may have been inspired to choose his protagonist, whose biography he had read in Diogenes Laertes's *Lives of the Philosophers*, by the impression "that what is passing and changing in human thoughts and systems strikes me nearly more tragically than those fates which one usually calls [. . .] real,"[1] it would be at least as appropriate to speak of the death of the prophet as it would be to speak of "the death of the philosopher,"[2] when it comes to Hölderlin's unfinished drama, *The Death of Empedokles*.

The suspension of prophetic address in the draft materials and poetological prose texts known as Hölderlin's *Empedokles* solicits a critical return to what Paul de Man once called "a persistent tendency to treat Hölderlin as a prophetic and eschatological poet, the precursor of a new historical era that his work helps to prepare" ("The Riddle" 211). With these words, de Man rightly pointed out the limitations of the hagiographic approach to Hölderlin adopted by members of the George school, among others—not least of all in relation to his *Empedokles*. It does not escape Max Kommerell, for example, that the role he assigns Hölderlin in his own text is tightly bound up with that of Hölderlin's dramatic figure, Empedocles, whom he calls "Hölderlin's unique, unrepeatable mysterium" in the final chapter of *Spirit and Letter in Poetry*, which is devoted to *Empedokles* (330). Yet whereas Empedocles attempts to speak the wrong word at the wrong time—because he places a wrong emphasis upon his own person—Kommerell announces Hölderlin's success as the prophet who can mediate between the gods and his people precisely where his protagonist fails. "In a genuine act of imparting," Kommerell writes, "Empedokles would merely be, so that the God could step through him, out into the people—and to mediate this way was granted him only in death" (328). He would merely be, in other words, what Hölderlin was, as Kommerell suggests, when he writes in the last sentence of his essay and his book, "Hölderlin, given his disposition, could experience only a historical happening that is ungraspably far for us and barely still thinkable as the real history of his soul" (357). Thus, Kommerell consigns him to the "prophetic mourning of becoming foreign among the most familiar" that he had evoked at the start of his essay (320). Yet it is symptomatic that Kommerell rarely quotes from Hölderlin's texts, which imply, upon close analysis, a very different structure of and for prophetic poetry than Kommerell elaborates. Showing a similar tendency in an otherwise very different reading of a different poetic work, Martin Heidegger writes in his lecture course on Hölderlin's "Germanien" that poets—and a fortiori Hölderlin—"foretell the coming being of a people in its history" (*Hölderlins Hymnen* 146).[3] Yet perhaps the problem is less "the tendency to treat Hölderlin as a prophetic and eschatological poet" than the neglect to read closely what those categories might mean, in a dramatic text where a prophetic word should have been delivered in person, and never was. Following de Man in his criticism of Heidegger's approach, Ian Balfour suggests alternatives, arguing that the very "openness" of Hölderlin's poetry "to divergent readings" is "part of the ambiguously prophetic character of his work" (178). Conceived in this way, its prophetic tendency cannot be located within one national history or one national language, not least because, in prophetic poems such as "Germania," "it is impossible to decide between history and allegory, because 'history' in the form of the fatherland especially is itself allegorical," and "always becoming other" (248–49).[4]

When, however—and without explicit reference to prophecy—readers seek to address Empedocles's divine calling, Empedocles has consistently been read as the representative figure for what Maurice Blanchot has called "the will to effect an irruption, by death, into the world of the invisible," and "to unite oneself to the element of fire, sign and presence of inspiration, to attain the intimacy of divine commerce" (*L'espace littéraire* 363).[5] While Empedocles's longing for fire is a trait that is drawn out throughout Hölderlin's drafts, Blanchot does not elaborate the specificity of this longing in distinction to Hölderlin's other remarks on "heavenly fire," nor does he analyze the relation of that longing to the many interruptions of speech, which occur, intermittently, throughout Hölderlin's versions. Instead, his remarks on Empedocles's longing are integrated into the context of other passages from Hölderlin's corpus, such as the poem "Wie wenn am Feiertage," where the poet is also said to have exposed himself "to the danger of incineration by fire" (*L'espace littéraire* 364). On the other hand, the differences among Hölderlin's drafts have most often been analyzed not with an eye to prophecy and inspiration, but according to Hölderlin's changing engagements with the genre of tragedy, the French Revolution, and the philosophy of speculative Idealism. Christoph Jamme suggests that, over each draft, tragic fate becomes transfigured according to the model of Christian sacrifice, such that Empedocles wishes to establish, through his sacrificial death, "a new reality" akin to the Christian "kingdom of God" (321).[6] Pierre Bertaux has interpreted Hölderlin's successive drafts as dramatic responses to the French Revolution (116–18), which interpretation Alexander Honold furthers in his more recent monograph, *Hölderlins Kalender: Astronomie und Revolution um 1800*.[7] Other readers of Hölderlin, such as Philippe Lacoue-Labarthe and Stanley Corngold, have construed the texts as successive experiments in an idealistic dramaturgy, through which Hölderlin strives to deny the scenic image and to present instead the speculative coincidence of life and death in person,[8] thus working to disintegrate the very speculative thought that sustains the drama.[9]

But what if the drama revolves around a mantic moment that both resists assimilation to Hölderlin's other remarks on prophetic poetry and heavenly fire and cannot be plotted along the lines of those generic, historical, and philosophical narratives that have organized much scholarship on *Empedokles*? And what if this unassimilable moment could be approached—for lack of any orienting framework—only in a way that is true to the language of Hölderlin; that is, in a way that follows the turns and ruptures of his rhetoric as closely as possible, in order to trace where they lead? This is not to say that excurses on other, related texts by Hölderlin should not enter into a reading of *Empedokles*; yet none could be taken as an interpretive key, and each would also need to be read closely in its own right. Even the cipher with which Hölderlin equates "the original" of tragic presentation and the "concealed ground of every nature" in a brief prose fragment that begins with the words "The meaning of tragedies" (*Sämtliche Werke: Frank-furter Ausgabe* 14: 383) need not be the meaning of *this* abortive tragedy. And if it were, it would not obviate the need to read *Empedokles* in its own right. For even if Hölderlin's thinking on tragedy shows the recurrence of many motifs; and even if this fragment, which has been carefully analyzed by scholars such as Lacoue-Labarthe, Peter Szondi, and Anja Lemke, was crucial to Hölderlin's thinking on tragic language, it would be a mistake to adopt it too hastily as the theoretical framework through which to read the utterances at stake in *Empedokles*. What Hölderlin says about "the meaning of tragedies"—whatever this should mean—may not be the same as the original word that Empedocles himself fails to speak, and the sign he fails to become. Peter Szondi has rightly cautioned against such leaps in approaching a singular poetic text, when he reminds readers in his *Studies of Hölderlin* "that in literary studies every single citation, before evidential force can be ascribed to it, must be no less carefully interpreted in itself than the passage for whose interpretation it is drawn upon as an argument or counterargument."[10]

Rather, beginning with a text peripheral to Hölderlin's drafts of his trag-edy—an ode entitled "Empedokles," which is the sole piece of writing to bear this name that Hölderlin published during his lifetime—the trajectory of this chapter will near *Empedokles* and the language of Hölderlin's tragic prophet, at some distance from the more familiar topoi within Hölderlin scholarship. This distance involves, too, taking seriously the radical for-eignness of *Empedokles*, which is at least as crucial a translation project as Hölderlin's Sophocles translations were, and not only because Empedocles's word should involve a translation of the language of Nature itself—and is thus not entirely unlike Hegel's later attempt to seduce Philosophy to teach German speaking in his *Phenomenology of Spirit*—or because the play should have culminated in the transfiguration of the prophet himself into a sign of burnt offering. For *Empedokles* also should have been a poem in which Hölderlin attempts to speak through another, and, through Empedocles, "to translate [*übertragen*] our own mind and our own experience to a for-eign analogical material [*in einen fremden analogischen Stoff*]," without which "nothing at all can be understood and brought to life," and "the right truth [. . .] goes missing. . . ."[11]

When Friedrich Hölderlin speaks of Empedocles in a letter addressed to his stepbrother, he says that he has completed a plan for a tragedy, whose "material [*Stoff*]" utterly "ravishes," or "tears [him] away [*hinreisst*]."[12]

When Hölderlin addresses Empedocles in an ode, Empedocles is the one who is enraptured by a "trembling longing." And the speaker, who retraces his trajectory into Aetna twice differently, is held back from following in the same way:

"Empedocles"
    Life, you seek it, seek, and a godly fire wells up and gleams deep from the earth to you, and you, in trembling longing, cast yourself downward into Aetna's flames.
    Thus the overaudacity of the queen melted pearls in wine; and she surely may! if only you had not sacrificed your riches, o Poet, in the seething chalice.
    But you are holy to me, as to the power of the earth that took you away, bold Slain One! And I would like to follow the hero into the depths, if love did not hold me back. (My translation)

"Empedokles"
Das Leben suchst du, suchst, und es quillt und glänzt
    Ein göttlich Feuer tief aus der Erde dir,
        Und du in schauderndem Verlangen
            Wirfst dich hinab, in des Aetna Flammen.

So schmelzt' im Weine Perlen der Übermut
    Der Königin; und mochte sie doch! hättst du
        Nur deinen Reichtum nicht, o Dichter,
            Hin in den gärenden Kelch geopfert.

Doch heilig bist du mir, wie der Erde Macht,
    Die dich hinwegnahm, kühner Getöteter!
        Und folgen möcht' ich in die Tiefe,
            Hielte die Liebe mich nicht, dem Helden. (5: 430)

From the outset, this is less a poem about Empedocles than it is about speaking to him, or more nearly, about speaking directly to "you"—and, indirectly, to the longing that draws "you" and "me" toward flames that tear "you" away, and nearly enrapture "me," too. With this, the minimal pair of any dramatic dialogue—but also speech per se, as well as its incendiary limits—is sketched most intensely, and in such a way that, from the outset, all terms appear on the verge of dissolution. Even as "Empedocles" temporarily materializes into a poem, then, and Hölderlin appears to near the tragic subject that "tears [him] away," the direction of address and the directness of this address reach only the most tenuous hold. Likewise, the limits that are drawn from strophe to strophe turn out to open vertiginously. Coming to a full stop, each is reprised in the next at a different, disparate point, "but [*aber*]" with conjunctions, which "thus [*so*]" indicate that each apparent limit is, ultimately, crossed and that the poem is torn from each halt, in turn, straight down to the end—from Empedocles's Aetna to Egypt, where Cleopatra once melted pearls in wine, to the verge of sheer, indefinite "depths [*Tiefe*]." Meanwhile, the longing, the love that moves the whole—that "wells up" as the source of speech and overwhelms the only "Poet" to speak of—crosses "you," the soliciting flames, and "me," in a dynamic that exposes the precariousness of this poetic speech, as well as Hölderlin's never-finished tragedy. And beyond this, it may trace, in a preliminary way, the rapidity of tragic time Hölderlin will articulate later, which is said to be held only for a moment with the prophetic speeches of Tiresias, as it tears man away into the eccentric sphere of the dead (16: 251).

The poet is the prophet of Empedocles, speaking for (*pro*) and to (*pro*) him, as one who can no longer speak—and Empedocles is the precursor and prophet for the poet, who, before (*pro*) anything was said, gave him a trajectory to speak of and drew him into the philological movement of love and words that follows. But to speak more precisely: Empedocles is the anonymous "hero" who has cast himself into Aetna; "I," one who would want to follow, if love did not "hold [*hielte*] me back." In the end, "love [*Liebe*]" would seem not only to spare "me" but also to recover, differently, the "life [*Leben*]" that was lost and sought from the start, and to temper the impetuous "longing" that impels Empedocles into the flames of Aetna. The cycle from destruction to preservation would seem to operate along the lines of an economy where the "sacrificed [*geopfert[e]*]" becomes recuperated by another as the "sacred [*heilig[e]*]," through an act of love that retains, rather than stretching forth in further longing (*Verlangen*). But this love is, strictly speaking, the love of another, attributed to neither Empedocles nor anyone else, and it is explicitly determined only by a restraint or reticence (*Zurückhalten*) that culminates in the end of speaking: beyond holding "me" back, it leads, through the last line, to the silence that follows it and ends the poem.

This trajectory alone suggests that love, although it seems to sustain the speaker rather than precipitate him, is not exactly the antinomy to the exorbitant longing of the first two strophes—an opposition that cannot be maintained longer than a moment. Rather, before it is so much as suggested, it is implicitly dissolved, insofar as the only lover in this poem is another: Cleopatra, who, according to Pliny the Elder,[13] had liquefied one of two pearls in wine in order to surpass her lover, Marc Antony, in wasting wealth on a meal. Over the analogy to her pearls, to which "you" and "I" are diverted, love operates first of all as a competition, whereby the mutual espousal of the lovers, the only promise that binds them, is their *sponsio*, or "convened dispute" (*Naturalis Historiae* 9.121)—and whereby the resolution of their dispute is the dissolution of their bond, commuted, as it were, to those two pearls. In Pliny's account, the pearls redouble the pair, and as they redouble, each member is impaired accordingly, as paired to each pearl as to each other. The pearl that dissolves turns out to be ominous for Marc Antony, marked only by an ablative absolute in Lucius Plancus's proclamation: "and he pronounced Antony vanquished, with omen [*victumque Antonium pronuntiavit omine*]" (9.121). And the other, "dissected [*dissectum*]," "is concomitant [*comitatur*]" with its "counterpart [*parem*]" (9.121): for Cleopatra's capture immediately follows, just as the second pearl has been intercepted by the arbiter of the couple's dispute. This Last Supper of pearls in wine is a communion of division alone between two entirely unequal halves—one that tends toward rapid and absolute disintegration, while the other, for all its inclination toward the first, is torn away elsewhere. And in this way, the royal couple and pair of pearls is also, even before the analogy of "Empedocles," an analogy—over which, however, each member is consumed or taken captive by another: a hyperanalogy that transfers beyond its terms on the one hand, and utterly dissolves on the other.[14]

When Empedocles casts his "riches [*Reichthum*]" into Aetna, as Cleopatra did her pearls; when he thereby disintegrates as they and Antony will have done; and when, over the near rhyme between "melted [*schmelzt'*]" and "chalice [*Kelch*]," the container of his act (phonetically) melts, too— one half of Pliny's analogy is drawn and analyzed even further, and in such a way that the distinctions among person, pearl, and goblet in the configuration Pliny depicts dissolve in one stroke. The comparison of Empedocles's self-sacrifice to Cleopatra's prodigal expenditure divides him into the "riches [*Reichthum*]" he once had or was and the "you" that "I" now address, thereby guaranteeing that a bare "you" can nonetheless be held holy, by "me." Yet "I" can only be, in the same stroke, as halved and had as you are dissolved, at once; and furthermore, by the same logic, "my" poetry, as your counterpart—and which I impart to only you, "o Poet"—must likewise dissolve. Conversely, the analogy Hölderlin espouses guarantees, at the same time, that I am only held back from following you into the "depths"—*these* depths of analogical, amatory exchange—by being held captive, myself. Thus, the ultimate hold of the poem is not love, but the "hero [*Held*]," the last word that marks its limit and stops "my" speaking, after the initial apostrophe has turned away from the modus of direct address; after "I" am articulated separately from "you" for the first time in the last strophe; and after the present tensions of seeking and seething fire have been recast as an act of the earth in the preterite tense, and thus separated from the time of speech in such a way that now nothing more—no further talk of "you" or "flames," and thus no talk of "me," either—could follow.

Prophecy—speaking for or in the place of another—can perhaps only go so far. Yet only when nothing more could follow, could the poem, properly speaking, have begun: with the end of the hero and the separation of his destiny from the one who lives to tell it; with the moment when the "divine fire [*göttlich Feuer*]" no longer immediately "wells up and gleams deep from the earth," but the ambivalent "power of the earth" is held sacred. This earth, however—which is as holy to me "as [*wie*]" you are, while holding you holy "as [*wie*]" I do—complicates any direct relation between "you" and "me," while remaining separate—and *thus* sacred—itself.[15] The structure of mediation resembles one that Paul de Man traces in an essay devoted to "Wordsworth and Hölderlin," but without specific mention of "Empedokles," when he writes of "the moment of active projection into the future," in which the self temporarily goes lost, until it can imagine itself again "in a past from which it is separated by the experience of a failure." He continues, to suggest that "interpretation is possible only from a standpoint that lies on the far side of this failure, and that has escaped destruction thanks to an effort of consciousness to make sure of itself once again," only to add: "but this consciousness can be had only by one who has very extensively partaken of the danger and failure" (58). Yet the breach between poet and "Poet" here—which doubling, according to de Man's analysis, also runs through Hölderlin's poetic oeuvre (62–63)—may also preclude the kind of recuperation he traces elsewhere in Hölderlin's corpus. Here, from the very beginning, everything starts after its end, when nothing could follow.

Already in the first line—to follow the order of Hölderlin's words— "you" are first named after what "you seek" ("life, you seek it [*Das Leben suchst du*]"), such that "life" gets left behind before the "seeking" begins. From the outset, "you" can no longer pursue what you seek—for it is already behind you—hence, seeking becomes absolute, as the verb doubles, this time without subject or object—"you seek, seek [*suchst du, suchst*]"—as though you could no longer seek anything, but the absolute itself: purification, "pyrification," in the fire of Aetna, which, at once, "wells up and gleams [. . .] to you." These flames, meanwhile, correspond and coincide with your seeking: they are coordinated with it by the conjunction "and" and narrated in the same tense, so that no moment in this sequence has priority over another. Similarly, the only end rhyme of the entire poem reflects the harmony in your "trembling longing [*in schauderndem Verlangen*]" and "in Aetna's flames [*in des Aetna Flammen*]." And insofar as both stand "*in*" an alignment that contains your fall—and insofar as the phrase "*you, in trembling longing*" is already a hyperbaton, before you have "*cast* yourself"—it is implied that the longing already burns; that the whole strophe turns in the throe of this cast; that it is one, instantaneous hyperbole, long gone down in flames.

"In the flames": Hölderlin's first draft of the ode begins where the first strophe of the published version will end, and in a way that emphasizes all the more the confusion of beginning and ending, the elimination of sequence and priority, that takes place with each approach to this fire in language:

> In the flames you seek life, your heart bids and beats and you follow and cast yourself downward into Aetna.

> In den Flammen suchst du das
>   Leben, dein Herz gebietet und pocht und
>   Du folgst und wirfst dich in
>   den Aetna hinab. (5: 428)

And this time, again, "you" were already inflamed before "you follow" the bidding of "your heart," as though you were already among the flames, as "you [. . .] cast yourself" toward them "into Aetna." And as for the flames themselves: they are also over and past your motions from start to finish, the hyperbole of your overthrow, and perhaps even the "hyperbole of hyperboles," to borrow the figure Hölderlin will evoke in his prose text that begins, "When the poet is once in the power of spirit [*Wenn der Dichter einmal des Geistes mächtig ist*]." For hyperbole aims at nothing less than the poetic attempt to surpass all figures—over and above synthesis and opposition, as well as their harmonic opposition—and to grasp thereby "the original poetic individuality, the poetic I" per se (14: 234, my translation).

Above all and below all, flames mark each instant throughout this ode, instantaneously, and in such a way that no moment of the ode could be held or taken for a moment at all. Like the "burning points" that David Farrell Krell has analyzed in Hölderlin's *Empedokles* and his poetological texts from this time, they elude grasp (*Lunar Voices* 24–25, 37–40).[16] Yet precisely because of these burning points, Hölderlin's triadic ode, with all its variants, is prophetic of the way he will begin a triad of poetological-cal fragments several years later, between his second and third unfinished drafts of *Empedokles*, recasting the ode in a prose that renders the plunge of Empedocles, the poetic language that might address him, and, ultimately, the possibility of language per se, still more radically contingent upon a prior conflagration that would also have been their end. There, Hölderlin situates the start of tragic language again with an ode that begins "in highest fire"—"The tragic ode begins in the highest fire [*Die tragische Ode fängt im höchsten Feuer an*]" (13: 868)[17]—and thus: as a tragedy of language before any drama and beyond any poem.

How might this language translate? As the tragic ode begins in the highest fire, fire is the matter that ravishes, that "tears away [*hinreißt*]," over and past every boundary, limit, or hold:

> The tragic ode begins in the highest fire; pure spirit, pure intensity has over-stepped its boundary, has failed to hold those alliances of life that necessarily and thus even without fire incline to contact, as it were, moderately enough, alliances that through their quite intense attunement become inclined to ex-cess, consciousness, reflection, or physical sensuality; and so, through excess [*Übermaas*] of intensity, the conflict has arisen, which the tragic ode invents at the very outset in order to present the pure.[18]
>
> Die tragische Ode fängt im höchsten Feuer an, der reine Geist, die reine Innigkeit hat ihre Grenze überschritten, sie hat diejenigen Verbindungen des Lebens, die nothwendig also gleichsam ohnediß zum Contact geneigt sind, und durch die ganz innige Stimmung dazu übermäßig geneigt werden, das Bewußtseyn, das Nachdenken, oder die physische Sinnlichkeit nicht mäßig genug gehalten, und so ist, durch Übermaas der Innigkeit, der Zwist entstanden, den die tragische Ode gleich zu Anfang fingirt, um das Reine darzustellen. (13: 868)

This fire is not the fire of Zeus that will incinerate Semele, giving birth to Dionysos, and with him, his tragedy, however crucial this moment will be for Hölderlin's poetics, as writers such as Bernhard Böschenstein have shown.[19] Nor is it the fire of Apollo that strikes Hölderlin, as he will write in a letter to Casimir Böhlendorff after his return from Bordeaux (19: 499). And it is certainly not the fire of Hegel's (Luther-inspired) hymn of hot devotion, which was to have been the first language of "the universal self-consciousness of all" (*Phänomenologie* 381) in his *Phenomenology of Spirit*. This fire and in it the "tragic ode"—which may name no genre before or beyond this text—begins, as it were, sui generis.[20] And beginning in flames, as the "alliances of life" have failed to be "held moderately enough," it initiates and ignites a barren genre with no generation, isolated, desolate, and desolating—a "tragische Öde." Nothing could follow this unprecedented eruption of desolation, and if this ode appears to have a history—"pure intensity *has* overstepped its boundary, *has* failed to hold"—this does not necessarily imply that an equilibrium had gone before it, but only that the boundaries or definitions that could make any such balance tenable first become evident once they are trespassed and set ablaze. Thus, the ode "invents at the very outset" the fiction of a past for a present that could not have been maintained for a moment.

From start to finish, each word of the text writes and overwrites the possibility that what is said could take place and that what is said to take place could ever be uttered purely. From start to finish, all that is proposed is an absolute, pure inception, which repeatedly loses hold, divides, and dissolves, in a series of reprisals, "in order to present the pure": for every step turns out to be another beginning, over and beyond the first.[21] According to an etymology that Hölderlin consciously, reflectively, or utterly unwittingly turns into a *figura etymologica* with the last clause of his sentence: "which the tragic ode invents at the very outset [*gleich zu Anfang fingirt*]," "anfangen [*to begin*]" implies, like the Latinate "fingieren [*invent*]," to touch and take hold. "Originally," write the Grimm brothers in their *German Dictionary*, it meant "to seize upon something (capere) [*ursprünglich an etwas fahen (capere)*]" (Grimm and Grimm 1: 325).[22] And so, the absolute beginning Hölderlin initially posits in apposition to "pure spirit, pure intensity" is repeated precisely in the holding on and holding in of that "intensity [*Innigkeit*]."[23] Still more than this, insofar as that intensity is "pure"—delimited and determined by nothing else, and therefore absolutely excessive—it has also already "arisen," stood out (*ent-standen*), existed and exited, from the very start. At once holding in and standing without, the initial intensity of the beginning parts through its "excess [*Übermaas*]" and redoubles again in and as the "conflict [*Zwist*]," which is literally rendered in the phrase "gleich zu An*fang fing*irt," where the words for "beginning" and "invention" touch and thus set the beginning at odds with itself. And even before this, the "conflict [*Zwist*]" alone—which implies at once the twisting and twining of separate strands as much as the twaining of two—reprises through its proper duplicity the way in which "pure *in*tensity" *ex*ceeds. Meanwhile, concomitant and intertwined with this deceptive inception, this "disinception," the inclination of the "alliances of life" cannot but decline, until they are no longer binding and already beyond grasp—as was anticipated by and from the beginning.

From the beginning, these are the operations of a rapid, incendiary language, the tongue of flames to "present the pure," which, in this context, in which one can only go too far, could not but be an impure word in its own right. Just after Hölderlin pairs two words of German origin and Latin invention—"zu Anfang fingirt"—"the pure [*das Reine*]" is presented in such a way that its Latin cognate "purus" immediately suggests itself, and not only as itself, but also as another word for the "fire"—in Greek: τὸ πῦρ, *tò pûr*—in which the tragic ode would have begun. If the tragic ode should present, and thereby translate, the pure that could have been before it, the passage that describes this purification recalls, yet again, that poetic fragment to which I repeatedly return: "But often as a firebrand / arises conf(used)usion of tongues [*Oft aber wie ein Brand / entstehet Sprachverw(irrt) irrung*]" (7: 377). With this conflation and conflagration of terms, Hölderlin's tragic ode suggests that the fire and the pure can be presented only when these words dissolve in a fire that transcends and incends each word of at least three languages (German, Greek, and Latin)—and that could thus be called the "impyrification" of the word. Thus, the ode to "Empedokles," as well as its reprisal in Hölderlin's prose-poem "The Tragic Ode," will have spoken of the fire, too, that breaks out in the text to follow his third draft of *Empedokles*, a prose piece that begins: "The fatherland in decline . . . [*Das untergehende Vaterland . . .*]." There, the language of tragedy begins in a "more heavenly fire [*himmlischer Feuer*]," offering nothing less than the possibility of a new language through the dissolution of all that was said or known before, and thus, paradoxically, of all that could still be said.[24] And above all, these texts from the so-called *corpus empedocleum* expose from the outset the fact—or fiction—that this language of flames is not one. Not only do Hölderlin's terms for it disintegrate into permutations of a fiery beginning that, since it has passed "its boundary," is, *per definitionem*, entirely dislimited and therefore never to begin definitively. They also each exceed, in turn, their proper senses as lexical items and incline toward other words of other tongues.

And beyond this point, where nothing more could follow and Hölderlin begins yet again, introducing a sequence from this instantaneous flash and tracing the further trajectory of the tragic ode—"It then goes further [*Sie gehet dann weiter*]"—the movement he bespeaks does not, properly speaking, come to speech, nor does it constitute a poem, as his later contrast of the "tragic ode" to the "tragic poem [*tragische Gedicht*]" at the very outset of his next prose fragment, "The General Basis [*Allgemeiner Grund*]," makes explicit (8: 868; Krell, *Death of Empedocles* 142). All the ode does is proceed from the utmost intensity—which Hölderlin now refers to as an "extreme of differentiation [*Extrem des Unterschiedens*]"—toward a "more modest intensity [*bescheidenere Innigkeit*]," before turning "back to its initial tone [*in den Anfangston zurück*]" (8: 868; Krell, *Death of Empedocles* 142). It thereby attains "the experience [*Erfahrung*] of, and insight [*Erkenntnis*] into, the heterogeneous"—through a motion that half echoes the tonal modulations Hölderlin will elaborate in other notes from around this time (14: 340–41, 369–72), and that half resembles the trajectory of a bildungsroman.[25] But even from the moment the ode is thus personified, it does not speak through the course it performs and perceives, but intends, extends, and even "falls [*fällt*]" to sentience of itself, in a dynamic of sheer tonality—which, itself another word for "tension,"[26] may never have referred in this fragment to anything that resounds, but only that which intends to. When, in "The General Basis," Hölderlin returns to this ode, he will call it the "unmediated language of sensibility [*unmittelbare Sprache der Empfindung*]," making plain: this is not yet language by any stretch, whether one turns to the resonance that this phrase had in the writings of Hölderlin's contemporaries, such as Johann Gottfried Herder, who uses it to describe the inarticulate vocalizations common to animals and men, and therefore no "language" in the proper sense;[27] or whether one hears in "Empfindung"—from *empfangen*, 'to receive'—the reception of the ode by itself, and thus the taking in and taking back of its ignitial, failed inception. In that case, however, its "language" would amount to no more than its self-withdrawal.

No more than its self-withdrawal, no sooner begun than burnt out, this "tragic ode" speaks as little as "you" did in Hölderlin's ode to "Empedocles." Nonetheless, as in that ode, this intensive instant also becomes the experience to and from which the poet would speak. It is also evoked, in retrospect, as the experience of a "poet [*Dichter*]" (13: 869) in the subsequent text on tragic poetry in Hölderlin's manuscript "The General Basis." And there, it will be imparted, at least in part, via an analogy that arises as abruptly here as it did then, with the leap to Cleopatra's pearls. For when Hölderlin goes further in his next prose fragment, the "sensibility [*Empfindung*]" of the tragic ode "no longer expresses itself immediately [*drükt sich nicht mehr unmittelbar aus*]"; it is "no longer the poet and his proper experience that appears" from this sheer emergency (13: 868–69; Krell, *Death of Empedocles* 142). At the same time, he continues, each poem "must have proceeded from poetic life and poetic actuality"—the very life whose limits were first felt in their transgression and failing, and which therefore must be "brought to life [*belebt werden*]" again—"because otherwise the right truth everywhere goes missing [*weil sonst überall die rechte Wahrheit fehlt*]" (13: 869; Krell, *Death of Empedocles* 143). And at this point, when nothing left is true, and right truth, missed; when the poet can no longer set forth his "experience"—which, if it is truly experience, will have to have perished from the start, in the highest fire—Hölderlin averts the devastating, logical conclusion of these premises—that, namely, truth could be nowhere and poetic life, a priori null and void—by suddenly turning elsewhere: "nothing at all can be understood and brought to life if we are unable to translate [*übertragen*] our own mind and our own experience to a foreign analogical material [*in einen fremden analogischen Stoff*]."[28]

Foreign, analogical material appears, then, to be the only possible vehicle by which truth, poet, and poem might not be utterly ravished and torn away, by diverting them, translating and transporting them over and past their proper logic, and thereby holding them back from the end they would have had to attain immediately before they could so much as begin.[29] The truth can only be preserved, withheld and held back—true to its name, *wahren*, 'to guard,' 'to ware'—by immediately disowning it, and the language of truth can only be foreign to its subject. To be sure, this alternative is eminently questionable. Does this logic not amount to the disowning of any "empirical visibility," and thus, to the disowning of the foreign protagonist as well, as Stanley Corngold has suggested in his reading of this passage (217–18)? Furthermore, "how could 'our own experience,'" as Corngold continues, "be preserved when our own 'true temporal and sensory connections' are annihilated" (217)? And to these impasses, one might add: in Hölderlin's "General Basis," any duration depends upon speaking from another time, as another—insofar as each sensation is exposed and extinguished to the degree that it is intense. "The most intense sensibility," Hölderlin writes, "is exposed to transitoriness to the degree that it has not denied truly temporal and sensuous relationships [*die innigste Empfindung ist der Vergänglichkeit in eben dem Grade ausgesezt, in welchem sie die wahren zeitlichen und sinnlichen Beziehungen nicht verläugnet*]" (13: 869, Krell 143). Thus, it is not only true that the most intensely personal speech can take place only through a most precarious impersonation; time itself must become untimely. Above all, the "General Basis [*Allgemeiner Grund*]" of the tragic poem, as of any other; the metaphoric ground upon which Hölderlin will found this poetics of "godly fire"—which is no ground, properly speaking, but a metaphor, a translation from the proper to the foreign, and, ultimately, a movement over nowhere—is, first of all, denial (*Verläugnung*), and, by way of denial, it lies.[30]

Repeating the verb "verläugnen" thrice, Hölderlin thus elaborates the structure of analogy:

Thus in the tragic dramatic poem too the divinity the poet senses and experiences in his own world expresses itself; the tragic dramatic poem too is for the poet an image of the living, of that which is and always was present to him in his own life; yet as this image of intensity everywhere *denies* its ultimate basis, and as it has to *deny* it ever more, to the degree that it everywhere approximates the symbol; the more infinite and ineffable the intensity is, that is, the nearer such intensity comes to the *nefas*, and the more rigorously and more coldly the image has to distinguish the human and his felt element in order to hold the sensibility fast within its boundaries, the less is the image capable of expressing that sensibility immediately; it has to *deny* sensibility in both its form and material; the material has to be a bolder more foreign likeness and exemplar of that sensibility, while the form has to bear more the character of counterposing and separating.[31] (13: 869; Krell 143, my emphases)

"Everywhere," the "ultimate basis" of "this image of intensity"—which is too an image of "the living," and an expression too of "divinity," as they are set in apposition, used nearly synonymously, and therefore intimately intertwined throughout this passage—is and must be denied. Insofar as this "denial" constitutes the "general basis" of the poem, the "basis" itself could be nothing other than an image for what is, ultimately, groundless. And it would have to be, then, at least as abyssal as the indefinite "depths," toward and from which the ode to "Empedocles" tends. "Everywhere"—where, that is, truth would always "go missing"—a ground is transported instead, as the denial of an "ultimate basis" that would be an ultimum, a "Leztes" or "last" that is the further than far, but no basis upon which anything but its proper fiction might begin to be laid.

As in Kant, whose discussion of analogy and the symbol in §59 "On Beauty as Symbol of Ethicality" from the *Critique of the Power of Judgment* Hölderlin reprises and reconfigures here—down to the "Ground," which Kant cites as his first example of the way "our language is full of such indirect presentations according to an analogy" (*Kritik der Urteilskraft* 713)—analogy does not relate four terms that subsist independently, such that, if three are given, the fourth could be deduced.[32] Analogy concerns, instead, relations, whereby the power of judgment carries out, as Kant puts it, a "duplicitous business [*doppeltes Geschäft*], first bringing a concept to bear upon an object of sensual intuition, and then the mere rule of reflection over that intuition upon an entirely different object, of which the first is only the symbol" and to which, he adds, "perhaps no intuition could ever directly correspond" (713, 714, my translation). Thus, too, "all of our knowledge of God is merely symbolic, as are all of our words for the operations of logic, from the "ground [*Grund*]," to anything "depending (being held from above) [*Abhängen (von oben Gehalten werden)*]" upon it, to "what follows [*Folge*]" from it (714). And so, over and above even the logical functions it should denote—which themselves depend upon analogy, in order to be articulated at all—analogy no longer relates concepts or objects of appearance, but carries out the presentation of sheer relations. Accordingly, analogy—despite its terms—no longer has a determinate or determinable halt: it may also get carried away, overshoot, and overturn into the excess it most intensely verges upon. This is a consequence that Kant will not draw from his radical reinterpretation of analogical presentation,[33] but Hölderlin, who follows Kant's reflections upon analogy further and thinks them through to their "ultimate basis," does exactly this, drawing out the way in which a logic of sheer relations necessarily implies their possible increase or decrease, ad infinitum. Hölderlin's analogy thus crosses limits—and beyond the limits of its proper terms, it also crosses the limits of those philosophical studies devoted to Hölderlin, which do not reflect upon the rhetoric of philosophy, in both senses of the genitive. In, for example, Dieter Henrich's reconstruction of Hölderlin's readings in Kant, Friedrich Heinrich Jacobi, and Fichte, his analysis of Hölderlin's reception of Kant's *Critique of the Power of Judgment* remains restricted to a discussion of the concept of beauty (266–85), rather than extending to the ways in which both Kant's and Hölderlin's writings exceed conceptual grasp. Yet henceforth, according to Hölderlin's analogy, even the "infinite" can exceed itself: "the more infinite and ineffable the intensity is, that is, the nearer such intensity comes to the *nefas*, [. . .] the more rigorously and more coldly the image has to distinguish the human and his felt element" (13: 869; Krell 143). And even if this critical distinction should take place "in order to hold the sensibility fast within its boundaries," that hold, as a matter of infinite gradations, is thoroughly imaginary and can also be no definitive end,[34] any more than denial itself has any limit—: "yet [. . .] this image of intensity everywhere denies its ultimate basis, and [. . .] has to deny it ever more. [. . .]" (13: 869; Krell 143).

As Hölderlin proceeds to call analogy "denying," and, ultimately, translates it with the foreign "*nefas*," this move reflects no arbitrary departure from Kant, but names that "duplicitous business" still more improperly than his predecessor. As in Kant, analogy opens and offers the only way to say what cannot be said directly at all—and says, thereby, what is unsayable. Thus, it must not only deny the unsayable in addressing it but also deny its unsayability; over and above denial (*Verläugnung*), it is, properly speaking: an "analaugy."[35] Analogously, the Latin *nefas*—which means "what is opposed to divine law" and comes from the negative particle "ne" and "fari," the verb for "to speak, to say"—says as much as well, as Susan Bernofsky has also pointed out (100). Moreover, since "nefas" can refer here only to the maximum "intensity," which is divine, the ultimate divine abomination conflates, conflagrates in this word with the divine itself, in a tension not unlike the "conflict [*Zwist*]" of the tragic ode, or, as Hölderlin will write several years later in his "Remarks to Oedipus," the way "the god and man pair and [. . .] the power of nature and the innermost core of man are becoming one in wrath [*wie der Gott und Mensch sich paart, und gränzenlos die Naturmacht und des Menschen Innerstes im Zorn Eins wird*]." With the difference that, in the later remarks, Hölderlin will interpret the nefarious "character of counterposing and separating" more infinitely, saying that "the boundless becoming-one purifies itself through boundless scission [*das gränzenlose Eineswerden durch gränzenloses Scheiden sich reiniget*]" (16: 257, my translation).[36] And before that, the more profane analogy of love and pairing that Hölderlin draws in the second strophe of "Empedocles" to the royal couple and pair of pearls—which are espoused only in *sponsio*, and which utterly dissect and dissolve, twice over—operates just as nefariously, in order to further near "you," who only burn and do not speak—*ne fas* . . . .[37]

Neither "you" nor "I" could speak alone, not even alone with each other, without another to intervene. Nothing between us translates directly, and when Hölderlin returns to the operation of analogy once more in the poetological prose text that begins, "When the poet is once in power of spirit . . . [*Wenn der Dichter einmal des Geistes mächtig ist . . .*]," written from back to front in the midst of the notebook now known as the *Stuttgarter Foliobuch*, he presents analogy as the only way that would permit the "I" to know itself as the "poetic I"—just as it is, more exactly, the only operation that would permit this "I" to know itself in its "three-fold property [*dreifachen Eigenschaft*]"—as "the known [*das erkannte*]," "the knowing one [*das Erkennende*]," and "the knowledge of both [*die Erkentniß beeder*]" (14: 233). This knowing will turn out to be the presentiment and precondition for language, too, as the last strain of this text indicates, where Hölderlin writes—"Is language not like the knowledge just discussed, and of which it was said that in it, as oneness, the unified [*Einige*, lit: 'oned'] was contained, and vice versa? [*Ist die Sprache nicht, wie die Erkenntniß von der die Rede war, u. von ihr gesagt wurde daß in ihr, als Einheit das Einige enthalten seie, und um(h)g|e(g)k|ehrt?*]" (14: 213). He then goes on to temporize this analogy—"Just as knowledge has presentiment of language, so too does language remember knowledge [*So wie die Erkentniß die Sprache ahndet, so erinnert sich die Sprache der Erkentniß*]" (14: 210)—through a chiasmus that draws knowledge and language together while keeping them apart, as the one leads to the other by way of its proper dissolution.[38] Alone, this knowledge, crossed with language, is never quite pure, like the pure fire of the tragic ode, and its fictive beginning. Its beginning is indeterminate, insofar as "poetic language appears here in the point of intersection between presentiment and remembrance" as Rainer Nägele has written in his monograph *Hölderlins Kritik der poetischen Vernunft* (23)—whereby this point could never be fixed once and for all.[39] And this knowledge alone is, as Hölderlin will prove again, testing the limits of thinking through knowing, absolutely impossible. For no one member of this trinity knows and is known at once, and none can be subject or object of knowing without the others. "I" can either know something and therefore fail to know myself and my knowing, or I can know only myself, knowing nothing else and therefore nothing at all—just as none, at the same time, knows or can be known without the separate articulation of each member.

Always all in one, and at any given time, only one of all—"all-ein"—and therefore none:[40] such is the "real contradiction [*reale Widerspruch*]" (14: 233) that unfolds here.[41] This contradiction cannot be resolved by turning to Hölderlin's philosophical reception of Jacobi's and Wilhelm Heinse's responses to Spinoza's monism—which was the most debated modern version of the Greek *hen kai pan*, "One and All"—or by focusing exclusively on the positive ways one might, as Henrich writes on *Hyperion*, describe a "course through the conflicts of one's formation and world experience [. . .] to the insight, in which a life collects and completes itself" (171). For this contradiction is also the one Empedocles will have uttered repeatedly throughout Hölderlin's drafts of the drama, as when he addresses himself in the second draft, in his opening monologue—"you [. . .] should have felt yourself free and great and rich in your proper world—and again alone, alas! and again alone? [*du [. . .] sollst / frei und groß und reich / In eigner Welt dich fühlen— / Und wieder einsam, weh! und wieder einsam?*]" (13: 826–27). For these words also indicate that he can only know and say his determination and "proper world" by addressing it to "you"; that the imperative to feel freedom must have failed; and that his "loneliness" stands alone, severed from him and "you" alike. Even as it culminates in an exclamation of proper pain (*Weh*)—in an expression of proper sensibility—this utterance, too, becomes radically uncertain, returning as a question in an echo that belongs to none and that calls even the repetition of this echo into question: "and again alone [*und wieder einsam*]?"[42]

No amount of talk from him to me to you can resolve this fundamental contradiction, but rather—

> when it [the I] is made determinately distinguishable through a third; when this third, insofar as it was chosen with freedom, and insofar too as it does not, in its influences and determinations, cancel out the pure individuality, but can be observed by it; where it [the pure individuality], then, observes itself at once as something determined through a choice, empyrically individualized, and characterized; only then is it possible that the I appears as oneness in harmonically opposed life, and conversely, that the harmonically opposed appears as oneness in the I and becomes an object in beautiful individuality.[43] (14: 233–32, my translation)

Nothing takes place but *"through"* a third—which cannot, from the outset, be the third of the "threefold property" named a few lines earlier in this text. For so long as that one can only ever be directly experienced as two—whether it be knowing and known, subject and object, or active and receptive; so long as each twofold configuration necessarily implies one-sidedness; and so long as this one-sidedness, opposed to another it cannot know and thus cannot truly oppose, can only cancel itself out; the transitivity that defines the "I" here—but most properly leaves it utterly indefinite—will have always been too rapid to constitute any relation or to lead anywhere. Hence, there must be two thirds, a second three, which makes the first "distinguishable [*unterscheidbar*]" to and for itself, which rends and renders it one in the first place.[44]

This transcendental deduction of the "poetic I," unlike Kant's, leads to another; this subject, unlike Fichte's, can only set itself elsewhere;[45] and this other is neither "you" nor "not-I"—both of which would be the immediate correlates of the "I," and thus participants in its proper annihilation—but what Hölderlin will soon call an "outer sphere [*äußere Sphäre*]," recalling his own directive that the poet transfer his mind and experience "to a foreign analogical material [*in einen fremden analogischen Stoff*]" (13: 869, 143). Unlike that formulation, too, however, Hölderlin's next sentence will go on to deny that any transference takes place in this displacement, in this ex-orbitant eduction through which the "I" becomes distinct by no longer remaining in itself or in its proper sphere. For, in writing next the imperative for "you," as for every "I"—"Set yourself *in with free choice* in harmonic opposition in with out an outer s[ph]ere, as you are in *harmonic* opposition in yourself, by nature, but in an unknowable way, so long as you remain in yourself" (14: 229, my translation)[46]—Hölderlin crosses out the "in" before the "outer sphere" that would have rendered this passage analogous to the "General Basis." And he replaces the "through" that had modified "choice" earlier in this text with "with."

With the phrase "with an outer sphere," Hölderlin translates his analogical sine qua non of poetic presentation to a structure where nothing is carried over or through, but is carried out and withheld at once. "You," no longer "in yourself," are without—but without entering in the outer, other sphere at all. The exigency of this outer sphere for any "you" or "I" opens no passage, but for an utterly precarious interval in which no one and nothing properly belongs, and all is held suspended. The point of suspension reached here is not unlike the verge of Aetna, although the sense of that topos, as well as the nature of the outer sphere it verges upon, will have to be analyzed further below. Alone, however, this halt to analogy would seem to suggest that, in its radical unboundedness, Hölderlin's earlier thinking on this structure had gone too far; that its motion would need to be held back halfway; and that speech, translation, and analogy—all alike—could take place only at a utopic point that would neither be proper nor foreign in the sense that it were ever proper to another. Rather, between expropriation and appropriation, it could occur solely at an instant of utterly improper standstill. In the ode to "Empedocles," the name for this suspension, for this third instance, was "love [Liebe]," and here as before, this instance proves instable, insofar as the possibility cannot be eliminated that this other sphere might still "in its influences and determinations, cancel out the pure individuality," whereby one displacement in either direction would lead to dissolution—either into the foreign "influences and determinations" that would "cancel the pure individuality" or into the properly threefold nullness from before. Hölderlin therewith suggests that the tension of mutual withholding and partial denial that "you" should seek to establish would be nearly as precarious as utter abandon, and that the one sphere may at any point prevail upon the other. But also without such an eventuality, this pure intensity at and of the limit, insofar as it is outside both spheres that delimit it, has already per definitionem overstepped, and thus cannot but incline toward contact—toward, that is, the conflagratory conflict that will have incinerated the tragic ode.

This is a consequence that Hölderlin will not explicitly draw from his radical reinterpretation of analogical presentation, though the implicit excess of the interval he seeks to point out is intimated in the way the "I" becomes "empyrically individualized [empyrischindividualisiert]," where Hölderlin conflates a transliteration of the Greek word ἔμπυρος (empyros), "that which is in the fire," with the German word "empirisch," "empirical." Elsewhere in Hölderlin's writings, "empirisch" is spelled with an *i*,[47] and even if the *y* were a slip of the pen, what Hölderlin writes out as "empyrischindividualisiert" tends nonetheless toward the flames in which Empedocles, the "tragic ode," "you," and "I" converge. And beyond this, Hölderlin's idiosyncratic, individualized spelling of the "empyrical" intimates, too, that his references elsewhere to "in the flames [*in den Flammen*]" and "in highest fire [*in höchstem Feuer*]" may themselves have been translations of the Greek word ἔμπυρος, and thus on the verge all along of the other sphere it touches upon.

In ancient Greek, ἔμπυρος not only means "that which is in the fire," as one might literally translate this composite from ἐν ('in') and πῦρ ('fire'). It also refers to those burnt offerings that would be made to the gods and from which mantics would read their divinations, as at the start of Pindar's eighth Olympian ode:[48]

> O mother, of the gold-crowned games, Olympia, ruler of truth, where men who are seers, marking with the things-in-the-fire [ἐμπύροις], probe Zeus of the silver thunderbolt to learn if he holds any word concerning mortals who are striving in their hearts to gain a great success and respite from their toils. (Race 137, trans. modified)

> Μᾶτερ, ὦ χρυσοστεφάνων
> ἀέθλων, Οὐλυμπία,
> δέσποιν' ἀλαθείας, ἵνα μάντιες ἄνδρες
> ἐμπύροις τεκμαιρόμενοι παραπει-
>   ρῶνται Διὸς ἀργικεραύνου,
> εἴ τιν' ἔχει λόγον ἀνθρώπων πέρι
> μαιομένων μεγάλαν
> ἀρετὰν θυμῷ λαβεῖν,
> τῶν δὲ μόχθων ἀμπνοάν (15: 164, lines 1–9)

Here, where Olympia is praised as the ruler of truth and situated as the utterly duplicitous place for prophecy; where, from the start, she splits between the place of contest and the higher Olympia of the gods, mantic men mark "things-in-the-fire," to "probe [παραπειρῶνται]"—that is, attempt, test, and provoke—Zeus. And they probe Zeus, the god of the gods and the god of the games—whose lightning here already redoubles the fires that solicit him—to experience whether "he holds any word." Here is, in other words—and in something other than words—the doubled burning point where the ground and the heavens meet "with the things-in-the-fire," which appears in the midst of the world and in the exact midst of the strophe, according to the edition of Christian Gottlob Heyne that Hölderlin had used as the basis for his translations.

At this precarious meeting of the mantics' signs and a word of Zeus, the more usual relationship of language to portents in antiquity reverses, and the mantics' signs solicit a divine word, rather than providing words for a divine sign. And beyond this point, the fire involves the world in at least one more way.[49] For here, the things of the world in the fire are marked (τεκμαιρόμενα) as signs only insofar as they are incinerated, destroyed, and dissolved. And should the mantic men who seek to "probe [παραπειρῶνται]" Zeus in this way—and who thereby set the world on trial by fire, too—be spared from imperiling themselves in this experience by operating askance and standing aside (παρά), the verb παραπειρῶνται, in the middle voice, also implies that these agents are the patients of their actions, and therefore almost as exposed to the contingency of earthly and heavenly fire as the things they burn. The experience of the para-empirical, then, for the sake of a word held by Zeus—which may remain withheld and may not be at all—is thus nearly empyrical for all involved. And furthermore, it proves to be the experience of a limit of language, where the precarious, thoroughly contingent possibility nearly emerges that flames might become tongues.

Similarly, Tiresias uses the word ἔμπυρος in Sophocles's *Antigone*, when he reports that he has heard an "unknown voice [ἀγνῶτ[α] φθόγγον]" (Hölderlin, *Sämtliche Werke: Frankfurter Ausgabe* 16: 368, line 998) of birds and, "fearing, made trial [lit: tasted] straightaway of the things-in-the-fire [ἐμπύρων] upon all-blazing altars [εὐθὺς δὲ δείσας ἐμπύρων ἐγευόμην / βωμοῖσι παμφλέκτοισιν]" (16: 368, lines 1002–03, my translation)—bringing "the things in the fire" even closer to the tongue over a relationship of taste, which Hölderlin will render: "Quickly I feared, and tasted the flame, upon all-enkindled alters [*Schnell befürchtet' ich, / Und kostete die Flamm', auf allentzündeten / Altären*]" (16: 369, my translation). And if Hölderlin would translate Sophocles after his attempts to render the tragedy of Empedocles were long abandoned, his translations of Pindar's epinician odes, or songs for athletic victors, appear in the same octavo as the clean copy of the second draft of *Empedokles*. This draft in particular bears traces of those epinicia and recasts the philosopher-poet into Aetna as an athletic victor, nearing the end: "It speeds for him, the pains, the flight, and like the chariot-driver, when the wheel begins to burn upon the track, the endangered one races only all the faster to the crown! [*Es Beschleunigen ihm / Die Schmerzen den Flug und wie der*

Wagenlenker, / Wenn ihm das Rad in der Bahn / zu rauchen beginnt, eilt, / Der Gefährdete nur schneller zum Kranze!]" (12: 394–95). In this passage, one finds the topoi, hyperbata, and syntactic inversions that, as Albrecht Seifert and Felix Christen have conveyed in their studies of his translations, mark Hölderlin's Pindar.[50] And indeed, his Pindar—especially the eighth Olympian Ode—will likewise speak to the fires of his *Empedokles* project, and all that is at stake with them—which, by analogy, addresses nothing less than mantic language, and its truth.

In the octavo, among other epinicians, and near to Empedocles and his fire, Hölderlin translates the opening of the eighth Olympian ode:

> Mother, o you of the golden-crowned contest, Olympia, you ruler of truth, where intimating [*ahnende*] men, concluding from holy flame, experience by Zeus, the bright-fulgurating one, when he by chance has a word, by men to be received, [men] striving after great virtues, in mind, and [after] the breathing from toils.

> Mutter, o du des goldgekrönten
> Kampfspiels, Olympia,
> Du Herrscherin der Wahrheit, wo ahnende Männer
> Aus heiliger Flamme schließend,
> Erfahren von Zeus, dem helleblizenden
> Wenn etwa er hat ein Wort von Männern
> Strebend nach großen
> Tugenden im Gemüthe zu empfangen
> Und der Mühen Umathmung (15: 165).

In this strophe alone, translation becomes a matter of displacement that exceeds an attempt to render Pindar's Greek into German or to grecize Hölderlin's mother tongue,[51] and goes further, with the displacement of and among the words in these verses themselves. To begin, "toils [*Mühen*]" turns to a turn of breath, which, neither exhalation nor inhalation, but rather a "breathing [*Athmung*]" "around [*Um*]," is a "breathing [*Umathmung*]" that surrounds the atmosphere with toil rather than its relief—to the letter: "der *Mühe Umathmung*"—and which is, above and before this, a toil in mind, or "*Gemüthe*," as well as its more proper, virtuous inversion, "*Tugend*." This vaporization of toil in and of language begins, as in Pindar, in the exact middle of the strophe, but here, more nearly, with the "experience by Zeus, the bright-fulgurating one [*Erfahren von Zeus, dem helleblizenden*]." Whereas the first several verses address the "Mother" in a fairly straightforward way, the experience of Zeus opens the strophe to the ambivalences that will culminate in the sheer dislimitation of linguistic toil. For the redoubling of "by Zeus [*von Zeus*]" and "by men [*von Männern*]," suggests that the word that is supposed to come from Zeus could also be a word from men, "to be received [*zu empfangen*]" by him. In other words, "ahnende Männer [. . .] erfahren von Zeus [. . .] wenn etwa er hat ein Wort von Männern," could, in a breathtaking turn, translate to: "intimating men experience from Zeus whether he has a word from men," as well as: "intimating men experience from Zeus whether he has a word about men." Furthermore, the designation of "Zeus" as "the bright-fulgurating one" already guarantees, with the active participle, that his holy fire answers the "holy flame" of "intimating men." Likewise, the immediately preceding verse suggests, with the ambiguity of "aus heiliger Flamme," that the lightning of Zeus in Hölderlin's Pindar may itself be that very holy fire. Either way, all around, the intimate contingency of "holy fire" and divine fulguration exposes the peril of this experience still more intensely than Pindar had in his version. And so, by the time the "men" return in the sixth verse of the strophe, they have lost their "intimating [*ahnende*]" disposition toward the flame and are merely "striving [. . .] to receive [*strebend* [. . .] *zu empfangen*]." Yet although they are active and receptive at once, they remain without an inkling—*keine Ahnung*—of what, empirically and empyrically, comes to pass, and thus become themselves, too, "in mind" as well as "virtue," utterly surrendered to their incendiary surroundings.

Hence the dissolution of language that follows. Hence, too, the shift from Pindar's "things-in-the-fire [ἐμπύροις]" to Hölderlin's "from holy flame [*Aus heiliger Flamme*]," marking an all-around exigency that opens to an outer atmosphere with no definite limits, and that is, at once, just as rapidly "closing [*schließend*]," since the boundary between openness and closure will have hereby been eliminated. Nothing is concluded here but an utterly other sphere of sheer toil, in and through the "word" from Zeus that burns his mantic men, and that burns in and through each word here—"der Mühen Umathmung." And by rendering the "mantic men [μάντιες ἄνδρες]" of Pindar "intimating men [*ahnende Männer*]," Hölderlin also emphasizes the proximity between these mantics and the "empyrically individualized [*empyrischindividualisierte*]" subject from his other text on "the poet in power of spirit . . . ," which, undivided from the fire, can only haltlessly dissolve, and which, on the verge of conflagration with an outer sphere, "has a presentiment of language [*die Sprache ahndet*]" (14: 210).

The foremost empyrical and empirical individual for Hölderlin, however, is another—: the poet who is so much "in power of spirit," who intones this spirit so intensely, and who thereby touches so closely upon another sphere that he provokes his devotee Panthea to exclaim: "the tone from his breast! in every syllable resounded all melodies! and the spirit in his word! [*der Ton aus seiner Brust! in jeder Silbe / klangen alle Melodien! und der Geist in seinem Wort!*]" (13: 699, my translation).[52] And ultimately, he touches so closely, to the point that this "excess of intensity [*Übermaas der Innigkeit*]" (13: 872)[53] will dissolve appearance and person alike, leaving the subject of this tragic öde, already from the very start of his tragedy, "silent and deathly deserted [*stumm und todesöde*]" (13: 709, my translation). He remains, then, foreign to even his closest disciple, Pausanias, who wonders: "Were you alone? The words I heard not, but the foreign death tone tolls for me still [*Warst du allein? Die Worte hört' ich nicht, / Doch schallt mir noch der fremde Todeston*]" (13: 707, my translation). The foremost empyrical and empirical individual for Hölderlin is, in other words, the foreign, tragic subject who both tears him away and appears to offer a foothold for thinking through tragic language and time, at once true to his name—with "fame [κλέος]" as the "grounded [ἔμπεδος]" one,[54] or famed for "impeding [ἐμποδίζειν]"[55]—and who, untrue to that wisdom, will cast himself "downward into Aetna's flames" to seek dissolutely the language, ground, and life he will have lost (5: 430). The foremost empyrical and empirical individual for Hölderlin is, in a word—Empedocles.

In a word, Empedocles, who is burned out from the very outset and already burning for a new word, seeks to utter and offer more than can be said and therefore nefariously approaches the burning point that would yield the divine word he never held, nor could have. Whereas in the tragedies of Sophocles, Tiresias, the fire-tasting mantic, intervenes with his word in the rapid course of tragic time and thereby temporarily interrupts its succession (16: 250), the tragedy of Empedocles is a tragedy of the mantic sign that never arrives and can only be sought. More nearly, it is a tragedy of the mantic sign that should have prophesied and translated not only a word of the gods but the pure, "pyrified" word of language as such, and that can, ultimately, only be thrice denied.

In the first version, Empedocles offers, in words, what is "hallowed" to and of himself—"mein Heiligtum" (13: 745)—bidding the Agrigentians:

> dare it! what you inherited, attained, what the mouth of the fathers told,
> taught you, law and custom, the names of the old gods, forget it boldly
> [. . .]. (My translation)

> wagts! was ihr geerbt, was ihr erworben,
> Was euch der Väter Mund erzählt, gelehrt,

Gesez und Bräuch, der alten Götter Nahmen,
Vergeßt es kühn [. . .]. (13: 745)

He thereby offers nothing other than the exorbitant imperative to forget
the foundational alliances of life, the names of the gods, the language of the
fathers' mouth (*Mund*), and, with all of this, the fathers' world (*mundus*). In
Empedocles's mouth, nothing is held holy or sacred but the sacrificial offering of language and world alike, so that the spirit might "catch fire on the
light of heaven [*an des Himmels Licht entzünde[n]*]" (13: 745, my translation),
and "the word [*das Wort*]," as well as "the law [*das Gesez*]"—now named
in the singular, with the definite article, as though they will have then
come to be determined for the first and only time—might be imparted
anew. With this, all becomes contingent upon nothing less than a holocaust
that cannot come from his words or the Agrigentians'—though with few
exceptions, such as Jürgen Söring's reading of *Empedokles*, the radicality
of Empedocles's imperatives to the Agrigentians has not been emphasized
in most scholarship on this drama.[56] Nonetheless, there is one holdup:
the forgetfulness Empedocles calls for would dissolve mother tongue and
fatherland alike—which, therefore, cannot be called for without at once
holding back this lethal dissolution.

Hence, Empedocles's words, too, will have to be denied and abandoned
as a sheer placeholder—"it speaks, when I am far, in my stead, the flowers
of heaven, flowering constellations [*es sprechen, wenn ich ferne bin, statt meiner
/ Des Himmels Blumen, blühendes Gestirn*]" (13: 746, my translation). Still
less than that, his words will have to be cast as a superfluous placeholder
for what needs none—"Divinely present nature / needs no speech [*Die
göttlichgegenwärtige Natur / Bedarf der Rede nicht*]" (13: 747; Krell, *Death of
Empedocles* 93)—and for what, although and because it is already "divinely
present [*göttlichgegenwärtig*]," cannot be promised. Ultimately, Empedocles's
last words to the Agrigentians amount to nothing more than a withdrawal
of all that he will have said—

What I said while I still while here, 'tis but little, yet the ray, perhaps, of
light takes't along to the still source that might bless you, downward through
dawning clouds. (My translation)

Was ich gesagt,
Dieweil ich hie noch weile, wenig ists,
Doch nimmts der Stral vieleicht des Lichtes zu
Der stillen Quelle, die euch seegnen möchte,
Durch dämmernde Gewölke mit hinab. (13: 751)

With this withdrawal, in advance of his own, all that is and has been said by Empedocles is, literally, reduced to a minimum—less than "it [*es*]," it is a single *s* ("nimmt*s*"), which hisses rather than speaks, which sizzles and peters out. Its trajectory is utterly contingent. And as a "perhaps [*vieleicht*]" also breaks the "ray [*Stral*]" from the "light [*Licht*]" in his syntax, the possibility is deflected further still that this *s* might, for an instant, encounter, let alone be borne by, the light. This most inconspicuous gesture comes from the one who proclaims to impart what is most "hallowed [*Heiligtum*]" to him, and who says earlier, "I want to say all to you [*Ich will dir alles sagen*]" (13: 707, my translation), but boils down to saying this *s*. He thus implies that this's all there is to say. But this is not all, and this "little [*wenig*]," still too much: Empedocles then goes further, approaching the rim of Aetna, about to plunge into the flames, in order to become himself a "thing in the fire"—a sign in person, in the dissolution of both person and sign; a mantic who conflates with his empyromancy; an empyrically individualized subject who does not speak and, in not speaking, but translating himself into a foreign matter, would express, receive, and be the unspeakable in person, all at once. At that point, however, Empedocles breaks off with "trembling longing [*schauderndes / Verlangen*]" (13: 755), on the verge of the catastrophic point where, in Hölderlin's ode to "Empedocles," he will have cast himself downward—and where he must remain, held back by the unspeakable longing he speaks out. Over Hölderlin's translation of these words from the ode "Empedocles" to Empedocles in person—no longer a "you," and not quite an "I"—the catastrophe spoken of before becomes spoken before it can befall, and thus becomes one that can, at the same time, only be denied in and through the attempt to say the end and the all of saying—again, Empedocles's "Heiligtum."

Such an end of saying can only be perpetuated and said again differently, and for all the differences among the three drafts of *Empedokles*, the retraction of Empedocles's words will go further, and from draft to draft, it will appear to have never gone far enough. This excess takes place, first of all, in the way each new version presents the progressive fulfillment of Empedocles's imperatives from the first draft and proves them to fail in and through that very fulfillment. Even when, in the second draft, the people of Akragas will be said to have already forgotten language, law, gods, and customs;[57] and after, in the third draft, that "uprising [*Aufruhr*]"—which stretches from field to house to temple (13: 943)—will be said to have not only occurred again but also resulted in "free firm bonds [*freie[n] veste[n] Bande[n]*]" (13: 944),[58] among the people the dissolution and renewal that Empedocles had once called for dissolves itself anew.

This dissolution follows most immediately from the fact that all of this is also said to have taken place through Empedocles's initiative alone. Contingent upon one person in this way, all that occurs so long as he lives would reflect nothing more than an excessive alliance to him in the sheer semblance of dissolution—as the opening words of Hermokrates and Mekades, with their ever more emphatic similes, make explicit at the very start of the second draft: "I know; like parched grass, humanity ignites [*Ich weiß, wie dürres Gras / Entzünden sich die Menschen*]" (13: 817; Krell, *Death of Empedocles* 114); "That One so moves the crowd seems to me as like when [*als wie wenn*] Jove's lightning bolt seizes the forest, and more terrible [*Daß Einer so die Menge bewegt, mir ists, / Als wie wenn Jovis Bliz den Wald / Ergreift, und furchtbarer*]" (13: 817, my translation). "As," "like": when the dissolution can be said to appear only in analogy to dissolution, dissolution too cannot but dissolve through analogy—as a mere appearance of itself, and therefore as the appearance of what, strictly speaking, cannot appear. As Corngold writes in his discussion of the "General Basis," "this *Verläugnung* takes place under a condition that in fact jeopardizes its work of negation" (217). Likewise, Hölderlin will go on in his later prose text on the "Basis of Empedocles" to deny the possibility that an individual could do more than appear to dissolve the problem of destiny, as this problem "can [. . .] never visibly and individually dissolve itself, since otherwise the universal would lose itself in the individual [*sich [. . .] niemals sichtbar und individuell auflösen kann, weil sonst das Allgemeine im Individuum sich verlöre*]" (13: 873). And, reprising the truth of analogy that he had traced earlier, Hölderlin goes on to say that no solution to destiny would be possible without its individual dissemblance—"from which onward, first then, the solution that was found will have to come to pass into the universal [*von dem aus dann erst, die gefundene Auflösung ins Allgemeine übergehen muß*]" (13: 873; Krell, *Death of Empedocles* 148). However, insofar as the necessitation of universal passage also recalls the imperative of dissolution that Empedocles utters and that the successive drafts of the drama refute—not least of all because an imperative could hardly constitute a dissolution, properly speaking, unless that imperative too were to dissolve—and insofar as the only dissolution to appear could still only be a merely apparent one, these remarks also intimate that the dissolution may itself be a fiction invented from the outset for something else entirely. Perhaps, then, the truth of Empedocles's tragedy lies elsewhere than the sphere of tragic dissolution, at least as the successive drafts appear to imagine it.

In that case, the prescriptions that Empedocles utters at first and that the people of Akragas seem subsequently to fulfill could *only* fail, because the imperatives and prophecies they do fulfill could not have truly been what they appear. And in any case, by the time the third draft begins, Empedocles's appearance upon Aetna seems to respond more nearly to one who addresses him alone, directly, and who, like "you" in Hölderlin's ode to "Empedocles," does not speak, but figures solely in Empedocles's address. To nature, to Aetna—"the mother [*die Mutter*]" who "spreads her arm [. . .] around him [*ihren Arm [. . .] um [ihn] breitet*]"—he says: "You call, you draw me near and nearer—[*Du rufst, du ziehst mich nah und näher an*—]" (13: 932, my translation). With this, he responds, in speaking, to an unspeakable contingency that he nears, voices, and denies at once in giving it voice. And still more than that, in breaking his call off with a dash—in at once holding it back and abandoning it utterly—he indicates not only that this open embrace has not yet drawn to a close but also that the gesture of the mother may open to the love of another, just as his attraction may likewise divert in another direction.

With these words, in other words, Empedocles also speaks to the ultimate contingency that is closing in and opening up, where, as he will put it later, the "dark mother [*Mutter*] spreads her arms of fire to the ether [*die dunkle Mutter / Zum Aether aus die Feuerarme breitet*] (13: 945), which ether "now [. . .] comes in his ray [*izt [. . .] in seinem Stral [kömt]*]" (13: 945). He speaks, in other words, to the impending touch between the heavenly fire of "Aether" and the fire of Aetna, the "Mother," who, like Pindar's Olympia, figures here as the duplicitous ground of incineration—and mantic prophecy. For, ultimately, he will proclaim himself to burn rather for the ray of ether, intending to follow its coming "as a sign [*zum Zeichen*]" that he is "affiliated with him [*ihm / Verwandt*]" (13: 945, my translation), and thereby to burn for the sign that he would be. This sign, in turn, would make him a "thing in the fire," which, marking only a relation to the fire, and disappearing without a trace, would not seek another word, as Pindar's mantics did, but be purified and absolved from all other words and signs, including the one he would have become in the flames. Pure prophecy.

This threefold affiliation would, on the one hand, mark *Empedokles* as a tragedy of empyromancy that reprises the birth of tragedy which Hölderlin had also translated around this time, insofar as the ether, whom Empedocles also calls the "Lord [*Herrscher*]," comes to him in a bolt of light and thereby recalls the coming of Dionysos announced in the prologue of Euripides's *Bacchae*, which Hölderlin had also translated.[59] There, Dionysos proclaims himself to come to Thebes—Hölderlin translates: "I come [*Ich komme*]"—and then goes on to recall his still earlier arrival there upon birth, as he stands before the monument of "flame, of the smoldering,

still living divine fire [*die rauchenden, noch lebend göttlichen Feuers Flamme*]"
(17: 635). For there, Zeus, coming in and as lightning, had fatally struck
his mother, Semele, who died as she gave birth to Dionysos. Similarly
incinerated in the fire of the father (and the mother), Empedocles would
be the pure sign of tragedy in his disappearance—whereby the meaning
of the tragedies, as Hölderlin will write elsewhere, might amount to such
a moment, where the sign = 0 (14: 380).[60] Yet at the same time, this tragic
purification of persona and language is not one, and not only because the
coming of the ray and the plunging of Empedocles remain suspended in
Hölderlin's unfinished draft. There is a second threefold most intimately
involved in this moment, which would be all else but a reduction of language and signs to such a vanishing point.

If, in Empedocles's words, the mother reaches her arms of fire to the
ether like a lover, "mindful of the former oneness [*eingedenk / Der alten
Einigkeit*]" (13: 945), Manes, the Egyptian seer who visits Empedocles on
Aetna and who figures as his double[61]—to the point that, for a moment,
Empedocles invites him to follow him below: "Then we follow, as a
sign that we are affiliated with him [the ray], down into the holy flames
[*Dann folgen wir, zum Zeichen, daß wir ihm / Verwandte sind, hinab in heil'ge
Flammen*]" (13: 945, my translation)—reminds us of something else. In
a couplet that addresses the same couple, differently, Manes says: "Yet
what flames from above only inflames, and what strives from below [only
inflames], the wild dissension [*Doch was von oben flammt, entzündet nur /
Und was von unten strebt, die wilde Zwietracht*]" (13: 942, my translation).
With this, Empedocles not only recasts the espousal of ether and Aetna as
sponsio but also pronounces it in a language of dissension that thoroughly
dissolves the possibility that a sign in these flames could ever be pure.
Just where the fire from above "only inflames [*entzündet nur*]" and would
seem to "inflame alone," at the exact point where the verse is about
to turn downward, the verb "entzündet" doubly lights "off [*ent-*]" and
"away [*ent-*]," catastrophically, turning out to be a zeugma that joins
this fire with the strivings of another "from below [*von unten*]."[62] Thus,
the apparently intransitive inflaming goes further to inflame "the wild
strife [*die wilde Zwietracht*]." No less absolute for this—for this "strife"
is the strife of the absolute—the inflaming here marks the splitting and
redoubling of the absolutely pure fire, pure πῦρ itself, and abandons it to
its wildest impurity.

This impurity is given a name when Pausanias, who would also like
to follow Empedocles below and is about to be sent away, addresses
him:

[A]nd should you climb into the groundless vale from that peak to haunt the forceful ones below, reconciling the Titans, and risk yourself into the hallowed sanctuary of the abyss, where, suffering, the heart of the earth conceals itself before day, and the dark mother tells her pains to you, o you son of the night of ether! I would follow you down. (My translation)

[S]tiegst du auch
Um die Gewaltigen, die drunten sind,
Versöhnend die Titanen heimzusuchen,
Ins bodenlose Thal, vom Gipfel dort,
Und wagtest dich ins Heiligtum des Abgrunds,
Wo duldend vor dem Tage sich das Herz
der Erde birgt und ihre Schmerzen dir
Die dunkle Mutter sagt, o du der Nacht
Des Aethers Sohn! ich folgte dir hinunter. (13: 947)

Although the talk of cosmic reconciliation ("Versöhnung") here is questionable—at least insofar as the sign Empedocles would ultimately strive to become is irreconcilable with any particular aim at all[63]—these words come near enough to Empedocles's intentions to give him pause. Empedocles answers: "So stay! [*So bleib!*]" (13: 947; Krell, *Death of Empedocles* 179). And in naming the Titans, the ones who "strive below" (13: 942),[64] Pausanias also gives the proper name to one half of the pair that Hölderlin evokes in more general terms, just after the "General Basis," at the outset of the "Basis for Empedocles"—"nature and art [*Natur und Kunst*]" (13: 870)—which he more properly or improperly names in another ode from around this time: "Nature and Art, or Saturn and Jupiter [*Natur und Kunst oder Saturn und Jupiter*]."

In general terms, it only follows that this exorbitant sphere would be evoked in this context.[65] If there were any utterly other, outer sphere upon which one could be contingent, into or with which an analogy could be drawn—it would have to something like this. It could not truly be the Greco-Italian world of Empedocles's Sicily, nor could it be Sophocles's Greece, but what both of these other other spheres touch upon most intensely—which is, for Hölderlin, always most intimately related to fire.[66] It would have to be, thought most radically, thought to the utmost extreme, Tartarus, where the Titans dwell with the dead, and still more extremely, the anonymous topos below, to which Hölderlin repeatedly returns in his late poetry, from the ode "Nature and Art" to the still less determinate "below" that ends "Celebration of Peace [*Friedensfeier*]": "for gladly it rests, insentient till it ripes, what is terribly laboring below [*Denn gerne fühllos ruht, / Bis daß es reift, furchtsamgeschäfftiges drunten]*" (8: 644).[67] And in the "Remarks on Oedipus," the "power of nature [*die Naturmacht*]" is similarly said to tear man away into the "eccentric sphere of the dead [*exzentrische Sphäre der Todten*]"—a power that the mantic Tiresias, as "Aufseher," oversees, and which Empedocles, drawn ever more nearly toward it, will more immediately attempt to understand (16: 251).

Below Aetna, however, as Hölderlin not only knew from his early studies of Hesiod and from his translation of Pindar's first Pythian Ode (15: 192–93) but also explicitly testifies in his earlier novel *Hyperion*,[68] there dwelled only one Titan: Typhon, who "would have ruled over all mortals and immortals" (Hesiod, *Theogony* 837), if Zeus had not stricken all his hundred heads with lightning, and in a moment where the entire cosmos trembles, but does not quite dissolve.[69] Alexander Honold also draws attention to the particular Titan that attracts Empedocles, glossing "his subterranean grumbling as the vital sign of a [. . .] rebellious spirit," of a lone one who would overturn all, and who thus figures appropriately for the revolution that, according to his reading, Hölderlin's drama was meant to stage (314).[70] But if Hölderlin's Hyperion, considering the "Titan of Aetna," laments the "one [*Eines*]" in us, "the uncanny striving to be All, which, like the Titan of Aetna, rages up from the depths of our essence [*das ungeheure Streben, Alles zu seyn, das, wie der Titan des Aetna, heraufzürnt aus den Tiefen unsers Wesens*]" (27)—this "all" of that striver is, first of all, all of language, and its excess.[71]

After naming him the child of the earth and Tartarus, Hesiod speaks of Typhon's hundred heads and hundred voices, saying:

And there were voices in all his terrible heads, launching all sorts of unspeakable [ἀθέσφατον] sound, for sometimes they emitted such sounds that were intelligible to the gods, and at others, in turn, [sounds] of a loud-roaring bull, in strength unrestrained, an omen of pride, and at other times, again, [sounds] like a lion with ruthless heart, and at others, again, like whelps, a wonder to hear, and at others, again, he hissed and the great mountains echoed. (My translation)

φωναὶ δ' ἐν πάσῃσιν ἔσαν δεινῆς κεφαλῆσι,
παντοίην ὄπ' ἰεῖσαι ἀθέσφατον · ἄλλοτε μὲν γὰρ
φθέγγονθ' ὥς τε θεοῖσι συνιέμεν, ἄλλοτε δ' αὖτε
ταύρου ἐριβρύχεω μένος ἀσχέτου ὄσσαν ἀγαύρου,
ἄλλοτε δ' αὖτε λέοντος ἀναιδέα θυμὸν ἔχοντος,
ἄλλοτε δ' αὖ σκυλάκεσσιν ἐοικότα, θαύματ' ἀκοῦσαι,
ἄλλοτε δ' αὖ ῥοίζεσχ', ὑπὸ δ' ἤχεεν οὔρεα μακρά. (829–35)

And Hölderlin knew this, too, for he will reprise these words of Hesiod in a word, at the very outset of the third draft of *Empedokles*, setting the tone for all that would have followed. Empedocles, in his opening monologue upon Aetna, reflects back upon his trajectory and recalls "the hundred-voiced, the sober laughter [*das hunderstimmige / Das nüchterne Gelächter*]" that "yelled [*gellt*]" all the way "in his ear [*im Ohre*]" (13: 931, my translation). Here, of course, this phrase most nearly relates to the voices of the people who expelled him. However, Empedocles's reflections will almost immediately give way to an address to nature, who calls him—"You call, you draw me near and nearer [*Du ruftst, du ziehst mich nah und näher an*]" (13: 932, my translation)—and insofar as the final "e" of the preterite "yelled [*gellte*]" is elided, making the verb indistinguishable from the present "yells [*gellt*]," the hundred voices he speaks of may also coincide with the one voice he addresses now, too.[72] Either way, these voices are certainly drawn near to each other in his monologue, and all of them draw Empedocles toward the rim of Aetna.

This nearly inconspicuous detail is most certainly no accident, for Hölderlin will have read in Diogenes Laertes's biography of Empedocles, the primary source that inspired and informed his drama, that Empedocles's tragedy is first of all the tragedy of Typhon: "Diodoros, the Ephesian writing about Anaxagoras says that he emulated [Empedocles], in practicing a tragic *typhon / pride* [τῦφον] [Διόδωρος δὲ ὁ Ἐφέσιος περὶ Ἀναξαγόρου γράφων φησὶν ὅτι τοῦτον ἐζηλώκει, τραγικὸν ἀσκῶν τῦφον]" (617, my translation).[73] And as he is the son of the earth, the language of that Titan *is* the language of nature that Empedocles addresses as it calls him—which is not the seemingly innocuous language of nature that Empedocles appears to bid the citizens of Akragas to hearken to in the first draft; nor a language of nature emitted in immediate pleasure and pain, as Herder had called it in his account of the origins of language; but one that comes closer to the desolating "unmediated language of sensibility [*unmittelbare Sprache der Empfindung*]" of the tragic ode and that nearly culminates in the dissolution of language there—or, perhaps, the "next best thing":

> open the windows of sky
> and let free, the night spirit
> the sky-storming one, he has cajoled our land
> with many tongues, unbound ones, and
> rolled the debris
> till this hour.

Das Nächste Beste.
>   offen die Fenster des Himmels
Und freigelassen der Nachtgeist
Der himmelstürmende, der hat unser Land
Beschwäzet, mit Sprachen viel, unbändigen, und
Den Schutt gewälzet
Bis diese Stunde. (Hölderlin, *Sämtliche Werke* [Beissner] 234; cf. Hölderlin,
>   *Sämtliche Werke: Frankfurter Ausgabe* 8: 745–46)

Under these auspices, Empedocles's will to die—"for die I will [*Denn Sterben will ich ja*]" (13: 932)—would be a will to strive (*Streben*); to dissolve in that striving, like the Titan of Aetna—"as a sign, that we are related to him [*zum Zeichen, daß wir ihm / Verwandte sind*]" (13: 945)—and to thereby reach the source and end of all that could not have been said in each saying, and of all that could ever be said. Under these auspices, the "trembling longing [*schaudernde Verlangen*]" for flames that was spoken in the ode to "Empedocles," that leads the speaker to indefinite "depths [*Tiefe*]," and that returns as an isolated exclamation, intensified, in Empedocles's last monologue (13: 755) would be a longing for an utterly nefarious language that most profoundly troubles the world and language alike. And under these auspices, the depths these speakers voice, the other sphere they almost touch, would be not the depths of a volcano, but the abysses that open up within each utterance of that longing, prophetic for other words that do not ultimately arrive, but that always had been nearing.

Ultimately, the longing of Empedocles all along announces nothing other than a longing for these depths, which begins to sithe and seethe through the remarks of Hölderlin on his tragedy, where the empyrical becomes enflamed; over his drafts of *Empedokles*, where a sheer *s* hisses through Empedocles's last words to the Agrigentians and nearly amounts to all he will have said; around the toil in language that singes Pindar's song in Hölderlin's translation of the eighth Olympian ode—"der Mühen Umathmung"; up to the "Empedocles" öde. And beyond this, one would have to say, too, that "Ver*langen*" only barely conceals the tongue, the *langue*, of another, and as "*Ver*langen," implies the distorting of at least both languages involved, in an incendiary splitting and *z*wisting of tongues that tears a way through every "you" or "me" . . .

DISCLOSURE

Just between you and me now, I know you may be wondering what, in these last pages, remains to be said. (But in case you have not read all the way, here is a somewhat lengthy parenthetical remark, for orientation: "I" am addressing "you" here, to pick up where the last chapter left off, and to pick up at a different point, according to the rhythm of repeated reprisal—of "taking up again" and "taking back"[1]—that has been operative throughout the book. Such a rhythm may be unsettling, but that would have been, you know, the point: to unsettle what may seem to be set in the languages of those writers I have been addressing, including my own, and to suspend what may seem to be their, or my, positive gestures, so that, in imparting and parting ways with their words, part of "that which still remains to be said within that which is said" might be said. I am quoting, of course, from the opening of Werner Hamacher's *Ninety-Five Theses on Philology* [3]—not to indicate a method, in the sense of a set of steps to follow in approaching literary or philosophical texts, but to make explicit, yet again, the demand that each chapter should have responded to, each time in a different way. Of course, I admit: the approaches that I have taken may have made for more difficult reading. But such difficulty is entailed in an attempt to reprise, in writing, the languages that one, as a reader, encounters and undergoes; to write with and from those languages; to further them by altering them, in ways that are surely deviant, but only insofar as they traverse and are traversed by the ways of others. Such a gesture is, wouldn't you agree, less arbitrary than the imposition of a set of vocabulary and argumentative conventions, such that any text is forced to conform to easily conveyable information, while whatever does not fit and cannot speak that way is suppressed, silenced, or simply passed over.)

To reprise: you may be wondering what, in these last pages, remains to be said. For surely you will have noticed that this book cannot have a conclusion, if by "conclusion" one understands the telos of the whole, the summary of a set of findings, or the ultimate consequence of a set of premises. You know by now that the readings presented here were, each time, the purpose of this book, and that no one of these readings was subordinated to an end in such a way that I could now sum them up—and thereby reduce them—or claim that each chapter "builds" upon the others. To construct such an edifice, or to assume such a façade of development, would be to diminish the importance of each reading. And in the worst case, putting each reading in the service of a conclusion would promote its singularity to be forgotten, and therefore amount to the pretense, in language, to deny language. In other words, it would amount to the neglect of the precondition for any reading, for any lection, namely—philology, which might be called "an affection for, friendship with, inclination to" the logos, or, "once again, otherwise [. . .] the inclination of language to a language that is, for its own part, inclination toward it or to another" (Hamacher, *Ninety-Five Theses* 11, 28). But I might also remind you that even Hegel's formidable attempt to mediate, conclusively, a language of absolute knowing with nothing left that is foreign to itself was lethal, and that the monumental achievement of the *Phenomenology* rests upon a plethora of foreign terms and figures that Hegel cannot entirely obliviate, even as he strives to translate them into a pure philosophical German. There were, in other words, plenty of loose ends in his endgame, and no fulfillment of *the* absolute spirit "with the rest, in the end, the shadows, the murmurs, all the trouble, to end up with."[2]

Without being oriented toward an end, the collection of readings in this volume was loosely drawn together via the ways in which oracular, prophetic, or mantic gestures in each text—and each time, different ones—exposed how several, seemingly monolingual writings that appear to be signed by G. W. F. Hegel, Wilhelm von Humboldt, Aeschylus, Friedrich Schlegel, and Friedrich Hölderlin[3] are crossed, many times over, by others. Retracing those intersections, was, each time, an attempt to disclose more of what is said in each text. For you will surely recall what Humboldt wrote: "in the scattered chaos of words and rules, which we tend to call a language, only the singularity brought forth through this or that speaking is there, and never fully, [but] also first in need of new labor" (*Gesammelte Schriften* 7: 46). And in laboring to open more in the language of each author—the "plus" of linguistic plurality[4]—each chapter was therefore, too, an attempt on my part to respond to the questions that Jacques Derrida posed in "Des tours de Babel," his analysis of the original plurality and confusion of tongues, via Walter Benjamin's essay "The Task of the

Translator": "How to translate a text written in several languages at once? How is the effect of plurality to be 'rendered'? And if one translates with several languages at a time, will that be called translating?" (Graham 196). Yet because those questions cannot be answered fully for any one instance of language; because they cannot be answered in the same way for any one or another, the theoretical implications of what Derrida addresses require, rather than obviate, further reading, explications, and elaborations—also beyond those you will have read in this book.

But what about the point that Derrida will address in further remarks on translation in another essay, "Les langages et les institutions de la philoso-phie"—namely, the presupposition of "an originary unity," which would underlie the task of translation, such that "all the differences would be but translations (in a sense that is not necessarily linguistic) of the same" (28)? There, Derrida will retrace the contours and limits of this presupposition in the writings of F. W. J. Schelling and Immanuel Kant, and he will it trace back to the instance of "holy Scripture," reprising a moment from his earlier analysis of Walter Benjamin's "The Task of the Translator," where it is said that the "interlinear version (of the Bible)" figures as "the *Urbild*, the prototypical ideal [. . .] of translation" ("Les langages" 26).[5] What about, in other words, "the theology of translation" (26), which any responsible discussion of prophecy and translation would have to con-front—and especially one that was begun under the auspices of "Des tours de Babel?" It was, after all, Derrida who indicated an affinity between the two modes, writing in his earlier essay: "In a mode that is solely anticipa-tory, annunciatory, almost prophetic, translation renders *present* an affinity that is never present in this presentation" (Graham 209–10). Of course, you could say that I have, for the most part, skirted around this issue—but I did so, because the passages of translation and prophecy that were traversed in this book trespass the monotheological register that they also evoke, and, beyond it, turn out to be moments of speaking for and through others, in ways that cannot be limited a priori by a theological term. If even the source of inspiration for Cassandra, a priestess of Apollo, is not one—if her voice carries not only "*the* god," as the chorus says at one point, but also the Furies—what unity could one presume to speak of? Therefore, I also cannot tell you what a "prophecy of language" is, either, which would entail providing a unifying horizon of definition. And I certainly cannot tell you what the language of prophecy could be—not least of all, because there is no such language, either in the sense of a system of words and rules that ever were there to be fixed and transmitted or in the sense of a transcendent source of signification that was to be prophetically revealed.

Insofar as "prophetic" was, implicitly and explicitly, an operative term in the texts that I have been addressing, the linguistic operations in which it was involved, and not definitions of this inconceivable mode of speech, were what I sought to retrace and impart—most partially—to you.

However, I can disclose yet again what you will have grasped by now: this book should have loosened the hold of certain assumptions about language—such as its supposed status as a grammatical and lexical system—which are taken for granted, especially when language is mistaken for an object, over, above, and about which one could speak or write without participating in it and thereby being crossed by it, without crossing the limits of every term and thereby thwarting any presupposed determination, without giving each trope a new turn. At this point, you might recall the extremes of Cassandra's utterances in the *Agamemnon*, where every term of her inspired speech marked an end point and turning point, a summons and aversion of what she says and sees, a transmission of the divinities that speak through her, and their dismissal.

Now one might object—I say "one," not "you"—that others have exposed the tenuousness of such assumptions, too. Take, for instance, Werner Hamacher's excursus on Francis Ponge's "objeu," a word with no English or French equivalent, which confounds "objet [*object*]," "je [*I*]," and "jeu [*play*]," and thus meddles profoundly with the basic structures of empirical knowledge, namely, its subject and object: "Language is the *objeu* of philology. [. . .] *Objeu* is the object that preserves in play its freedom not to ossify into the object of a subject. It is the counterplay against the objectification of a thing by naming it. Each word and language as a whole may be such an *objeu*. In the *objeu*, language plays against language" (*Minima* 54). It is surely true that Hamacher's remarks on philology—among others'—have marked my readings profoundly. And his—most important—work calls for further reading, further commentary along the lines he sets forth. It would be a mistake to assume, in a reading of any philological writing, however insightful it may be, that the questions of language or philology have therefore been settled, or that "this has been done." For should one adopt such a position or posture, one would have imposed a model of understanding drawn from the objective, empirical sciences and an ideology of progress—and thereby rejected a priori what was at stake, *en jeu*, from the outset. And one would have overlooked, too, that to claim that "this has been done" with any kind of rigor, one would also have to say what "this" is, elaborate it differently, and thereby demonstrate that nothing has, in fact, been said or done—at least nothing that could ever be the same. Strictly speaking, if the ethos of dismissal implicit in the protest "this has been done" were to become a habit that regulates the play of language in philosophy and literature, then there would be no reason to return to literary or philosophical texts at all—or to anything that had been written or said before—so that, far from advocating "new" and innovative approaches to writing, one would have to end up declaring: game over.

To repeat: I can offer you no closure here—not without contradicting everything that was advocated in the readings presented in each chapter. I could only put the stakes of those readings somewhat differently, by proposing, for instance, that the languages of those writers whom I address should have been traced in and as "singular plural" instances of speech. I borrow these words from another—Jean-Luc Nancy—who articulates "singular plural" primarily as an ontological structure—as "the primordial requisite of ontology, or of the first philosophy" (*Être singulier pluriel* 77)—but who addresses language throughout, since, from the outset, "*being itself*" is emphatically said to be "*given to us as sense*" (20).[6] But in one passage, his language touches especially closely upon points that have been of foremost importance throughout this book: "A language is always a mêlée of languages, something midway between Babel, as total confusion, and glossolalia, as immediate transparency [*Une langue est toujours une mêlée de langues, quelque chose à mi-chemin de Babel comme confusion totale et de la glossolalie comme transparence immédiate*]" (178–79). Again, Babel and Pentecost are evoked, in a pronunciation of the plurality of any given language—albeit very differently than in the quotation with which this book began: "But often as a fire / arises confusion of tongues [*Oft aber wie ein Brand / entstehet Sprachverw(irrt)irrung*]." And again, even toward the ends of this spectrum, from confusion to transparency, from Babel to "glossolalia"—which is another word for Pentecost, which cannot be properly named here, without determining it and thereby obscuring its immediate transparency—at no point is language ever simply onefold. Perhaps something of the infinite refractions of oneness and noneness—1/0 and 0/1—through which Schlegel, as you may recall, parses the language of the world resonates in the continuum of obscurity and clarity that is evoked here. But unlike Schlegel's formulation, this continuum pertains only to the relative lucidity of language, nor is it a homogeneous one, when it comes to the languages that are evoked in speech at any given moment. And still more critically, the limits that Nancy evokes are prescribed by no system of measure, mathematical or otherwise. Rather, confusion and transparency are utterly contingent upon what comes to pass in each instant of language, and what does not—which cannot, ultimately, be decided, so long as the subjects and destinations of an address themselves arise together, in each moment of address, none being prior in time or rank to the others. Have these words touched you? I am not one to say. And no one could say in advance where the longing for language—or the *Verlangen* for the *langue*, of another—should halt.

So what remains to be said? Everything. And again: everything, otherwise . . .

Acknowledgments

This book is about nothing other than writing for and through others, in ways often unknown to the writer herself. And if this means that I certainly could not address or name all of those to whom I will have owed thanks, I think first of those with whom I have read with the most, beginning with Rainer Nägele—with whom I still read, even more often than we hear from one another, and certainly more than I could know or say.

But this book is also indebted to many, without whose philology—whose care and inclination for other words and for the words of others—it could not have been written. These readers and writers are, first of all, those philologists from Yale University and the Goethe University in Frankfurt am Main who read and commented upon earlier drafts of the chapters in this book: Werner Hamacher, John Hamilton, Shinobo Iso, Carol Jacobs, Jason Kavett, and Henry Sussman. They include my colleagues and mentors from the University of Notre Dame and Brown University, who have been colleagues in the true, etymological root of the term, coreaders: Susan Bernstein, Rebecca Haubrich, Thomas Kniesche, David Farrell Krell, Robert Norton, Marc Redfield, Gerhard Richter, Thomas Schestag, Zachary Sng, and Jane Sokolosky. I would like to express special thanks to Michael Levine, whose conversations and encouragement were critical, at a time when the outcome of this project was most uncertain. And my deep thanks goes to the readers for Fordham University Press, Ian Balfour, Jan Miezskowski, and Jan Plug; to the editors of the LitZ series, Brian McGrath and Sara Guyer; and to Tom Lay, whose interventions at various stages of the project urged me to improve the text when it had seemed finished to me, but would have been incomplete.

The publication of this book was generously supported by the German Studies Department at Brown University and the Office for the Dean of Faculty. The editors of *differences* have kindly permitted me to reprint "Yes—Yet—Hegel's Oracle" in modified form as the first chapter of this book. I would like to thank Annalisa Palmieri Briscoe from the Sicardi Gallery and Marty Stein from the Museum of Fine Arts, Houston, for their assistance in locating and procuring permissions to reproduce Léon Ferrari's *Sin titulo* (1979–1981) on the cover of this book. I am also indebted to all of my students, who have taught me about the importance of dialogue to academic writing—but most of all, to Aine Doyle and Blake Wilcox, who not only assisted me in research for this book through the UTRA summer research program at Brown University but who also read and commented on drafts of various chapters from this book, and thereby made its contents more communicable.

I am most thankful to my closest friends, with whom I am always speaking and writing—also in this book—Tea Alagic, Marta Machabeli, and Betiel Wasihun. I would like to thank Joan and Joseph Mendicino, whose love and support taught me the care that I bring to reading, and try to carry out through the pages that follow.

And beyond this, for now, I thank you, who are reading this, here, and now—

Notes

Introduction

1. Hölderlin, *Sämtliche Werke: Frankfurter Ausgabe* 7: 377. All translations throughout this book, unless otherwise noted, are mine.

2. And even this "confusion of tongues" is confused. For in Hölderlin's text, as Ben Robinson reminded me in the context of a workshop at Northwestern University, the word "Sprachverwirrung" is written, as the transcription of the manuscript reflects, "Sprachverw(irrt)irrung" (7: 377). The word—if it is one—could be said to vary incessantly between the substantivized past participle "sprachverwirrt" ("language confused") and the noun "Sprachvewirrung" ("language confusion").

3. I will distinguish my own translations of "Des tours de Babel" from the English translation of Joseph F. Graham by referring to his name in my parenthetical references to his version of the text.

4. The Hebrew word "lip," as Derrida points out early in his text, is the word for "language" in that language, in distinction to the "tongues" one encounters in Greek, Latin, French, and English—to name a few (Graham 193).

5. In his examples of the "Babelian book" and the "Babelian performance," Derrida echoes precisely the first examples J. L. Austin cites for the performative in *How to Do Things with Words*: the "*contractual*" and "the declaratory ('I declare war')" (7). For the context of the "Babelian performance" is the contraction of an insoluble debt—but intended, enacted, and uttered by no one in particular—and the sentence Derrida draws from *Finnegan's Wake* to exemplify the "Babelian performance" is none other than "And he war." Derrida declares this sentence to be not only a statement in "at least English and German," but also "the declaration of war (in English) of he who says, 'I am that I am,' and that thus was (*war*)" (Graham 196). Thus, Derrida renders the "Babelian performance" one that suspends the "I"; unsettles the status of a decisive "act"; and disrupts the temporal coherence of any moment of agency—which are all preconditions for Austin's speech-act theory.

6. He most likely derives this assertion from Wilhelm von Humboldt, whom he will address explicitly, in admiring terms, later in his book (79–86).

7. For example, this formulation, "the saying of the said," is meant to resonate with Martin Heidegger's reflections on language—for the "way to language [*Weg zur Sprache*]" is formulated in a similar way: "to bring language as language to language [*Die Sprache als die Sprache zur Sprache bringen*]" (*Unterwegs zur Sprache* 242). But "saying" implies a singular instance of speech, unlike any other, and therefore more than any one that could be reprised, while "said" indicates a pastness that necessarily differs from an instance of "saying." "The saying of the

said" thus already demarcates a difference that opens the said to other sayings, and thus to a future. At the same time, if the phrase "saying of the said" evokes Heidegger's famous sentence, it must also evoke Theodor W. Adorno's variant thereof, when he writes that Hölderlin strives, in his poetry, "to bring language itself to speaking [*Sprache selbst zum Sprechen zu bringen*]" (*Noten zur Literatur* 478). Already here, with what seems to be simply put, how could one univocally decide upon the source of a phrase, or the languages it speaks and brings to speech, properly speaking?

8. All quotations from the New Testament are cited on the basis of Nestle and Nestle's *Novum Testamentum*. Quotations from the German Bible are based on Luther's translation in *Werke: Kritische Gesamtausgabe*. Quotations from the Hebrew Bible in English are based on *The New Oxford Annotated Bible*.

9. Rather, this chapter of the Acts of the Apostles begins with a gathering at an indefinite location, which remains unnamed.

10. In the Greek version of this chapter, the verb used here for the distribution of goods is the same verb that was used for the distribution of tongues among the Apostles (Acts 2.3): διαμερίζω.

11. When the *Homburger Folioheft* is read from front to back, the words "der Vatikan" appear on the page that follows the poetic fragment in question. Yet they are printed in Friedrich Beißner's edition of the poems as the title of the fragment. Beißner supports his editorial decision by noting that Hölderlin recorded this text "from back to front [*von hinten nach vorne*]," as Hölderlin was sometimes wont to do (*Sämtliche Werke* 381). Whatever its relationships may be to the poetic text in its vicinity, "der Vatikan" belongs to the poem in a tradition of readings that includes commentators such as Beißner and, more recently, Anke Bennholdt-Thomsen and Alfredo Guzzoni. It may thus be understood as its belated name, in more senses than one, which is due to the interventions of more than one author in the text. For a more nuanced discussion of the problems involved in conferring titular status to "der Vatikan," see Bennholdt-Thomsen and Guzzoni 138.

12. My thanks to Jonas Rosenbrück for pointing out this sense of the word and sharing this reference during the context of a workshop at Northwestern University.

13. In their reading, Bennholdt-Thomsen and Guzzoni consider the apocalyptic scene primarily in relation to Richard Chandler's travel narratives from the late eighteenth century, which Hölderlin had also drawn upon for his composition of *Hyperion*. They conclude: "In distinction to *Hyperion*, Chandler no longer serves in the affirmative evocation of ancient localities here [. . .], but in the demonstration of a post-antiquity condition, with which Hölderlin could fill the gap between the ancient and modern and pose the question of the [. . .] possibility of [. . .] Hesperian culture" (159–60).

14. For an excellent discussion of the immense importance of Schiller to Hölderlin, see Laplanche, who, in an analysis that owes much to Lacanian psychoanalysis, traces the ways in which Schiller seems to be articulated in Hölderlin's writings as occupying the position of the father for him—with the most disastrous consequences. Of course, if Schiller is truly the "Nom du Père," or "Name of the Father,"

one could argue for an even closer proximity between Hölderlin's "Vatikan," where the words of his father's tongue grow confused, and Babel. For according to Derrida's analysis of Genesis, "Babel" is the name God declaims for himself, and in the French version of Derrida's text, it is all the more evident that this is to be understood as "son nom de père" (207).

15. Bennholdt-Thomsen and Guzzoni stress this moment as marking a return to an "architectonics [. . .] of divine nature into which culture has changed back, and from which culture will form itself" (159).

16. Lawrence Venuti reads Berman in a similar way, writing in his monograph *The Translator's Invisibility*, "The 'foreign' in foreignizing translation"—the modus of translation he sees Berman to espouse—"is not a transparent representation of an essence that resides in the foreign text and is valuable in itself, but a strategic construction whose value is contingent on the current target-language situation. Foreignizing translation signifies the difference of the foreign text, yet only by disrupting the cultural codes that prevail in the target language" (21). Yet in Venuti's seeking to develop a strong terminology for translation, both in his discussions of "foreignizing" and in his decision to retain critical categories such as "target language" (18), the division between the proper and the foreign remains firmly in place, even as he argues for an understanding of translation "as a locus of difference" (42).

17. One of the most insightful monographs devoted to challenging assumptions regarding the borders of language—in this case, those that have been tacitly assumed to distinguish language from reality, politics, and history—is Jan Plug's *Borders of a Lip: Romanticism, Language, History, Politics*.

The Pitfalls of Translating Philosophy: Or, the Languages of G. W. F. Hegel's *Phenomenology of Spirit*

1. "Luther hat die Bibel, Sie den Homer deutsch reden gemacht,—das größte Geschenk, das einem Volke gemacht werden kann; denn ein Volk ist so lange barbarisch und sieht das Vortreffliche, das es kennt, so lange nicht als sein wahres Eigentum an, als es [es] nicht in seiner Sprache kennen [lernt];—wenn Sie diese beiden Beispiele vergessen wollen, so will ich von meinem Bestreben sagen, daß ich die Philosophie versuchen will, deutsch sprechen zu lehren."

2. In a similar vein, Hans-Georg Gadamer traces the ways in which Hegel's dialectic emerges and departs from that of his Greek predecessors, most notably Plato in his *Parmenides* (see esp. Gadamer 5–34). The Greek language, as well as the specificity of Hegel's German, figures prominently in his analysis, which culminates in remarks such as: "It is his affinity with [the Greeks] in the matter of speculation itself, which Hegel half guesses from the Greek texts and half forcibly extracts from them. Here Hegel experiences the linguistic suppleness of Greek thought relative to what is closest to him and most central to his thinking: his own roots in his native tongue, the wisdom of its sayings and its plays on words, and, moreover, in its power of expression in the spirit of Luther, German mysticism, and the Pietist heritage of his Schwabian homeland" (33). In Gadamer's essay, however, the accent is placed less

upon the coincidence of diverse languages that inform Hegel's thought than upon the immanence of speculative logic that renders both Hegel's German and Plato's (and Aristotle's) ancient Greek the bearers of "speculative content and [. . .] the 'expression' in which spirit presents itself" (33).

3. Other recent studies of this kind include the interesting discussion of the problems involved in translating Hegel into modern Greek—given the centrality of ancient Greek terms to his own German—in Georgia Apostolopoulou's piece, "Probleme der neugriechischen Hegel-Übersetzung."

4. For an excellent discussion of the famous "end" of art that, according to Hegel, is reached in Attic comedy, see Hamacher, "(Das Ende der Kunst mit der Maske)."

5. "Formell kann das Gesagte so ausgedrückt werden, daß die Natur des Urtheils oder Satzes überhaupt, die den Unterschied des Subjects und Prädicats in sich schließt, durch den speculativen Satz zerstört wird."

6. Hegel writes, "Das Denken, statt im Uebergange vom Subjecte zum Prädicate weiter zu kommen, fühlt sich, da das Subject verloren geht, vielmehr gehemmt, und zu dem Gedanken des Subjects, weil es dasselbe vermißt, zurückgeworfen [. . .]" (44). The chiastic form of speculative dialectics is discussed in Gasché's introduction to Warminski (xv–xxvi), who works through this rhetorical structure, implicitly, in his elaboration of the example of the example in Hegel (and Heidegger) (95–179). Although, of course, Hegel would never explicitly reflect upon this rhetorical figure that makes the logic of the dialectic possible, it will become one of the central ways in which Theodor Adorno will, in the wake of Hegel, work to articulate a dialectic without closure; on this, see Nelson.

7. "Die Wissenschaft darf sich nur durch das eigne Leben des Begriffs organisieren [. . .]."

8. For a far more nuanced discussion of the structure of "Aufhebung" in Hegel's language, see Jean-Luc Nancy's *La remarque spéculative*, where he proceeds from a careful reading of Hegel's remark on "Aufhebung" in the *Science of Logic*—and opens a reading that attends to the resistances of grammar within the texts of Hegel to the operations Hegel proposes.

9. Werner Hamacher reads the organic metaphors that carry through Hegel's texts in relation to the genealogy of Father and Son in Hegel's Christology—what Hegel elsewhere calls "the infinite tree of life" (qtd. in Hamacher, *Pleroma* 125; see also 129–31)—writing: "since the ontological copula 'is' proves to be a genealogical copula here, it can be said more precisely that the son begets himself as the father who in turn begets himself as his son. [. . .] In the speculative circle of generation every moment relates to the position of its own father, to the position of its own grandson. Hegel's text itself, [. . .] as a spiritually inspired speech about spirit, shows itself here to be the logos, the language and the truth of Being [. . .]. Hegel's langue—an economy of autogeneration—would be the pure, surplusless and remnantless transition from the son to the father, from being to consciousness, a sacramental transubstantiation in the speculative mass which he reads" (*Pleroma* 127).

10. For this reason, I have translated all passages from Hegel's German myself. The translations are integral to my argument and interpretation and can be checked

against his German in the notes. In many ways, this project is undertaken in response to the critical passages in Hegel's prose that indicate, as Hamacher puts it, the
"philological task [. . .] which necessarily completes the philosophical task and indicates its limits" (*Pleroma* 5).

11. Hegel's remark on the language of philosophy is, to an extent, purely conventional. It echoes, for example, Fichte's footnote on the language of philosophy
at the start of his propaedeutic text, "Ueber den Begriff der Wissenschaftslehre
oder der sogenannten Philosophie," which reflects his own aspiration to translate
philosophy into German and makes the stakes of this translation more forcefully
clear than Hegel does in his letter. There, Fichte asserts that the nation in which
philosophy is first formulated as a system, so that it no longer constitutes a love of
knowledge, but knowledge itself, would also be worthy to confer this philosophy
(or science) "all remaining technical expressions [*Kunstausdrücke*] from out of its
own language" and would enjoy "a decisive preponderance over other languages
and nations" (118). These intentions might be read as the philosophical complement to what Comay, reading Fichte's *Reden an die deutsche Nation* and *Staatslehre*,
considers to be Fichte's location of (French) revolutionary self-determination
within the German language itself, writing: "developing autonomously in supposedly uninterrupted continuity, and unpolluted by foreign contaminants, the German *Ursprache* incarnates the transcendental project of free self-fashioning" (12). In
his text on the *Begriff der Wissenschaftslehre*, the (yet-hypothetical) transition from a
love of wisdom (φιλοσοφία) to a science of knowledge (*Wissenschaft*) already takes
the form of a translation from Greek to a German term—and Fichte judiciously
avoids foreign *termini technici* in his text—despite the fact that, at this point, only
Fichte's striving for translation and knowing has been established. (German-speak-
ing Philosophy would also thus mean the end of "Philosophy"—but for the fact
that it remains, with each anticipation of this end, suspended between traditional
"philosophy" and a desire to transcend it. The "oder [*or*]" between "doctrine of
the science of knowledge" and "so-called philosophy" in Fichte's title is one trace
of this suspension.)

12. At the start of his essay "Fragmentation, Contamination, Systematicity: The
Threats of Representation and the Immanence of Thought," Thompson writes: "It
follows then that such a system must be able to account for the conditions of its own
possibility wholly and completely from within itself. Accordingly, it cannot appeal
to the extrinsic, to the merely transient, in order to establish itself as a whole or to
ground any moment of its totality. What then about what is perhaps the most fundamental of these conditions, the medium whereby the system itself is presented,
that is, what about language? What could be more mired in the domain of the contingent, the empirical, and the singular?" (35). Similarly, Lau writes, at the start of
"Language and Metaphysics," "At first glance, Hegel's critique of the propositional
form seems to lead inevitably to a cul-de-sac, for no matter how skeptical he is about
this linguistic form, he has no other choice but to develop and to present his philosophy as well as this very critique by means of it" (55). But for both authors, as for
Adorno, the generalization of "language" as the source of trouble presupposes that
language is a homogeneous medium—in this case, German.

13. For a reading of other problems that enter into Adorno's construal of literality or "Wörtlichkeit" here and elsewhere, see Weber 229–50. Weber also alludes to the monolingual presuppositions underlying Adorno's discussion, when he analyzes the passage in which Adorno describes learning a term from a foreign language through examining its appearance in different contexts. Such a procedure serves less to allow the sense of the word to be fixed, as Adorno suggests, but rather, as Weber argues, to "open [. . .] it to constant transformation" (242).

14. Bloch also quotes the letter to Voss that is cited above, but reads it less as a suggestion that the *Phenomenology* should be read as a work of translation than as Hegel's implicit rejection of previous German philosophy, since, as he points out, Christian Wolff had already undertaken the articulation of metaphysics in German (22).

15. Several exceptions include Franco Lo Pipero's reading of Hegel's discussion of writing in his *Encyclopedia*, "Die Buchstabenschrift ist 'die intelligentere'," in which he traces Hegel's thesis on the intelligence of alphabetic script to the many senses the Greek terms for written characters and letters, *gramma* and *stoicheion*, have in Plato's dialogues. In her essay "The Language of Hegel's Speculative Philosophy," Angelica Nuzzo alludes to the ways in which "Hegel's vocabulary is rich in new expressions that either do not belong to the German philosophical language at all (as in the case of expressions such as *Ansichsein* and *Fürsichsein* that rather translate the scholastic Latin of *in se* and *per se*) or do violence to language through the way in which they are employed" (76). In his monograph *The Spirit and Its Letter*, John Smith presents a thorough reading of Hegel's language in the context of his rhetorical education, very much in the spirit of the philological work pursued in this chapter. Werner Hamacher's *Pleroma* and Jacques Derrida's *Glas* are still the strongest readings of the consequences of Christology, the Eucharist, and the Holy Family for Hegel's language and philosophy—as well as the structure of Hegel's "speculative sentence" (*spekulativer Satz*) and the kind of hermeneutics it implies.

16. "Das *Orakel* sowohl des Gottes der künstlerischen, als der vorhergehenden Religionen ist die nothwendige erste Sprache desselben [. . .]."

17. When Bloch refers to the oracle in passing, he cites only from the preface to the *Phenomenology*, where Hegel speaks against those who appeal to their "internal oracle," and thereby explain that they have "nothing further to say," bringing speech to a halt (Bloch 315). In his article on this passage from the *Phenomenology*, Richard Velkey elaborates solely the moment when Hegel speaks of the daimon of Socrates, in order to illustrate his broader claim that Socrates initiates "the great turning-inward of consciousness" from the ethical world of the Greeks (590), but in so doing shares similarities with Hegel's later formulations of the modern absolute monarch, which similarities, in turn, "cast some doubt" on the rationality Hegel seems to accord the monarch in his text (591). In his recent commentary on the *Phenomenology*, Ludwig Siep merely summarizes the systematic function of the oracle in Hegel's text, without examining its implications for Hegel's thinking on language and philosophy more broadly, writing: "Even in his later *Philosophy of Right*, Hegel continued to accord an essential role to the oracle qua ultimately decisive authority in the Greek conception of

the state. The oracle usurps the most important decisions away from rational, self-conscious judgment. It contains elements of chance and inscrutable fate. All this must be overcome through the liberation of the principle of rational knowledge. But for the history of religion, the oracle represents a necessary step in the 'subjectivization' of the divine" (214).

18. In his preface to Malabou's *The Future of Hegel*, Derrida writes, "If I understand correctly, what you find admirable in this book is that, at the same time, it is a gift of idioms and a particular type of philosophical writing. Yes, and also, which is extremely rare, the art of cultivating something like a performative writing of which the force be philosophical, or, better, reflexive: reflecting upon the very possibility of the philosophical" (xiv). Along different lines, Nuzzo argues against attempts on the part of writers such as Thomas Seebohm to formalize Hegel's dialectic into an iterable, schematic grammar. Instead, through readings of passages from Hegel's *Science of Logic*, she seeks to demonstrate "that the language in which Hegel's philosophy is written is constitutive of the dialectical method that structures speculative philosophy as system. Language is not simply the static *medium*, given once and for all, in which method is carried through; language, for Hegel, is itself method" (77).

19. "Daß die Form des Satzes aufgehoben wird, muß nicht nur auf *unmittelbare* Weise geschehen, nicht durch den bloßen Inhalt des Satzes. Sondern diese entgegengesetzte Bewegung muß ausgesprochen werden; sie muß nicht nur jene innerliche Hemmung, sondern diß Zurückgehen des Begriffs in sich muß *dargestellt* seyn. Diese Bewegung, welche das ausmacht, was sonst der Beweis leisten sollte, ist die dialektische Bewegung des Satzes selbst."

20. This "yes" is, arguably, the crux of the *Phenomenology* that marks the end of all the previous transformations of self-consciousness and translations of foreign texts that Hegel had traced before and will trace in his subsequent chapters on "Religion" and "Absolute Knowing." For this reason alone, it is be crucial to address it at least obliquely, marking the tensions that operate against this affirmation. In her discussion of the "reconciling 'yes,'" Comay shows it to be yet another iteration of the temporal disjointedness she elaborates in relation to the French Revolution (127), which disjointedness also characterizes the oracle.

21. "Das *Orakel* sowohl des Gottes der künstlerischen, als der vorhergehenden Religionen ist die nothwendige erste Sprache desselben, denn in seinem *Begriffe* liegt ebensowohl, daß er das Wesen der Natur als des Geistes ist, und daher nicht nur natürliches sondern auch geistiges Daseyn hat."

22. "Insofern dies Moment erst in seinem *Begriffe* liegt, und noch nicht in der Religion realisiert ist, so ist die Sprache für das religiöse Selbstbewußtseyn Sprache eines *fremden* Selbstbewußtseyns. Das seiner Gemeine noch fremde Selbstbewußtseyn *ist* noch nicht *so da*, wie sein Begriff fodert."

23. "Das Selbst ist das einfache und dadurch schlechthin *allgemeine* Fürsichseyn; jenes, aber, das von dem Selbstbewußtseyn der Gemeine getrennt ist, ist nur erst ein *einzelnes*."

24. "—Der Inhalt dieser eignen und einzelnen Sprache ergibt sich aus der allgemeinen Bestimmtheit, in welcher der absolute Geist überhaupt in seiner Religion gesetzt ist.—"

25. It is clear from the context that Hegel's usage of the word "Strom"—"the devotion kindled in all is the spiritual current [*die Andacht in allen angezündet ist der geistige Strom*]" (380)—most likely refers to a current that is analogous to electricity.

26. "[D]er Geist hat als dieses allgemeine Selbstbewußtseyn Aller seine reine Innerlichkeit ebensowohl als das Seyn für Andre als das Fürsichseyn der Einzelnen in Einer Einheit."

27. "Diese Sprache unterscheidet sich von einer andern Sprache des Gottes, die nicht die des allgemeinen Selbstbewußtseyns ist."

28. "Dieses ist mit den mannichfachen Kräfften des Daseyns und den Gestalten der Wirklichkeit als mit einem selbstlosen Schmucke angekleidet; sie sind nur eignen Willens entbehrende Boten seiner Macht, Anschauungen seiner Herrlichkeit und Stimmen seines Preises."

29. Hegel's rhetoric here suggests an, albeit historically insupportable, etymological relation between the homonymous words "name" (*Nahme*) and "taking" (*Nahme*), between the dynamic of taking that the sentence describes and the proximity of these words to "perceiving" (*Wahr-nehmen*), which Hegel glosses earlier in the *Phenomenology* as an act of "taking true" (70). This passage I have quoted reads in full: "Der Inhalt, den diß reine Seyn entwickelt, oder sein Wahrnehmen ist daher ein wesenloses Beyherspielen an dieser Substanz, die nur *aufgeht*, ohne in sich *niederzugehen*, Subject zu werden und durch das Selbst ihre Unterschiede zu befestigen. Ihre Bestimmungen sind nur Attribute, die nicht zur Selbstständigkeit gedeihen, sondern nur Nahmen des vielnahmigen Einen bleiben" (371). To proximate this homonymy in English, I have chosen to render "Nahme" "token/take-in."

30. This interpretation could be confirmed by turning to the many moments Hegel explicitly addresses Spinoza, as in the *Wissenschaft der Logik*, in which he avails himself of a similar rhetoric (e.g., 376–79).

31. The light-essence that Hegel speaks of here cannot, strictly speaking, be exclusively identified with any particular religion. His condensed presentation resonates with ancient Iranian Zoroastrianism, Judaism, and the light of the Johannine Word, as Walter Jaeschke has argued in his monograph, *Die Vernunft in der Religion* (209–15). However, Hegel's association of God with light—and light as his clothing—is especially evocative of those passages from the Hebrew Bible to which Hegel will also explicitly return in the *Lectures on Aesthetics*. In *Aesthetic Ideology*, Paul de Man traces Hegel's imagery to the Psalms, arguing that the depiction of light as God's clothing not only illustrates, as Hegel suggests, "the insignificance of the sensory world as compared to the spirit," but also exposes how "spirit posits itself as that which is unable to posit." "This declaration" of light as God's clothing—and thus, too, God's *fiat lux*—is therefore "either meaningless or duplicitous" (113–14).

32. Having called it "pure force" (*reine Kraft*), he writes, "sie ist das Wort, das noch keine Articulation an ihm hat"; later on the same page, Hegel renames it "matter" (*Materie*) and writes, "–Sie ist das finstre sich nicht mittheilende Insichseyn [. . .]" (36).

33. Hegel emphasizes that the distinctions that arise for the "Light-Essence" are never "fastened [*befestig[t]*]"; any figurations that arise are just as soon "consumed [*verzehr[t]*]" and their differences, "dissolved [*aufgelöst*]" (371). That organization in

the sense of organic life is the next step in the unfolding of Hegel's religious logos is clear from the way the next "natural religion" is the religion of plants and animals. For a reading of this passage from light to life, see Derrida, *Glas* 265–76.

34. "[Sie ist] das verschwindende Daseyn; [. . .] so bleibt sie [. . .] zu sehr in das Selbst eingeschlossen, kommt zu wenig zur Gestaltung, und ist, wie die Zeit, unmittelbar nicht mehr da, indem sie da ist."

35. In his gloss on the imagery of the baker and the fire of devotion, Luther aligns the baker with the king of Ephraim, then writes of the passage, "it means to say, they burn so hotly in idolatry that they are not to be brought away from it with any inflicted suffering [*wil also sagen, Sie brennen so heiß in Abgöttery das sie mit keiner Plage davon zu bringen sind*]" (Luther, *Werke* 11.2: 197). For a very different interpretation that aligns the imagery of the oven with the repeated regicides and political turmoil in Ephraim, see Paul, who also provides an extensive bibliography on this passage.

36. This remark is occasioned by the occurrence of the name Camarim, which, Luther writes, "means hot, great devotion [*Andacht*]. And burning incense [*reuchern*] had the value for them that the singing and praying of monks has for us in the churches. For overall in the Scriptures incense means prayer [*lautet als von hitziger grosser andacht. Und das reuchern galt bey inen, als bey uns die Moenche singen und beten in den Kirchen. Denn Reuchwerg bedeutet allenthalben gebet in der Schrifft*]" (*Werke* 9.2: 85).

37. It is also worth noting the title of the often-reprinted collection of prayers during the Reformation, *Feuerzeug christlicher Andacht* (1536). For the history of the book, see Shevchenko.

38. In this respect, the language of the oracle structurally resembles the French Revolution within Hegel's system as Comay analyzes it—as that which is "forever unattainable because always already achieved" or surpassed (23).

39. "Der allgemeine Geist des Aufgangs, der sein Daseyn noch nicht besondert hat, spricht also ebenso einfache und allgemeine Sätze vom Wesen aus, deren substantieller Inhalt in seiner einfachen Wahrheit erhaben ist, aber um dieser Allgemeinheit willen, dem weiter sich fortbildenden Selbstbewußtseyn zugleich trivial erscheint."

40. McCumber explicitly acknowledges a tension analogous to the one between proper and foreign speech that I am tracing, when he writes, toward the end of his monograph, "Hegel's System, if I am right about it, never claims to be 'true' of extraphilosophical discourse, to say nothing of extralinguistic reality itself. It is a linguistic ideal [. . .] engaging in various types of interplay with discourses outside it. Those interplays proceed via a double set of meaning transformations, in which both the System and historical language drop and add markers from the definitions of the words they contain or form" (332). The questions that I am posing are therefore not intended to imply a contradiction to his reading, but a complication of it, insofar as the problem becomes one of reading Hegel's text, when the "discourses" it involves are articulated in multiple languages at once, to the point where the "System" cannot, as such, hold together.

41. Hegel borrows and translates these lines from Sophocles's *Antigone*, "das sichre und ungeschriebene Gesetze der Götter das ewig lebt, und von dem niemand

weiß, von wannen es erschien" (381). In Greek, the passage reads: [τὰ] ἄγραπτα κἀσφαλῆ θεῶν νόμιμα [. . .] [ἅ] ἀεί ποτε ζῆ [. . .] κοὐδεὶς οἶδεν ἐξ ὅτου φάνη (lines 454–57).

42. I quote in full: "ebenso hohlt das allgemeine Bewußtseyn das Wissen vom Zufälligen von den Vögeln, oder von den Bäumen oder von der gährenden Erde, deren Dampf dem Selbstbewußtseyn seine Besonnenheit nimmt; denn das Zufällige ist das Unbesonnene und Fremde." If it may seem unusual to translate "Besonnenheit" and "das Unbesonnene" as "enlightenment" and "unlit," it is important to remember that the entire chapter on religion reflects a dialectic of light and dark, and that Apollo, the god of the oracle, is also the god of the sun (*Sonne*), so that these German words, which usually mean "prudence" and "the imprudent," cannot but evoke the lumenology that pervades these passages in Hegel's text.

43. "[S]o liegt dieser Selbstbestimmung die Bestimmtheit des besondern Charakters zum Grunde; sie ist selbst das Zufällige; und jenes Wissen des Verstands, was dem Einzelnen nützlich ist, daher ein eben solches Wissen als das jener Orakel oder des Looses."

44. E.g., Lev. 16.8, 1. Chron. 26.14, Acts 1.26.

45. See Benjamin, "Schicksal und Charakter." For a passage in antiquity that signals the translation of the stamp of a coin to the character of a person, see Euripides, *Medea* (lines 516–19): "O Zeus, why did you send clear signs to men of gold that is impure, but of men, not one stamp appears upon the body with which one could see through the bad one?" (ὦ Ζεῦ, τί δὴ χρυσοῦ μὲν ὃς κίβδηλος ἦι / τεκμήρι' ἀνθρώποισιν ὤπασας σαφῆ, / ἀνδρῶν δ' ὅτωι χρὴ τὸν κακὸν διειδέναι / οὐδεὶς χαρακτὴρ ἐμπέφυκε σώματι;).

46. In the *Phenomenology*, Hegel speaks of the works of Egypt—the pyramids; obelisks; animal, hybrid, and human statues—as "diese zweydeutigen sich selbst räthselhaften Wesen" (375). Here, however, his accent upon the riddle is far less emphasized than it is in the later *Lectures on Aesthetics* and *Lectures on a Philosophy of History*, on which see Tucker, who discusses Hegel's riddle as an indication of the riddle itself (61), as well as previous interpretations of its significance for Hegel's aesthetics by Peter Szondi, *Poetik und Geschichtsphilosophie*, and de Man, *Aesthetic Ideology* (Tucker 60–77).

47. On Hegel's insistence on the Word from the prologue to the Gospel of John, see Rosenkranz 193. However, Hegel does not adhere to the Johannine word uncritically, which is, as he writes in an early, fragmentary text on Christianity, only the "*more* authentic reflection-language [*eigentliche*here. . . *Reflexionssprache*]" in comparison to the other gospels, in which there "remains always the Jewish principle of antinomy of thought against reality, of the reasonable against the sensual [*bleibt immer das jüdische Prinzip der Entgegensetzung des Gedankens gegen die Wirklichkeit, des Vernünftigen gegen das Sinnliche*]" ("*Der Geist des Christenthums*" 473, 475, my emphasis). For an excellent reading of Hegel's early translation and commentary of the prologue to the Gospel of John, see Hamacher, *Pleroma* 124–42.

48. "Noch fehlt dem Werke aber die Gestalt und Daseyn, worin das Selbst als Selbst existirt;—es fehlt ihm noch diß, an ihm selbst es auszusprechen, daß es eine innre Bedeutung in sich schließt, es fehlt ihm die Sprache, worin der erfüllende Sinn selbst vorhanden ist."

49. The most thorough commentary on Hegel's adoption of this notion, as well as his reading of Aristotle's *Metaphysics*, remains Ferrarin's monograph, in which he also takes great care to show where Hegel departs from his Greek predecessor, offering instead a "translation of Aristotelian themes" that reflects "his desire to comprehensively account for what he took to be the great new Aristotelian principle, even going beyond what Aristotle left unexplained, unsaid, or in principle ineffable" (119). When, for example, it comes to Hegel's interpretation of the triad of potency, actuality, and entelechy that coincide in the Aristotelian notion of God as the unmoved mover, Ferrarin writes: "Something that is at the same time unmoved and moving cannot be conceived by Hegel otherwise than [as] the activity of realizing itself" (119).

50. More recently, Peter Wake meditates upon the ontotheological significance of love in Hegel's early writings on Christianity, writing: "The law, as a *concept*, as a command, as an *ought*, binds reason and inclination together artificially, in 'opposition to reality,' as Hegel says [. . .]. To cancel this cleavage is to reach a point where reason *is* inclination, where inclination conforms to reason *immediately*. We desire doing what we are supposed to do. This is *love*—a modification of *life*, or life *qua* praxis. *Life* continues to be Hegel's word for the *hen kai pan*, and, as *eine Modifikation des Lebens*, this *point* of reconciliation—love—*is*. Unlike the law, which is made real only in an infinite future, love is present" (144). However, love can only be fulfilled, as Wake later points out, following Hamacher's reading of shame in Hegel's early Christian writings, via withdrawal: "This is the double bind in which Jesus finds himself. It is the insoluble tragedy of love, as manifested in the son of man. By choosing to struggle against the fate of his people in the name of the beauty of his relation with the divine, he sacrifices the communal bonds of family and political life. It also means [. . .] that Jesus, as individual, as personality, must be sacrificed so that the disciples' dependence on him as an external point of authority ceases. Only his irrefutable mortality could reveal their shared essence. Jesus's individual self is sacrificed to revive concrete, but corrupted, life. Yet he and his disciples *flee* from life in all its concrete forms. To remain within the spirit of his people would allow him to grasp only fragments of his nature and would lead it to become contaminated" (191).

51. "Das weiter gebildete Selbst, das sich zum *Fürsichseyn* erhebt, ist über das reine Pathos der Substanz, über die Gegenständlichkeit des aufgehenden Lichtwesens Meister, und weiß jene Einfachheit der Wahrheit, als das *ansichseyende,* das nicht die Form des zufälligen Daseyns durch eine fremde Sprache hat, sondern *als das sichre und ungeschriebne Gesetze der Götter das ewig lebt, und von dem niemand weiß, von wannen es erschien.*" To avoid confusion between Hegel's usage of "Herr" ("Lord," but often translated "master") in the so-called "master-servant dialectic" and his much rarer usage of the word "Meister," I have chosen to translate the latter term in terms of its Latin roots, "magus," "greater," and "-ter," "agent."

52. I quote in full: "Die *Existenz* des reinen Begriffs, in den der Geist aus seinem Körper geflohen, ist ein Individuum, das er sich zum Gefässe seines Schmerzens erwählt. Er ist an diesem, als sein Allgemeines und seine Macht, von welcher es Gewalt leidet,—als sein Pathos, dem hingegeben sein Selbstbewußtseyn die Freyheit

verliert. Aber jene positive Macht der Allgemeinheit wird vom reinen Selbst des Individuums, als der negativen Macht, bezwungen. Diese reine Thätigkeit, ihrer unverlierbaren Krafft bewußt, ringt mit dem ungestalteten Wesen; Meister darüber werdend hat sie das Pathos zu ihrem Stoffe gemacht und sich ihren Inhalt gegeben, und diese Einheit tritt als Werk heraus, der allgemeine Geist individualisirt und vorgestellt."

53. "[D]ie allgemeine Wahrheit, die vom Lichtwesen geoffenbart wurde, [tritt] hier ins Innre oder Untre zurück."

54. Hegel had cited the same passage earlier and translated it into verse, just before the transition from "Reason" to "Spirit" (236).

55. For example, in his monograph, *On Germans and Other Greeks*, Schmidt sums the problem of tragedy for Hegel thus: "Conflict, contradiction, negation, sacrifice, and death saturate the life of spirit so thoroughly and are so native to it that they define the very truth of spirit, and to hold fast to this truth, to pay tribute to the complexity of life, is the task of thinking. The dynamic of tragedy, the economy of the idea of the tragic, presents a thinking which would answer to this task with the supreme challenge. This, then, is the highest moment for thinking: to grasp the tragedy of spirit speculatively, that is, as a unity which is a unity precisely because it is lodged in the antinomy of its own contradictions" (90).

56. "—Wenn ich Zeit hätte, so würde ich suchen, es näher zu bestimmen, wieweit wir—nach Befestigung des moralischen Glaubens die legitimierte Idee von Gott jetzt rückwärts brauchen, z.B. in Erklärung der Zweckbeziehung u.s.w., sie von der Ethikotheologie her jetzt zur Physikotheologie mitnehmen und da jetzt mit ihr walten dürften. Dies scheint mir der Gang überhaupt zu sein, den man bei der Idee der Vorsehung—sowohl überhaupt, als auch bei Wundern und, wie Fichte, bei Offenbarung—nimmt u.s.w.—"

57. Writing against one line of interpretation that would take the many fulfillments of Old Testament prophecy in the Gospel of John as a matter of the "comparison of similarity of situations [*Vergleichung von Aehnlichkeit der Situationen*]," Hegel remarks that John sees a "relation only in spirit [*Beziehung nur im Geiste*]," so that "the objective view upon it as a coincidence of something real, of something individual, falls away [*die objektive Ansicht derselben als eines Zusammentreffens von Wirklichem, von Individuellem, weg[fällt]*]" (*"Der Geist des Christenthums"* 514).

58. Hegel writes, "Was wir etwa unter dem Gesichtspunkt eines Instruments der göttlichen Vorsehung ansehen würden, darin sah Johannes ein vom Geist Erfülltes, da der Charakter der Ansicht Jesu und seiner Freunde nichts so entgegengesetzt sein konnte, als dem Gesichtspunkte, alles für Maschine, Werkzeug, Instrument zu nehmen, sondern vielmehr der höchste Glauben an Geist war; und da, wo man Einheit des Zusammentreffens von Handlungen erblickt, denen für sich diese Einheit, die Absicht des Ganzen der Wirkung mangelt, und diese Handlungen (wie die des Kaiphas) als ihr unterworfen, von ihr ohne Bewußtsein in ihrer Beziehung auf die Einheit beherrscht, geleitet, als Wirklichkeiten und Instrumente betrachtet, sieht Johannes Einheit des Geistes [. . .]" (515).

59. In the *Critique of Judgment*, Kant describes the structure of a *causa finalis* such that "the parts of the same produce one another reciprocally, on the whole both ac-

cording to their form and their connection, and so [produce] a whole out of their proper causality, whose concept again, in turn, [. . .] could be judged to be the cause of the same, according to a principle, [and], consequently, to be the connection of effecting causes and, at the same time, as the effect through ultimate causes [*die Teile desselben einander insgesamt ihrer Form sowohl als Verbindung nach wechselseitig und so ein Ganzes aus eigener Kausalität hervorbringen, dessen Begriff wiederum umgekehrt [. . .] Ursache von demselben nach einem Prinzip sein, folglich die Verknüpfung der wirkenden Ursachen zugleich als Wirkung durch Endursachen beurteilt werden könnte*]" (*Kritik der Urteilskraft* 736).

60. In writing about the so-called bad infinity, it is important to note that "schlecht," the word for "bad" in German, is phonetically and, perhaps, etymologically, closely related to "schlicht," or "plain," "straight," "even." See Grimm and Grimm 15: 655.

61. I quote in full: "Man kann umgekehrt einer gewissen Verbindung, die aber mehr in der Idee als in der Wirklichkeit angetroffen wird, durch eine Analogie mit den genannten unmittelbaren Naturzwecken Licht geben. So hat man sich bei einer neuerlich unternommenen gänzlichen Umbildung eines großen Volks zu einem Staat des Worts *Organisation* häufig für Einrichtung der Magistraturen usw. und selbst des ganzen Staatskörpers sehr schicklich bedient. Denn jedes Glied soll freilich in einem solchen Ganzen nicht bloß Mittel, sondern zugleich auch Zweck und, indem es zu der Möglichkeit des Ganzen mitwirkt, durch die Idee des Ganzen wiederum seiner Stelle und Funktion nach bestimmt sein" (*Kritik der Urteilskraft* 738).

62. "[Die gegenständliche wirkliche Welt hat] für das Selbst alle Bedeutung eines Fremden, so wie das Selbst alle Bedeutung eines von ihr getrennten, abhängigen oder unabhängigen Fürsichseyns verloren."

63. "Die *Substanz* und das allgemeine, sichselbstgleiche, bleibende Wesen,—ist er der unverrückte und unaufgelöste *Grund* und Ausgangspunkt des Thuns Aller,— und ihr Zweck und Ziel, als das gedachte *Ansich* aller Selbstbewußtseyn."

64. I quote: "diese Sittlichkeit, als dieser lebendige, selbstständige Geist, der als ein Bryareus erscheint, von Myrien von Augen Armen und den andern Gliedern, deren jedes ein Absolutes Individuum ist, ist ein absolut allgemeines, und in Bezug auf das Individuum, erscheint jeder Theil dieser Allgemeinheit, jedes was ihr angehört, als ein Object, als ein Zweck [. . .]."

65. "Oracle" comes from *orare* ["to speak"] and the diminutive ending -*culum*.

66. "Ihr [. . .] Wille war frei, gehorchte seinen eigenen Gesetzen, sie kannten keine göttlichen Gebote, oder wenn sie das Moralgesetz ein göttliches Gebot nannten, so war es ihnen nirgend, in keinem Buchstaben gegeben, es regierte sie unsichtbar (Antigone)."

67. In his text, Hegel presents life as the moment when the opposition implied by law is overcome, when the Latinate "anti-nomies" [*entgegen-gesetzte*]—which had cloven Kantian reason and which Hegel translates here into German—conflow in "only one pure oneness" (*nurEine Einheit*), which is to be called "the onefold essence of life, the soul of the world, [. . .] the universal blood." I cite here from the earlier chapter on "Force and Understanding," where he writes: "Es bestehen beyde unterschiedne, sie sind *an sich*, sie sind *an sich* als *entgegengesetzte*, d.h. das entgegengesetzte

ihrer selbst, sie haben ihr Anderes an ihnen und sind nur Eine Einheit. Diese einfache Unendlichkeit, oder der absolute Begriff ist das einfache Wesen des Lebens,
die Seele der Welt, das allgemeine Blut zu nennen, welches allgegenwärtig durch
keinen Unterschied getrübt noch unterbrochen wird, das vielmehr selbst alle Unterschiede ist, so wie ihr Aufgehobenseyn, also in sich pulsirt, ohne sich zu bewegen,
in sich erzittert, ohne unruhig zu seyn" (99).

68. This time, Hegel translates the quotation from Antigone in verse: "nicht etwa
jetzt und gestern, sondern immerdar / lebt es, und keiner weiß, von wannen es erschien"—but with colloquialisms such as "etwa." Thus, it is at once more formal and
more particular than his later rendering of these verses in the chapter on religion,
and in line with his remarks on the tautological, universal singularity of every claim
to rights.

69. As a commentary on these verses, Hegel writes: "They *are*. If I ask about their
emergence and constrict them to the point of their origin, I have transgressed them;
for now I am the universal, and they, the conditional and limited. [. . .] The ethical disposition consists in precisely remaining, uncrazed, fixed in what is right, and
holding back from all moving, shaking, and retracing of the same.—A depositum
is made with me; it *is* the property of another, and I recognize it, *because it is so*, and
hold myself unwaveringly in this relation [*Sie sind. Wenn ich nach ihrer Entstehung
frage, und sie auf den Punkt ihres Ursprungs einenge, so bin ich darüber hinausgegangen; denn
ich bin nunmehr das Allgemeine, sie aber das bedingte und beschränkte. [. . .] Die sittliche
Gesinnung besteht eben darin, unverrückt in dem fest zu beharren, was das Rechte ist, und
sich alles Bewegens, Rüttelns, und Zurückführens desselben zu enthalten.—Es wird ein Depositum bey mir gemacht; es ist das Eigenthum eines Andern, und ich anerkenne es, weil es
so ist, und erhalte mich unwankend in diesem Verhältnisse*]" (236). Here, Hegel returns
to the problem of the tautological categorical imperative and its translation from a
purely formal law to the living polis, which he had addressed at length in his essay,
"Ueber die wissenschaftlichen Behandlungsarten des Naturrechts, seine Stelle in
der praktischen Philosophie, und sein Verhältniß zu den positiven Rechtswissenschaften." For a reading of the Kantian resonance of Hegel's discussion of the "Depositum" problem, which Hegel adopts from Kant's *Critique of Practical Reason*, see
Schulte. At the same time, however, because this passage appears on the threshold of
ancient Greek ethicality, it is overdetermined in ways that invite one to think of the
initial confusion of possessions, if not "deposits," in the *Iliad*, too; namely, the prize
women over whom Achilles and Agamemnon will begin their fateful quarrel.

70. On this etymological sense of the term, see Oehler's commentary to Aristotle's *Categories* (*Aristoteles: Kategorien* 76, 98).

71. "[S]ie macht ihn hierdurch zum Genossen eines Gemeinwesens, welches
vielmehr die Kräffte der einzelnen Stoffe und die niedrigen Lebendigkeiten, die gegen ihn frey werden und ihn zerstören wollten, überwältigt und gebunden hält." He
speaks of burial as an act that "weds the relative to the womb of the earth [*vermählt
den Verwandten dem Schoße der Erde*]" on the same page.

72. "Sein Pathos ist nicht die betäubende Naturmacht sondern die Mnemosyne,
die Besinnung und gewordne Innerlichkeit, die Erinnerung des vorhin unmittelbaren Wesens."

73. See *Vorlesungen über die Ästhetik III* 331, 335. That such a book is essential to the coherence of any people, is clear from Hegel's remarks in his *Vorlesungen über die Philosophie der Weltgeschichte*, where he contrasts the hieroglyphic writing of Egypt with the foundational epic and religious texts of Judea, Greece, and India: for all their writing, the Egyptians "do not possess such a book as the Jews have, no Homer, no Ramayana [*besitzen nicht so ein Buch, wie es die Juden haben, keinen Homer, kein Ramayana*]," which also means that they have no language in any "proper" sense: "But they have not had any national work of language [*Aber sie haben kein Nationalwerk der Sprache gehabt*]" (462).

74. "Die Handlung ist die Verletzung der ruhigen Erde, die Grube, die durch das Blut beseelt, die abgeschiednen Geister hervorruft, welche nach Leben durstend, es in dem Thun des Selbstbewußtseyns erhalten."

75. This connection is not at all surprising, given the fact that the pathos of the epic singer is, Hegel writes, "Mnemoysne" (389). Likewise, the sections of the *Encyclopedia* that concern Krell and Derrida revolve the entire time around memory, and thus, as Krell puts it later in his chapter, "Mnemosyne" (226).

76. "Das Bild wird ertötet, und das Wort vertritt das Bild. [. . .] Die Sprache ist die Ertötung der sinnlichen Welt in ihrem unmittelbaren Dasein, das Aufgehobenwerden derselben zu einem Dasein, welches ein Aufruf ist, der in allen vorstellenden Wesen wiederklingt."

77. Similarly, Malabou writes, in her reading of Hegel's remarks on language for the students in Nuremberg: "If Hegel shows that philosophical language, in its true form, implies the rejection of a ready-made philosophical idiom, it is not because he wants to retain the purity of a national origin, but because, contrary to expectation, he wants to preserve the strange and alien character of any and all language, that is, to preserve the irreducibility of its place and time" (170).

78. Here, my conclusion resonates closely with what Krell says of the shafts and pits of memory, in and beyond Hegel's *Encyclopedia*: "And why should we object that he merely preserves the element unconsciously, preserves it in his text, as long as the shaft comes to gape, as long as Hegel's hearers and readers come to stumble onto the very verge of it? To interiorize something that remains obstinately outside and resists all incorporation—contingency, adversity, language, the past—is to remain subject to perpetual egress" (*Of Memory* 230).

79. For an analysis of the openness that is also implicit in this—strange—articulation of affirmation and community, see Comay 132.

80. Here I adopt the translation Pahl cites and adapts from Pinkard in the context of her analysis of this triumphant turn at the end of the *Phenomenology* (85). See Pahl 83–99.

81. "Von Ihnen erfahre ich, daß bei Frommann oder vielleicht gar bei mir eine Logik herauskommen solle; zugleich theologischen Unterricht zu geben,——und zwar der den Trichtern, durch welche er weiter ans Volk kommen sollte, gemäß ist,——und Logik schreiben, wissen Sie wohl, wäre Weißtüncher und Schornsteinfeger zugleich sein, Wiener Tränkchen nehmen und Burgunder dazu trinken;—der ich viele Jahre lang auf dem freien Felsen bei dem Adler nistete und reine Gebirgsluft zu atmen gewohnt war, sollte jetzt lernen, von den Leichnamen verstorbener oder (der mod-

ernen) totgeborner Gedanken zehren und in der Bleiluft des leeren Geschwätzes
vegetieren; [. . .]—eine Berührung, deren Gedanke mir eine Erschütterung durch
alle Nerven gibt, als ob die christliche Kirche eine geladene galvanische Batterie
ware, ε, ζ, η u.s.w.—Herr! gib, daß dieser Kelch vorüber gehe! [. . .] Ihr Hgl,"
Hegel to Niethammer, November 1807 (Briefe 196–98).

Language at an Impasse, in Passing: Wilhelm von Humboldt's *Agamemnon* Translation

1. "Schliesslich muss ich noch bemerken, dass ich dieselbe im Jahr 1796 anfieng,
sie 1804 in Albano umarbeitete und endigte, und dass seitdem nicht leicht ein Jahr
verstrichen ist, ohne dass ich daran gebessert hätte. Ich sage dies nicht, um mir diese
Sorgfalt zum Verdienst anzurechnen, sondern damit es zur Entschuldigung diene,
wenn vielleicht an dieser oder jener Stelle die Leichtigkeit und Geschmeidigkeit
vermisst würde, die durch häufigeres Umarbeiten oft verloren geht. / Frankfurt am
Main, am 23. Februar, 1816" (*Gesammelte Schriften* 8: 146).

2. In his essay, Hans-Jost Frey focuses on the passages in which Humboldt,
through imagery that recurs in his aesthetic and linguistic writings, describes the
emergence of a word. Frey offers a compelling reading of the way the foreignness
that, according to Humboldt, translation should preserve corresponds to the way a
"not entirely assimilable foreignness from aesthetics" continues to mark Humboldt's
philosophy of language, and in so doing, "holds" his thinking "in motion" (61).

3. In his monograph, *Guillaume de Humboldt et la Grèce: Modèle et histoire*, Quillien
merely lists Humboldt's translation of the *Agamemnon* among other works in ancient
Greek that Humboldt had engaged with, to illustrate his philological expertise (21).
In *Apeliotes*, Trabant writes, "[i]n the preface to his *Agamemnon*-translation, there
are interesting remarks on language" (164), within a list of those brief publications
that had appeared before Humboldt, after his release from ministerial duties, would
publish more treatises on language through the Prussian Academy, to which he be-
longed. In his subsequent book, *Traditionen Humboldts*, a brief reference to the *Agamemnon* introduction occurs in a similar list, this time of those works that preceded
Humboldt's speech before the academy in 1820, "Über das vergleichende Sprach-
studium in Beziehung auf die verschiedenen Epochen der Sprachentwicklung" (100).
In two passages, Tilman Borsche cites excerpts from Humboldt's introduction to
the *Agamemnon*, to illustrate Humboldt's later assertions that every language, for all
its structural differences to others, can express everything (242), and that the emergence of language necessarily eludes cognition (308).

4. All citations and translations from the *Agamemnon* in this book are taken, unless otherwise noted, from Eduard Fraenkel's edition, though I have modified translations of many passages to adapt them more closely to the morphemes of the Greek.
The drama will be cited by line number. Fraenkel's commentary will be cited by
volume and page number. The edition that Wilhelm von Humboldt used for the
text was a work in progress, namely, the one that Gottfried Hermann had been
preparing, and that would be published posthumously—after Hermann had made
further changes to the text. For several examples of those instances where the tex-

tual basis for Humboldt's translation must have differed from the text Hermann ultimately established, see Mendicino 324–25. Otherwise, in August or September 1792, Humboldt writes of working with Christian Gottfried Schütz's Aeschylus-edition (Humboldt to Friedrich August Wolf, *Briefe* 22).

5. Insightfully noting the parallel between the formulation "mit Einem Schlag" and Leibniz's assertion that the monads arise "tout d'un coup," Trabant remarks that the "parallelism" is "interesting" (*Traditionen Humboldts* 84), but provides no further commentary on the implications of such a rhetoric for either thinker. When he returns later to Humboldt's proposal that language as a whole flashes up all at once, he notes solely that this origin is not conceived successively, but as a "'strike [*Schlag*],' a lightning flash" (120). Likewise, Ernst Cassirer, who takes Wilhelm von Humboldt as his inspiration for the first volume of his *Philosophie der symbolischen Formen*, quotes Humboldt's remarks from "Ankündigung einer Schrift über die Vaskische Sprache," in which Humboldt emphasizes language as a wonder—"as a true, inexplicable wonder it breaks out of the mouth of a nation [*als ein wahres, unerklärliches Wunder bricht sie aus dem Munde einer Nation*]" (Cassirer 99). But he says nothing about this wondrous outbreak qua wonder, concluding: "thus a nation is also, in this sense, a spiritual form of humanity, characterized through a determinate language, individualized in relation to an ideal totality" (99).

6. Force is crucial to Müller-Sievers's larger argument that Humboldt's linguistic philosophy develops in response and relation to the natural philosophy of his time, and that a model of epigenesis, stamped by violence, becomes the way in which Humboldt articulates the possibility for the "limit between the two regions"—of meaning and phonetic matter—to be "passed," and for the production of poetry and prose to take place (148).

7. Henri Meschonnic has rightly criticized this tendency, however, arguing for a Humboldt philology that would not reduce his texts to a grammar of abstract principles. In his essay on Humboldt's "Über die Aufgabe des Geschichtschreibers," Meschonnic performs an extraordinary analysis of the nuances of Humboldt's prose, demonstrating through a comparison of translations of this essay how Humboldt's writing cannot be reduced to the sense each word has in a dictionary (353), nor can its sense be rendered without an attentiveness to the rhythmic elements of alliteration that shape it (381). For the "labor of the concept" in philosophical writing cannot be grasped apart from that writing, nor can it be approximated, on the assumption that one can "touch its form without altering the sense" (380). However, in his essay "La difficulté de Humboldt," Denis Thouard argues for a hermeneutics that would complement such a "poetic" reading, and that would attend more closely to the argumentative dimension of Humboldt's texts (see esp. 20–24).

8. "Denn Uebersetzungen sind doch mehr Arbeiten, welche den Zustand der Sprache in einem gegebenen Zeitpunkt, wie an einem bleibenden Massstab, prüfen, bestimmen, und auf ihn einwirken sollen, und die immer von neuem wiederholt werden müssen, als dauernde Werke."

9. Further comparisons between Humboldt's published version of the *Agamemnon* and his draft materials are hindered by the current state of the critical edition of his works, which reproduces only one undated earlier variant of several passages from

the drama. For a brief description of the many original draft materials that the editor, Albert Leitzmann, consulted while editing the text, see his commentary (*Gesammelte Schriften* 8: 222–23).

10. Reading a passage from Humboldt's introduction to the *Agamemnon* in which Humboldt describes the emergence of a word in analogy to the work of an artist, Thouard writes, "The invention of a word is, in effect, comparable to the work of the artist by which objects are resolved into ideas, dissolved; said otherwise, they are modifiable and determinable, separable and relatable, which confers an autonomy to the world of the language, a milieu by and despite of which we comprehend one another in comprehending the world, the accord and harmony (two musical words), that incessantly forms and unforms between the speakers-auditors [*L'invention d'un mot est en effet comparable au travail de l'artiste, par lequel les objets sont résolus en idées, dissous; autrement dit, ils sont modifiables et déterminables, séparables et reliables, ce qui confère une autonomie au monde de la langue, milieu par quoi et malgré quoi on se comprend en comprenant le monde, l'accord et l'entente (deux mots musicaux) se faisant et se défaisant incessamment entre les locuteurs-auditeurs*]" ("La difficulté de Humboldt" 5).

11. "Die Sprache, in ihrem wirklichen Wesen aufgefasst, ist etwas beständig und in jedem Augenblicke Vorübergehendes"; "Sie [die Sprache] ist nemlich die sich ewig wiederholende Arbeit des Geistes."

12. He writes, for example, on the same page in *On the Diversity of Human Language Structure*: "Immediately and strictly speaking, this definition is the definition of each instance of speaking; but in the true and essential sense one can only, so to speak, see the totality of this speaking as language. For in the dispersed chaos of words and rules that we tend to call language it is only the singularity produced through that speaking that is present, and this, never entirely, also from the start in need of new labor [*Unmittelbar und streng genommen, ist dies die Definition des jedesmaligen Sprechens; aber im wahren und wesentlichen Sinne kann man auch nur gleichsam die Totalität dieses Sprechens als die Sprache ansehen. Denn in dem zerstreuten Chaos von Wörtern und Regeln, welches wir wohl eine Sprache zu nennen pflegen, ist nur das durch jenes Sprechen hervorgebrachte Einzelne vorhanden und dies niemals vollständig, auch erst einer neuen Arbeit bedürftig*]" (7: 46).

13. He writes at a later point in *On the Diversity of Human Language Structure*, "this [autoactivity of language-building force] always handles each singularity in language always so, as if at once the entire web to which it belongs were instinctively present to it" [*diese [Selbstthätigkeit der sprachbildenden Kraft] [behandelt] jedes Einzelne immer so, als wäre ihr zugleich instinctartig das ganze Gewebe, zu dem das Einzelne gehört, gegenwärtig*]" (7: 80).

14. Humboldt writes of this force, "no bridge conducts [man], in his synthesizing consciousness of the phenomenon in each blink of an eye, to this unknown foundational essence [*keine Brücke führt ihn in verknüpfendem Bewusstseyn von der Erscheinung im jedesmaligen Augenblick zu diesem unbekannten Grundwesen hin*]" (6: 127).

15. This ontological tendency in Humboldt's writing is most clearly articulated in the section of *On the Diversity of Human Language Structure* that is devoted to the verb, where he writes: "Through one and the same synthetic act, it [the verb], through being, binds the predicate together with the subject, such that being [*das*

Seyn], which passes over, with the energetic predicate, into an acting [*in ein Handeln*], is attributed to the subject itself, and thus what is thought as merely bindable becomes a condition or process in reality. One does not think merely of the striking lightning, but the lightning is itself that which drives down [. . .]" (7: 214). Angela Esterhammer emphasizes that the synthesis the verb effects between subject and predicate "brings a totally new entity into being" (121), as evidence of a metaphysics of positing (122). In his essay "Der Weg zur Sprache," Heidegger suggests that Humboldt's determination of the essence of language "as energeia" derives from Leibniz's *Monadologie*, where force is understood "as the activity of a subject," and thus as a positing, too, on the part of a sovereign subject (*Unterwegs zur Sprache* 238). Borsche also elaborates the relation between Humboldt's notion of force and Leibniz's philosophy, as mediated by Humboldt's teacher Johann Jacob Engel, with reference to Humboldt's notes (136–37). If, however, language is also essentially characterized by need and privation, Humboldt's rhetoric would depose any subject, including language itself, from its force, and expose the powerlessness without which it could not work.

16. Trabant also stresses the importance of alterity to Humboldt's writings on language, focusing first on the way in which each speaker must be understood by others within his proper linguistic community, in order to be understood at all (*Traditionen Humboldts* 41–43). He attributes the necessary diversity of languages to the way in which, for Humboldt, "the connection of sensuality and understanding in the word always individualizes itself necessarily in various languages" (44). However, he does not discuss the possibility that also resonates in Humboldt's rhetoric: namely, that each individual language may itself be in need of others, and that the complement to the actuosity implied in Humboldt's—Aristotelian—rhetoric is not only possibility but also privation, which turns every work, finished or not, into labor. This possibility is implicit on the page in which Humboldt says that each singular instance of speech is "never complete, and also first in need of new labor," when he shifts from speaking of a labor of "language [*Sprache*]" to "languages [*Sprachen*] as a labor of spirit" (7: 46).

17. On the affirmation of this more human need, see also di Cesare 43.

18. Thus, the dynamics of force that Humboldt describes entail not only "autoactivity and receptivity [*Selbsttätigkeit und Empfänglichkeit*]," as Borsche writes (144), but also a lack that would exceed such reciprocity.

19. This is what Meschonnic also strives to do throughout his essay on Humboldt's "Über die Aufgabe des Geschichtschreibers"—through translations of Humboldt, and through a sharp critique of the ways other translators have transferred their presuppositions to Humboldt's "original."

20. Meschonnic emphasizes the importance of substantivized participles and adjectives in the neuter in Humboldt's grammar, but does not comment specifically on this passage (355–56).

21. He writes, "Da jede schon einen Stoff von früheren Geschlechtern aus uns unbekannter Vorzeit empfangen hat, so ist die, nach der obigen Erklärung, den Gedankenausdruck hervorbringende geistige Thätigkeit immer zugleich auf etwas schon Gegebenes gerichtet, nicht rein erzeugend, sondern umgestaltend" (7: 47).

22. In his most recent work, Gerhard Richter reflects at length upon the radical unknowability that haunts the structure of inheritance and that renders it an inexhaustible problem of interpretation, posing the important question, "Wie wäre die Aufgabe des Erbens aufzufassen, wenn diese Aufgabe nicht nur als Herausforderung und als etwas zu Bewältigendes, sondern auch als etwas potenziell Unlösbares sichtbar würde, als etwas also, das die Auf-gabe als ein resigniertes Auf-geben zur Folge haben mag?" (36).

23. Heidegger uses the word "dimension" in a related way, in his essay "Die Sprache," where he writes: "The di-fference [Unter-Schied] is neither distinction nor relation. The di-fference [Unter-Schied] is, in the highest case, dimension for world and thing. But in this case, 'dimension' also no longer means a region on hand for itself, in which this and that settles. The di-fference is *the* dimension, insofar as it measures world and thing in that which is proper to each [*Der Unter-Schied ist weder Distinktion noch Relation. Der Unter-Schied ist im höchsten Fall Dimension für Welt und Ding. Aber in diesem Fall meint 'Dimension' auch nicht mehr einen für sich vorhandenen Bezirk, worin sich dies und jenes ansiedelt. Der Unter-Schied ist* die *Dimension, insofern er Welt und Ding in ihr Eigenes er-mißt*]" (*Unterwegs zur Sprache* 23). However, I would not suggest that the dimensioning that takes place in Humboldt's text opens a measure for the proper, but distances every proper instant of speech from ever being "itself."

24. "Allein in der Einwirkung, die jedes auf das Nachfolgende ausübt, wird diejenige [Einwirkung] deutlich, welche es selbst von seiner Vorzeit erfahren hat."

25. Other passages in which Humboldt uses this term in the first part of *On the Diversity of Human Language Structure* alone include, for example, 7: 19–20, 22,, 29, 34, 35, 36, 40, 54, 59, 60, 63, 64.

26. Several pages after this passage, he will reformulate this metaphor: "Man kann die Sprache mit einem ungeheuren Gewebe vergleichen, in dem jeder Theil mit einem andren und alle mit dem Ganzen in mehr oder weniger deutlich erkennbarem Zusammenhange stehen. Der Mensch berührt im Sprechen, von welchen Beziehungen man ausgehen mag, immer nur einen abgesonderten Theil dieses Gewebes, thut dies aber instinctartig immer dergestalt, als wären ihm zugleich alle, mit welchen jener einzelne nothwendig in Uebereinstimmung stehen muss, im gleichen Augenblick gegenwärtig" (7: 70).

27. "Durch denselben Act, vermöge welches der Mensch die Sprache aus sich heraus spinnt, spinnt er sich in dieselbe ein, und jede Sprache zieht um die Nation, welcher sie angehört, einen Kreis, aus dem es nur insofern hinauszugehen möglich ist, als man zugleich in den Kreis einer andren Sprache hinübertritt."

28. After his description of the spider's sphere of activity, Herder writes, "Now however—man has no such uniform and narrow sphere, where only one work awaits him:—a world of businesses and determinations lies around him—His senses and organization are not sharpened towards one: he has senses for all and thus for each single one, weaker and duller senses—His forces of the soul are spread over the entire world [*Nun aber—Der Mensch hat keine so einförmige und enge Sphäre, wo nur eine Arbeit auf ihn warte:—eine Welt von Geschäften und Bestimmungen liegt um ihn—Seine Sinne und Organisation sind nicht auf Eins geschärft: er hat Sinne für alles und natürlich auch für jedes Einzelne schwächere und stumpfere Sinne*]" (713). With this unlimited range,

then, man's language is absolutely not "instinctive [*instinktmäßig*]" (714; cf. 716), but a product of his "freedom [*Freiheit*]" according to Herder (716).

29. It may even be a coinage of Aristotle's. The word does not appear, as di Cesare has remarked, before Aristotle in the extant corpus of ancient Greek texts (32).

30. "Die Sprache, in ihrem wirklichen Wesen aufgefasst, ist etwas beständig und in jedem Augenblicke Vorübergehendes. Selbst ihre Erhaltung durch die Schrift ist immer nur eine unvollständige, mumienartige Aufbewahrung, die es doch erst wieder bedarf, dass man dabei den lebendigen Vortrag zu versinnlichen sucht. Sie selbst ist kein Werk (Ergon), sondern eine Thätigkeit (Energeia). Ihre wahre Definition kann daher nur eine genetische seyn. Sie ist nemlich die sich ewig wiederholende Arbeit des Geistes [. . .]."

31. The scholarly articles and monographs that address Humboldt's sentence on "Energeia" are numerous. In addition to the ones I explicitly engage, Leonard Jost's monograph, *Sprache als Werk und wirkende Kraft*, offers helpful insights. In it, he elaborates other sources from which Humboldt may have been inspired in his formulation of language as "Energeia," including, for example, James Harris's Aristotelian and Neoplatonic writings on aesthetics, which Humboldt had already encountered in 1785. (Jost 37–40). The second part of Jost's monograph, which is devoted to the "Auffassung der Sprache als Energeia seit Humboldt," sketches many important subsequent interpretations of Humboldt's sentence. For another, different genealogy of Humboldt's "Energeia," see Aarsleff, who traces it back to the French Enlightenment texts Humboldt had been reading between 1797 and 1799 and beyond, including several essays by Dominique-Joseph Garat, Nicolas Beauzée's encyclopedia entry on energy, and Denis Diderot's *Lettre sur les sourds et muets*.

32. Josef Voss ultimately agrees with Heidegger, although he argues that Humboldt's usage of ἐνέργεια must be understood in part through Aristotle's usage of the term in the *Metaphysics*, the *Nicomachean Ethics*, and *De anima*.

33. In this respect, di Cesare furthers the interpretation that Eugenio Coseriu promotes in "Der Mensch und seine Sprache," where he speaks of Humboldt as a proponent of "the Aristotelian *enérgeia*, the actousity, which precedes potentiality (*dynamis*)" (143).

34. Esterhammer adopts a similar interpretation of Humboldt's definition of language as "Energeia" in *The Romantic Performative*, placing an emphasis on what she calls "intersubjective speech acts" (114). In his monograph on Humboldt and the philosophy of nature, Müller-Sievers proposes another likely Aristotelian source for Humboldt's ἐνέργεια: namely, Aristotle's text *De generatione animalium*, where masculine force is said to impart form to life, while the female body is conceived as the potential material recipient of that force (Müller-Sievers 23–24).

35. However, for an excellent, more nuanced reading of force (*Kraft*) in Humboldt in the context of contemporary natural science, see Müller-Sievers 89–115.

36. I borrow this word—if it is one—from Werner Hamacher's *Für—die Philologie* (85) (see English translation by Groves in Hamacher, *Minima Philologica*, trans. Diehl and Groves, 155), where it occurs in a different, but related context: namely, the question of philology, and the distance it bespeaks, in precisely the measure it

furthers and develops what has been said before: "Philology is, to the extent that it is a setting forth and continuing onward and an unfolding, repetition. But even before it can be the repetition of a given word or work, it must be a repetition of the distance from which it receives this given word and gives it an answer, the distance from which this given word itself became either an answer to a word that preceded it or even an answer to no word [*Die Philologie ist in dem Maß, in dem sie Fortsetzung und Enfaltung ist, Wiederholung. Aber noch bevor sie die Wiederholung eines gegebenen Wortes oder Werkes sein kann, muß sie die Wiederholung der Entfernung sein, aus der sie das gegebene Wort empfängt und ihm eine Antwort gibt, und aus der jenes Wort selbst Antwort auf ein vorangegangenes oder auf kein Wort geworden ist*]" (trans. Groves in *Minima* 154. / Hamacher, *Für—die Philologie* 77–78). What I am in the process of drawing out in Wihelm von Humboldt's remarks on translation between languages—from the way each instant of language is, only as it is radically instable; to the way that speaking is always involved in and in need of translation; to the way a structure of privation is inherent in every instance of speech and every sentence one might posit—converges at many points with Hamacher's writings on philology, as when he writes, early in *Für—die Philologie* (4), "For in the sphere of language nothing is self-evident, and so much needs [*bedarf*] elucidation, commentary, and elaboration" (trans. Groves, *Minima* 109). In his *95 Thesen zur Philologie*, he writes in the third thesis (3): "The fact that languages must be philologically clarified indicates that they remain obscure and reliant upon further clarifications. The fact that they must be expanded philologically indicates that they never suffice. Philology is repetition, clarification, and multiplication of impenetrably obscure languages" (English trans. Diehl in Hamacher, *Minima* 5). The reading of Wihelm von Humboldt that is developed here may be read as an answer to and furtherance of the demands of philology, set forth in this way.

37. Aristotle writes, "But in it [energeia], there is the telos and the praxis [ἀλλ' ἐκείνῃ ἐνυπάρχει τὸ τέλος καὶ ἡ πρᾶξις]" (*Aristotle's Metaphysics* 1048b 22–23).

38. For an elaboration of the unsettling function the adverb ἅμα performs in Aristotle's analysis of time in the fourth book of the *Physics*, see Derrida's essay "Ousia et grammè," where he exposes the way in which Aristotle's description hinges upon "a certain *simultaneity* of the non-simultaneous," as marked by the insistence of this word throughout Aristotle's discussion (63–64)

39. His commentators often emphasize this, before proceeding to argue for the centrality of this single sentence. See, e.g., di Cesare 31, Voss 485.

40. "Auch diese [idealische Gestalt in der Phantasie eines Künstlers] kann nicht von etwas Wirklichem entnommen werden, sie entsteht durch eine Energie des Geistes, und im eigentlichsten Verstande aus dem Nichts; von diesem Augenblick an aber tritt sie ins Leben ein, und ist nun wirklich und bleibend" (8: 129–30).

41. In his article on the perfect tense in ancient Greek, C. J. Ruijgh shows that this form denotes "the state which is the continuation of the action denoted by the verbal stem"; when the stem itself denotes a state, it refers to "the permanence of this state" (345).

42. "Bei jeder neuen Bearbeitung habe ich gestrebt immer mehr von dem zu entfernen, was nicht gleich schlicht im Texte stand. [. . .] Vor Undeutschheit und

Dunkelheit habe ich mich zu hüten gesucht, allein in dieser letzteren Rücksicht muss man keine ungerechte, und höhere Vorzüge verhindernde Foderungen machen. Eine Uebersetzung [. . .] darf keine Dunkelheit enthalten, die aus schwankendem Wortgebrauch, schielender Fügung entsteht; aber wo das Original nur andeutet, statt klar auszusprechen, wo es sich Metaphern erlaubt, deren Beziehung schwer zu fassen ist, wo es Mittelideeen auslässt, da würde der Uebersetzer Unrecht thun aus sich selbst willkührlich eine den Charakter des Textes verstellende Klarheit hineinzubringen. Die Dunkelheit, die man in den Schriften der Alten manchmal findet, und die gerade der Agamemnon vorzüglich an sich trägt, entsteht aus der Kürze und der Kühnheit, mit der, mit Verschmähung vermittelnder Bindesätze, Gedanken, Bilder, Gefühle, Erinnerung und Ahndungen wie sie aus dem tief bewegten Gemüthe entstehen, an einander gereiht werden."

43. "Ein solches Gedicht ist, seiner eigenthümlichen Natur nach, und in einem noch viel andrem Sinn, als es sich überhaupt von allen Werken grosser Originalität sagen lässt, unübersetzbar."

44. He writes, "dass, so wie man von den Ausdrücken absieht, die bloss körperliche Gegenstände bezeichnen, kein Wort Einer Sprache vollkommen einem in einer andren Sprache gleich ist. Verschiedene Sprachen sind in dieser Hinsicht nur ebensoviel Synonymieen; jede drückt den Begriff etwas anders, mit dieser oder jener Nebenbestimmung, eine Stufe höher oder tiefer auf der Leiter der Empfindungen aus. Eine solche Synonymik der hauptsächlichsten Sprachen, auch nur (was gerade vorzüglich dankbar wäre) des Griechischen, Lateinischen und Deutschen, ist noch nie versucht worden, ob man gleich in vielen Schriftstellern Bruchstücke dazu findet, aber bei geistvoller Behandlung müsste sie zu einem der anziehendsten Werke werden" (8: 129).

45. For a bibliography and discussion of the French Enlightenment projects of synonym lexica that form the background for Humboldt's discussion here, see Hassler and Gauger.

46. It would exceed the scope of this chapter to describe and analyze the ontological premises Nancy sets forth, but to give a sense of the way Nancy addresses singular-plural origins in his book, I quote one of his remarks on the creation of the world: "That is why that which one calls 'the creation of the world' is not the production from nothing of a pure something, which could not but implode into the nothing from which it never would have departed, but rather, it is the explosion of presence in the original multiplicity of its partition" (20–21). He will come to discuss the symbolic explicitly later, in terms of "the real of relation to the extent that it represents itself," and as a "placing-with [*mise-avec*]" (79). And although he does so with a different accent than the one Humboldt places, what Nancy writes about symbolic unity—"social being does not recur henceforth to any assumption in an interior or superior unity. Its unity is entirely symbolic: it is completely of the with"—could also be written of Humboldt's synonymics and symbols (Nancy 80).

47. "Ein Wort ist so wenig ein Zeichen eines Begriffs, dass ja der Begriff ohne dasselbe nicht entstehen, geschweige denn fest gehalten werden kann; das unbestimmte Wirken der Denkkraft zieht sich in ein Wort zusammen, wie leichte Gewölke am heitren Himmel entstehen. Nun ist es ein individuelles Wesen, von

bestimmtem Charakter und bestimmter Gestalt, von einer auf das Gemüth wirkenden Kraft, und nicht ohne Vermögen sich fortzupflanzen."

48. For a reading of Humboldt's clouds in relation to John Locke's discussion of
language as that which clouds ideas, "a mist before our eyes," see Thouard, "La difficulté de Humboldt" 8–9, where he also sketches Trabant's discussions of this metaphor
in Humboldt's œuvre. In his reading of this passage, Frey draws attention to the way
the "cloud [Wolke]," as a word, recurs throughout Humboldt's poetry and prose as the
privileged figure of indetermination (45), which can also, in other passages, "stand for
the 'confusing and null swarm' of thoughts," and thus mean "the opposite of what it
should clarify in the introduction to the Agamemnon" (43). He then suggests that the
analogy between word and cloud in Humboldt's introduction, which precedes Humboldt's comparison of the emergence of a word to the creative vision of the artist, reflects Humboldt's attempt to approach language via aesthetics, but necessarily fails,
because the word that thereby arises is not utterly original and isolated, like the work
of an artist, but necessarily the "word of a language" (55). Frey then goes on to suggest that the tension that arises between Humboldt's simile and his line of argument
is what allows Humboldt to approach translation "not as an attempt to say the same
otherwise," but to near it "from difference" (57), which lends Humboldt's writings
on language their productive energy (61). To the other instances of cloud imagery in
Humboldt's writing that Frey analyzes, however, it would be appropriate to list in
this context the foreign one: namely, the passage from Pindar's second Pythian Ode,
which Humboldt translated in 1804, where Ixion, who believes he is sleeping with
Hera, copulates with a deceptive cloud image instead. That cloud will give birth to
the Centaur, "a foreigner in the circle of men and foreign in the seats of the gods [in
der Menschen / Kreis ein Fremdling und fremd in der Götter Sitzen]" (8: 95), which will bear
progeny of its own, who later become a threat to man. Humboldt depicts the scene
thus: "for, groping after flattering deception, he embraced a false image, a naught
cloud formation, the fool [Denn nach schmeichelnder / Täuschung Trugbild haschend uma-
rmte / ein nichtiges Wolkengebild der Thor]" (8: 94). One of the most rigorous analyses of
the clouding of words, however, is Hamacher's essay on Walter Benjamin, "The Word
Wolke—if It Is One," where he begins with a discussion of one possible consequence
of the morphological similarity between "Wolke" and "Wort," writing: "'cloud' is,
in a certain sense, the forgetting of ascertained meaning, of linguistic convention and
everything that can enter into its space" (147).

49. He writes, "Wenn man sich die Entstehung eines Worts menschlicher Weise
denken wollte (was aber schon darum unmöglich ist, weil das Aussprechen desselben
auch die Gewissheit, verstanden zu werden, voraussetzt, und die Sprache überhaupt
sich nur als ein Produkt gleichzeitiger Wechselwirkung, in der nicht einer dem andern zu helfen im Stande ist, sondern jeder seine und aller übrigen Arbeit zugleich
in sich tragen muss, gedacht werden kann), so würde dieselbe der Entstehung einer
idealen Gestalt in der Phantasie des Künstlers gleich sehen" (8: 129).

50. "Ueberall, wo die Freiheit sich in Schranken der Endlichkeit bewegt, giebt es
zwar eine Reihe bestimmender, ihr im Augenblick des Wirkens fremder Einflüsse,
sie kann aber auch, wie ein Blitz aus dem wolkenlosen Aether, plötzlich aus denselben heraustreten, und selbstbestimmend werden."

51. "[D]a es nun die Eigenthümlichkeit des Wortes ist, diesen Begriff durch den Ton, wie durch einen elektrischen Schlag, hervorzurufen, so strahlt die Wirkung desselben durch die ganze Seele nach allen Richtungen hin."

52. "Die intellectuelle Thätigkeit, durchaus geistig, durchaus innerlich und gewissermassen spurlos vorübergehend, wird durch den Laut in der Rede äusserlich und wahrnehmbar für die Sinne. [. . .] Sie ist aber auch in sich an die Nothwendigkeit verknüpft, eine Verbindung mit dem Sprachlaute einzugehen; das Denken kann sonst nicht zur Deutlichkeit gelangen, die Vorstellung nicht zum Begriff werden. [. . .] Die Uebereinstimmung des Lautes mit dem Gedanken fällt indess auch klar in die Augen. Wie der Gedanke, einem Blitze oder Stosse vergleichbar, die ganze Vorstellungskraft in Einen Punkt sammelt und alles Gleichzeitige ausschliesst, so erschallt der Laut in abgerissener Schärfe und Einheit. Wie der Gedanke das ganze Gemüth ergreift, so besitzt der Laut vorzugsweise eine eindringende, alle Nerven erschütternde Kraft."

53. Esterhammer also remarks upon Humboldt's references to lightning in passing, calling it "a recurrent Romantic image for instantaneous power, or for a phenomenon whose existence seems to be pure action" (115).

54. He cites from this chapter of Creuzer's second edition of *Symbolik und Mythologie der alten Völker* (1819) in his *Foundational Traits of the Universal Language Type* (*Gesammelte Schriften* 5: 428) and indicates an ambivalent rereading of this work in his epistolary exchanges with Friedrich Gottlieb Welcker, writing to the classical philologist on 15 December 1822, "I am alternately attracted and repelled by it" (*Wilhelm von Humboldts Briefe* 67), and it can be no mere accident that, with this formulation, he uses the very same terms that Kant had used to describe the fundamental ambivalence of the sublime.

55. "Es ist wie ein plötzlich erscheinender Geist, oder wie ein Blitzstrahl, der auf Einmal die dunkele Nacht erleuchtet. Es ist ein Moment, der unser ganzes Wesen in Anspruch nimmt, ein Blick in eine schrankenlose Ferne, aus der unser Geist bereichert zurückkehrt."

56. "Hier waltet das Unaussprechliche vor, das, indem es Ausdruck sucht, zuletzt die irrdische Form, als ein zu schwaches Gefäß, durch die unendliche Gewalt seines Wesens zersprengen wird. Hiermit ist aber sofort die Klarheit des Schauens selbst vernichtet, und es bleibet nur ein sprachloses Erstaunen übrig."

57. All references to the *Iliad* and the *Odyssey*, as well as the Homeric Hymns, are taken from Allen's edition and quoted by book and line number, or, in the case of the Homeric Hymns, by line number alone.

58. In the "Homeric Hymn to Hermes," Zeus is also called, not insignificantly, the "agent of signs [σημάντωρ]" (line 367).

59. For several passages that illustrate the prevalence of this register in Humboldt's writings, see above, note 4.

60. He writes that language is "nicht ein Werk der Nationen, sondern eine ihnen durch ihr inneres Geschick zugefallene Gabe" (7: 17), where "inneres Geschick" implies "inner destiny" in the sense of being sent, and thus oriented toward that which is given to the nation and falls to it "through [*durch*]" this destiny. The dynamic intersection of the "through" and the "to" implicit in Humboldt's vocabulary here

corresponds to the complex temporality of the "Energeia" and "Einwirkung" that pervades his discussions of language.

61. "Man hat bei Beurtheilung der Sprachen und Nationen viel zu wenig auf die gewissermassen todten Elementen, auf den äusseren Vortrag geachtet; man denkt immer Alles im Geistigen zu finden. Es ist hier nicht der Ort dies auszuführen, aber mir hat es immer geschienen, dass vorzüglich der Umstand, wie sich in der Sprache Buchstaben zu Silben, und Silben zu Worten verbinden, und wie diese Worte sich wieder in der Rede nach Weile und Ton zu einander verhalten, das intellektuelle, ja sogar nicht wenig das moralische und politische Schicksal der Nationen bestimmt oder bezeichnet."

62. In "Über die Aufgabe des Geschichtschreibers," Humboldt refers to anything that "follows invariable laws" and that would thus be like "clockwork, driven by mechanical forces" as "dead [*todt*]" (4: 48). For a thorough discussion of the difference between dead mechanisms and living, self-forming matter around the time of Humboldt's writing, see Müller-Sievers, esp. 49–50, 57–63.

63. Along the lines of his thesis that the organic model of epigenesis underlies the structure of linguistic force in Humboldt's writing, Müller-Sievers writes in relation to a similar passage: "Thus, the generation of language presents itself as the epigenetic overcoming [*Überwindung*] and 'convincing' / 'over-generating' [*'Überzeugung'*] of the dead" (158).

64. "[D]ie Sprache [ist] durch die Empfindungen der früheren Geschlechter durchgegangen [. . .] und [hat] ihren Anhauch bewahrt [. . .] in denselben Lauten der Muttersprache" (7: 62).

65. Although he strictly denies the possibility of crossing this cleft, Humboldt adds: "In that one thus acknowledges that one stands at a limit over which neither historical research nor free thought can cross over, one must nonetheless truthfully note the fact and the immediate consequences from it [*Indem man also bekennt, dass man an einer Gränze steht, über welche weder die geschichtliche Forschung, noch der freie Gedanke hinüberzuführen vermögen, muss man doch die Thatsache und die unmittelbaren Folgerungen aus derselben getreu aufzeichnen*]" (7: 39).

66. Here one may be reminded of the way Derrida remarks, on the confusion of tongues: "[It] takes place as a trace or as trait, and this place takes place even if no empirical or mathematical objectivity pertains to its space" (Graham 208).

67. "Alle Sprachformen sind Symbole, nicht die Dinge selbst, nicht verabredete Zeichen, sondern Laute, welche mit den Dingen und Begriffen, die sie darstellen, durch den Geist, in dem sie entstanden sind, und immerfort entstehen, sich in wirklichem, wenn man es so nennen will, mystischem Zusammenhange befinden, welche die Gegenstände der Wirklichkeit gleichsam aufgelöst in Ideen enthalten, und nun auf eine Weise, der keine Gränze gedacht werden kann, verändern, bestimmen, trennen und verbinden können."

68. Among Humboldt's contemporaries, the symbol is often discussed as the sensuous incorporation of an idea. In an exemplary passage from the *Maximen und Reflexionen*, Johann Wolfgang von Goethe writes, "Symbolics transform the appearance [*Erscheinung*] into an idea, the idea into an image, and in such a way, that the idea remains always and infinitely effective and unreachable in the image and, even

if it were spoken in all languages, would remain unspeakable" (470). Humboldt uses the word "symbol" in a similar way, when he writes in *Latium und Hellas, oder Betrachtungen über das classische Alterthum* that the Greeks "handled everything [. . .] symbolically, and were therein gifted with such fortunate tact that the purity of the idea was as protected as the individuality of reality.—Here, the determination of the concept of the symbol [is crucial] as well as the warning not to separate the visible from the invisible, as though one were merely the husk of an otherwise independent other" (3: 137). For a survey and bibliography of the notion of the symbol from Leibniz's text from 1684, *Meditationes de cognitione, veritate et ideis* to the Kantian and Romantic symbol, see Galland-Szymkowiak. One of the best analyses of the symbol in key texts of European Romanticism remains, however, de Man, "The Rhetoric of Temporality."

69. "Im Symbol wird Sinnliches und Unsinnliches, einander gegenseitig durchdringend, als Eins angesehen, [. . .]; Idee und Körperstoff fallen zusammen."

70. Humboldt makes a similar attempt to limit the symbolic potential of language already in *Foundational Traits of the Universal Language Type*, when he asserts that the word shares properties of the symbol and the sign, but is inherently different from both, insofar as the components of the word—this time, conceived as a combination of concept and voiced sounds—do not subsist apart from one another, whereas the signified of any sign is presumably independent from the latter. Conversely, the sensual, "natural form [*Naturform*]" that the idea penetrates in the symbol can subsist independently of the latter and even be abandoned by it, "like the body, when the soul leaves it" (5: 428–29). And although words themselves can function as symbols, Humboldt asserts that the preponderance of symbols can overpower the further motion of thought and speech.

71. "Unter allen Werken der Griechischen Bühne kommt keines dem Agamemnon an tragischer Erhabenheit gleich. So oft man dies wundervolle Stück von neuem durchgeht, empfindet man tiefer, wie bedeutungsvoll jede Rede, jeder Chorgesang ist, wie alles Einzelne, wenn gleich äusserlich scheinbar locker verbunden, innerlich nach Einem Punkt hinstrebt, wie jeder aus zufälliger Persönlichkeit geschöpfte Bewegungsgrund entfernt ist, wie nur die grössesten und dichterischsten Ideen die überall waltenden und herrschenden sind, und wie der Dichter dergestalt alles bloss Menschliche und Irrdische vertilgt hat, dass es ihm gelungen ist, das reine Symbol der menschlichen Schicksale, des gerechten Waltens der Gottheit, des ewig vergeltenden Verhängnisses hinzustellen, das unerbittlich Schuld durch Schuld so lange rächt, bis ein Gott mitleidsvoll die zuletzt begangene versöhnt."

72. In his discussion of the dynamic sublime, where it is a question of force, Kant says that this prospect presents itself through such phenomena as "towering thunderclouds in the sky, closing in with lightning and crashing, volcanoes in their entire destructive violence" (*Kritik der Urteilskraft* 596), as well as war (598). All of these works of nature "make our capacity to resist, in comparison with their force, into a meaningless smallness [*zur unbedeutenden Kleinigkeit*]" (596)—and thus nullify. Reading different passages from Humboldt's oeuvre, Müller-Sievers also emphasizes the resonance between Humboldt's writings on language and the rhetoric of the dynamic sublime (157).

73. The indebtedness that follows from the structure of the symbol in Humboldt's presentation thus resonates very closely with the infinite debt and need to translate that follows the (de)construction of Babel, in Derrida's reading of Genesis (Graham 199–201).

74. "Kassandra *füllt* den schrecklichsten Moment des Stücks aus, den zwischen Agamemnons Eintritt in den Pallast, bei dem sein Schicksal nicht mehr zweifelhaft ist, und seiner Ermordung" (my emphasis).

75. In saying that Cassandra "fulfills" a moment, Humboldt also evokes Kant's description of actual intensity in the *Critique of Pure Reason*, where the apprehension of the real takes place "only in the blink of an eye [*nur einen Augenblick*]" (*Kritik der reinen Vernunft* 267), and in terms of fulfillment or lack. In the *Critique of Pure Reason*, Kant speaks of reality as the degree of intensity of an apprehended sensation (*Empfindung*), and in terms of its relative fulfillment (*Erfüllung*) or lack (*Mangel*), along a scale from 1 to 0 (265–74). Any full apprehension takes place, Kant insists, "only in the blink of an eye [*nur einen Augenblick*]," and therefore before any duration or succession (267). Thus, in evoking the fulfillment of a moment, Humboldt, who had professed Kant to be a "Codex" of philosophy as indispensible as the "Codex juris" is in legal matters (letter to Christian Gottfried Körner 27 October 1793 [*Ansichten über Aesthetik* 2]), also implies a maximum intensity of sensation and the real at this point in the *Agamemnon*. For an excellent analysis of this passage from Kant's first critique, see Hamacher, "Intensive Sprachen."

76. For these, see Bernhardi 23–26, where he traces the beginning of language from inarticulate, vocal cries that imitate the source of sensation. Humboldt had studied this book and recommended it to friends, as testified in his letters to Friedrich August Wolf (see Mattson's edition, *Briefe* 367–70, 598). Thus, in a certain measure, Humboldt also revokes his later assertion that all language begins with "articulate sound." At the very start of his discussion of language elements in *On the Diversity of Human Language Structure*, Humboldt defines "the articulated sound [*den articulirten Laut*]" as "the foundation and essence of all speaking [*die Grundlage und das Wesen alles Sprechens*]" (7: 65). Otherwise, he refuses all myths of origins, explicitly rejecting as senseless any "imagined state of nature [*eingebildeten Naturstand*]" from which one might derive human language from "needs [*Bedürfnisse*]"—for which, he points out, "inarticulate sounds would have sufficed [*unarticulirte Laute ausgereicht [hätten]*]" (7: 61). With these words, Humboldt writes in opposition to narratives such as Condillac's, where children in the desert first speak "as a consequence of the need that presses them [*en conséquence du besoin qui les pressoit*]" (195).

Prophecy, Spoken Otherwise: In the Language of Aeschylus's *Cassandra*

1. This assumption has, of course, been challenged in scholarship on Aeschylus. See, for example, Jean Bollack and Pierre Judet de la Combe's discussion of Agamemnon's murder in relation to the larger problems of the justice of Zeus that arise in the *Oresteia* trilogy (1: cxiii –cxiv), as well as James I. Porter's excellent reading of the way in which echoes and repetitions in the text render the murder itself a dead event (43–44).

2. This pattern of revenge has been linked closely to the motif of sacrifice in Froma Zeitlin's landmark analysis of the *Oresteia*, "The Motif of the Corrupted Sacrifice in Aeschylus' *Oresteia*."

3. While Laura McClure (79–80, 97–98) and Annie Bonnafé have discussed the way in which Clytemnestra, through her vocabulary, characterizes herself as a warrior, neither has explicitly addressed this lexical parallel, which further supports their claims.

4. This observation comes very close to the way in which Porter describes the problem of ambiguity more generally in his reading of the *Agamemnon*, when, after commenting on the circular logic that governs the chorus's portrayal of the rape of Helen—when Helen is described as "the Erinys that the Greeks approximate, in order to lay their claim to Helen, and so on"—he concludes, "this ravaged logic of cause and effect [. . .] is the very root of the play's magnificent ambiguities and ironies" (35).

5. Longinus's *On the Sublime* will be cited by chapter and section, according to Russell's edition. I continue to refer to the author of this treatise as "Longinus," although his authorship has been disproven, in order to avoid writing the longer phrase "the anonymous author of *On the Sublime*" throughout the text. After all, "Longinus" is the proper name that has been historically associated with the treatise, and no one knows who, exactly, composed it.

6. Frequently throughout his treatise, Longinus uses the nominal form of this verb, ἔκπληξις, to describe the experience of the sublime. In his commentary, Russell writes, "ἔκπληξις is surprise or fear which 'knocks you out'" (122). It has received less critical attention, however, than Longinus's other central terms, φαντασία and ἐνάργεια, though readers generally distinguish it as a moment of stupefying astonishment that exceeds the evidential quality of ἐνάργεια (see Bompaire 335; Manieri 77–85; Webb 101–03). For a discussion of all three terms in the history of Greco-Latin thought, see Manieri.

7. For a discussion of the usage of the term ἔκπληξις ("awe-striking," "amazement," "terror") in the synopsis, in comparison to its usage in the scholia to the *Eumenides* and *Ajax*, see Easterling 25–28.

8. Before this scene, it is used only once, when the messenger from Troy comes to announce the impending arrival of Agamemnon and confesses his longing for the fatherland. There, the chorus describes the relation that had bound the soldiers abroad to citizens at home as one in which they were mutually "smitten with desire for those who returned the longing [τῶν ἀντερώντων ἱμέρωι πεπληγμένοι]" (544). The conjunction between the verb for striking and the noun for longing returns when Apollo's desire for Cassandra is articulated thus: "Being smitten—even he, a god—with desire? [μῶν καὶ θεός περ ἱμέρωι πεπληγμένος;]" (1204).

9. For an excellent analysis of the permutations that the usage of πλήσσω undergoes in the drama, see Porter, who argues that by the time Agamemnon himself claims to be struck, his outcries are "utterly preempted," and thus "utterly unexpressive of any personal content" (44), to the point that one might say, with Porter, that Agamemnon's death "never occurs, or rather occurs only in the dead space of a dead spectacle" (43). My own opening suggestion that the death of the tragic hero may be

beside the point comes very close to the conclusions Porter draws, but through the analysis of a different set of passages than those he analyzes, and under the auspices of prophecy. In this respect, I attempt in the following pages to respond to his call for further "commentative scrutiny" (31).

10. For a discussion of her prolonged silence, which nearly leads one to believe that she is a silent actor, or κωφὸν πρόσωπον, see Knox, "Aeschylus and the Third Actor" 109–24; and Taplin 316–22.

11. In his monograph on time and ritual in the *Oresteia*, Widzisz argues that the "mixing of ritual registers" Cassandra performs in addressing a dirge to Apollo was perceived by the chorus as blasphemous (63), citing its remark, "Once more with ill-omened sounds [δυσφημοῦσα] she invokes the god whom it in no wise befits to be present at lamentations" (1078–79). McClure also reads the chorus's response to Cassandra's mourning cries as one that suggests a fear of "dangerous," because "sacrilegious," speech (*Spoken like a Woman* 96).

12. In archaic Greece, the mantic was the figure who received divine inspiration, and the prophet, the one who formalized the mantic's message—most often, in dactylic hexameters—as Gregory Nagy shows in *Pindar's Homer* (ch. 6).

13. All citations from the other tragedies of Aeschylus are taken from Denys Page's edition (*Aeschyli septem*) and cited by line number.

14. However, Seth Schein argues differently: "What is different about Cassandra is that she is not interpreting bird-signs but actually seeing and emotionally responding to exceptionally gruesome and vividly-described events, including her own murder. In thus witnessing her own death, she transcends a boundary of experience which was, for the Greeks, one of the defining limits of the human condition. An audience in turn experiences, in part vicariously and in part through emotional identification, all the pain and horror of this transcendence, of what we might call Cassandra's ceasing to be human" (11–12). Yet this horror is not necessarily all that captivates the chorus, especially not when they exclaim their wonder over Cassandra's speech, suggesting that, in addition to Schein's important insights, there must be at least one other ground for the unsettling effects of Cassandra's prophecies.

15. Humboldt's interpretation is most likely informed by the scholia of the medieval editor of Aeschylus, Demetrius Triclinius, whose glosses Humboldt had already sought to procure in 1792 and was reading intensively by 31 March 1793, as he testifies in letters to Friedrich August Wolf from August or September 1792 (*Briefe* 22, 46). In his gloss on ἀλλόθρουν πόλιν, Triclinius writes, "in [εἰς]" (Smith, *Scholia* 192), which, construed with "speaking [λέγουσαν]," would mean "speaking in regard to an other-speaking city."

16. In his reading of the prophetic and symbolic language in the *Agamemnon*, J. Michael Degener also reflects upon the irresolvable complexities of speech in Aeschylus in a way that circumvents reductive approaches to the text, but he concentrates primarily upon Calchas's prophecies and the ambiguities of the signs that surround the sacrifice of Iphigenia at Aulis.

17. On the editorial problems of the text, see Fraenkel 3:579–81; Judet de la Combe 2: 538; and West, *Studies* 214.

18. For an excellent discussion of the sense of semblance indicated in the verb ἔοικα and its derivatives, see Jean-Pierre Vernant's article "Figuration et image," in which he shows that εἰκών does not, originally, refer in Greek to the copy of a stable original, but to a dynamic of resemblance by which the graces confer to each individual semblance to oneself. The body appears, he writes, as a "bearer of values: beauty, nobility, force, agility, elegance, the brilliance of Charis [*porteur de valeurs: beauté, noblesse, force, agilité, élégance, éclat de la charis*]" (236), which values make up semblance in the Greek sense. Dissimilitude, on the other hand, results from the destruction of these values, such that one is reduced to a "non-personne" (238). Dissimilarity amounts, in other words, to the destruction of one's image per se. These reflections are further developed in his later article on Pandora, "Les semblances de Pandora."

19. However, as Scott has pointed out, the dochmiac rhythms of her strophes are very close to the iambic trimeter that was used for tragic dialogue (*Musical Design* 8–9).

20. Thalmann's argument is developed over the course of two extensive articles devoted to the fourth stasimon and the Cassandra scene, in which he analyzes Aeschylus's references to physiological functions and deduces their respective relations to the experience of emotion and knowledge. Particularly helpful is the distinction he draws between the "heart [καρδία]," which receives emotions, and the "breast [φρήν]," which should usually hold "control over these less rational parts," but does not in the case of the chorus's overwhelming fear in this scene ("Speech and Silence 1" 109–11).

21. Here, I refer to the line in which Cassandra replies to the chorus's assertion, "I do not understand who will accomplish the design [τοὺς γὰρ τελοῦντας οὐ ξυνῆκα μηχανήν]" (1253), with the remark, "And yet I know the speech of Hellas all too well [καὶ μὴν ἄγαν γ᾽ Ἕλλην᾽ ἐπίσταμαι φάτιν]" (1254). In his monograph, Goldhill provides an incisive critique of those analyses of the play that rest upon the assumption of psychological interiority as the "transcendental source" of language, such that "the inconsistencies of language, the play, are limited by an appeal to the (in-)consistency of human character; language becomes transparent, thus [. . .] the openness of language, the production of meaning in difference[. . .] must be limited and defined precisely according to the (already) postulated character" (70).

22. On the function of deictic pronouns and tense as ways of modulating distance to the events that are narrated, see especially Egbert Bakker's monograph, *Pointing at the Past*. In it, he engages the issues of visualization, not only via Erich Auerbach's famous reading of Homer in *Mimesis* (Bakker 56–70) but also through the chapter of Longinus's treatise *On the Sublime* that concerns me here (Bakker 154–76). In her comparison of Timotheus's and Aeschylus's *Persians*, Pauline LeVen also analyzes the temporal deixis of tense in terms of *enargeia* (194–202). For a detailed analysis of Longinus's remarks on *enargeia* and *phantasia*, a history of both concepts, and an extensive bibliography, see Rosenmeyer, "ΦΑΝΤΑΣΙΑ und Einbildungskraft."

23. In a different context, Ernst Neustadt has also remarked on the power of Cassandra's language to form the visions of the chorus, though he suggests that her song completes and confers clearer contour to the indeterminate dread the

chorus had voiced in its previous stasimon (261), and thus adopts a different interpretive tendency than the reading I offer here, where the chorus's concord
with Cassandra does not at all lead to clearer insight into its or her words, but
takes place blindly.

24. Longinus, too, suggests this disappearance effect, when he associates
poetic instances of *enargeia* with the violence of "astonishment [ἔκπληξις]"
(15.2), and goes on to say that the shapes they hew (τὸ πλάσμα) "fall out into
the impossible [προεκπῖπτον τὸ ἀδύνατον]" (15.8), most likely exploiting the
resonance between the stroke of ἔκπληξις and the phonetically similar Greek
word for 'shape': πλάσμα. This violence illustrates, too, the explosive potential
of *plast*icity that Malabou traces elsewhere, in Hegel's writings, which not only
forms the controlled contours of sculpture and habit but also "explodes its own
reserves," demarcating the moment "where form forms itself and at the same
time deforms itself, where it acquires consistency and bursts out like a bomb"
(187).

25. In his analysis of the *Agamemnon*, Goldhill also stresses the tension between
what he calls "two different modes of communication, showing and speaking" in
the structures of communication and exchange throughout the drama (9). What I
am trying to do here, however, is to think further about the implications of light as
speech; that is, about the moments when the difference between these two modes
threatens to be elided.

26. "Die nun, als Gefangene, dienende Königstochter löst nach und nach ihr
starres Schweigen; bricht erst in Wehklagen, blosse unarticulirte Laute und Ausrufungen, dann in Weissagungen aus; anfangs in dunkle; darauf [. . .] entfernt sie
jedes Dunkel; unverhüllt soll der Seherspruch der Sonne entgegentreten."

27. The name "Apollo," according to K. C. Guthrie, may also be foreign (901).

28. In his *Treatise on the Origins of Language*, Herder evokes the "weak Ach" and
"fiery O" in his discussion of the initial, immediate "language of nature" that proceeds from sensory reception (*Empfindung*) (699–700).

29. See Judet de la Combe 2: 429–31.

30. The dochmiac rhythm of Cassandra's opening lyrics and of the song of
the Danaids in Aeschylus's *The Suppliant Women* also supports my claim, for,
as Mary Bachvarova has shown, there is a resemblance between the dochmiac
rhythm—which frequently occurs in contexts of mourning—and cretic-pae-
onic rhythms, which tend to be used in very different contexts—namely:
hymns to Apollo, which suggests "a common origin" that she locates in apotropaic prayer (29).

31. In *Les mères en deuil*, Loraux retraces these sanctions (28–36), which are also
discussed at length in her earlier work *L'invention d'Athènes* 44–45. For a further discussion of this legislation, see Alexiou 14–23.

32. This similarity between the insatiability of Cassandra's cries and what is later
described as a daemonic physiological and erotic insatiability for blood would reaf-
firm the close connection between mourning and rage—and the indelible memory
of loss—that Loraux traces in her book, especially in her discussion of the relationship between *mênis*, or "rage," and memory (*Mères en deuil* 68).

33. In her article on the *Oresteia*, Gloria Ferrari, examining both the surviving literary corpus and ancient vase paintings, deduces: "as a rule, that is, there is no *goos* without a corpse" (31).

34. For the associations between ὀτοτοτοῖ and lament, see Judet da la Combe, who cites similar passages from *Andromache* and the *Choephoroe* (430). He also cites the passage in question from *The Suppliant Women*, but emphasizes only the way in which the cry is provoked by a sudden "commencement"—in the latter case, of terror—without associating the cry with the imperative that follows it: "ἀπότρεπε," or "turn-away," from which the English word "apotropaic" derives.

35. For the difficulties of βοᾶν (and proposed corrections of it), along with arguments for ὢ πᾶ (rather than ὢ βᾶ) see Friis Johansen and Whittle 3: 219–22. For the scansion of these verses as a combination of dochmiacs and iambics, see Johansen and Whittle 3: 362 and West, *Aeschyli* 481–82.

36. It is crucial that this refusal is specifically articulated in terms of Cassandra's refusal to be a mother. Only when the chorus asks her, "Did you also come to the work of children, as is custom?" (1207), does she reveal the cause of her punishment by Apollo: for she "gave consent, then deceived Loxias" (1208). Thus, although Cassandra will not, like the Danaids, kill her husband, her refusal of children with a god is drastic, and most likely underlies the connection between her threnody and the song of Procne, the mother who killed her child and is thereafter condemned to lament and descry her crime perpetually. For a discussion of the nightingale as the figure for the murderous mother, see Loraux, *Les mères en deuil* 87–100. As Loraux points out, the Danaids will compare themselves to Procne, too (90).

37. On the erotic dimension of persuasion in ancient Greek language and religion, see Pirenne-Delforge. McClure comes close to suggesting that Cassandra's lack of persuasion has to do with her sexual relations to Apollo—specifically, her refusal to bear him children—when she analyzes the passage in which Cassandra's laments are compared to those of the nightingale: "The reference to the Procne myth is interesting from another perspective as well, since the story chronicles the silencing of a woman for infanticide; when transformed into a bird, her speech is restored and takes the form of a lament, a socially accepted speech genre for women in ancient Greece" (*Spoken like a Woman* 95).

38. See Mitchell-Boyask 275, where he also cites the connections that Christiane Sourvinou-Inwood draws between marriage and abduction. However, he does not draw the connection between Cassandra's vocabulary in this scene and that of the Danaids. Lexically, ἄγω, the verb Cassandra uses for Apollo in this passage, can specifically mean "to marry" in collocations such as "to lead a woman [ἄγεσθαι γυναῖκα]." For references, see Liddell and Scott, *sv.* ἄγω.

39. Bernard Knox writes, for example, "in Cassandra's possessed song the past, present, and future of Clytemnestra's action and Agamemnon's suffering are fused in a timeless unity which is shattered only when Agamemnon in the real world of time and space (which is also the false world of mask and stage) screams aloud in mortal agony" ("Aeschylus and the Third Actor" 114). Examining a different aspect of her language, Thomas Rosenmeyer writes of Cassandra's turn from song to iambic dialogue, when she says that her oracle "will no longer peer [. . .] from behind veils,"

but "shine" and "reach the rising sun": "coming where it does, on the boundary between hallucination and explanation," the distinctions blur between "tenor" and "vehicles" in what might otherwise seem to be a metaphoric construction. Instead, there takes place what he calls a "blending of disparate spheres" (*Art of Aeschylus* 125).

40. For time, used as a passive participle (χρονισθείς) in reference to periods of maturation, see *Agamemnon* 727; the same verb (χρονίζω) in the active form refers to delaying (148, 847, 1356). Michael Theunissen addresses *chrónos* in epic poetry as the whole of time—in contrast to and as the fulfillment and truth of the singular time of day—in his extensive study of temporality in the poetry of Pindar (see esp. 41). That the whole of time has everything to do with the rule and justice of Zeus is argued in Jacqueline de Romilly's earlier monograph (57–78). This relationship of all time to the decisive time of a day is especially emphasized when, upon Orestes's murder of Clytemnestra and Aegisthos in Aeschylus's *Choephoroe*, the chorus speaks of "the time that fulfills all" (παντελὴς χρόνος), which, at this moment, shall swiftly (τάχα) enter the house that has lain prostrate to the ground for "all too much time" (πολὺν ἄγαν χρόνον) (965, 963–64).

41. In the Pythagorean table of opposites that Aristotle retraces in the first book of the *Metaphysics*, the female aligns with the limitless, or ἄπειρον (986 a22–26). Most commentators, however, have trouble with the word ὅρος in this passage, which usually means "limit," but is modified by its opposite: "fast-passing [ταχύπορος]," and appears with the verb ἐπινέμεται, meaning "to spread." Opposing those who emend it to ἔρος, Fraenkel reads it as deriving from ὁρίζειν, which is used in Sophocles's corpus to mean "to set a norm, to make a rule, establish a line of conduct as binding"—and Fraenkel translates accordingly, "a woman's ordinance" (2: 244). However, in their commentary, Jean Bollack and Judet de la Combe argued persuasively that "the *horos*, in fact, is *poros*," for it is preceded by lines that fault women in power for "agreeing to give thanks before the thing itself has appeared" (2: 484). Thus, they conclude: "the limit that woman assigns to things is itself without limit, when she rejoices over a phenomenon before it has been produced [. . .], and it is this uncontrolled adhesion, which, in an uncontrolled movement, spreads" (487).

42. Goldhill also comments at length on the phrase "female limit [θῆλυς ὅρος]," but does not discuss the relationship between this delimitation of speech and the fires that blaze throughout Argos, rendering it similar to the city that has been destroyed. Instead, he writes: "ὅρος can mean 'definition,' 'limit,' rule.' The phrase seems to imply 'a female's laying down, saying that such a thing is such and such,' a reading that Denniston-Page reject as 'so odd, crabbed and obscure,' and Fraenkel dismisses as unparalleled. It is, however, as I hope to show, a summing up in the discourse we have been considering. Female determination as evinced by Clytemnestra's description of the passage of the beacons, which in some ways reduced language as a means of communication to the visible passage of light, can be called πιθανός, 'likely to persuade,' precisely because it bridges (as we have seen *peitho* is intended to do) the heuristic gap between addresser and addressee; indeed it removes, erases that gap. But it is ἄγαν πιθανός because by this unifiication, this reduction to a single signifier (the beacon) of the difference in which meaning is constituted, we have not the intended single meaning, the limitation implied by ὅρος, but rather, as the sec-

ond speech of explanation of Clytemnestra showed, we have a complete open-endedness of meanings—ἐπινέμεται, 'it spreads over'" (40–41).

43. This epithet is discussed at length in the context of Aeschylus's usage of the adjective κροκοβαφής in Judet de la Combe 2: 455–57.

44. For arguments that the outpouring of "the dyings of saffron [κρόκου βαφὰς]" (239) at Iphigenia's sacrifice refers to her blood, and not to her robes, as Fraenkel has suggested, see Bollack and Judet de la Combe, L'Agamemnon d'Eschyle 2: 300–03.

45. In Aeschylus's dramas, the rays of the sun also penetrate sharply, like a spear. The adjective that accompanies the first reference to the rays of the sun in the drama, τόρος (254), refers both to sharpness and, as an extension of this sense, clarity. This usage implies from the very start that the rays of the sun are sharp, and in the Persians, the vocabulary of the messenger to describe the rays of the sun implies that it does the same thing that a warrior would do with a spear: the sun "drives [them] through [διῆκε]" penetrating the ice of the water to create a "pathway [πόρον]" with its flame (504–05).

46. Others have noticed the visionary power of Clytemnestra's speeches, when she narrates with what will turn out to be astonishing accuracy the return voyage of the Argives, so that she seems, as Aya Betensky has argued, to "actualize[] what she imagines" (14). This power would mark another similarity between Clytemnestra's language and Cassandra's prophecies.

47. For an excellent study of this word and its significance for archaic Greek poetry and thought, see Fränkel 23–29 and, more recently, Theunissen 45–78.

48. Earlier references to the reversal of the sun and stars' course in relation to Atreus and Thyestes's first dispute are to be found in the choral lyrics of Euripides; see Orestes 996–1012 and Electra 699–730. (These works are cited by line number according to Diggle's edition.). According to Plato's Stranger in the Statesman, this reversal came to pass, apparently, as a "testimony in favor of Atreus" (269a 4)—but there can be no favorable version of this portent, since the reign of Atreus leads to Thyestes's feast. As Euripides's Electra tells it, the "change [μεταβολή]" involved in this cosmic turn maps onto an "exchange [ἀμοιβόν]" of "deaths for deaths [θανάτους θανάτων]" (1006–06).

49. I quote in full: "Bearer of good tidings may the morning be, coming, as the proverb goes, from (or: taking after) the kindly mother [μητρὸς εὐφρόνης πάρα]!" (264–65). For a further discussion of the way this proverb alludes to Night and to her progeny, the Furies, see Ferarri 19–24, as well as Lynn-George.

50. In addition to the verse in which Cassandra speaks of the fire that "comes over" her (1256), there is, before this, another one in which the chorus characterizes her speech as "rushing [ἐπισσύτους], god-bearing [θεοφόρους], void burning-pangs [ματαίους δύας]" (1150–51). It is worth noting that the Greek word for "pangs" here, δύη, comes from Indo-European roots that first of all signal incendiary fire, as Pierre Chantraine traces it in his Dictionnaire étymologique 1: 300–01. In this context, where fire is crucial to the pains of Cassandra's prophecy—as well as the rhetoric of the drama as a whole—this etymological sense of the term has resonance, as Judet de la Combe indicates in his translation: "the sufferings that burn [les souffrances qui brûlent]" (2: 480).

51. There, the ghost of Clytemnestra reproaches them for sleeping and failing to catch Orestes: "In dream you hunt the prey, and you howl the very things the hound [κύων] does, who never abandons his concern for murder" (132). Later, when the Erinyes are awake, they rejoice at the scent of mortal blood—"The scent of mortal blood grins toward me" (253)—a rejoicing that Helen Bacon also associates with hunting dogs ("Furies' Homecoming" 49). Although others have pointed out the role of Cassandra as a huntress within the context of the Erinyes in the *Agamemnon*, none has worked through the consequences of this relationship for an understanding of her prophetic speech and the god that speaks through her. See the excellent studies on hunt and sacrifice in the *Oresteia* by Zeitlin and Vidal-Naquet.

52. Fraenkel translates this adverb to modify the action of Cassandra: "And bear ye witness unto me as in close pursuit I scent out the track of ills enacted long ago"; however, the proximity of the adverb to the imperative "bear witness" (μαρτυρεῖτε), together with the way it, like μαρτυρεῖτε, would require a dative—and the noun in the dative here is the participle "scenting" (ῥινηλατούσηι) to describe Cassandra's action—it seems plausible that the adverb could continue to describe what the chorus should do: namely, bear witness *and* run along with Cassandra.

53. For an excellent reading of the famous torch race that first announces the capture of Troy as a signal for, above all, the Erinyes, see Ferrari 19–24.

54. It has been frequently recognized that Clytemnestra otherwise dominates the language and action of every other episode, making Cassandra's scene with the chorus all the more significant. See, for example, Betensky; Humboldt 8: 123–24; Goldhill 96; and Rosenmeyer, *The Art of Aeschylus* 70–74, where he qualifies the assumption that Clytemnestra is on stage for nearly all of the play, but nonetheless affirms her extraordinary force of presence.

55. It should be noted that the chorus expresses wonder only in response to Cassandra's and Clytemnestra's language in the drama, in the passages cited here and above, as well as the passage immediately following the murder of Agamemnon, when they tell Clytemnestra, who boasts of her deeds, "we wonder at your tongue [θαυμάζομέν σου γλῶσσαν]" (1399). The only object of wonder, it would seem, is language, and the rare usage of this verb in the drama as a whole makes the connection between the two female protagonists all the more striking.

56. See, for example, the analysis of the phrase "blinding oracles [ἐπαργέμοισι θεσφάτοις]" (1113) above.

57. This rhetorical parallel has not gone unnoticed; as Fraenkel notes in his commentary, "in the ear of the spectator, who guesses what she has in mind to do, the words must have rung like a travesty of the repeated τὸ δ'εὖ νικάτω of the parados" (2: 178), but he does discuss the effect of these words upon the chorus.

58. In his article "Wort und Geschehen in Aischylos' *Agamemnon*," Ernst Neustadt drew attention to precisely this feature of the drama, going so far as to write at the outset of his text: "No remaining Greek tragedy is so pervaded by the daemonic as Aeschylus' *Oresteia* is" (243). More recently, Franziska Geisser has devoted a monograph to daemons and spirits in Aeschylus, but in her commentary on these lines, she suggests that the chorus is simply initially misled to recognize "only the influence of a madness-inducing daemon in Cassandra's unholy laments," while

it later learns "that Apollo is the god who inspires Cassandra" (297). When she cites the passage in which a daemon is said to fall upon Clytemnestra, the similar collocation of subject and verb is not discussed, though this time, Geisser concludes: "that what concerns the daemon and alastor for Clytemnestra it is entirely in earnest" (327). Such a reading affirms, at once, the familiar "chain of bloody deeds in the house" and a divine order, but it can do so only by eliding other important aspects of the language that complicate and disturb all of these things in the text.

59. Citing George Thomson's commentary, Jean-Pierre Vernant also notes the way in which the absent Helen whom Menelaus appears to chase in the house is a figure whom he mourns, and he adds that this mourning converges with that of the women of Argos, who mourn in the same choral ode "the presence-absence of their husbands [*la presence-absence de leur mari*]" (*Figures, idoles, masques* 26–27). Goldhill also notes how the phantasm of Helen recalls the Nekyia of Homer's *Odyssey*, but emphasizes instead the relationship between desire and imagination here: "The expression is applicable to the desires of dreams, a paradigmatic example of the insubstantiality of vision, and to the modality of the visible in general. The modality of the visible is likened to the insubstantiality of dreams, and thus again implies the doubts of the chorus concerning the nature of the message and its proof offered by Clytemnestra" (47).

60. In his essay "Styx et serments," Bollack shows through a reading of Hesiod that, besides the waters of the Styx, this daughter of the Ocean and Thetis is presented as composed of rock that delimits even the ocean itself—and thus corresponds to the notion of the "oath," or ὅρκος as a derivative of ἕρκος, "enclosure." "If the Styx is that ultra-oceanic, rocky and terrifying barrier," he writes, "it truly holds the universe enclosed and is its closure, just as the ἕρκος surrounds the domain of a frontier" (22). The taking of an oath by the Styx would therefore not designate "the object upon which the oath is sworn," but "the enclosure with which the one who swears surrounds himself" (31).

61. The best analysis of this line can be found in McClure, *Spoken like a Woman* 80–92, where she argues that the alliterations and assonances here and in Clytemnestra's preceding verses operate as "incantatory elements" (89) typical of magical formulae in ancient Greece and render her speech "a perverted form of an erotic spell that works death rather than love" (92).

Prophetic Poetry, ad Infinitum: Friedrich Schlegel's *Daybreak*

1. The first reference to *Aurora* in relation to prophecy can be found among Schlegel's philosophical notes, recorded in Paris in 1802. (*Kritische Friedrich-Schlegel-Ausgabe* 18: 458). Explicit references to *Aurora* as prophetic poetry begin to occur with greater frequency around 1807 within Schlegel's literary notebooks (see, e.g., 17: 78, 81, 93). When Schlegel writes of prophetic poetry, however, he refers to a genre that may never come to be, placing it under the auspices of a "perhaps": "a proper *prophetic* genre, perhaps" (17: 28). And even when Schlegel records his last notes on *Aurora* in 1823—while still conceiving it as prophetic poetry—he asserts that such a poetry had never hitherto been made: "and so a properly *Christian* epic,

and, at the same time, prophetic poem would be found, which *Dante, Milton*, and *Klopstock* have sought in vain" (17: 471).

2. Schlegel writes in an entry from his literary notebooks in 1808: "Philosophy, too, transitions in its highest fulfillment into poetry, upon the presentation of mystical Catholic philosophy, the poem *Aurora* should follow, according to the old idea, just not immediately at first [*Auch [Philosophie] in ihrer höchsten Vollendung geht in Poesie über, auf die Darstellung d[er] myst.[isch] katholischen Philosophie folge das Poem Aurora nach der alten Idee, nur freilich nicht gleich zum Anfang*]" (17: 149). In his reading of other fragments that mostly come from Schlegel's earlier writings, Balfour emphasizes "the hypothetical character" of Schlegel's "pronouncements even when they come in the form of the most apodictic or self-assured statements" (40).

3. Before Lacoue-Labarthe and Nancy, Maurice Blanchot emphasized in *L'entretien infini* the crisis that Romanticism provokes—in the sense of κρινεῖν, 'to decide,' as well as its latter-day derivatives—precisely because its representative writers and texts were characterized by "the exigence or experience of contradictions," which "makes for the confirmation of its vocation of disorder, a menace for some, a promise for others, and for still others, an impotent menace, a sterile promise" (516). However, even those writers such as Blanchot, Lacoue-Labarthe, and Nancy who caution against drawing a sharp distinction between the "early" and "late" Schlegel concentrate in their analyses on the early texts and thus call for complementary readings of the later ones. Meanwhile, the tendency among scholars to draw such a distinction—which pivots upon Schlegel's official religious conversion—continues to inform, for example, Elizabeth Millan-Zaibert's very thorough reading of the philosophical implications of his work in relation to Kant, Fichte, and Jacobi, among others. In order to define the chronological scope of her study, *Friedrich Schlegel and the Emergence of Romantic Philosophy*, she writes, "Yet Schlegel's Romantic thought extended beyond these years, with 1808 (the year he converted to Catholicism) marking his break from many of the philosophical convictions that shaped his romantic thought" (2). For a nuanced presentation of the complexities involved in Schlegel's conversion, see the recent collection of essays edited by Winfried Eckel and Nikolaus Wegmann, *Figuren der Konversion*.

4. For further studies that elaborate and qualify the connection between the "literary absolute" of Romantic writing and current critical theory, see Bernstein and Hillis-Miller and Asensi (142–82).

5. I deliberately translate a fragment from Lacoue-Labarthe and Nancy's French translation of the following excerpt from *Athenaeum* fragment 116: "de ne pouvoir qu'éternellement devenir, et jamais s'accomplir," as though it were part of their argument. For not only do they integrate Schlegel's description of progressive universal poetry into their description of the fragment; the slight differences between their French translation and Schlegel's German also stresses a tendency in the latter that supports their reading. The German sentence in question reads: "Die romantische Dichtart ist noch im Werden; ja das ist ihr eigentliches Wesen, daß sie nur ewig werden, nie vollendet sein kann [*The romantic kind of poetry is still in becoming; yes, that is its proper essence, that it can only become, never be completed*]" (2: 183). Here, the clause denoting perpetual becoming is positive (albeit modified with a limiting

adverb), "ewig nur werden [. . .] kann," and the clause denoting accomplishment, negative: "nie vollendet sein kann." Because, however, the adverb "only [*nur*]" is rendered in French via the negation "ne . . . que," the negative particle "ne" affects both portions of the double clause, accenting the way that, as Lacoue-Labarthe and Nancy rightly argue, the limitation of the fragment—its nonachievement—is precisely what constitutes its infinity (63). Also, the German "vollendet sein [*be completed*]" implies a statal passive, while the French "s'acclompir" operates grammatically as an active reflexive verb, and thus already subtly underscores the importance of organic "autoformation" to the articulation of the fragment that Lacoue-Labarthe and Nancy will elaborate later in their book (70–71).

6. This tension is evident in Lacoue-Labarthe and Nancy's reading of the fragment, on which see above.

7. I have cited the text and translation according to the dual-language edition of Andrew Weeks, but have occasionally modified his translations. In his edition, the original German appears on the even-numbered pages, while the English translation appears on the facing pages. When referring to both pages, I distinguish them in the parenthetical page references with a "/." For a publication history of *Aurora*, see Ferdinand van Ingen's commentary in his edition of *Aurora* and *de signatura rerum* (832–40).

8. The most recent and exhaustive monograph on the Romantic reception of the writings of Jacob Böhme is Paola Mayer's book *Jena Romanticism and Its Appropriation of Jakob Böhme*, where she advances the claim that the Romantics appropriated Böhme in a variety of ways to serve their purposes of constructing "a Romantic version of idealism" (6), and that Schlegel's and Schelling's serious engagements with Böhme began "long after the demise of Jena Romanticism (in 1805 for Schlegel, in 1809 for Schelling)" (6–7). She argues that the long-standing presupposition of Böhme's influence upon the Romantics is an effect of a "hagiographic myth" that "the Romantics themselves deliberately created" (11). According to Mayer, this myth primarily involved casting Böhme in the role of a "poet-prophet who could be used to secure sacral authority for *Poesie*," which was propounded by a variety of writers, often with little evidence of further engagement "with Böhme's works themselves" (16). Marshall Brown argues that the Romantics were attracted to Böhme by the version of dualism he articulated, in particular, the doctrine of "two Centres," a spiritual and a corporeal one, which inhere in every thing (135), such that the divinity of earthly matter "must be continually generated or produced" (138). For an earlier elaboration of Novalis's reception of Böhme, as initiated through his exchange with Ludwig Tieck, see Feilchenfeld, esp. 32–34. Hegel's reception of Böhme is discussed extensively in Magee 36–50.

9. Elsewhere, in his philosophical notebooks, Schlegel speaks of Böhme's philosophy precisely as the philosophy of the word, writing: "The word is the essence of man [.] Böhme's φσ [philosophy] is the φσ [philosophy] of the *Word* [*Das Wort ist das Wesen des Menschen [.] Böhme's φσ [Philosophie] ist die φσ [Philosophie] des* Wortes]" (18: 490).

10. "*Beschreibung der natur wie alles gewesen und im anfang worden ist: wie die Natur vnd Elementa Creatürlich worden (ist.) sind Auch von beyden qualitäten*

Bösen und gutten wo Hehr alle ding seinen vrsprung Hatt vnd wie es ietzt stehed und wircked. vnd wie es am Ende dieser zeit werden wirdt. auch wie Gottes / vnd der Hellen Reich beschaffen ist vnd wie alles auß rechtem grunde in erkendnis des Geistes in wallen Gottes. mit fleiß gesetelled / durch Jacob Böhmen in Görlitz Im Jahr 1612" (74).

11. This description already signals the beginning and end of nature, with purification by fire. However, it would be misleading to omit that, after succinctly introducing the significance of his simile—"The garden of this tree signifies the world; the field, nature; the stem of the tree, the stars; the branches, the elements; and so the fruit growing on this tree mean human beings. The sap in the tree means the clear divinity. Now the men have been made from nature, stars and elements, God the Creator prevails in all like the sap in the entire tree. But nature has two qualities in itself until the judgment of God, a praiseworthy heavenly and holy one and a fierce hellish and thirsty one" (79)—the seemingly clear alignments Böhme establishes give way to an elaborate allegory, in which the sap splits into one that provides life and another that dessicates (79), before the tree itself is redoubled by another, planted by the devil (who had seemed contained within the first), while the first tree, in turn, is now said to be solely "sacred, good and potent" (91). Moreover, the distinction between the tree and nature—initially, "the field" that contains it (79)—likewise dissolves, as the struggle between the "heavenly and hellish realm" is both set "in nature" and set as a prenatal figure in its own right. For this "realm," which Boehme splits between two modifiers ("heavenly," "hellish"), but names in the singular, stands "in great labor as a woman giving birth" (83). For a fuller analysis of the complexities of the prologue, see Schuff.

12. Steven Konopacki suggests that it is only around 1620 that "the introduction of an alchemical and cabalistic component into phonology occurs" (2). He also convincingly suggests that Böhme's analyses of consonants in *Aurora* are related to Böhme's association of the flesh with "Begreifflichkeit," or "conceivability"—hence, "the tongue is instrumental in directing the breath stream toward the articulators [consonants], directing the *Geist* towards *Begreifflichkeit*" (15).

13. When amid these notes Schlegel writes that the liquids *r* and *l*, as well as the sibilant *s*, are "ονοματοποιητικοι [*onomotopoietics*]" (16: 379), recalling the *Cratylus*—where *r*, the sibilants, and *l* are discussed in that order, as eminently experesssive of motion (426c 1–427d 2)—this designation might be taken in a more radical sense of *poiesis* than is usually meant by the word. It might be taken to indicate, namely, that the sounds give birth to things in and as their names. Michel Chaouli's sustained analysis of these pages along the lines of chemistry (161–69)—which register is certainly also evoked by Schlegel's vocabulary of "affinities [*Verwandtschaften*]" among phonemes (16: 378)—could thus be complemented by considering the ways in which his rhetoric is inflected by Böhme. Such an elaboration would, however, exceed the scope of this chapter.

14. Böhme writes, "Now, however, the divinity is not separate [*abe getheilt*] from the external birth, not in the sense that there would be two things up to now in this world. Else the human being would have no hope. And in that case this world would not stand in the power and love of God. Rather, the divinity is con-

cealed in the external birth" (510–13). The world itself, however, is, since Lucifer's fall, "the house of tribulation or hell [*das Haus der tribsal oder der Hellen*]" (154/55), or "encompassed by hell and death" (352/53). Yet because Lucifer himself was born of God (386/87), this death would have always been a potential in God. Hence, when Böhme outlines the seven qualities, or motions, that make up all of nature in the first chapter of his book, each is accordingly discussed as a "source [*Quelle*]" or "mother [*Mutter*]" of life and as a "source" or "house of death [*Haus des Todes*]" (117–25). In his monograph on Böhme, Alexandre Koyré emphasizes, "light and shadows, if one reprises this classical comparison, oppose one another, but not as the being and non-being of the light, for the shadows *are* just as much as the light" (73). As O'Regan puts it, following Koyré (247), the critical word "quality" itself is, for Böhme, critical in its double resonance, on the one hand as a "*Quell*, which points to a surging, pulsating force'" and on the other, as "*Quahl*, which means pain" (41).

15. Böhme refers repeatedly to "die Euserliche begreiffligkeit" (510), or bodily "begreiffligkeit" (522, 756) which Weeks translates as "the external palpability" (511, 757). (However, "begreiffligkeit" also means, more broadly, conceivability and graspability, and thus contains both mental and physical objects.) Conversely, "all of what is in spirit stands in ungraspability [*alles des was im Geiste in der vnbegreiffligkeit stehed*]" (520/21), and although Böhme adds that spirit *can* grasp itself, nothing said of it can be grasped properly in words. Hence, he cannot but pledge not to mean what he says when he describes the heavens, on which see below.

16. For a list of further epithets to denote the namelessness of God, see O'Regan 32, who will also go on to complicate the "apophatic" character of divinity in Böhme's oeuvre.

17. O'Regan also speaks of the diabolical split in and through the visible world as a scission—writing, "Lucifer decides against the doxological posture" (43)—which the Apocalypse would ultimately purge. However, he does not comment upon the doubling of scissions that structure Böhme's remarks in *Aurora*, because he is primarily concerned with elaborating the more general patterns of Böhme's thought, which come to fruition in the later works, for which, he writes, "*Aurora* cannot function as the interpretive key" (131).

18. Thus Böhme can also write, "For the right heaven is everywhere, also in the place where you stand and go [*Den der rechte Himmel ist allendhalben / Auch ahn dem orte wo du stehest vnd gehest*]" (554/55). Koyré emphasizes this co-location as well (162–63)

19. My thanks to Blake Wilcox for his translation suggestion and for his assistance in tracking down the scholarly literature on Schlegel's reception of Böhme.

20. Here I quote from van Ingen's edition, which includes this final chapter, while Weeks's does not. Böhme's sentence reads in German: "Ich bescheide den Gott-liebenden Leser / daß diß Buch MORGENROTE nicht ist vollendet worden / dan der Teufel gedachte feyer-abend damit zu machen / weil er sahe / daß der Tag darinnen wolte anbrechen" (497).

21. I refer here to the etymology of "diabolic," from διαβάλλειν, "to throw or cast across," and "set at variance" (LSJ, s.v.).

22. This claim for the importance of Böhme to Schlegel's project holds true, even if, as Mayer asserts, Schlegel begins to take some distance from this Protestant mystic around the time of his decision to convert to Catholicism. Mayer traces the shifts in Schlegel's engagement with Böhme, from his earliest attested encounter with *Aurora* around 1798 through his more intensive engagement with Böhme's theosophy in the lectures he delivered in Cologne (113–78). She notes a tendency on Schlegel's part, beginning around 1805, to praise Böhme, while criticizing Böhme's suggestion that "creation [is] ineluctably evil" in setting Lucifer together with God from the beginning (145–46). However, she does not discuss the fragments devoted to Schlegel's *Aurora* project quoted in this chapter, except for the longer one on the dithyrambs that I address below—and where I will also address her interpretation in more detail. Neither she nor other commentators on the Romantics' reception of Böhme, such as Marshall Brown, draw attention to the resonance of Böhme's eschatological thinking in Schlegel's philosophical and poetic plans (see Brown 129–41). Recent discussions of Schlegel's anticipation of the end of the world in his late lectures, notes, and poetry include Keiner 157–69, 188–92, Oesterle 110–18, and Malinowski 231 (where she asserts, however, that Schlegel alters "the par for course apocalyptic interpretation and opposes to it the prospect of a better future"). However, none of these writers devote significant attention to *Aurora*.

23. "Die π[Poesie] d.[er] Aurora (als Ahndung des Neuen Evang[eliums] <Apokalypse pp>) muß nicht wie eine *Art* und *Form* der Poesie behandelt werden—sondern das innre Wesen d[er] π[Poesie] muß hier durchaus neu und magisch erzeugend und mit constitutiver Gewalt hervorbrechen.—Sie müßte also nicht als Element des Epos sondern als außer aller Reihe ganz für sich betrachtet werden."

24. "Poesie" implies "making," as derived from its Greek root, ποιεῖν—and as others have observed, such as Hamacher and Lacoue-Labarthe and Nancy (278–84), the Romantics took this sense of the word seriously in developing their program of transcendental poetry—with serious consequences for the positional logic of Fichte. See esp. Hamacher, *Entferntes Verstehen* 195–234.

25. For this reason, *Aurora* should also be absolved from the two commingled senses of "genre" that Jacques Derrida retraces near the beginning of his essay "The Law of Genre," namely: nature and law, biology and typology (*Parages* 253). Derrida's remarks on genre emerge out of a commentary on Lacoue-Labarthe and Nancy's discussion of the issue in *L'absolu littéraire* (see *Parages* 255–56, 259), as well as Gérard Genette's essay "Genres, 'Types,' Modes." It is, of course, not entirely clear whether one might understand "form" in its pairing with "kind [*Art*]" in a way that aligns precisely with the supposedly artificial "law" that Derrida pairs with "nature" in his essay. Nonetheless, Schlegel's words seem to bespeak a similiarly structured opposition, if Peter Szondi's argument be generalized: namely, that "form" differs in Schlegel's literary-theoretical remarks from "kinds of poetry [*Dichtarten*]," in such a way that the latter refers to historically specific generic conventions, and the former, to the "formal, technical moments of an artwork, which in themselves may be ahistorical and eternally different from one another, but which, through their concretization in a singular artwork, participate in its historicity and stand in ever different, historically determined functional contexts" ("Friedrich Schlegels" 194).

26. The phrase "constitutive Gewalt" is political in register and would refer to the force that constitutes the constitution, and thus the foundation, for any laws of any state institution. In a variant of this phrase (and of the terms of Jean-Jacques Rousseau and Immanuel Kant), Schlegel comments on the state constitution and its fictional status in his review of Kant's *Zum ewigen Frieden* from 1796, "Essay on the Concept of Republicanism, Occassioned through the Kantian Text on Perpetual Peace [*Versuch über den Begriff des Republikanismus veranlaßt durch die Kantische Schrift zum ewigen Frieden*]," on which see below.

27. The German reads: "Sie wird gewiß kommen, die Zeit eines neuen ewigen Evangeliums, die uns selbst in den Elementarbüchern des Neuen Bundes versprochen wird." Schlegel distinguished this pronunciation of Lessing's as preeminently important, first in the 1801 continuation of his early essay on Lessing from 1797, where he appends the poem "Something That Lessing Said." In it, he cites and adapts Lessing's pronunciation of the coming time of a new evangelium, to the exclamatory, "The new evangelium will come! [*Es wird das neue Evangelium kommen!*]." Later, in an essay that Schlegel includes in the third volume of his selected edition of Lessing's works from 1804, "On the Character of Protestants," he calls this "announcement of a new evangelium" the "most important point [*wichtigste Punkt*]" of Lessing's confession of faith and reprints his own poem (*Lessings Geist* 3: 21, 22).

28. Given Schlegel's attentiveness to etymology and the morphemes of individual words, it is not impossible to hear in the verb "behandeln," which usually means "to treat," the transformation of "handeln," or "act" into a transitive verb, via the prefix "be-," so that one might translate "behandeln" with "to turn into praxis or action."

29. There, the note reads as a series of equations between kinds of poetry and working titles for projects, the first two of which allude also to works of Böhme— *Aurora* and *De signatura rerum*—"(Note. Absolute π [Poetry] = Aurora / Systematic <universal> = The Nature of Things / Transcendental = Dodecamerone)."

30. It may be objected that the term "Epos," given Schlegel's constant reconsiderations of genre, from his earliest studies in classical philology through to his last poetic tables of categories, may mean much more, or at least something entirely different, than "word" or "myth." Nonetheless, insofar as Schlegel has already dimissed any treatment of *Aurora* as a "kind and form" of poetry, "Epos" could only mean here the utmost limit of poetic genres and forms—from which *Aurora*, too, would have to differ—and thus would have to be taken in its double sense, as both the word (*epos*) and as the original, amorphous production of poetry, before any formal divisions—including the division of poetry from philosophy, law, and natural science—as Schlegel had characterized it a decade earlier in his discussion of epic "legend" and "myth" in his *History of the Poetry of the Greeks and Romans* (1: 422–23, 455–56, 543).

31. The German text reads: "Die Konstitution ist der Inbegriff der permanenten Verhältnisse der politischen Macht, und ihrer wesentlichen Bestandteile. Die Regierung hingegen ist der Inbegriff aller transitorischen Kraftäußerungen der politischen Macht. Die Bestandteile der politischen Macht verhalten sich untereinander und zu ihrem Ganzen, wie die verschiedenen Bestandteile des Erkenntnisvermögens untereinander und zu ihrem Ganzen. Die konstitutive Macht entspricht

der Vernunft, die legislative dem Verstande, die richterliche der Urteilskraft und die exekutive der Sinnlichkeit, dem Vermögen der Anschauung. Die konstitutive Macht ist notwendig diktatorisch: denn es wäre widersprechend, das Vermögen der politischen Prinzipien, welche erst die Grundlage aller übrigen politischen Bestimmungen und Vermögen enthalten sollen, dennoch von diesen abhängig machen zu wollen; und eben deswegen nur transitorisch. Ohne den Akt der Akzeption würde nämlich die politische Macht nicht repräsentiert, sondern zediert werden, welches unmöglich ist.—Die Konstitution betrifft die Form der Fiktion und die Form der Repräsentation."

32. Armin Erlinghagen, in his study of the concept of "the whole" in Schlegel's corpus, also notices that this passage, among other, similar formulations, bespeaks a "simultaneously productive and receptive factum," where "factum" is glossed etymologically, in accordance with Schlegel's usage: "that which is made [*Hervorgebrachtes*]" (41–42). However, in accenting almost exclusively the productive potential of this structure, he attends less to the way Schlegel's sentence entails privations and negations ("without [*ohne*]," "not [*nicht*]," "impossible [*unmöglich*]"), which develop a logic of their own and invite the consideration that the definition of political power, which proceeds *via negativa*, may itself point to its impossibility. The resonance and etymological connection between the German word for "power [*Macht*]" and "impossible [*unmöglich*]" also reinforce this more negative reading.

33. Of course, *poiesis* never could do this, even in light of the primacy of "imagination" (*Einbildungskraft*) that Schlegel and many of his friends from the Jena circle had maintained. For the productivity that would thereby be implied could only be endlessly continued—or deferred. Again, the best analysis of the centrality and de-centering effects of poetry in Schlegel's thinking—as a consequence of Schlegel's interpretations of Fichte and Kant—is Hamacher, *Entferntes Verstehen* 195–234. La-coue-Labarthe and Nancy also emphasize the impossibility that the poetry the early Romantics called for could be produced or realized, as a consequence of its projected or presupposed absoluteness and infinity (263–88, esp. 266–67).

34. See 16: 325, 500, 505, 509; 17: 78, 99; 18: 459; 19: 84.

35. For notes that reflect the first possibility, see 16: 399, 422; 18: 439; the second, 16: 277, 17: 81, 18: 459; and the third, 16: 310, 311; 17: 60, 165.

36. For these three alternatives, see 16: 399, 403, 421; 18: 472, 473 on the first; 16: 350, 383, 470, 473 on the second; and 16: 320, 387, 425 on the third. Given the frequency of remarks on *Aurora* throughout Schlegel's notes, it should also be noted that none of these lists is exhaustive, but merely an indication of where, among other passages, one finds these tendencies registered in Schlegel's plans.

37. The German text reads: "Aurora schon nothwendig, um an die Stelle des *Paradise lost* und des *Messias* etwas andres ächt poetisches und christliches zu sezen."

38. As Schlegel had once said of philosophy in his lectures on transcendental philosophy in Jena 1800–01: "Of philosophy one could say what an Italian poet said of God: Philosophy is a circle, whose center is everywhere and whose periphery is nowhere [*Von der Philosophie könnte man sagen, was ein Italiänischer Dichter von Gott sagte: Die Philosophie ist ein Zirkel, dessen Centrum überall und dessen Peripherie nirgends ist*]" (12: 11).

39. Here I refer not only to those passages in which Schlegel explicitly designates *Aurora* a "central poem" (e.g., 16: 355, 17: 106) but also to those constellations
of poetic projects that Schlegel maps in diagrams, often setting *Aurora* in the center
(e.g., 16: 368, 402, 472).

40. Thus, in his introduction to the seventeeth volume of the *Kritische Fried-
rich-Schlegel Ausgabe*, Behler takes up disparate passages devoted to *Aurora* as an example of how "it would be incorrect to ascribe to an arbitrarily drawn strand from
these plans a greater significance than the others or to assume that there were a line
of development between these temporally disparate plans in, for example, the sense
of a greater or more encompassing Christian or Catholic tendency" (17: xiv). Although this observation is true in many respects, there are similarities among many
of the fragments written under the sign of "Aurora" and at least several signs that indicate a more specific direction for the project toward the end of Schlegel's writing.
Schlegel's *Aurora* could never be an object of pure positivistic or empirical inquiry,
but this should not exclude a priori an attempt to read what Schlegel wrote of it and
notice the—never quite consistent—trajectory his notes took.

41. See also 16: 173, 200, 277, 311, 324, 328, 333, 374, 401, 404, 423, 427, 436, 474.

42. For instances of the first designation, see 16: 198, 374, 386; for the second, see
16: 173, 481; 17: 70, 81.

43. In his notebooks with remarks on literature and poetry recorded between
1817 and 1820, Schlegel writes of *Edda*: "Remarkable, HOW MUCH THAT IS TRUE
is contained in the *Edda* on the *downfall of the world* (the twilight of gods and night
and Lokes's victory)—and then the glorification that follows [*Merkwürdig, WIE VIEL
WAHRES in der* Edda *über den* Untergang der Welt *(die Götterdämmerung und Nacht und
Lokes Sieg)—und die dann folgende Verklärung enthalten ist*]" (17: 449).

44. "Es könnte ein Gedicht Statt finden, als *Abschied* von der *bisherigen* Poesie—
und Wendepunkt des Uebergangs zu der neuen Poesie—zur *Aurora*. Erst muß es in
die heil[ige] *Einöde* in die *Nacht* führen—aus der dann die neue Morgenröthe em-
porblüht."

45. Earlier in the book of the Hebrew prophet, the new growth that Isaiah announces is associated explicitly with blooming, as it is in Schlegel's note—"The wilderness and the dry land shall be glad, the desert shall rejoice and blossom; like the
crocus it shall blossom abundantly [*Aber die Wüsten vnd Einöde wird lustig sein / vnd
das Gefilde wird frölich stehen / vnd wird blühen wie die Lilien.*]" (Isa. 35.1)—whereby this
particular flower is also the one that Böhme recurs to, repeatedly, as when he ends
De signatura rerum with the pronunciation, on and for those who find God: "Then
a lily blooms over mountain and vale, in all ends of the earth: he who seeks there,
finds. Amen [*dann eine Lilie blühet vber Berge vnd Thal / in allen Enden der Erden: Wer
da suchet der findet. Amen*]" (788). Likewise, the final advertisement of *De tribus principiis* reads: "The lily will not be won in war or strife but in a friendly humble spirit
of love, with good reason, which will break and dispel the smoke of the devil, and
grow green for a time [*Die Lilie wird nicht im Krieg oder Streit gewonnen werden; sondern
in einem freundlichen demüthigen Liebe-Geiste, mit guter Vernunft, der wird den Rauch des
Teufels zerbrechen und vertreiben, und grünen eine Zeit*]" (482).

46. Of lyric poetry, he will write in 1812: "Most commensurate to the *idea* of the lyrical poem are the *apocalyptic future* songs" (17: 406).

47. Other remarks to this end include his statement, "In the *Encomium of the Spirits,* the *entire idea of this new poetry* of the Last Judgment according to all traits of the Apocalypse could be—entirely spoken and not merely suggested" (17: 470), and his proscription: "From *biblical* history only *tragic presentation of the downfall of the Antichrist* may be taken up" (17: 473). Furthermore, since Schlegel also repeatedly considers composing *Aurora* in hieroglyphs (e.g., 16: 317, 324, 377; 17: 70, 393), and since the marginal note he appends to his last note on *Aurora* from 1823 prescribes the *"whole, typical image and holy hieroglyphic language* of the Bible" (17: 471), it is also thinkable that his last major poetic work, which breaks off betimes, like Böhme's, is the continuation of *Aurora*: namely, "The Song of Hieroglyphs; or, Echoes and Images of Time and Future," which is drawn above all from the Apocalypse of John, but also entails many other images from the Old and New Testaments. For a discussion of the background of this poem and an exhaustive account of its biblical allusions, see Anstett.

48. In her monograph on the dithyramb, Francesca Fantoni also refers to this fragment, but like Mayer, she does not perform a detailed reading of it. Instead, she focuses on the way in which the fragment illustrates what she attempts to reconstruct as Schlegel's "concept of the dithyramb [*Begriff des Dithyrambos*]," which, she asserts, entails the "enthusiasm traditionally bound with the dithyramb" in ancient poetics, but in such a way that its "dynamic of law and freedom" informs Schlegel's project of "progressive universal poetry" (64). This transformation of the ancient genre to a modern form, she argues, takes place via Schlegel's reading of Plato's prose—especially his prose concerning love—as dithyrambic (53–57). Regarding the fragment in question, she cites several passages from it as evidence for the way "Schlegel wanted [. . .] to shape the genre of the dithyramb with modern, Christian motifs," in accordance with the "ideal of a new mythology" outlined in his *Conversation on Poetry* (161).

49. "Zu den Dithyramben. Die Διθ[Dithyramben] = Kosmogonie + παθ / o[absolutes Pathos]. Die Welt als χα[Chaos], und χα[Chaos] für die Welt.—Das *Universum* ist ewig und unveränderlich, aber die *Welt* als κοσμος ist im ewigen Werden.— *Evangelium der Poesie*; also *Poesie der Poesie*.—<Es muß anfangen mit d[em] *Geist* und s.[einer] innren Schöpfungskraft.—> Orgien der Fantasie; Poesie zum Schluß als das Wort des Rätsels.—Chöre von Kindern, Mädchen, Jünglingen, Müttern, Männer, Priestern pp—den Ursprung d[er] Welt singen die Priester.—Die Mutter und die Kinder müssen die Liebe ausdrücken / die Jünglinge und Mädchen die Natur.—Alleg.[orie] <vom> *Baum des Lebens / Quell d[er] Freude*—die *Liebe* ist d[er] göttliche Funken durch d[en] das todte Universum zur Natur belebt wird, und durch die Vernunft erhebt s.[ich] die Natur wieder zur Gottheit.—Das Ganze = Mysterien der Natur—und Orgien der Schönheit oder der Liebe.—Alle Bilder sind wahr.—<Alle Bilder sind wahr.> *Licht* ist Leben und Liebe; alle Materie ist menschlich und alle Form göttlich. Die Rückkehr zu den Elementen ist das was eigentl[ich] d[en] Menschen von Thieren und Pflanzen unterscheidet.—*Paradies.*—Ansicht d[er] Mahlerei? *Adam und Eva.*—Der Himmel innerlich wie im Böhme.—Fülle d[er] Alleg[orien]

und Gesichte.—*Darstell[un]g des Himmels.*—Ein *Lichtreich* wie im Dante.—Die Menschheit ein unmittelbarer Ausfluß der Gottheit.—Auch Thiere, Pflanzen und Elemente idealisirt nach d[em] Charakter jener. Unmittelbares Anschauen der Sonne, und auch sonst urspüngl.[icher] Sinn der jezt verlohren ist. Vernehmen der Musik d[er] Sphär[en] der Liebe in der Natur. Spielende Engel wie im Böhme. Die primitive Sprache so viel als möglich nachgebildet. / *Titanen* sehr gut um die wilde Natur d[er] Menschen nach d[er] ersten Explosion zu bezeichnen.—Die Wildheit nach d[er] erst[en] Explosion—die goldne Zeit nach der ersten zufälligen Revoluzion—Dann wieder eine zufällige Störung; sonst würde das Zeitalter der Liebe ewig gewesen sein."

50. Looking to Schlegel's other notes on the genre testifies only to the impossibility of determining its form, as when he calls the "Dithyrambic Phantasy [Διθ *[Dithyrambische] Fant[asie]]*" the "unform, antiform and superform," for which the "material" must be "absolutely absolute and absolutely universal" (16: 119). Fantoni also cites and analyzes this passage and its implications for generic form (159–60).

51. The narrative of a second kindling of light and life on earth follows in the seventeenth chapter of Böhme's *Aurora*, where the deadening of matter through Lucifer's burnout is narrated (504–09). In this passage, the word "spark [*funcke*]" is used solely with reference to Lucifer's "rage [*zorn*]." Elsewhere, however—in accordance with the premise that Lucifer also is a manifestation of God's light, and that God is a "twofold god [*zwifacher Gott*]" (508/09)—the same word will be used for the life-giving light that remains concealed in man (e.g., 110/11).

52. In his monograph on Böhme, Koyré traces the word "chaos" to the works of Paracelsus, where it refers to the confused indistinction of a germ before its development, and thus figures as a *potentia ad esse*, in which, as Böhme writes in the *Clavicula*, the "possibility of revelation and outward birth [*Ausgeburt*] lies" (71). Whether or not Schlegel had read *Mysterium magnum* by this time, the word could come from Böhme, insofar as "chaos" was already noted as one of Böhme's signature terms in exchanges between Novalis and Tieck, in ways that resonate with its usage in that work. In a letter from 23 February 1800 to Tieck—who was in Jena at the time (i.e. near Schlegel)—Novalis wrote, "I am now reading Jacob Böhme [. . .] and beginning to understand him as he has to be understood. One sees in him throughout the forceful spring with its swelling, driving, forming and mixing powers, which bear the world outward from within.—A genuine chaos full of dark desire and wonderful life—a veritable microcosm going asunder [*Jacob Böhme lese ich jetzt [. . .] und fange ihn an zu verstehn, wie er verstanden werden muß. Man sieht durch aus in ihm den gewaltigen Frühling mit seinen quellenden, treibenden, bildenden und mischenden Kräften, die von innen heraus die Welt gebären.—Ein ächtes Chaos voll dunkler Begier und wunderbaren Leben—einen wahren, auseinandergehenden Microcosmus]*" (4: 322–23). The second time Böhme uses the word "chaos" in *Mysterium magnum*, it is illustrated through the example of man as microcosmos: "You are the small world from the greater one, your external light is a chaos of suns and the stars, else you could not see sunlight" (10). Furthermore, Novalis's previous familiarity with Paracelsus suggests a usage of "chaos" in the sense that Böhme had adopted (and adapted) from the alchemist. All of these exchanges speak for

the possibility that Schlegel could have encountered "chaos" in association with Böhme through his friends and used the word in this way.

53. Given Schlegel's subsequent reference to the poem "To the Germans" on the same page as his fragment on the dithyrambs—in one of several further reflections on the dithyrambs—the fragment must date from around 1800. On a page from his philosophical notebook dated 1799, he reformulates the triad of his opening equation on the dithyrambs in the following entries: "The universum perhaps merely a historical concept that comprises the world, humanity, reason, nature—is χαος, πᾶν and κοσμος at once;" "πᾶν = χαος + κοσμος.—κοσμος is only thinkable through and with an infinite reason" (18: 312). These notes reflect an attempt to think the "all" as the πᾶν, under which sign—in the formula ἑν καὶ πᾶν "one and all"—contemporary writers such as Hölderlin, following Jacobi, were thinking through a new pantheism developed along the lines of Spinoza's philosophy. By reformulating the πᾶν in a sentence on the simultaneous conjunction of cosmos and chaos, however, Schlegel intervenes and shifts the basis for considering the unifying principle of all through his articulation of chaos and order. Meanwhile, by designating the "all" a "*historical* concept" that would "at once" encompass all that takes shape and takes place—and dissolves—Schlegel also suggests that the primary problem of philosophy is first of all a problem of history and temporality. When, later, he replaces the term πᾶν with the term "Dithyrambs"—which originally denoted inspired songs sung for Dionysos, as well as Dionysos himself—Schlegel suggests that the "all" may be thought as a divine subject of song in every possible turn of the phrase. If, moreover, "chaos" is inspired by Böhme—for whom it contains the germ of eternity and temporality within it ("da alles innen lieget was Ewigkeit und Zeit ist" [*Mysterium magnum* 6]), the theological implications of Schlegel's statement are all the more complex. Either way, with the dithyrambs, the philosophical and theosophical problem becomes broken off, resumed, and pursued as a poetic one. For a different commentary on the relationship between chaos and system, see Frank 47–48.

54. In his lectures on philosophy in Cologne, Schlegel designates the world—or the "World-I [*Welt-Ich*]"—as a problem of "cosmogony [*Kosmogonie*]" (12: 410) and elaborates it as a genesis of the becoming of the world. But it is also—and first of all—a matter of time and its divisions, from which he deduces the laws of history: that every development must reach the critical point of return to its (transformed) beginning or conversion into its opposite (12: 412–19, esp. 417). These passages will have to be analyzed closely, but for now it is already clear that, when it comes to cosmogony, a historical concept is in question, one that could never coincide with a historical datum or factum, but that determines all such moments, and that, as such a determinant, belongs not to history proper, but to philosophy—which marks "the utmost limit points [*die äußersten Grenzpunkte*]," the "beginning and end [*Anfang und Ende*]" of all history (13: 15). Still more than this, however, the future of the cosmos—its ultimate fulfillment and tendency toward this end—is, according to Schlegel, only possible to articulate in poetry: "it would be easy to show here [*Es wäre hier leicht zu zeigen*]," he writes, "that also according to form, prophecy could be nothing other than poetry [*daß auch der Form nach jene Weissagung nichts als Poesie sein könne*]" (13: 55).

55. In a philosophical notebook entry from 1802, he will assert: "A cosm.[ogony] that is at once πφ [prophecy] could only be called *Aurora* [*Eine Kosm.[ogonie] die zugleich πφ [Prophetie] ist, kann nur Aurora heißen*]" (18: 439). On the same page as his note on the dithyrambs, but only in the margins, he will write later: "NOTE All of this for Aurora [*NOTA Zur Aurora alles dieß*]" (16: 199).

56. This may be one further way in which the fragment is connected with other notes on dithyrambs, for Schlegel had written earlier in his literary notebooks that the dithyramb is "outside/apart from any relation to an object [*außer Beziehung auf ein Objekt*]" (16: 149).

57. See Schelling I,7: 154–56. In the notes to the critical edition of this work, the editors emphasize that the notion of a first explosion is first proposed here (I,7: 413). In a letter from 10 August 1799, Schlegel writes to his brother August Wilhelm that Schelling had sent him his book—most likely the *Entwurf*—and that he cannot receive it soon enough (24: 307).

58. The German passages reads: "[I]st die Natur [. . . .] ursprünglich nur Producitivität, es kann also in dieser Productivität nichts bestimmtes seyn, (denn alle Bestimmung ist Negation), also kann es auch durch sie nicht zu Producten kommen." Between the topic of nature and the specific statement "for all determination is negation," the resonance of Schelling's remarks with Spinoza's famous dictum from his letter to Jarig Jelles, where he writes, "determination is negation [*determinatio negatio est*]" (*Opera* 4: 240), is unmistakable. Hence, he seems to confront here the problem of difference in nature that arises in Spinoza's work, where the accent falls upon positivity and upon nature as a *causa sui*.

59. This problem arises, of course, from the writings of Fichte, whose "I" should be pure activity and actuality, always setting itself, and with it, its ontological status. For this "I" could never come to consciousness, if it were not for the hindrance (*Hemmung*) of what it does not set, which Fichte calls the "non-I." In different terms, Schelling and Schlegel are equally concerned with articulating the relation between the unconditional and the conditioned, the infinite and the finite, the active subject and the states it suffers.

60. "Die Natur muß ursprünglich sich selbst Object werden, diese Verwandlung des reinen Subjects in ein Selbst-Object ist ohne ursprüngliche Entzweyung in der Natur selbst undenkbar."

61. Later in the *Entwurf*, he writes: "Identity gone forth from difference is indifference, the third [between opposition and a striving after identity] is thus a *striving after indifference*, which is determined through difference itself, and through which, in turn, this is determined. [. . .] There is here no first and second, but difference and striving after indifference is, temporally, straightout one and at once [*Identität aus Differenz hervorgegangen ist Indifferenz, jenes Dritte also ein Streben nach Indifferenz, das durch die Differenz selbst, und wodurch hinwiederum diese bedingt ist [. . .] Es ist hier kein Erstes und kein Zweites, sondern Differenz und Streben nach Indifferenz ist der Zeit nach schlechthin Eines und zugleich*]" (I,8: 63).

62. For a different account of Schlegel's engagement and distantiation from Schelling around this time, largely through a reading of Schlegel's Jena lectures on

transcendental philosophy and Schelling's *System des transzendentalen Idealismus*, see Peter 20–59.

63. This premise is no longer, however, accepted in mathematics as it was around the turn of the nineteenth century, on which see Maor.

64. In his study on Novalis, Howard Pollack also elaborates the way the infinitely great and infinitesimally small figure in his thinking on analogy, if not allegory, writing: "thus, the meaning of calculus for Novalis, the paradox in which it lives, is precisely its ability to bridge the two models of unification: continuity based on the transition generated by the infinitely small and analogy which goes on to infinity" (137).

65. Schlegel presents $0/1$ in analogy to the infinitely great $1/0$, as the representation of an approximation to zero, through the infinitestimally small. In his Jena lectures, Schlegel will reformulate his formulas precisely along these lines, in the context of a discussion of consciousness, writing "*consciousness* is so to speak $+ a - a \ldots$ a becoming and vanishing zero [*eine werdende und verschwindende Null*]," taking up the rhetoric of infinitesimal calculus, which entails "vanishing quanta [*verschwindende Größen*]." He then turns everything around in the next sentence: "the infinite is a limitless potentiated 1, from all sides [*Das Unendliche ist eine gränzenlos potenzierte 1, nach allen Seiten*]" (12: 25). The two quanta he names are already entailed in the series $+ a - a \ldots$, depending upon whether one ends with $+ a - a \ldots$ ($= 0$, ad infinitum), or the reverse: $+ a - a + a$ ($= 1$, *ad infinitum*). And the fact that Schlegel is talking about one series, and not two, is made explicit in his next sentence: "From *the* infinite, consciousness arises [*Aus dem Unendlichen entsteht das Bewußtseyn*]" (12: 25, my emphasis). Schlegel's inversion of the infinite ($1/0$) into an ultimate minimum ($0/1$), and vice versa, is also discussed in Smith, "Friedrich Schlegel's" 253.

66. In his excellent analysis, Frank does not enter into the differences between the remarks with which Schlegel addresses this duality and the cosmological derivations that Schlegel performs in his lectures in Jena (1800–01) and Cologne (1805–06). There, largely in response to Schelling, Schlegel proceeds from the premise of a scission, in every moment, between a productive infinity and infinite nullity, which are one. Frank cites and insightfully comments on Schlegel's philosophical notebooks from the period that concerns me here, but does not emphasize the mathematical formulas Schlegel drafts in order to represent the structures of time and space. Doing so yields a more differentiated discussion of simultaneity and allegory as well, which Frank discusses in ways that my commentary approaches (Frank 28–32), but that I also depart from in my analysis of Schlegel's logic of the *simul*—the simultaneous and the similar—on which see below.

67. However, this magic would be a most unpredictable one, for whereas Menninghaus accents self-referentiality in his reading of Novalis, Balfour rightly notes, in his reading of Novalis's "Monolog": "Paradoxically, the very autonomy of mathematics is what constitutes its similarity to 'ordinary' language, and so the 'autonomous' is not at all singular" (41). And for Schlegel, it is clear: the law (*nomos*) of any one, self (*autos*) or other, is always less than autonomous; no autonomy, but auto*tomy*. In his monograph on translation in the age of Goethe, Berman also discusses the predilection of Schlegel and Novalis for mathematics as one that belongs to a larger project, in which language itself would be "non-referential," or "a pure formaliza-

tion" (144). He, too, relates this nonreferentiality (or autoreferentiality) to an allegorical mode of presentation (144).

68. Insofar as the infinite one is thought of, from the start, as an infinite becoming, the splitting of one is the scansion of time that first makes a differentiation of moments thinkable. Schelling elaborates this implication at the start of his draft, when he introduces the problem of productivity in nature under the sign of time and intellect, which are here synonymous—time being the "infinite series in which our intellectual infinity evolves" (I,8: 42). Furthermore, both time and intellect are, at first, neither temporal nor conscious, until the breach "in each moment [*in jedem Moment*]" of our "acting [*Handeln*]"—that is, thinking—which he here calls "Reflexion" and praises as the "secret artifice through which our existence obtains *duration* [*geheime Kunstgriff, wodurch unser Daseyn Dauer erhält*]" (I,8: 42).

69. Schlegel writes: "Abstracted from all content, there is a peculiar rule of becoming:—becoming can be a gradually incrementing one, one which lawfully grows in a particular way, in increasing, incrementing progression; and to the extent that time and temporal relations are regarded here already, two more sorts of becoming offer themselves to us, which are different from those;—in opposition to the becoming that lawfully unfolds in time, thinkable, too, are also namely an *infinitely fast becoming*, and in opposition to this, an *infinitely slow one*" (12: 416). Before this passage, on the same page, he writes of time and space that the latter is "a spiritual essence, *complete* in itself [*ein geistiges, in sich* vollendetes *Wesen*]," while the former is "incomplete like the world itself [*unvollendet wie die Welt selbst*]," which division between completion and incompletion, thought infinitely, might be read as the reprisal of his earlier note: "time = 0/1 space = 1/0" (18: 420). Only according to these terms, which pervade his thinking on time from the time of Schelling's *Entwurf* onward, can it be explained that Schlegel speaks of temporality as a dynamic of polarity and indifference—with the implication that each pole operates simultaneously—in later fragments, on which see below. And only on this premise can it be explained that time and space are not essentially different, but themselves part of a continuum for Schlegel—such that, in the beginning as in the end, he will identify the future with space (cf. 12: 435, 19: 64).

70. Schlegel will also repeat this sentence in his Lessing essay (2: 116)—but with an accent upon understanding and knowing rather than being. This accent, while consonant with Schelling's notions of the identity of intellect and time, takes his proposition in a very different direction. What is more, Schlegel introduces this reformulation of Schelling in terms of the differences and crossings of philosophy, poetry, and philology, with crucial implications for his thinking on each. It would not be possible to pursue these implications in this chapter, but for an excellent reading of these passages and the broken structure of self-affection that is therein implied, see Hamacher, "For—Philology" (*Minima* 127–31).

71. The translation offered here is based on David Farrell Krell's translation of Heidegger's translation of the fragment in his essay on the "Anaximander Fragment [*Spruch Anaximanders*]" (Heidegger, *Early Greek Thinking* 20).

72. In a very different context, Jacques Derrida comes to a very similar reading of the implications of Aristotle's usage of *hama,* or 'simultaneously,' in his discussion of the 'now' in the *Physics.* See Derrida, "Ousia et grammè."

73. Early in his monograph, Frank comes to a similar conclusion and even speaks of an infinite series, writing, "Schlegel's infinite series is, with regard to its immanence of the absolute, a pure chaos" (28), but he does not note the chasm implicit in this chaos—which Schlegel also most likely takes up from the opening of Hesiod's *Theogony*—or reflect upon the simultaneity that creates a rift in infinity, along the lines Schlegel sketches. Frank implicitly addresses this rift, however, when he later cites a remark by Schlegel on the "relation of twofold infinities [*Verhältnis zweier Unendlichkeiten*]" (72) in the context of a discussion of "infinite oneness" and "infinite fullness." What is primarily at stake for me in this chapter, however, is the possibility that this twofold structure may follow from Schlegel's considerations of oneness itself.

74. Of course, there are other particular instances of chiasm that open into a chasm and that have been noted in other contexts. However, the effects of the structure are contingent on its singular context. In his introduction to Warminski's *Readings in Interpretation,* Rodolphe Gasché makes a similar remark in the context of a discussion of de Man's and Derrida's particular evocations of this figure (xxv).

75. The importance of mathematics to the structure of Romantic reflection—and Romantic thinking on language—is elaborated by Menninghaus in both *Unendliche Verdoppelung* and "Die frühromantische Theorie von Zeichen und Metapher," though in the former work, he emphasizes primarily the doubling implicit in thinking toward the infinite, and not the fractioning that is equally crucial to Schlegel, whose consequences I delineate, in part, here. In his article, he attributes the Romantics' interest in considering language mathematically to the way in which mathematics was considered by writers such as Kant to be "a pure construction of the human spirit" (49), which leads his own considerations in a very different direction from mine as well.

76. The German reads: "Aus der *Allegorie* (Erklärung vom Daseyn der Welt) folgt, daß in jedem Individuo nur so viel Realität ist, *als es Sinn, als es Bedeutung, Geist hat.*" In this text, which reflects the lectures on transcendental philosophy that Schlegel held in Jena between 1800 and 1801, he introduces allegory just after he poses the following question, which shows itself to be nothing other than another, negative formulation of the problem of natural productivity and annihilation, as he had posed it in his philosophical notes and, implicitly, in his draft on the dithyrambs: "Why does the play of nature not run its course into nullity, so that absolutely nothing exists? [*Warum läuft das Spiel der Natur nicht in einem Nu ab, so daß also gar nichts existirt?*]" (12: 39). The close relationship between this text and his note on the dithyrambs is evident, too, from the way that its operative terms are, again, chaos and world, albeit ordered differently, as when he writes: "*chaos* arose for us from the elements and identity [*[uns] entstand [. . .] das Chaos aus den Elementen und der Identität*]" (12: 40).

77. This semantic structure is noted by Frank as well in—nearly—identical terms (31).

78. Smith, "Friedrich Schlegel's" 250 also notes the relationship of allegory to Schlegel's continuum of 0/1 and 1/0, but only in passing.

79. Novalis, in the context of his own mathematical studies, draws the same conclusion, writing in one notebook: "Matter is divisible *ad infinitum,* because it is individual—undivided. [*Die Materie ist theilbar ins unendliche, weil sie* individuell—*ungetheilt ist*]" (Hardenberg 2: 67).

80. For the Eleatic Visitor's description of the "other [τὸ ἕτερον]," which he will later call the proper designation for "what is not [μὴ ὄν]" (257 b8–c3), in terms of relations (πρὸς τί, 'toward,' 'in relation to'), see 258 c12–d7. The "as" structure of what is, is articulated most clearly in the definition of the true and false speech (263 b4–9). For an extremely thorough discussion of this "as" and "toward" structure, see Heidegger, *Platon: Sophistes,* esp. 430–33, 563–64.

81. On these plans, see Behler's commentary in 19: 535–38. The majority of scholarship on Plato and Schlegel tends to remain centered upon the importance of the *Symposium* to his early fragments and the *Gespräch über die Poesie* (e.g., Mergenthaler) or more generally on the importance of the dialogic form and irony to his thinking (e.g., Hamlin). Frank refers to Schlegel's multiple mentions of the "ὄντως ὄν des Plato" (26), but does not discuss them in detail or situate them in the context of the *Sophist,* a dialogue in which the formulation occurs frequently. However, it is telling for any assessment of Schlegel's reception of Plato that, around 1800, he takes up the problem of the truth of images that guides the entire dialogue of the *Sophist.* Furthermore, in his notes, he repeatedly returns to the formulation that concerns the participants of that dialogue. For the *Sophist* also revolves around the question of the ability to say what "truly" or "really" is (ὄντως ὄν)—which Schlegel ultimately describes as a poetic possibility, writing of the plural, "οντως οντα"—"only poetry can and should present [them]" (18: 345). This pluralization and poeticization of true being is of a piece with his emphatic remark: "all images are true" (16: 199).

82. It is crucial to the logic of the dialogue that, from the start, the making of images was introduced as nothing other than a construal and reproduction of proportions—"according to the symmetries of the paradigm in length and width and depth, and in addition to these, colors" (235 d7–e1). The Eleatic Visitor recurs to this trope repeatedly, as when he says, "cutting then along the width [. . .] [let us now cut] lengthwise" (266 a1–2). That is, the image is considered from the start as a logos in the sense of "proportion," and not primarily as an object of visual perception. Moreover, the Eleatic Visitor's first discussion of false speeches follows immediately from his evocation of the reproduction of all things—in imagistic likeness—as a distortion of proportions. For such speeches make "the small things *appear* as great ones, the difficult ones as easy [ὥστε σμικρὰ μὲν φαίνεσθαι τὰ μεγάλα, χαλεπὰ δὲ τὰ ῥάδια]" (234 d6–7, my emphasis). The importance of proportion to both the Eleatic Visitor's discussion of images and the logos is addressed in Villela-Petit, who cites Gadamer's and Stenzel's previous discussions of this relation (77), but in the particular context of the visual arts of Plato's time (76–80).

83. Although speech is most explicitly thematized at the end of the Eleatic Visitor's dialogue, the premise that knowing depends upon saying is implicit throughout. For example, the Eleatic Visitor remarks that those thinkers who refuse to call anything another—that is, to predicate it—and thereby utter its "sharing in the experience of another [κοινωνία παθήματος ἑτέρου]" (252 b9–10) cannot know what they say. They also do not speak anything that they know, since their own words refute them: for example, when it comes to "'to be,'" the Eleatic Visitor argues, "they are forced in some way [. . .] to make use, too, of 'apart' and 'from others,' and 'according to itself,' and myriad others, which they are powerless to shut out [εἴργεσθαι] and not take up together in those speeches." "Thus," he concludes, "they are in need of no other refutations" (252 c2–5). This premise is something the Eleatic Visitor takes from his "father" (241 d5) and teacher Parmenides himself—with the argument that not being cannot be, because it cannot be said, for in saying "not being" one attributes being to it, as well as the status of a something and a number. In using the verb εἴργεσθαι ('shut out') he also recalls the sentence of Parmenides that he had quoted before and decided to dare to violate—namely, "May you never let this thought overcome you, he says, that nonbeing is / but shut [εἶργε] this way out as you seek" (237 a 8–9).

84. Villela-Petit also notes the way that the dialogue itself produces the appearance of the sophist (56).

85. For all the rigor and detail of his commentary on this passage (*Platon* 452–55), Heidegger skips over this part of the sentence, and thus the possibility that a speech (λόγος) could lack reason (or its homonym: λόγος). Yet he carefully traces the argument of the Eleatic Visitor that one can say neither that words are something different nor that they are the same as the things they name. If words were different things from what they name, that would mean that there are two separate things, and that words, remaining separate, never speak of anything at all. But if one says they are the same, then words are the names for nothing else but themselves, and if one still insists that a name is the name of something, then "the name is the name alone of a name, being nothing else [τὸ ὄνομα ὀνόματος ὄνομα μόνον, ἄλλον δὲ οὐδενὸς ὄν]" (244 d3–9, see Heidegger, *Platon* 452). This logic bears out, too, in the near liquefaction of "name" and "alone" in the Eleatic Visitor's sentence, through the permutations of ov / oμ / vo that make up these two names.

86. That is, the syntactic conjunction of noun (ὄνομα) and verb (ῥῆμα), which make up the minimal units of predication.

87. One could also say that words *are* the images that the Eleatic Visitor first lists by name—but not exhaustively—when he introduces the pretensions of makers of likenesses to make "you and me, and all other living beings and trees [. . .] and the sea and earth and sky and gods and all other things"—toward the opening of the dialogue (233 e5–6, 234 a 3–4). And in his list, incidentally—aside from you and me—he names precisely the first topoi that occur in the cosmogony of Hesiod. This insertion of "you and me" is, however, critical, because it will be you and me, the pronominal shifters of the dialogue—and therefore also no general community of speakers of a language, but the participants in a particular exchange, as it is happen-

ing—who ultimately decide and speak the true and false in the end (see below, n. 88).

88. The dialogue thus seems to suggest that truth can be decided only with other words of another, which has everything to do, in turn, with the Eleatic Visitor's persistent and ostentatious ventriloquism of the other philosophers he evokes and refutes, as well as the extended debate at the start of the dialogue over whether the Eleatic Visitor should present an extended speech of his own or engage in dialogue. The decisive function of direct speech in the ultimate decision of truth vs. falsehood is a relatively inconspicuous detail that does not tend to be addressed in many major commentaries on the dialogue; see e.g., Heidegger, *Platon* 599–610, Rosen 293–308, Ambuel 170–75. However, one might read the further consequences of this premise for verification in Schlegel's lecture devoted to psychology in Cologne, albeit in a very modified form that also opposes Fichte's division of the "I [*Ich*]" from the "Non-I [*Nicht-Ich*]," when he distributes all knowing between each partial and individual "I" and an "opposite-I [*Gegen-Ich*]," which is "at once a you, he, we [*zugleich ein Du, Er, Wir*]" (12: 337).

89. The German text reads: "Es gibt zweierlei Ewigkeit durch Vernichtung der Pole (der Zukunft und Vergangenheit) und durch Vernichtung der Gegenwart—als der bindenden hemmenden Indifferenz.—Völlige Gegenwart wäre Todt.—Ewigkeit ist unendliche Zeitfülle nicht Zeitabwesenheit."

Empedocles, Empyrically Speaking: Friedrich Hölderlin's *Tragic Öde*

1. I quote from his letter to Isaak von Sinclair from 24 December 1798. The German text reads: "Ich habe dieser Tage in Deinem Diogenes Laertes gelesen. Ich habe auch hier erfahren, was mir schon manchmal begegnet ist, daß mir nemlich das Vorübergehende und Abwechselnde der menschlichen Gedanken und Systeme fast tragischer aufgefallen ist, als die Schicksaale, die man gewöhnlich allein die wirklichen nennt [. . .]" (*Sämtliche Werke: Frankfurter Ausgabe* 19: 343) For a thorough discussion of Hölderlin's engagement with ancient sources on the historical Empedocles, see Hölscher and Kranz.

2. With this phrase, I refer to Theresia Birkenhauer's lengthy monograph on Hölderlin's *Empedokles* project, *Legende und Dichtung*. In the first part of her book, she reconstructs Hölderlin's earlier plans to compose a tragic drama on the death of Socrates, and situates these plans within the context of contemporary interpretations of Socrates's suicide (16–95).

3. As Jennifer Anna Gosetti-Ferencei points out, Heidegger also depicts Hölderlin as a prophetic poet in his *Erläuterungen zu Hölderlins Dichtung*, when, for example, he poses the series of questions: "Who speaks here? Hölderlin himself. But who, here and now, is Hölderlin himself? The one whose essence finds its fulfillment in the 'willing' that this wind [from 'Andenken'] is and should be as it is" (qtd. in Gosetti-Ferencei 77), but that such remarks do not fully speak to the images and language of Hölderlin's poem, and the experience of a different, far more singular nature that is imagined therein (Gosetti-Ferencei 80).

4. In her monograph, *"Das Heilige sei mein Wort,"* Bernadette Malinowski touches upon *Empedokles* only briefly, drawing attention to the way, in Hölderlin's second draft, Empedokles is accused by Hermokrates, the priest of Akragas, of proclaiming himself a god and attempting to dominate nature with his word (140). But she restricts her remarks to only a few pages within her broader study of Hölderlin's poetological prose texts and "Patmos."

5. Eric Santner makes remarks to a similar effect in his excellent monograph devoted to the ways in which Hölderlin's poetry challenges the "narrative vision of history as *Heilsgeschichte*," which, he argues, has often been read as "the dominant text in the writings of Hölderlin" (25). There he writes: "the image of dissolution, of incineration, be it by a bolt of lightning or by the fires of Mt. Aetna, is one to which the poet is drawn over and over again as by a strange, irresistible, and yet deadly seduction" (60). He then presents a reading of the later poems, in which this desire is countered by a sober attentiveness to "concrete particulars" that resist subsumption in any narrative (121). His focus upon "paratactic forms" and upon narrative structures—inspired by Theodor Adorno's famous essay on Hölderln's late lyrics, "Parataxis"—differs from the figures of rupture that I examine in this chapter, because I do not concentrate on their effects upon narrative structures, as Santner does, or upon figures of conceptual and predicative synthesis, as Adorno does (see *Noten zur Literatur* 471–72).

6. For another interpretation that reflects this line of argumentation, see Kurz.

7. The first prominent proponent of this hypothesis is Bertaux. For an alternative and more nuanced reading of the relation between Hölderlin's drama and the French Revolution, see Szondi, "Der Fürstenmord." More recently, Alexander Honold has argued that "Empedokles is the abbreviation for Hölderlin's interpretation of temporal history [*Zeitgeschichte*] as an experimental situation" (322), which should take place in coordination with nature and lead to the establishment of a new calendar. In his historicizing approach to the drama, he reads the changes to each draft in synchrony with events such as Napoleon's appointment as first consul (321), and in relation to the festivals and cults established in France during the Revolution—as well as the new revolutionary calendar that had been introduced.

8. See also Birkenhauer, who argues that Hölderlin's drafts represent various stages in his "reflection on tragic form" (588), and Söring.

9. This hypothesis is argued at length in Lacoue-Labarthe's celebrated essay "Le césure speculatif," where he reads Empedocles's desire as one that would allow him to be the "One-Whole [*Un-Tout*]" of the speculative subject (60). One might say that this chapter is devoted to an explication of the linguistic implications of that desire.

10. The German text reads, "daß in der Literaturwissenschaft jeder einzelne Beleg, bevor ihm Beweiskraft zugeschrieben wird, nicht weniger sorgfältig für sich interpretiert werden muß als die Stelle, für deren Deutung er als Argument oder Gegenargument herangezogen wird" ("Traktat" 19).

11. Hölderlin 13: 868–69; Krell, *Death of Empedocles* 142. Throughout, I have relied upon David Farrell Krell's excellent translation of Hölderlin's *Empedokles* drafts and the prose texts that belong to the *Empedokles* corpus. However, I have occasion-

ally modified his translations when it seemed important to bring out additional resonances and interpretive possibilities offered by the original German text.

12. Friedrich Hölderlin to Karl Gok, August 1797 (19: 291).

13. Hölderlin's readings in Pliny go back at least to his time at the Tübinger Stift, where he cites him in an essay on the "Geschichte der schönen Künste unter den Griechen: Biß zu Ende des Perikleischen Zeitalters" (17: 51, 59).

14. This complex structure therefore involves more than the "motifs of fermentation and decomposition" that Honold perceptively draws attention to, but does not elaborate further (317).

15. For an excellent discussion of the sacred in Hölderlin, its relationship to nature and, before even this, the "force that opens to the sacred" within nature, see Blanchot, *La part du feu* 115–32. Blanchot draws explicitly and implicitly on the language of Hölderlin's drafts of *Empedokles*, where nature is proclaimed "the totality, without boundaries [*la totalité sans bornes*]" (119), and where the "repose [*repos*]" of nature that Blanchot will address (121–22) is spoken by Pausanius, Empedocles's disciple throughout Hölderlin's drafts (Hölderlin 13: 709).

16. And Krell does so in a language that—punctuated by excerpts from Hölderlin's letters and poetry—speaks to and from the texts he addresses exceptionally closely. Many of the passages he discusses will be retraced here, but with a different accent, and in other directions that Hölderlin's—and his—text open toward.

17. Here I depart from Krell's translation "supernal fire" (*Death of Empedocles* 142), since the "höchste Feuer" Hölderlin speaks of here may be as infernal as it is supernal, and may therefore be "highest [*höchst*]" in the sense of an extreme intensity, where no difference would subsist between the high and the low.

18. This translation is a modified version of the one Krell offers (*Death of Empedocles* 142).

19. This is a point that Balfour also emphasizes in *The Rhetoric of Romantic Prophecy* (182–83).

20. Attempts have been made to anchor the "tragic ode" in terms of Hölderlin's doctrine of the "alternation of tones [*Wechsel der Töne*]" (Lewis; Ryan, "Hölderlins Dichtungsbegriff" 33–36, *Hölderlins Lehre vom Wechsel der Töne* 107–10) or in terms of the composite word "tragedy" (τραγ-ῳδία)—so that the phrase would accentuate tragedy in its character, not as drama, but as inspired, Dionysian song (ῳδή) (Dahlke 206–07). Nonetheless, such attempts do not emphasize strongly enough that this ode has no precedent in the canon of poetic genres, which was already troubled by Friedrich Schiller's articulation of a system based on adjectival designations, such as "naive," "sentimental," "satirical," "idyllic," which, in turn, form no fixed categories, but can recombine in different ways (see, e.g., *Über naive und sentimentalische Dichtung* 728), and by the broader tendency in the eighteenth and early nineteenth centuries that Peter Szondi discusses in his lectures on "Antike und Moderne in der Ästhetik der Goethezeit" and "Hegels Lehre von der Dichtung" (*Poetik und Geschichtsphilosophie*). Around this time, a fixed, prescriptive "Gattungspoetik" begins to give way among major writers to a historical-philosophical investigation of aesthetics. Unprecedented even in light of his contemporaries' reconsiderations of genre,

however, Hölderlin's "tragic ode" may well designate an ode that flares up only in this singular text, with no other poetic existence.

21. This structure of reprisal has also been recently analyzed by Hannah Vandegrift Eldridge in the context of the prose text that begins, "Wenn der Dichter einmal des Geistes mächtig ist. . . ." She observes: "Hölderlin calls repeatedly for a further step for the completion of his oppositional structures, either remarking in the texts that something more is required or noting in paratexts that the text does not achieve its goal" (449).

22. For a lengthy discussion of Hölderlin's interest in etymology, in relation to his contemporaries, see Zuberbühler.

23. "Innigkeit," which might be translated as "intimacy," "intensity," or "inwardness," stubbornly resists, as so many of Hölderlin's words do, a definitive translation. I have chosen to adopt "intensity" with Krell, who discusses the difficulties of reading this term—as well as the problems involved in Heidegger's lengthy exegesis of "Innigkeit" as the "highest force of being-there [höchste Kraft des Daseins]" in his lecture course on Hölderlin's "Germanien" (Hölderlins Hymnen 117)—in Lunar Voices (40–45). Françoise Dastur makes strong arguments in favor of intensity as well (50–51).

24. A most rigorous reading of this essay, along with its consequences for Hölderlin's thinking of the tragic rapidity of time and the caesura, as Hölderlin will articulate it in his later "Remarks" on Oedipus and Antigone, is Hamacher, "Parusie, Mauern."

25. The ode's "experience" and "insight," which are the preconditions for its return to its "initial tone," are attained by "going outward [ausgehen]." This verb, in turn, repeats no less than three times in Hölderlin's second sentence, evoking a more radical German equivalent for e-ducation (literally: "to lead outward") than "Bildung" or "Erziehung." Furthermore, the ode is personified through Hölderlin's discussion of the way the ode's proper "original more lofty more godlike bolder intensity appears to it to be extreme," and the way it "receives" or "comes to appreciate [empfindet]" its opening tone as an "opposition" (13: 868; Krell, Death of Empedocles 142). Of course, it is questionable to what extent the category of the bildungsroman, like the conflict of the tragic ode, is ab initio an invention, nor do those works known as bildungsromans ever truly lead to the return of the full-fledged educated protagonist that should culminate his arc of formation. For an excellent discussion of the problems involved in this genre, see Redfield.

26. The word "Ton" comes from the Greek τόνος, which means "stretch" or "tension," and via this metaphor, comes to denote musical "pitch."

27. See Herder 697–702. His treatise on the Origins of Language opens with the sentence: "All vehement sentient receptions [Empfindungen], and the most vehement among the vehement, the painful sentient receptions [Empfindungen] of one's body, all strong passions of one's soul exteriorize themselves immediately in cries, in tones, in wild, inarticulate sounds. A suffering animal as well as the hero Philoctetes, when pain attacks it, will whimper, will groan, and [it would do so] were it even abandoned on a desert island, without a glimpse, trace or hope of a helpful neighboring creature. It is as though it breathed more freely, in that it gives its burning, anxious

breath air" (697). He will go on to argue that human language, and thus language proper, is produced with the distinctions man draws—without necessarily uttering a word—through free reflection (719–27).

28. Hamacher traces a similar motion of diversion in another context, addressing the "Remarks to Antigone," where he writes: "Halt, Haltung und Erhaltung werden im Ausweichen, einer lateralen Bewegung des Vergleichens und Übergehens, gewonnen [. . .]" ("Parousie, Mauern" 133).

29. Jean-François Courtine also emphasizes the importance of translation or transfer—*Übertragung*—into foreign material in Hölderlin's poetological texts on tragedy, relating these passages to Hölderlin's remark that "the tragic poem [. . .] is the metaphor of a unique intellectual intuition." Of this "metaphor," he writes, "it seems, then, that [it] must be understood, if you will, to the letter, as designating the trans-port, the transposition, the transfer or the trans-lation (with the deviation that every translation necessarily induces [. . .] in the explication of something unsaid that is essential to the 'source-language'); but the transfer here does not affect simply a name, conforming to the strict Aristotelian problem of *lexis*, but more generally, it affects an element, a tonality or a tone, a sphere, to deport them in that which is always relatively 'improper' or 'foreign'" (49–50).

30. The German verb *verläugnen*—which translates, too, the Greek ἀπαρνέομαι, the verb for Peter's thrice repeated denial of Christ (Matt. 26.33–35, Mark 14.30–31, Luke 22.34)—comes from Gothic and Old High German roots ("laugnen," "lougnan") that signal negation and concealment (Grimm and Grimm 12: 340). Thus, it truly comes close, phonetically and semantically, to the German verb "lügen," "to lie," which derives from the Gothic "liugan," "whose proper sense is assumed to be 'conceal'" (Grimm and Grimm 12: 1272). Heidegger, in his reading of these texts, also accents the denial of the poet, writing that Hölderlin's remarks suggest that the achievement of poetic expression lies most in the way poetic language "leaves the unsayable unsaid, in and through its saying [*das Unsagbare ungesagt [läßt], und zwar in ihrem und durch ihr Sagen*]" (*Hölderlins Hymnen* 119). It would be important to go still further, however, and see how the displacements and duplicities involved in poetic denial affect the status of the "unsayable" as well as what is said.

31. The German text reads: "Auch im tragischdramatischen Gedichte spricht sich also das Göttliche aus, das der Dichter in seiner Welt empfindet und erfährt, auch das tragischdramatische Gedicht ist ihm ein Bild des Lebendigen, das ihm in seinem Leben gegenwärtig ist und war; aber wie dieses Bild der Innigkeit überall seinen lezten Grund in eben dem Grade mehr *verläugnet* und *verläugnen* muß, wie es überall mehr dem Symbol sich nähern muß, je unendlicher, je unaussprechlicher, je näher dem nefas die Innigkeit ist, je strenger und kälter das Bild den Menschen und sein empfundenes Element unterscheiden muß um die Empfindung in ihrer Gränze vestzuhalten, um so weniger kann das Bild die Empfindung unmittelbar aussprechen, es muß sie so wohl der Form als dem Stoffe nach *verläugnen*, der Stoff muß ein kühneres fremderes Gleichniß und Beispiel von ihr seyn, die Form muß mehr den Karakter der Entgegensezung und Trennung tragen" (my emphases).

32. See also Kant's explicit remark to this effect in the *Critique of Pure Reason* (*Kritik der reinen Vernunft* 278).

33. For close analyses of Kant's intervention in his chapter on analogy from the *Critique of the Power of Judgment*—which begins, importantly, with his reinterpretation of the philosophical *and* aesthetic term "hypotyposis" as "the production of the reality of our concepts, and with it the life of the mind and its powers"—see Gasché 202–18, 210; and Beaufret 77–109.

34. The best discussion of the significance of the infinitesimal for Hölderlin's language, as well as the way it inflects the comparatives that are insistent throughout his poetry and poetological prose texts, is Hamacher, "Parusie, Mauern" 99–108.

35. The nominal Gothic formation 'analaugns,' which Hölderlin most likely did not know, is attested for 'κρυπτός' 'concealed,' 'encrypted' (Grimm and Grimm 12: 340).

36. The translation I offer here is an adaptation of Pfau 107. Earlier in the "Remarks," Hölderlin will speak of Oedipus's "*nefas*" as the moment where he "interprets the saying of the oracle too infinitely [*den Orakelspruch zu unendlich deutet*]" (16: 251, Pfau 102). Then, his spirit, "in wrathful presentiment [. . .], knowing all [*in zorniger Ahnung [. . .] alles wissend*]" interprets it to refer to the particular murder of Laios, "and then too takes the sin as infinite [*und dann auch die Sünde als unendlich nimmt*]" (16: 252; Pfau 103, trans. modified). Thus, Oedipus takes the particular and the infinite, man and god—in wrath—as one.

37. Together, the elements of the Latin composite *nefas* also build the negation of the second-person singular, present conjugation of "fari"—"fas," "you speak."

38. Knowledge can no longer *be*, properly speaking, when language remembers it, any more than language can be, so long as it is only a presentiment of knowledge. Each gives way to the other, then, in abandon. This "decline or transition"—this "Untergang oder Übergang" (14: 140)—thus recalls the structure of tragic dissolution that Hölderlin traces in his prose text "The Fatherland in Decline [*Das untergehende Vaterland*]," which immediately follows Hölderlin's third and last incomplete draft of *Empedokles*. There, he writes of the way, in any one world of relations, the possibilities of all relations "are therein to be intimated [*darinn zu ahnden*]." They then become released as possibilities in the dissolution of a fatherland—its world and language—while the particular possibility that emerges therefrom would entail "both the sensibility of the dissolution and the remembrance of the dissolved [*sowohl die Empfindung der Auflösung als die Erinnerung des Aufgelösten*]" (14: 142; Krell, *Death of Empedocles* 153). Hence, Hölderlin continues, "the thoroughgoing originality of every genuinely tragic language [*das durchaus originelle jeder ächttragischen Sprache*]" (14: 142; Krell, *Death of Empedocles* 153) is a language of dissolution, arising from the dissolution of what was previously only intimated, and remembering the dissolution of what was. That process of remembrance, however, would also, strictly speaking, have to entail the dissolution of that very intimation or presentiment, and could therefore remember nothing.

39. For an excellent analysis of this passage, see also Nägele's earlier monograph, *Text, Geschichte und Subjektivität* 161–67.

40. In the literal sense of the word, Hölderlin will speak of this noneness as "this being-alone [*dieses Alleinseyn*]" (14: 230).

41. In *Extase de la raison*, Jean-François Courtine stresses the way in which Hölderlin exposes and exponentiates the contradiction implicit in Fichte's self-pos-

iting subject in his philosophical prose writings (29). He also traces in his work Hölderlin's departure from Schelling's *Vom Ich als Prinzip der Philosophie* (see also 53). With particular reference to Hölderlin's Empedocles as the one against the all, he writes: "the all cannot sense itself except in its parts and when those parts become 'total.' [. . .] It is up to the part to suffer, to undergo the uni-ty; the properly tragic pathos is that of *Vereinzelung*, of the concentration upon the self to the point of complete dissidence" (60).

42. For discussions of other distorted echoes in this drama, as well as their implications for the status of this dramatic subject, see Corngold 225. See also Nägele's discussions of echoes in Hölderlin's late hymns in *Hölderlins Kritik der poetischen Vernunft* 84–86, "Ancient Sports and Modern Transports" 247–49 and *Echoes of Translation* 39–41.

43. "[W]enn es [das Ich] durch ein drittes bestimmt unterscheidbar gemacht wird, wenn dieses Dritte, in so ferne es mit Freiheit erwählt war, insofern auch in seinen Einflüssen und Bestimmungen die reine Individualität nicht aufhebt, sondern von dieser betrachtet werden kann, wo sie dann zugleich sich selbst als ein durch eine Wahl bestimmtes, empyrischindividualisirtes, und karakterisirtes betrachtet, nur dann ist es möglich, daß das Ich im harmonischentgegengesetzten Leben als Einheit, und umgekehrt das harmonischentgegengesetzte, als Einheit im Ich erscheine und in schöner Individualität zum Objecte werde."

44. For another reading of this threefold, in which its Christian implications are addressed, see Balfour 241–45.

45. Hölderlin indicates, however, that his thinking here is an intensive engagement with Fichte, when he reprises and unsettles the basic proposition of the *Doctrine of Knowing*, "The I sets itself [*Das Ich setzt sich*]," in passages such as, "But when now too the I would want to set itself [. . .] [*Aber wenn nun auch das Ich sich sez[(t)]en wollte . . .]*" (14: 222).

46. "Seze dich *in mit freier Wahl* in harmonische Entgegensezung in mit äuß einer äußeren S[ph]äre, so wie du in dir selber in *harmonischer* Entgegensezung bist, von Natur, aber unerkenbarer weise so lange du in dir selbst bleibst."

47. For example, in his early essay that begins, "There is a state of nature . . . [*Es giebt einen Naturzustand . . .]*," Hölderlin writes, "There is an aspect of the *empirical* faculty of desire, the analogue of what is called nature, which is most prominent where necessity and freedom, the restricted and unrestricted, the sensuous and the sacred seem to unite [. . .] [*Es giebt eine Seite des* empirischen *Begehrungsvermögens, die Analogie dessen, was Natur heißt, die am auffallendsten ist, wo das notwendige mit der Freiheit, das Bedingte mit dem Unbedingten, das Sinnliche mit dem Heiligen sich zu verbrüdern scheint [. . .]]*" (17: 134; Pfau 33, my emphasis). So, too, in a letter to his stepbrother Karl Gok of 1797—which shortly follows the letter in which he tells of the tragic matter that "tears him away"—Hölderlin writes, "The idealistic mind does best to make the *empirical*, the earthly, the limited its element [*Der idealische Kopf thut am besten, das* Empirische, *das Irrdische, das Beschränkte sich zum Elemente zu machen*]" (19: 292, my translation and emphasis).

48. This is not the only sense that "in the fire" has: in Plato's dialogue *Protagoras*, when Protagoras relates the myth of Prometheus to his auditors, he says that

Prometheus stole "the fiery art of Hephaistos [κλέψας τὴν [. . .] ἔμπυρον τέχνην τὴν τοῦ Ἡφαίστου]" (321e, my translation) and gave it to men. Here the word has a broader sense than mantic arts alone; the art that Prometheus transmits is the production of fires that protect men from the cold of winter, allow men to cook, forge metals, etc. Nonetheless, ἔμπυρος is often used in relation to prophetic speech and burnt offerings in those texts by Pindar and Sophocles that Hölderlin would most intensively engage with. A recent summary of the evidence and the types of encoding involved in ancient divination and "empyromancy" can be found in Boncherre.

49. On the divine signs of ancient Greek mantics, see Nagy, *Greek Mythology and Poetics* 202–22.

50. A certain intimacy between the words from this draft—written at the start of the octavo—and the Pindar translations—written from back to front—is plausible, regardless of whether this draft was written before or after, and despite the fact that these words, spoken by Empedocles's female disciple Panthea, recall a similar formulation from the first draft of the drama, where Empedocles, immediately after learning of his exile, says: "O, my gods! In the stadium I directed the chariot, so (must) I race once without care upon the burning wheel [. . .], so I would wish (also) to return to you (and) immediately the racing is dangerous," [*Ach meine Götter! Im Stadium lenkt ich den Wagen [. . .] so (muß) eil ich / Einst unbekümmert auf rauchendem rad [. . .] / So möcht (auch) zu euch zurück, (und) ist gleich die Eile gefährlich]*" (12: 166–67). Even though the date of these translations is contested, Pindar was important to Hölderlin from his earliest studies in Tübingen, whose song he "would nearly call the *summum* of poetic art [*das* Summum *der Dichtkunst*]" (17: 62), and the syntactic and stylistic differences between the first and second drafts of *Empedokles* suggest an ever closer proximation to the language that will appear in the Pindar translations, and beyond them, in the late odes of Hölderlin.

51. For a nuanced discussion of the way in which the operation of translation, especially in the case of Hölderlin, cannot be reduced to either one of these models, see Nägele, "Vatertext und Muttersprache"; as well as Christen 9–16.

52. Hölderlin redoubles these words of Panthea in his later "Basis for Empedocles": "nature appeared, with all her melodies, in the spirit and in the mouth of this man, and so intensely and ardently and personally, as though his heart were her own, and the spirit of the element dwelled among mortals in human guise [*die Natur [. . .] erschien mit allen ihren Melodien im Geiste und Munde dieses Mannes, und so innig und warm und persönlich, wie wenn sein Herz das ihre wäre, und der Geist des Elements in menschlicher Gestalt unter den Sterblichen wohnte*]' (13: 875–76; Krell, *Death of Empedocles* 150).

53. Incidentally, this phrase appears, over and beyond Hölderlin's initial fragment on the tragic ode, exactly three times in the "Basis of Empedocles [*Grund zum Empedokles*]" (see 13: 870, 872, 874).

54. I am not the first to make this observation; in a different context, Krell glosses ἔμπεδος as "steadfast" and considers the relationship of Empedocles to his name (*Lunar Voices* 16).

55. My thanks to Shinobo Iso for drawing my attention to this resonance.

56. Jamme, for example, speaks of Empedocles's promise primarily in positive terms in his essay on the concurrence of Hölderlin's *Empedokles* and Hegel's *Geist des*

Christenthums (317). In her monograph *Stern und Blume,* Anke Bennholdt-Thomsen emphasizes the way Hölderlin's protagonist performs a "Rückerstattung" of a direct language of nature—again in predominantly positive terms (236–42). More recently, Véronique Fóti writes that Empedocles "advocates a radical and creative forgetting of the established cultural, sociopolitical, and religious orders, admonishing the people to give themselves over to all-transforming Nature [. . .]," as his words should constitute an act of honoring "the elements [. . .] in an awareness of their intrinsic sacrality" (34–35). Although this is certainly true, his promise and admonitions are also utterly lethal—Empedocles introduces his imperative with the remark: "The great pleasure is given to men that they rejuvenate themselves. And out of *the purifying death,* which they choose for themselves at the right time, emerge, as Achilles from the Styx, the people [*Menschen ist die große Lust / Gegeben, daß sie selber sich verjüngen. / Und aus dem reinigenden Tode, den / Sie selber sich zu rechter Zeit gewählt, / Erstehn, wie aus dem Styx Achill, die Völker*]" (13: 744, my translation and emphasis). Söring, however, stresses the radicality of this call (122); and for another reading of a different text of Hölderlin that emphasizes the "Todeslust" involved in his poetics, see Nägele, *Text, Geschichte und Subjektivität* 161.

57. The archon of Akragas says in the new opening scene: "He should be their god, their king. [. . .] Still they speak much that is incomprehensible of / from him, and heed no law and no necessity and no custom [*Er soll ihr Gott, / Er soll ihr König seyn. [. . .] Noch sprechen sie viel Unständiges / Von ihm und achten kein Gesez / Und keine Noth und keine Sitte*]" (13: 818).

58. In her thorough study of all three drafts of the drama, Birkenhauer also draws attention to this relation among the drafts, albeit with a different accent—namely, with an accent upon the way in which Hölderlin's attempt to write the "death of the philosopher [*Tod des Philosophen*]" leads to an experiment in dramatic form that does not correspond to the models of classical poetics. In her analysis, she writes that Hölderlin does not begin each draft "von vorne [*from the beginning*]," but repeatedly begins from where he left off last (418).

59. Hölderlin translated only the first twenty-four verses of Dionysos's prologue, most likely around 1800. See 17: 627. For an analysis of the significance of this translation to Hölderlin's poetics, see Böschenstein.

60. Hamacher reads this passage as a radicalization of the infinitesimal approximation that had structured Kant's discussions of the sensory reception (*Empfindung*) of the real in his first critique, where 0 could not be reached, and he analyzes in detail its consequences for Hölderlin's language ("Parusie, Mauern" 110–12). In her reading of Hölderlin's *Empedokles* project together with his "Remarks" on Sophocles, Lemke also considers the "sacrificial death [*Opfertod*]" of Empedocles in analogy to this passage on the meaning of tragedy (414), but in a vocabulary borrowed from semiotics.

61. For a discussion of this doubling, as well as the excess of figures that Manes stands for here, see Krell, *Lunar Voices* 46. For a different interpretation of Manes as the double of Pausanius, who would therefore have already returned, aged and transformed, almost immediately after Empedocles has sent this young disciple to Egypt, see Warminski 12–17.

62. This is not the only possible construal of these verses, as Krell shows in his translation, "What flames on high is inflammation, nothing more / What strives from down below is savage discord" (*Death of Empedocles* 184), but it certainly is a possible one, and one that is closely related to the central problem of the drama, as well as the poetological prose texts that speak to it.

63. For this reason, I cannot agree with Jamme's assertion that the plunge of Empedocles into Aetna would allow him, like Christ, to effect a reconciliation of man and world and thereby participate in a decisive turn of historical time. The only figures who speak of a coming reconciliation are Pausanias and Manes, who says, "The one, however, the newborn savoir, grasps / The rays of heaven tranquilly, and lovingly / He takes mortality unto his bosom, and / the World's strife grows mild in him [*Der Eine doch, der neue Retter faßt / Des Himmels Stralen ruhig auf, und liebend / Nimmt er, was sterblich ist, an seinen Busen, / Und milde wird in ihm der Streit der Welt*]" (Krell, *Death of Empedocles* 184; 13: 942). When Empedocles himself speaks of such a moment, he will claim that "it has already happened" before—"Es ist geschehn"—and that the land is now about to perish without any doing of his own. Hence, whether a new dissolution—the real one—would follow, and whether Empedocles's suicide would have any historical effects, is left uncertain, and there is little to suggest that it has, in his eyes, any direct relation to the call that is attracting him to the rim of the volcano.

64. This "striving" is, in fact, their name, as Hesiod derives it from τιταίνω, 'stretch,' in his *Theogony* (209).

65. In "Die Bedeutung der Titanen in Hölderlins Spätwerk," Bennholdt-Thomsen sees the Titanic underground of Sicily and Aetna as a crucial mythological and structural principle in Hölderlin's *Empedokles* project (231). She also cites several other passages from Hölderlin's oeuvre that suggest that these mythological figures transgress their own chaotic nature and come to have language, citing the passage from "The Next Best One / The Nearest Best One [*Das nächste Beste*]" (232–33), which I quote below. The discussion of the particular figure of Typhon that I offer here further supports the interpretation she presents of the exceptional status of Titanic language.

66. The most famous document in which Hölderlin considers "the fire from the sky [*das Feuer vom Himmel*]" to be "originally [. . .] natural [*ursprünglich [. . .] natürlich*]" for the Greeks is his letter from 4 December 1801 to Casimir Ulrich Böhlendorff—whereby what is natural is precisely what cannot be mastered, and thus, in a sense, foreign. Hence, Hölderlin writes: "The Greeks were so little masters over the holy pathos, because it was inborn to them, while, to the contrary, they were exceptional in their gift of presentation" (*Sämtliche Werke: Frankfurter Ausgabe* 19: 492). One of the best analyses of the complexities of the relationship Hölderlin traces in this letter between the natural and the foreign remains Peter Szondi's essay "Überwindung des Klassizismus."

67. It would exceed the scope of this chapter to enter into the debate on what, precisely, this "furchtsamgeschäfftiges" refers to at the close of "Friedensfeier," and whether it refers to anything that could be named, without distorting the sense of the passage (a problem that also arises in attempts to identify the "Fürsten des Festes" in this poem, which Szondi discusses in detail in his essay of that name). Seifert

traces and contests the various interpretations in which this topos is identified with Tartarus and construed as the indication of the Titans' impending resurrection and insurrection (678–722). What is most important, though, is that Hölderlin's evocation of a "below" at the end is topologically related to the end toward which Empedocles tends.

68. This is the project that, as Paul de Man and Anja Lemke have argued, continues over and beyond its completion with *Empedokles*. In "Keats and Hölderlin," de Man offers a reading of the affinity between these two works, as well as with Keats's *Endymion*. Lemke takes the affinity between these two works—over Aetna—as the starting point of her essay on *Empedokles*.

69. This trembling is accented in Hesiod's account of Typhon's battle with Zeus, from the quaking of Olympus (πελεμίζετ' 842) to the trembling of Hades and all the Titans of Tartarus (τρέε 850), from the boiling of the land (ἔζεε 847) to the groaning of the earth (ἐπεστεναχίζε, στενάχιζε 843, 858). (Here, as in Pausanias's words to Empedocles, mother earth, the mother of Typhon, groans, tells her pain, twice over.) In his different—and therefore differently illuminating—reading of Hölderlin's *Empedokles* project, Krell also touches suggestively upon the significance of Typhon for the drama in *The Tragic Absolute* 237, 239.

70. He also explores the dialectical relation between this figure of volcanic force and Empedocles, "who can hardly expect" its "outbreak" and instead "comes to meet it" (214).

71. Dastur connects this passage from *Hyperion* to Hölderlin's *Empedokles* project as well (40–41), but within the context of a reading of the drama as a tragedy of time (41), in which she unfolds the implications of Hölderlin's early remark in his so-called Frankfurt Plan for the drama; namely, that Empedocles suffers the law of succession.

72. Hence, Krell reads "gellt" as a present-tense verb, translating this passage: "not without effect I still can hear / The clamor of a hundred voices in my ear, / The chilling laughter, when the dreamer, / The jester, went weeping on his way" (*Death of Empedocles* 172).

73. If, by that time, the adjective τῦφος had come to mean "pride," nothing would be more characteristic of Hölderlin's translation practice than to take it for the proper name—as he also does in many of his Pindar translations. For a thorough discussion of what he calls, in the strongest sense of the phrase, Hölderlin's "Übernahme von Namen," which might be translated as a "taking over of names," but also "overnaming of names," see Christen 52–53.

Disclosure

1. I owe these thoughts on reprisal to the work of Jean-Luc Nancy, who spoke of the rhythm of reprisal at length in his lecture "Image/Danse."

2. I hope you will forgive me—or at least hear me out—in borrowing these words from Samuel Beckett's *Endgame* as a further response to Hegel (Beckett 80)—words that I cannot comment further upon here. After all: "it's finished, nearly finished, it must be nearly finished . . ." (Beckett 1).

3. When I write of signatures here, I have, of course, Jacques Derrida's analyses of the signature in mind, in, for example, his essay "Signature, évenément, con-texte."

4. Nancy derives the word "pluriel" from the Latin "comparative of *multus*," writing "this is not 'numerous,' it is 'more / plus.' It is an increase or an excess of the origin, in the origin" (*Être singulier pluriel* 59–60).

5. These remarks also echo those of Antoine Berman, to whose *L'épreuve étranger* Derrida refers in his essay, writing that what he proposes to do will be in "homage, in a way, to that book" ("Les langages" 27). For in his opening analysis, Berman addresses the rhetoric of fidelity and betrayal that often comes into play when it comes to translation (whether one speaks of "faithful" translations, or appeals to the Italian adage *traduttore traditore*), underscoring the theological underpinnings of that rhetoric, its indications of the "sacralisation" of mother tongues (15). At the same time, however, Derrida departs radically from the cultural and political structures according to which Berman frames his argument—most markedly in his analysis of the metaphysical implications of the German words he proceeds to analyze, which share the root "Bild [*image*]."

6. Nancy exposes thinking itself as "addressed [*adressée*]," because "the sense is in the address, and not in the discourse (but it is in the address of the discourse)" (13–14). Shortly after, he writes that "the sense of being" is not to be "some property that would come to qualify, fulfill, or finalize the 'brute given' of being [. . .] but the given of being, the given that is given with the very fact that we comprehend something—whatever it may be and however confused it may be—when we say 'being' [. . .]: *being itself is given to us as sense*" (20).

Works Cited

Aarsleff, Hans. "The Context and Sense of Humboldt's Statement That Language 'ist kein werk (ergon), sondern eine tätigkeit (energeia).'" *The History of Linguistics 2002*. Ed. Eduardo Guimarães and Diana Luz Pessoa de Barros. Amsterdam: John Benjamins, 2007. 197–206.

Adorno, Theodor W.. *Drei Studien zu Hegel: Gesammelte Schriften*. Ed. Rolf Tiedemann et al. Vol. 5. Frankfurt: Suhrkamp, 1997. 247–381.

———. *Noten zur Literatur*. Frankfurt: Suhrkamp, 1981.

Aeschylus. *Aeschyli septem quae supersunt tragoedias*. Ed. Denys Page. Oxford: Clarendon, 1972.

———. *Agamemnon*. Ed. and trans. Eduard Fraenkel. 3 vols. Oxford: Clarendon, 1950.

Alexiou, Margaret. *The Ritual Lament in Greek Tradition*. Cambridge: Cambridge UP, 1974.

Ambuel, David. *Image and Paradigm in Plato's Sophist*. Las Vegas: Parmenides, 2007.

Anstett, Jean-Jacques. "Friedrich Schlegels 'Hieroglyphenlied.'" *Stoffe, Formen, Strukturen: Studien zur deutschen Literatur: Hans Heinrich Borcherdt zum 75. Geburtstag*. Ed. Albert Fuchs and Helmut Motekat. Munich: Hueber, 1962. 304–14.

Apostolopoulou, Georgia. "Probleme der neugriechischen Hegel-Übersetzung." *Übersetzen, verstehen, Brücke bauen: Geisteswissenschaftliches und literarisches Übersetzen im internationalen Kulturaustausch*. Ed. Arnim Paul Frank et al. Berlin: Schmidt, 1993. 239–47.

Aristotle. *Aristoteles Peri Poietikes: Mit Einleitung Text und Adnotatio critica, exegetischem Kommentar, kritischem Anhang und Indices Nominum, Rerum, Locorum*. Ed. Alfred Gudeman. Berlin: de Gruyter, 1934.

———. *Aristotelis categoriae et liber de interpretatione*. Ed. L. Minio-Paluello. Oxford: Clarendon, 1949.

———. *Aristoteles: Kategorien*. Ed. Klaus Oehler. Berlin: Akademie, 2006.

———. *Aristotelis Physica*. Ed. W. D. Ross. Oxford: Clarendon, 1950.

———. *Aristotle's Metaphysics*. Ed. W. D. Ross. 2 vols. Oxford: Clarendon, 1924.

Austin, J. L. *How to Do Things with Words*. Ed. J. O. Ursmon and Marina Sbisà. 2nd ed. Cambridge: Harvard UP, 1975.

Bachvarova, Mary R. "Sumerian *Gala* Priests and Eastern Mediterranean Returning Gods: Tragic Lamentation in Cross-Cultural Perspective." *Lamentation: Studies in the Ancient Mediterranean and Beyond*. Ed. Ann Suter. Oxford: Oxford UP, 2008. 19–52.

Bacon, Helen. "The Furies' Homecoming." *Classical Philology* 96.1 (2001): 48–59.

Bakker, Egbert J. *Pointing at the Past: From Formula to Performance in Homeric Poetics*. Washington: Center for Hellenic Studies, 2005.

Balfour, Ian. *The Rhetoric of Romantic Prophecy*. Stanford: Stanford UP, 2002.

Beaufret, Jean. *Dialogue avec Heidegger: Philosophie moderne*. Paris: Minuit, 1973.

Beckett, Samuel. *Endgame*. New York: Grove Press, 1958.

Benjamin, Walter. "Die Aufgabe des Übersetzers." *Gesammelte Schriften*. Ed. Rolf Tiedemann and Hermann Schweppenhäuser. Vol. 4. Frankfurt: Suhrkamp, 1972. 9–21.

———. "Der Begriff der Kunstkritik in der deutschen Romantik." *Gesammelte Schriften*. Ed. Rolf Tiedemann and Hermann Schweppenhäuser. Vol. 1. Frankfurt: Suhrkamp, 1974. 7–122.

———. "Schicksal und Charakter." *Gesammelte Schriften*. Ed. Rolf Tiedemann and Hermann Schweppenhäuser. Vol. 2. Frankfurt: Suhrkamp, 1977. 171–79.

Bennholdt-Thomsen, Anke. "Die Bedeutung der Titanen in Hölderlins Spätwerk." *Hölderlin-Jahrbuch* 26 (1986–87): 226–54.

———. *Stern und Blume: Untersuchungen zur Sprachauffassung Hölderlins*. Bonn: Bouvier, 1967.

Bennholdt-Thomsen, Anke, and Alfredo Guzzoni. *Analecta Hölderliana: Zur Hermetik des Spätwerks*. Würzburg: Königshausen & Neumann, 1999.

Berman, Antoine. *L'épreuve de l'étranger: Culture et traduction dans l'Allemagne romantique: Herder, Goethe, Schlegel, Novalis, Humboldt, Schleiermacher, Hölderlin*. Paris: Gallimard, 1984.

Bernhardi, Ferdinand August. *Anfangsgründe der Sprachwissenschaft: Faksimile-Neudruck der Ausgabe Berlin 1805*. Stuttgart-Bad Cannstatt: Frommann–Holzboog, 1990.

Bernofsky, Susan. *Foreign Words: Translator-Authors in the Age of Goethe*. Detroit: Wayne State UP, 2005.

Bernstein, Susan. "Re-re-re-reading Jena." *MLN* 110.4 (1995): 834–55.

Bertaux, Pierre. *Hölderlin und die Französische Revolution*. Frankfurt: Suhrkamp, 1969.

Betensky, Aya. "Aeschylus' *Oresteia*: The Power of Clytemnestra." *Ramus: Critical Studies in Greek and Roman Literature* 7.1 (1978): 11–25.

Birkenhauer, Theresia. *Legende und Dichtung: Der Tod des Philosophen und Hölderlins Empedokles*. Berlin: Vorwerk 8, 1996.

Blanchot, Maurice. *L'entretien infini*. Paris: Gallimard, 1969.

———. *L'espace littéraire*. Paris: Gallimard, 1955.

———. *La part du feu*. Paris: Gallimard, 1949.

Bloch, Ernst. *Subjekt-Objekt: Erläuterungen zu Hegel*. Frankfurt: Suhrkamp, 1962.

Bodammer, Theodor. *Hegels Deutung der Sprache*. Hamburg: Meiner, 1969.

Böhme, Jacob. *Aurora (Morgen Röte im auffgang, 1612)* and *Fundamental Report (Gründlicher Bericht, Mysterium Pansophicum, 1620)*. Ed. and trans. Andrew Weeks. Leiden: Brill, 2013.

———. *Morgenröte [und] De signatura rerum*. Ed. Ferdinand van Ingen. Frankfurt: Deutscher Klassiker Verlag, 2009.

———. *Mysterium magnum, oder Erklärung über Das Erste Buch Mosis (1623)*. Stuttgart–Bad Cannstatt: Frommann–Holzboog, 1958.

———. *De tribus principiis, oder Beschreibung der Drey Principien Göttliches Wesens (1619)*. Ed. Will-Erich Peuckert. Stuttgart–Bad Cannstatt: Frommann–Holzboog, 1960.

Bollack, Jean. "Styx et serments." *Revue des études grecques* 71 (1958): 1–35.

Bollack, Jean, and Pierre Judet de la Combe. *L'Agamemnon d'Eschyle: Le texte et ses interpretations*. 5 vols. Lille: Presses universitaires de Lille. 1981–.

Bompaire, Jacques. "Le pathos dans le *Traité du sublime*." *Revue des études grecques* 86 (1973): 323–43.

Boncherre, Pierre. "Divination." *A Companion to Greek Religion*. Ed. Daniel Ogden. Malden: Blackwell, 2007. 145–59.

Bonnafé, Annie. "Clytemnestre et ses batailles: Éris et Peithô." *Architecture et poésie dans le monde grec: Hommage à Georges Roux*. Lyon: Maison de l'Orient et de la Méditerranée Jean Pouilloux, 1989. 149–57.

Borsche, Tilman. *Sprachansichten: Der Begriff der menschlichen Rede in der Sprachphilosophie Wilhelm von Humboldts*. Stuttgart: Klett-Cotta, 1981.

Böschenstein, Bernhard. *Frucht des Gewitters: Hölderlins Dionysos als Gott der Revolution*. Frankfurt: Insel, 1989.

Bourgeois, Bernard. "Traduction philosophique et échange culturel." *Revue Philosophique de la France et de l'Étranger* 195.4 (2005): 469–80.

Brown, Marshall. *The Shape of German Romanticism*. Ithaca: Cornell UP, 1979.

Butler, Judith. *Subjects of Desire: Hegelian Reflections in Twentieth-Century France*. New York: Columbia UP, 1987.

Cassirer, Ernst. *Philosophie der symbolischen Formen*. Ed. Claus Rosenkranz. Vol. 1. Hamburg: Meiner, 2001.

Chantraine, Pierre. *Dictionnaire étymologique de la langue grecque*. 4 vols. Paris: Klincksieck, 1968.

Chaouli, Michel. *The Laboratory of Poetry: Chemistry and Poetics in the Work of Friedrich Schlegel*. Baltimore: Johns Hopkins UP, 2002.

Christen, Felix. *Eine andere Sprache: Hölderlins 'Große Pindar-Übertragung.'* Basel: Urs Engeler, 2007.

Comay, Rebecca. *Mourning Sickness: Hegel and the French Revolution*. Stanford: Stanford UP, 2011.

Condillac, Etienne de. *Essai sur l'origine des connaissances humaines*. Paris: Galilée, 1973.

Corngold, Stanley. "Disowning Contingencies in Hölderlin's 'Empedocles.'" *The Solid Letter: Readings of Friedrich Hölderlin*. Ed. Aris Fioretos. Stanford: Stanford UP, 1999.

Coseriu, Eugenio. *Sprache: Strukturen und Funktionen. XII Aufsätze*. Ed. Uwe Peterson. Tübingen: Tübinger Beiträge zur Linguistik, 1970.

Courtine, Jean-François. *Extase de la raison: Essais sur Schelling*. Paris: Galilée, 1990.

Creuzer, Friedrich. *Symbolik und Mythologie der alten Völker, besonders der Griechen: In Vorträgen und Entwürfen*. Vol. 1. Leipzig: Leske, 1810.

Dahlke, Karin. *Äußerste Freiheit: Wahnsinn / Sublimierung / Poetik des Tragischen der Moderne: Lektüren zu Hölderlins* Grund zum Empedokles *und zu den Anmerkungen zum Oedipus und zur Antigonä*. Würzburg: Königshausen & Neumann, 2008.

Dastur, Françoise. *Hölderlin: Le retournement natal: Tragédie et modernité et nature et poésie*. La Versanne: Encre marine, 1997.

Degener, J. Michael. "The Caesura of the *Symbolon* in Aeschylus' *Agamemnon*." *Arethusa* 34.1 (2001): 61–95.

de Man, Paul. *Aesthetic Ideology*. Ed. Andrzej Warminski. Minneapolis: U of Minnesota P, 1997.

———. "Keats and Hölderlin." *Comparative Literature* 8.1 (1956): 28–45.

———. "The Rhetoric of Temporality." *Blindness and Insight: Essays in the Rhetoric of Contemporary Criticism*. Minneapolis: U of Minnesota P, 1983. 187–228.

———. "The Riddle of Hölderlin." *Critical Writings 1957–1978*. Ed. Lindsay Waters. Minneapolis: U of Minnesota P, 1983. 198–213.

———. "Wordsworth and Hölderlin." *The Rhetoric of Romanticism*. New York: Columbia UP, 1984.

Derrida, Jacques. "Des tours de Babel." *Psyche: Inventions of the Other*. Trans. Joseph F. Graham. Vol. 1. Stanford: Stanford UP, 2007. 191–225.

———. "Des tours de Babel." *Psyché: Inventions de l'autre*. Paris: Galilée, 1987. 203–35.

———. *Glas*. Paris: Galilée, 1974.

———. "Les langages et les institutions de la philosophie." *Texte* 4 (1985): 9–39.

———. "Ousia et grammè." *Marges de la philosophie*. Paris: Minuit, 1972. 31–78.

———. *Parages*. Paris: Galilée, 1986.

———. "Le puits et la pyramide: Introduction à la sémiologie de Hegel." *Marges de la philosophie*. Paris: Minuit, 1972. 79–127.

———. "Signature, événement, contexte." *Marges de la philosophie*. Paris: Minuit, 1972. 365–93.

di Cesare, Donatella. "Die aristotelische Herkunft der Begriffe ἔργον und ἐνέργεια in der Sprachphilosophie Wilhelm von Humboldts." *Energeia und Ergon: Sprachliche Variation, Sprachgeschichte, Sprachtypologie; Bd. II: Das sprachtheoretische Denken Eugenio Coserius in der Diskussion*. Tübingen: Narr, 1988. 29–46.

Diels, Hermann. *Die Fragmente der Vorsokratiker: Griechisch und Deutsch*. Berlin: Weidmann, 1903.

Diogenes Laertes. *Diogenis Laertii Vitae Philosophorum*. Ed. Miroslav Marcovich. Vol. 1. Stuttgart: Teubner, 1999.

Easterling, Pat. "*Agamemnon* for the Ancients." *Agamemnon in Performance: 458 BC to AD 2004*. Ed. Fiona Macintosh, Pantelis Michelakis, and Edith Hall. Oxford: Oxford UP, 2005. 23–36.

Eckel, Winfried, and Nikolaus Wegmann, eds. *Figuren der Konversion: Friedrich Schlegels Übetritt zum Katholizismus im Kontext*. Paderborn: Schöningh, 2014.

Eldridge, Hannah Vandegrift. "Poetology as Symptom in Friedrich Hölderlin." *German Quarterly* 86.4 (2014): 444–63.

Erlinghagen, Armin. "Das Konzept des 'Ganzen' in Friedrich Schlegels Poetik, 1793–1804: Ein systematischer Aufriss auf der Grundlage seiner Traktate über Lessing und des unveröffentlichten Notizhefts Studien des Alterthums." *Athenaeum* 22 (2012): 15–63.

Esterhammer, Angela. *The Romantic Performative: Language and Action in British and German Romanticism*. Stanford: Stanford UP, 2001.

Euripides. *Fabulae*. Ed. J. Diggle. 3 vols. Oxford: Oxford UP, 1978–94.

———. *Medea*. Ed. Donald Mastronarde. Cambridge: Cambridge UP, 2002.

Fantoni, Francesca. *Deutsche Dithyramben: Geschichte einer Gattung im 18. und 19. Jahrhundert*. Würzburg: Königshausen & Neumann, 2009.

Feilchenfeld, Walter. *Der Einfluss Jacob Böhmes auf Novalis*. Berlin: Ebering, 1922.

Ferrari, Gloria. "Figures in the Text: Metaphors and Riddles in the *Agamemnon*." *Classical Philology* 91.2 (1997): 1–45.

Ferrarin, Alfredo. *Hegel and Aristotle*. Cambridge: Cambridge UP, 2001.

Fichte, Johann Gottlieb. "Grundlage der gesammten Wissenschaftslehre als Handschrift für seine Zuhörer." *Werke, 1793–1795*. Ed. Reinhard Lauth et al. Stuttgart–Bad Cannstatt: Frommann–Holzboog, 1965. 173–451.

———. "Ueber den Begriff der Wissenschaftslehre oder der sogenannten Philosophie." *Werke, 1793–1795*. Ed. Reinhard Lauth et al. Stuttgart–Bad Cannstatt: Frommann–Holzboog, 1965. 91–172.

Finkelstein, Naomi. "Unmentionables: The Erinyes as the Culmination of Alpha Privative and Negated Language in Aeschylus' *Oresteia*." Diss. Columbia University, 2010.

Fletcher, Judith. *Performing Oaths in Classical Greek Drama*. Cambridge: Cambridge UP, 2012.

Foley, Helene P. *Female Acts in Greek Tragedy*. Princeton: Princeton UP, 2001.

Fóti, Véronique M. *Epochal Discordance: Hölderlin's Philosophy of Tragedy*. Albany: SUNY P, 2006.

Foucault, Michel. *Les mots et les choses: Une archéologie des sciences humaines*. Paris: Gallimard, 1966.

Frank, Manfred. *Das Problem "Zeit" in der deutschen Romantik: Zeitbewußtsein und Bewußtsein von Zeitlichkeit in der frühromantischen Philosophie und in Tiecks Dichtung*. 2nd ed. Paderborn: Schöningh, 1990.

Fränkel, Hermann. *Wege und Formen frühgriechischen Denkens: Literarische und philosophiegeschichtliche Studien*. Ed. Franz Tietze. 2nd ed. Munich: Beck, 1960.

Frey, Hans-Jost. "Übersetzung und Sprachtheorie bei Humboldt." *Übersetzung und Dekonstruktion*. Ed. Alfred Hirsch. Frankfurt: Suhrkamp, 1997. 37–63.

Gadamer, Hans-Georg. *Hegel's Dialectic: Five Hermeneutical Studies*. Trans. P. Christopher Smith. New Haven: Yale UP, 1976.

Gasché, Rodolphe. *The Idea of Form: Rethinking Kant's Aesthetics*. Stanford: Stanford UP, 2003.

Galland-Szymkowiak, Mildred. "Le changement de sens du symbole entre Leibniz et Kant." *Revue germanique internationale* 4 (2006): 73–91.

Gauger, Hans-Martin. *Die Anfänge der Synonymik: Girard (1718) und Roubaud (1785); Ein Beitrag zur Geschichte der lexikalischen Semantik; Mit einer Auswahl aus den Synonymiken beider Autoren*. Tübingen: Narr, 1973.

Geisser, Franziska. *Götter, Geister und Dämonen: Unheilsmächte bei Aischylos— zwischen Aberglauben und Theatralik*. Sauer: Munich, 2002.

Goethe, Johann Wolfgang von. *Maximen und Reflexionen. Werke: Hamburger Ausgabe in 14 Bänden*. Ed. Erich Trunz. Vol 12. Munich: Beck, 1988. 365–547.

Goldhill, Simon. *Language, Sexuality, Narrative: The* Oresteia. Cambridge: Cambridge UP, 1984.

Gosetti-Ferencei, Jennifer Anna. *Heidegger, Hölderlin, and the Subject of Poetic Language: Toward a New Poetics of Dasein*. New York: Fordham UP, 2004.

Grimm, Jacob, and Wilhelm Grimm et al. *Deutsches Wörterbuch*. 32 vols. Leipzig: Hirzel, 1956–.

Guthrie, K. C. "The Religion and Mythology of the Greeks." *The Cambridge*

Ancient History. Ed. I. E. S. Edwards et al. Vol. 2. Cambridge: Cambridge UP, 1975. 851–905.

Hamacher, Werner. "(Das Ende der Kunst mit der Maske)." *Sprachen der Ironie—Sprachen des Ernstes.* Ed. Karl Heinz Bohrer. Frankfurt: Suhrkamp, 2000. 121–55.

———. *Entferntes Verstehen: Studien zu Philosophie und Literatur von Kant bis Celan.* Frankfurt: Suhrkamp, 1998.

———. *Für—die Philologie.* Basel: Urs Engeler, 2009.

———. "Intensive Sprachen." *Übersetzen: Walter Benjamin.* Ed. Christiaan L. Hart Nibbrig. Frankfurt: Suhrkamp, 2001. 174–235.

———. *Minima Philologica.* Trans. Catherine Diehl and Jason Groves. New York: Fordham UP, 2015.

———. "Parusie, Mauern: Mitteilbarkeit und Zeitlichkeit, später Hölderlin." *Hölderlin–Jahrbuch* 34 (2004–05): 93–142.

———. *Pleroma—Reading in Hegel.* Trans. Nicholas Walker and Simon Jarvis. Stanford: Stanford UP, 1998.

———. "The Word Wolke—if It Is One." *Benjamin's Ground: New Readings of Walter Benjamin.* Ed. Rainer Nägele. Detroit: Wayne State UP, 1988. 147–75.

Hamlin, Cyrus. "Platonic Dialogue and Romantic Irony: Prolegomenon to a Theory of Literary Narrative." *Canadian Review of Comparative Literature* 3.1 (1976): 5–26.

Hardenberg, Friedrich von (Novalis). *Schriften.* Ed. Richard Samuel et al. 4 vols. Darmstadt: Wissenschaftliche Buchgesellschaft, 1968.

Hassler, Gerda. "Lafaye's *Dictionnaire des synonymes* in the History of Semantics." *The Emergence of Modern Language Sciences: Studies on the Transition from Historical-Comparative to Structural Linguistics in Honor of E. F .K. Koerner.* Ed. Shiela Embleton et al. Amsterdam: John Benjamins, 1999. 27–39.

Haym, Rudolf. *Herder nach seinem Leben und seinen Werken dargestellt.* Vol. 1. Berlin: Gaertner, 1880.

Hegel, G. W. F. *Briefe an und von Hegel.* Ed. Johannes Hoffmeister. Vol. 1. Hamburg: Meiner, 1952.

———. "Differenz des Fichte'schen und Schelling'schen Systems der Philosophie."*Jenaer kritische Schriften.* Ed. Hartmut Buchner and Otto Pöggeler. Hamburg: Meiner, 1968. 1–92.

———. *Enzyklopädie der philosophischen Wissenschaften im Grundrisse (1827).* Ed. Wolfgang Bonsiepen and Hans-Christian Lucas. Hamburg: Meiner, 1989.

———. *"Der Geist des Christenthums": Schriften, 1796–1800.* Ed. Werner Hamacher. Frankfurt: Ullstein, 1978.

———. *Hegels theologische Jugendschriften.* Ed. Herman Nohl. Tübingen: Mohr, 1907.

———. *Jenaer Systementwürfe III.* Ed. Rolf-Peter Horstmann and Johann Heinrich Trede. Hamburg: Meiner, 1976.

———. *Nürnberger Gymnasialkurse und Gymnasialreden (1808–1816).* Ed. Klaus Grotsch. Vol. 10. Hamburg: Meiner, 2006.

———. *Phänomenologie des Geistes.* Ed. Wolfgang Boniespen and Reinhard Heede. Hamburg: Meiner, 1980.

————. *System der Sittlichkeit: Schriften und Entwürfe (1799–1808)*. Ed. Manfred Baum and Kurt Rainer Meist. Hamburg: Meiner, 1998.

————. "Ueber die wissenschaftliche Behandlung des Naturrechts, seine Stelle in der praktischen Philosophie, und sein Verhältnis zu den positiven Rechtswissenschaften." *Jenaer kritische Schriften*. Ed. Hartmut Buchner and Otto Pöggeler. Hamburg: Meiner, 1968. 417–85.

————. *Vorlesungen über die Ästhetik III*. Ed. Eva Moldenhauer and Karl Markus Michel. Frankfurt: Suhrkamp, 1986.

————. *Vorlesungen über die Philosophie der Weltgeschichte*. Ed. Johannes Hoffmeister. Vol. 2. Hamburg: Meiner, 1955.

————. *Wissenschaft der Logik: Die Objektive Logik (1812/1813)*. Ed. Friedrich Hogemann and Walter Jaeschke. Hamburg: Meiner, 1978.

Heidegger, Martin. *Early Greek Thinking*. Trans. David Farrell Krell and Frank A. Capuzzi. San Francisco: Harper & Row, 1984.

————. *Erläuterungen zu Hölderlins Dichtung*. Stuttgart: Klostermann, 1981.

————. *Hölderlins Hymnen: "Germanien" und "Der Rhein."* Ed. Susanne Ziegler. Frankfurt: Klostermann, 1989.

————. *Platon: Sophistes*. Ed. Ingeborg Schüßler. Frankfurt: Klostermann, 1992.

————. *Unterwegs zur Sprache*. Ed. Friedrich-Wilhelm von Herrmann. Frankfurt: Klostermann, 1985.

Henrich, Dieter. *Der Grund im Bewußtsein: Untersuchungen zu Hölderlins Denken (1794–1795)*. Stuttgart: Klett-Cotta, 1992.

Herder, Johann Gottfried. *Frühe Schriften: 1764–1772*. Ed. Ulrich Gaier. Frankfurt: Deutscher Klassiker Verlag, 1985.

Hermann, Gottfried. *Aeschyli Tragoediae*. Ed. Moritz Haupt. 2 vols. Berlin: Weidmann, 1859.

Hesiod. *Theogonia; Opera et Dies; Scutum; Fragmenta Selecta*. Ed. Friedrich Solmsen et al. Oxford: Clarendon, 1990.

Hillis-Miller, J., and Manuel Asensi. *Black Holes: J. Hillis-Miller; or Boustrophedonic Reading*. Stanford: Stanford UP, 1999.

Hölderlin, Friedrich. *Hyperion, oder der Eremit in Griechenland*. Frankfurt: Stroemfeld/Roter Stern, 1979.

————. *Sämtliche Werke*. Ed. Friedrich Beißner. Vol. 2. Stuttgart: Kohlhammer, 1951.

————. *Sämtliche Werke: Frankfurter Ausgabe; Historisch-kritische Ausgabe*. Ed. D. E. Sattler et al. 20 vols. Frankfurt: Stroemfeld/Roter Stern, 1975–2008.

Hölscher, Uvo. *Empedokles und Hölderlin*. Frankfurt: Insel, 1965.

Homer. *Opera*. Ed. Thomas W. Allen. 5 vols. Oxford: Clarendon, 1902–12.

Honold, Alexander. *Hölderlins Kalender: Astronomie und Revolution um 1800*. Berlin: Vorwerk 8, 2005.

Humboldt, Wilhelm von. *Aeschylos Agamemnon: Metrisch übersetzt*. Leipzig: Fleischer, 1816.

————. *Ansichten über Aesthetik und Literatur: Briefe an Christian Gottfried Körner*. Ed. F. Jones. Berlin: L. Schleiermacher, 1880.

————. *Briefe an Friedrich August Wolf*. Ed. Philip Mattson. Berlin: de Gruyter, 1990.

———. *Gesammelte Schriften*. Ed. Albert Leitzmann. 17 vols. Berlin: Behr, 1903–36.

———. *Wilhelm von Humboldts Briefe an F.G. Welcker*. Ed. Rudolf Haym. Berlin: Rudolf Gaertner, 1859.

Hyppolite, Jean. *Genèse et structure de la phénomenologie de l'esprit de Hegel*. Paris: Aubier, 1946.

Jacobs, Carol. "Dusting Antigone." *MLN* 115.5 (1996): 890–917.

Jaeschke, Walter. *Die Vernunft in der Religion: Studien zur Grundlegung der Religionsphilosophie Hegels*. Stuttgart-Bad Cannstatt: Frommann–Holzboog, 1986.

Jamme, Christoph. "Liebe, Schicksal, Tragik: Hegels 'Geist des Christentums' und Hölderlins 'Empedokles.'" *"Frankfurt aber ist der Nabel dieser Erde": Das Schicksal einer Generation der Goethezeit*. Ed. Christoph Jamme and Otto Pöggeler. Stuttgart: Klett-Cotta, 1983. 300–24.

Johansen, H. Friis, and Edward W. Whittle, eds. *Aeschylus: The Suppliants*. 3 vols. Copenhagen: Fr. Bagges kgl. Hofbogtrykkeri, 1980.

Jost, Leonard. *Sprache als Werk und wirkende Kraft: Ein Beitrag zur Geschichte und Kritik der energetischen Sprachauffassung seit Wilhelm von Humboldt*. Bern: Paul Haupt, 1960.

Judet de la Combe, Pierre. *L'Agamemnon d'Eschyle: Commentaire des dialogues*. 2 vols. Villeneuve-d'Ascq: Septentrion, 2001.

Kant, Immanuel. *Kritik der reinen Vernunft*. Ed. Jens Timmermann. Hamburg: Meiner, 1998.

———. *Kritik der Urteilskraft: Schriften zur Ästhetik und Naturphilosophie*. Ed. Manfred Frank and Véronique Zanetti. Frankfurt: Deutscher Klassiker Verlag, 1996.

Keiner, Astrid. *Hieroglyphenromantik: Zur Genese und Destruktion eines Bilderschriftmodells und zu seiner Überforderung in Friedrich Schlegels Spätphilosophie*. Würzburg: Königshausen & Neumann, 2003.

Kern, Walter. "Eine Übersetzung Hegels zu *de anima* III,4–5." *Hegel-Studien* 1 (1961): 49–88.

Kitzbichler, Josefine, Katja Lubitz, and Nina Mindt, eds. *Theorie der Übersetzung antiker Literatur in Deutschland seit 1800*. Berlin: de Gruyter, 2009.

Knox, Bernard M. W. "Aeschylus and the Third Actor." *American Journal of Philology* 93.1 (1972): 104–24.

Kojève, Alexandre. *Introduction à la lecture de Hegel*. Ed. Raymond Queneau. Paris: Gallimard, 1947.

Kommerell, Max. *Geist und Buchstabe der Dichtung: Goethe, Schiller, Kleist, Hölderlin*. Frankfurt: Klostermann, 1944.

Konopacki, Steven A. *The Descent into Words: Jakob Böhme's Transcendental Linguistics*. Ann Arbor: Karoma, 1979.

Koyré, Alexandre. *La philosophie de Jacob Boehme*. Paris: Vrin, 1929.

Kranz, Walther. *Empedokles: Antike Gestalt und romantische Neuschöpfung*. Zurich: Artemis, 1949.

Krell, David Farrell, trans. *The Death of Empedocles: A Mourning Play*. By Friedrich Hölderlin. Albany: SUNY P, 2008.

———. *Lunar Voices: Of Tragedy, Poetry, Fiction, and Thought*. Chicago: U of Chicago P, 1995.

———. *Of Memory, Reminiscence, and Writing: On the Verge*. Bloomington: Indiana UP, 1990.

———. *The Tragic Absolute: German Idealism and the Languishing of God*. Bloomington: Indiana UP, 2005.

Kurz, Gerhard. "Poetik und Geschichtsphilosophie der Tragödie bei Hölderlin." *Text und Kontext* 5.2 (1977): 15–36.

Lacoue-Labarthe, Philippe. *L'imitation des modernes*. Paris: Galilée, 1986.

Lacoue-Labarthe, Philippe, and Jean-Luc Nancy. *L'absolu littéraire: Théorie de la littérature du romantisme allemand*. Paris: Seuil, 1978.

Laplanche, Jean. *Hölderlin et la question du père*. 2nd ed. Paris: Presses Universitaires de France, 1969.

Lau, Chong-Fuk. "Language and Metaphysics: The Dialectics of Hegel's Speculative Proposition." Surber, *Hegel and Language* 55–74.

Lemke, Anja. "'Nichts als Zeit'—zum Zusammenhang von Sprache, Gott und Geschichte in Hölderlins Tragödienkonzeption." *"Es bleibet aber eine Spur/ Doch eines Wortes": Zur späten Hymnik und Tragödientheorie Friedrich Hölderlins*. Ed. Christoph Jamme and Anja Lemke. Munich: Wilhelm Fink, 2004. 401–18.

Lessing, Gotthold E. *Werke 1778–1781*. Ed. Arno Schilson and Axel Schmitt. Frankfurt: Deutscher Klassiker Verlag, 2001.

LeVen, Pauline A. *The Many-Headed Muse: Tradition and Innovation in Late Classical Greek Lyric Poetry*. Cambridge: Cambridge UP, 2014.

Lewis, Charles. "Hölderlin and the Möbius Strip: The One-Sided Surface and the 'Wechsel der Töne.'" *Oxford German Studies* 38:1 (1999): 45–60.

Liddell, Henry George, and Robert Scott. *A Greek-English Lexicon*. 9th ed. Oxford: Clarendon, 1940.

Lindorfer, Bettina, and Dirk Naguschewski, eds. *Hegel: Zur Sprache; Beiträge zur Geschichte des europäischen Sprachdenkens; Festschrift für Jürgen Trabant zum 60. Geburtstag*. Tübingen: Narr, 2002.

Longinus. *On the Sublime*. Ed. D. A. Russell. Oxford: Clarendon, 1964.

Lo Pipero, Franco. "Die Buchstabenschrift ist 'die intelligentere': Zu den griechischen Quellen einer These Hegels." Lindorfer and Naguschewski 145–52.

Loraux, Nicole. *L'invention d'Athènes: Histoire de l'oraison funèbre dans la "cité classique."* 2nd ed. Paris: Payot, 1993.

———. *Les mères en deuil*. Paris: Seuil, 1990.

Luther, Martin. *Werke. Kritische Gesamtausgabe: Die Deutsche Bibel*. Ed. Paul Pietsch et al. 12 vols. Weimar: Böhlau, 1906–61.

Lynn-George, M. "A Reflection on Homeric Dawn in the Parodos of Aeschylus' *Agamemnon*." *Classical Quarterly* 43.1 (1993): 1–9.

Magee, Glenn Alexander. *Hegel and the Hermetic Tradition*. Ithaca: Cornell UP, 2001.

Malabou, Catherine. *The Future of Hegel: Plasticity, Temporality and Dialectic*. Trans. Lisabeth During. London: Routledge, 2005.

Malinowski, Bernadette. *"Das Heilige sei mein Wort": Paradigmen prophetischer Dichtung von Klopstock bis Whitman*. Würzburg: Königshausen & Neumann, 2002.

Manchester, Martin L. *The Philosophical Foundations of Humboldt's Linguistic Doctrines*. Amsterdam: John Benjamins, 1985.

Manieri, Alessandra. *L'immagine poetica nella teoria degli antichi: Phantasia ed enargeia.* Pisa: Istituti Editoriali e Poligrafici Internazionali, 1998.

Maor, Eli. "Thou Shalt Not Divide by Zero!" *Math Horizons* 11.2 (2003): 16–19.

Mayer, Paola. *Jena Romanticism and Its Appropriation of Jakob Böhme: Theosophy—Hagiography—Literature.* Montreal: McGill-Queen's UP, 1999.

McClure, Laura. *Spoken like a Woman: Speech and Gender in Athenian Tragedy.* Princeton: Princeton UP, 2009.

McCumber, John. *In the Company of Words: Hegel, Language, and Systematic Philosophy.* Evanston: Northwestern UP, 1993.

Mendicino, Kristina. "Interrupting the Origin: Hegel, Humboldt and Hölderlin's Prophecies of Language." Diss. Yale University, 2012.

Menke, Christoph. *Tragödie im Sittlichen: Gerechtigkeit und Freiheit nach Hegel.* Frankfurt: Suhrkamp, 1996.

Menninghaus, Winfried. "Die frühromantische Theorie von Zeichen und Metapher." *German Quarterly* 62.1 (1989): 48–58.

———. *Unendliche Verdoppelung: Die frühromantische Grundlegung der Kunsttheorie im Begriff absoluter Selbstreflexion.* Frankfurt: Suhrkamp, 1987.

Mergenthaler, May. *Zwischen Eros und Mitteilung: Die Frühromantik im Symposium der "Athenäums-Fragmente."* Paderborn: Schöningh, 2012.

Meschonnic, Henri. *Poétique du traduire.* Paris: Verdier, 1999.

Millan-Zaibert, Elizabeth. *Friedrich Schlegel and the Emergence of Romantic Philosophy.* Albany: SUNY P, 2007.

Mitchell-Boyask, Robin. "The Marriage of Cassandra and the *Oresteia*: Text, Image and Performance." *Transactions of the American Philological Society* 136.2 (2006): 269–97.

Mueller-Vollmer, Kurt. "From Form to Signification: The Humboldt-Herder Controversy." *Johann Gottfried Herder: Language, History, and the Enlightenment.* Ed. Wulf Koepke. Columbia: Camden House, 1990. 9–25.

Müller, Götz. "Jean Pauls 'Rede des todten Christus vom Weltgebäude herab, daß kein Gott sei.'" *Religionsphilosophie und spekulative Philosophie: Der Streit um die Göttlichen Dinge (1799–1812).* Ed. Walter Jaeschke. Hamburg: Meiner, 1994. 35–55.

Müller-Sievers, Helmut. *Epigenesis: Naturphilosophie im Sprachdenken Wilhelm von Humboldts.* Paderborn: Schöningh, 1993.

Nägele, Rainer. "Ancient Sports and Modern Transports: Hölderlin's Tragic Bodies." *The Solid Letter: Readings of Friedrich Hölderlin.* Ed. Aris Fioretos. Stanford: Stanford UP, 1999. 247–67.

———. *Echoes of Translation: Reading between Texts.* Baltimore: Johns Hopkins UP, 1997.

———. *Hölderlins Kritik der poetischen Vernunft.* Basel: Urs Engeler, 2005.

———. *Text, Geschichte und Subjektivität in Hölderlins Dichtung: "Unessbarer Schrift gleich."* Stuttgart: Metzler, 1985.

———. "Vatertext und Muttersprache: Pindar und das lyrische Subjekt in Hölderlins späterer Dichtung." *Le Pauvre Holterling* 8 (1988): 39–52.

Nagy, Gregory. *Greek Mythology and Poetics.* Ithaca: Cornell UP, 1990.

———. *Pindar's Homer: The Lyric Possession of an Epic Past.* Baltimore: Johns Hopkins UP, 1990.

Nancy, Jean-Luc. *Être singulier pluriel.* Paris: Galilée, 1996.

————. "Image/Danse." Dance in/and Theory. Brown University, 11 April 2014. Lecture.

————. *Le partage des voix*. Paris: Galilée, 1982.

————. *La remarque spéculative: (Un bon mot de Hegel)*. Paris: Galilée, 1973.

Nelson, Jeffrey T. "Maxima Immoralia? Speed and Slowness in Adorno's *Minima Moralia*." *Theory and Event* 4.3 (2000).

Neustadt, Ernst. "Wort und Geschehen in Aischylos' *Agamemnon*." *Hermes* 64.2 (1929): 243–65.

The New Oxford Annotated Bible. Ed. Michael D. Coogan et al. 3rd ed. Oxford: Oxford UP, 2001.

Novum Testamentum: Graece et Latine. Ed. Eberhard Nestle and Erwin Nestle et al. 6th ed. Stuttgart: Deutsche Bibelgesellschaft, 2008.

Nuzzo, Angelica. "The Language of Hegel's Speculative Philosophy." Surber, *Hegel and Language* 75–91.

Oesterle, Ingrid. "Romantische Poesie der Poesie der Apokalypse: Neue Kunst, neue Mythologie und Apokalyptik in der Heidelberger Romantik und im Spätwerk Friedrich Schlegels." *Poesie der Apokalypse*. Ed. Gerhard Kaiser. Würzburg: Königshausen & Neumann, 1991. 103–28.

O'Regan, Cyril. *Gnostic Apocalypse: Jacob Boehme's Haunted Narrative*. Albany: SUNY P, 2002.

Pahl, Katrin. *Tropes of Transport: Hegel and Emotion*. Evanston: Northwestern UP, 2012.

Paul, Shalom M. "The Image of the Oven and the Cake in Hosea VII 4–10." *Vestum Testamentum* 18.1 (1968): 114–20.

Peradotto, John J. "Some Patterns of Nature Imagery in the *Oresteia*." *American Journal of Philology* 85.4 (1964): 378–93.

Peter, Klaus. *Idealismus als Kritik: Friedrich Schlegels Philosophie der unvollendeten Welt*. Stuttgart: Kohlhammer, 1973.

Pfau, Thomas, trans. *Friedrich Hölderlin: Essays and Letters on Theory*. Albany: SUNY P, 1988.

Pinkard, Terry. *Hegel's Phenomenology: The Sociality of Reason*. Cambridge: Cambridge UP, 1996.

Pirenne-Delforge, Vinciane. "Le culte de la persuasion *peithô* en grèce ancienne." *Revue de l'histoire des religions* 208.4 (1991): 395–413.

Plato. *Opera*. Ed. Jonathan Burnet. 5 vols. Oxford: Clarendon, 1900–07.

Pliny. *Naturalis Historiae Libri XXXVII*. Ed. Carolus Mayhoff. Vol. 2. Leipzig: Teubner, 1909.

Plug, Jan. *Borders of a Lip: Romanticism, Language, History, Politics*. Albany: SUNY P, 2003.

Pollack, Howard. "Novalis and Mathematics Revisited." *Athenaeum* 7 (1997): 113–40.

Porter, James I. "Patterns of Perception in Aeschylus." *The Cabinet of the Muses: Essays on Classical and Comparative Literature in Honor of Thomas G. Rosenmeyer*. Ed. Mark Griffith and Donald J. Mastronarde. Atlanta: Scholars Press, 1990. 31–56.

Quillien, Jean. *Guillaume de Humboldt et la Grèce: Modèle et histoire*. Lille: Presses Universitaires de Lille, 1983.

Race, William H., trans. *Pindar: Olympian Odes; Pythian Odes.* Cambridge: Harvard UP, 1997.

Redfield, Marc. *Phantom Formations: Aesthetic Ideology and the* Bildungsroman. Ithaca: Cornell UP, 1996.

Reiff, Richard August. *Geschichte der unendlichen Reihen.* Tübingen: Laupp, 1889.

Reinhardt, Karl. *Aischylos als Regisseur und Theologe.* Bern: Francke, 1949.

Richter, Gerhard. *Verwaiste Hinterlassenschaften: Formen des gespenstischen Erbens.* Berlin: Matthes & Seitz, 2016.

Romilly, Jacqueline de. *Le temps dans la tragédie grecque.* Paris: Vrin, 1971.

Rosen, Stanley. *Plato's* Sophist: *The Drama of Original and Image.* New Haven: Yale UP, 1983.

Rosenkranz, Karl. *Georg Wilhelm Friedrich Hegels Leben.* Darmstadt: Wissenschaftliche Buchgesellschaft, 1963.

Rosenmeyer, Thomas G. *The Art of Aeschylus.* Berkeley: U of California P, 1982.

———. "ΦΑΝΤΑΣΙΑ und Einbildungskraft: Zur Vorgeschichte eines Leitbegriffs der europäischen Ästhetik." *Poetica* 18.3–4 (1986): 197–248.

Ruijgh, C. J. "Observations sur l'emploi onomastique de κεκλῆσθαι vis-à-vis de celui de καλεῖσθαι, notamment dans la tragédie attique." *Miscellanea tragica in honorum J.C. Kamerbeek.* Ed. J. M. Bremer, S. Radt, and C. J. Ruijgh. Amsterdam: Hakkert, 1976. 333–95.

Russon, John. *Reading Hegel's* Phenomenology. Bloomington: Indiana UP, 2004.

Rusterholz, Peter. "Jakob Böhmes Naturbild und der Stilwandel der Dichtung vom 17. zum 18. Jahrhundert." *Gott, Natur und Mensch in der Sicht Jacob Böhmes und seiner Rezeption.* Ed. Jan Garewicz and Alois Maria Haas. Wiesbaden: Harrassowitz, 1994. 209–21.

Ryan, Lawrence J. "Hölderlins Dichtungsbegriff." *Hölderlin-Jahrbuch* 12 (1961–62): 20–41.

———. *Hölderlins Lehre vom Wechsel der Töne.* Stuttgart: Kohlhammer, 1960.

Santner, Eric L. *Friedrich Hölderlin: Narrative Vigilance and the Poetic Imagination.* New Brunswick: Rutgers UP, 1986.

Schein, Seth L. "The Cassandra Scene in Aeschylus' *Agamemnon.*" *Greece and Rome* 29.1 (1982): 11–16.

Schelling, Friedrich Wilhelm Joseph. *Werke.* Ed. Wilhelm G. Jacobs, Jörg Jantzen, and Hermann Quinn. 10 vols. Stuttgart–Bad Cannstatt: Frommann-Holzboog, 1976–.

Schiller, Friedrich. *Gedichte: Nationalausgabe.* Ed. Norbert Oellers. Vol. 2. Weimar: Böhlau, 1983.

———. "Über naïve und sentimentalische Dichtung." *Theoretische Schriften.* Ed. Rolf-Peter Janz et al. Frankfurt: Deutscher Klassiker Verlag, 1992. 706–810.

Schlegel, Friedrich. *Kritische Friedrich-Schlegel-Ausgabe.* Ed. Ernst Behler et al. 35 vols. Paderborn: Schöningh, 1958–.

———. *Lessings Geist aus seinen Schriften, oder dessen Gedanken und Meinungen zusammengestellt und erläutert von Friedrich Schlegel.* 3 vols. Leipzig: Hinrichs, 1810.

Schmidt, Dennis J. *On Germans and Other Greeks: Tragedy and Ethical Life.* Bloomington: Indiana UP, 2001.

Scholem, Gershom. "Über Klage und Klagelied." *Tagebücher nebst Aufsätzen und*

Entwürfen bis 1923. Ed. Karlfried Gründer et al. Vol. 2. Frankfurt: Jüdischer Verlag, 2000. 128–33.

Schuff, Karin. "Zahlenkomposition und prophetisches Selbstverständnis: Die Komposition der Vorrede zu Jacob Böhmes *Morgen-Roete im Aufgangk*." *Daphnis* 31 (2002): 491–528.

Schulte, Michael. *Die "Tragödie im Sittlichen": Zur Dramentheorie Hegels*. Munich: Fink, 1992.

Scott, William C. "The Confused Chorus ('Agamemnon' 975–1034)." *Phoenix* 23.4 (1969): 336–46.

———. *Musical Design in Aeschylean Theater*. Hanover: UP of New England, 1984.

Seifert, Albrecht. *Untersuchungen zu Hölderlins Pindar-Rezeption*. Munich: Fink, 1982.

Shevchenko, Nadezda. *Eine historische Anthropologie des Buches: Bücher in der preußischen Herzogsfamilie zur Zeit der Reformation*. Göttingen: Vandenhoeck & Ruprecht, 2007.

Siep, Ludwig. *Hegel's* Phenomenology of Spirit. Trans. Daniel Smyth. Cambridge: Cambridge UP, 2014.

Simon, Josef. *Das Problem der Sprache bei Hegel*. Stuttgart: Kohlhammer, 1966.

Smith, John H. "Friedrich Schlegel's Romantic Calculus: Reflections on the Mathematical Infinite around 1800." *The Relevance of Romanticism*. Ed. Dalia Nassar. Oxford: Oxford UP, 2014. 239–57.

———. *The Spirit and Its Letter: Traces of Rhetoric in Hegel's Philosophy of Bildung*. Ithaca: Cornell UP, 1988.

Smith, Ole Langwitz, ed. *Scholia Graeca in Aeschylum*. Vol. 1. Leipzig: Teubner, 1976.

Söring, Jürgen. *Die Dialektik der Rechtfertigung: Überlegungen zu Hölderlins Empedokles-Projekt*. Frankfurt: Athenäum, 1973.

Sophocles. *Fabulae*. Ed. H. Lloyd-Jones and N. G. Wilson. Oxford: Clarendon, 1990.

Spinoza, Baruch. *Ethik in geometrischer Ordnung dargestellt: Lateinisch–Deutsch*. Ed. Wolfgang Bartuschat. Hamburg: Meiner, 2007.

———. *Opera*. Ed. Carl Gebhardt. 4 vols. Heidelberg: Winter, 1925.

Steiner, George. *After Babel: Aspects of Language and Translation*. Oxford: Oxford UP, 1975.

Steinthal, Heymann, ed. *Die sprachphilosophischen Werke Wilhelm's von Humboldt*. Berlin: Dümmler, 1884.

Surber, Jere Paul, ed. *Hegel and Language*. Albany: SUNY P, 2006.

———. "Hegel's Speculative Sentence." *Hegel-Studien* 10 (1975): 210–30.

Szondi, Peter. "Er selbst, der Fürst des Fests: Die Hymne *Friedensfeier*." *Hölderlin-Studien*. Frankfurt: Suhrkamp, 1970. 62–92.

———. "Friedrich Schlegels Theorie der Dichtarten." *Euphorion* 64 (1970): 181–99.

———. "Der Fürstenmord, der nicht stattfand: Hölderlin und die französische Revolution." *Einführung in die literarische Hermeneutik*. Ed. Jean Bollack. Frankfurt: Suhrkamp, 1975. 409–26.

———. *Poetik und Geschichtsphilosophie: Studienausgabe der Vorlesungen*. Ed. Jean Bollack et al. Vol. 1. Frankfurt: Suhrkamp, 1974.

———. "Traktat über philologische Erkenntnis." *Hölderlin-Studien*. Frankfurt: Suhrkamp, 1970. 9–34.

———. "Überwindung des Klassizismus: Der Brief an Böhlendorff vom 4. Dezember 1804." *Hölderlin-Studien*. Frankfurt: Suhrkamp, 1970. 95–118.

Taplin, Oliver. *The Stagecraft of Aeschylus: The Dramatic Use of Exits and Entrances in Greek Tragedy*. Oxford: Clarendon, 1977.

Thalmann, William G. "Speech and Silence in the 'Oresteia' 1: 'Agamemnon' 1025–1029." *Phoenix* 39.2 (1985): 99–118.

———. "Speech and Silence in the 'Oresteia' 2." *Phoenix* 39.3 (1985): 221–37.

Theunissen, Michael. *Pindar: Menschenlos und Wende der Zeit*. Munich: Beck, 2000.

Thompson, Kevin. "Fragmentation, Contamination, Systematicity: The Threats of Representation and the Immanence of Thought." Surber, *Hegel and Language* 35–53.

Thouard, Denis. "La difficulté de Humboldt." *Dossiers HEL* 1 (2002). <http://htl.linguist.jussieu.fr/dosHEL.htm>. 1–24.

———. "L'epos spéculatif: *La phénomenologie de l'esprit* comme *Iliade* et comme *Odyssée*." Lindorfer and Naguschewski 231–46.

Trabant, Jürgen. *Apeliotes, oder Der Sinn der Sprache: Wilhelm von Humboldts Sprach-Bild*. Munich: Fink, 1986.

———. *Traditionen Humboldts*. Frankfurt am Main: Suhrkamp, 1990.

Trippe, Rosemary. "Art of Memory: Recollecting Rome in Giovanni Marcanova's *Collectio antiquitatum*." *Art History* 33.5 (2010): 766–99.

Tucker, Brian. *Reading Riddles: Rhetorics of Obscurity from Romanticism to Freud*. Blue Ridge Summit: Bucknell UP, 2011.

Underhill, James W. *Humboldt, Worldview and Language*. Edinburgh: Edinburgh UP, 2009.

Velkey, Richard L. "On Possessed Individualism: Hegel, Socrates' Daimon, and the Modern State." *Review of Metaphysics* 59.3 (2006): 577–99.

Venuti, Lawrence. *The Translator's Invisibility: A History of Translation*. London: Routledge, 1995.

Vernant, Jean-Pierre. "Figuration et image." *Métis* 5.1–2 (1990): 225–38.

———. *Figures, idoles, masques*. Paris: Julliard, 1990.

———. "Les semblances de Pandora." *Le métier du mythe: Lectures d'Hésiode*. Ed. Pierre Judet de la Combe and Philippe Rousseau. Villeneuve d'Ascq: Presses Universitaires du Septentrion, 1996. 381–92.

Vidal-Naquet, Pierre "Chasse et sacrifice dans l' 'Orestie' d'Eschyle." *Mythe et tragédie en grèce ancienne*. Ed. Jean-Pierre Vernant and Pierre Vidal-Naquet. 2 vols. Paris: Maspero, 1972. 1: 133–58.

Villela-Petit, Maria. "La question de l'image artistique dans le *Sophiste*." *Études sur le Sophiste de Platon*. Ed. Pierre Aubenque and Michel Narcy. Naples: Bibliopolis, 1991. 53–90.

Voss, Josef. "Aristote et la théorie énergétique du langage de Wilhelm von Humboldt." *Revue Philosophique de Louvain* 72.15 (1974): 482–508.

Wake, Peter. *Tragedy in Hegel's Early Theological Writings*. Bloomington: Indiana UP, 2014.

Warminski, Andrzej. *Readings in Interpretation: Hölderlin, Hegel, Heidegger*. Introd. Rodolphe Gasché. Minneapolis: U of Minnesota P, 1987.

Webb, Ruth. *Ekphrasis, Imagination and Persuasion in Ancient Rhetorical Theory and Practice*. Farnham: Ashgate, 2009.

Weber, Samuel. *Theatricality as Medium*. New York: Fordham UP, 2004.

West, Martin L. *Aeschyli Tragoediae*. Stuttgart: Teubner, 1990.

———. *Studies in Aeschylus*. Stuttgart: Teubner, 1990.

Widzisz, Marcel Andrew. Chronos *on the Threshold: Time, Ritual, and Agency in the* Oresteia. Lanham: Lexington, 2012.

Zeitlin, Froma. "The Motif of the Corrupted Sacrifice in Aeschylus' *Oresteia*." *Transactions and Proceedings of the American Philological Society* 96 (1965): 463–508.

Ziche, Paul. *Mathematische und naturwissenschaftliche Modelle in der Philosophie Schellings und Hegels*. Stuttgart-Bad Cannstatt: Frommann–Holzboog, 1996.

Zuberbühler, Rolf. *Hölderlins Erneuerung der Sprache aus etymologischen Ursprüngen*. Berlin: E. Schmidt, 1969.

Index

Sara Guyer and Brian McGrath, series editors